Phantom Dream™

VOLUME 3

NATSUKI TAKAYA

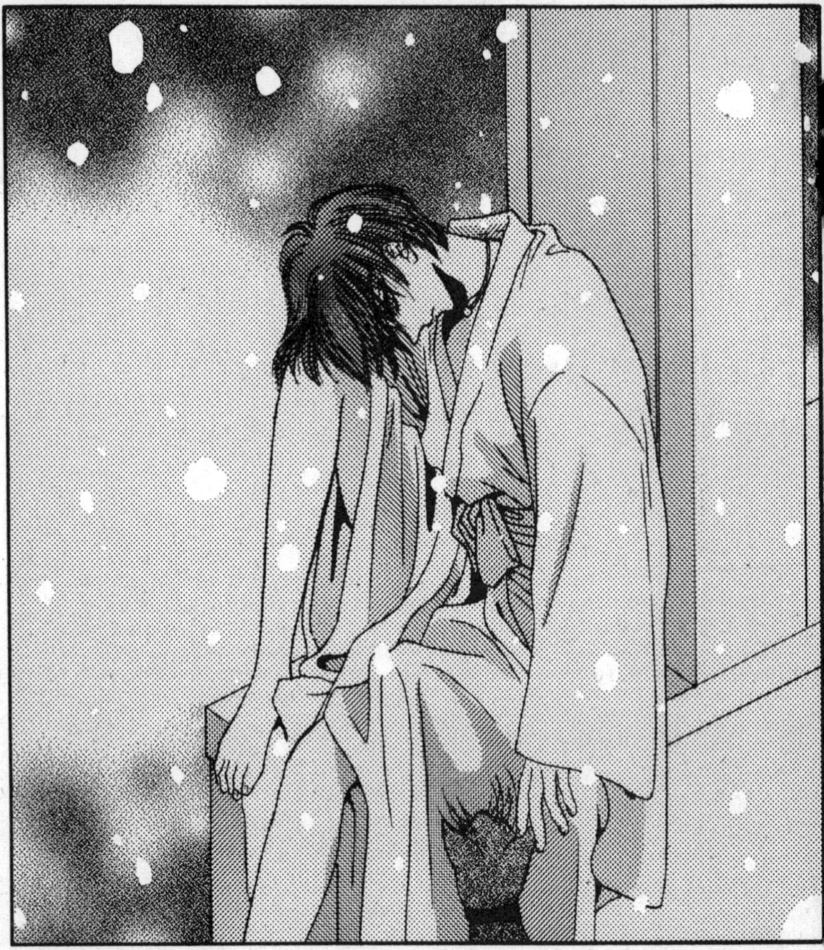

Phantom Dream Volume 3
Written by Natsuki Takaya

Translation - Beni Axia Conrad
English Adaptation - Ysabet Reinhardt MacFarlane
Copy Editor - Shannon Watters
Retouch and Lettering - Star Print Brokers
Production Artist - Michael Paolilli
Graphic Designer - Al-Insan Lashley

Editor - Lillian Diaz-Przybyl
Print Production Manager - Lucas Rivera
Managing Editor - Vy Nguyen
Senior Designer - Louis Csontos
Director of Sales and Manufacturing - Allyson De Simone
Associate Publisher - Marco F. Pavia
President and C.O.O. - John Parker
C.E.O. and Chief Creative Officer - Stu Levy

A  Manga

TOKYOPOP Inc.
5900 Wilshire Blvd. Suite 2000
Los Angeles, CA 90036

E-mail: info@TOKYOPOP.com
Come visit us online at www.TOKYOPOP.com

GENEIMUSOU by Natsuki Takaya © Natsuki Takaya
1995 All rights reserved. First published in Japan in
1996 by HAKUSENSHA, INC., Tokyo English language
translation rights in the United States of America and
Canada arranged with HAKUSENSHA, INC., Tokyo
through Tuttle-Mori Agency Inc., Tokyo
English text copyright © 2009 TOKYOPOP Inc.

ISBN: 978-1-4278-1091-5

First TOKYOPOP printing: August 2009
10 9 8 7 6 5 4 3 2 1
Printed in the USA

Phantom Dream

Volume 3

By Natsuki Takaya

HAMBURG // LONDON // LOS ANGELES // TOKYO

STORY SO FAR:

OUR STORY BEGINS NEARLY A THOUSAND YEARS AGO, WHEN A YOUNG GIRL, SUIGEKKA, WHO WAS BELIEVED TO BE ALL-POWERFUL, WAS SECRETLY REVERED AS THE GUARDIAN OF JAPAN. HER CONSTANT COMPANIONS WERE TWO MAGICIANS, HIRA AND SAGA. HIRA WAS DEEPLY IN LOVE WITH SUIGEKKA, BUT AFTER HER DEATH, HE CHANGED.

CALLING HIMSELF THE KING OF THE GEKKA FAMILY, HIRA TOOK IT UPON HIMSELF TO REINVENT THE WORLD. HIS SPELLS GAVE HIM POWER OVER JASHIN, THE DARKNESS WITHIN HUMAN HEARTS, AND THROUGH HIS INFLUENCE, THE PEOPLE THREW OFF THEIR WEAK EMOTIONS TO BECOME STRONG JAKI.

THE GEKKA FAMILY DREAMS OF A WORLD WHERE ONLY SUCH PEOPLE EXIST.

HOWEVER, SAGA OPPOSED HIM. USING SPELLS OF PROTECTION, HE EXORCISED THE JAKI AND BECAME THE FIRST SHUGOSHI OF THE OTOYA FAMILY. NOW, TAMAKI OTOYA, THE SHUGOSHI WHO INHERITED THE LONG-DEAD SAGA'S BLOOD, AND EIJI, A JAHOUTSUKAI WHO INHERITED THE BLOOD OF KING HIRA, HAVE INHERITED THEIR ANCIENT CONFLICT AS WELL.

JASHIN: POWERFUL NEGATIVE EMOTIONS, WHICH IF LEFT UNCHECKED TRANSFORM PEOPLE INTO JAKI.

JAKI: A TYPE OF DEMON OR MALEVOLENT BEING CREATED WHEN A HUMAN LOSES CONTROL OF EXTREME ANGER, HATE AND FEAR.

JARYOKU: BLACK MAGIC. A POWER THAT STEMS FROM JASHIN.

JAHOUTSUKAI: BLACK MAGICIAN. ONE WHO SPECIALIZES IN USING JARYOKU.

SHUGOSHI: A TYPE OF PRIEST WHO HAS THE POWER TO EXORCISE JASHIN. LITERALLY, A PROTECTOR.

GOSHI: ONE TASKED WITH DEFENDING THE SHUGOSHI. A HEREDITARY POSITION OCCUPIED BY MEMBERS OF THE OTOYA BRANCH FAMILIES.

JUZU: PRAYER BEADS.

SHUHOU: A PROTECTIVE AVATAR UNIQUE TO EACH SHUGOSHI. THEY TAKE ON DIFFERENT FORMS: TAMAKI'S IS A BIRD, WHILE HIS GRANDFATHER'S WAS A DRAGON.

SHICHIBOUJIN: A SHIELD OF PROTECTION. LITERALLY, A SEPTAGRAM--A SEVEN-POINTED STAR WITHIN A CIRCLE.

SHIEKI: A MAGICAL SERVANT THAT DOES THE SHUGOSHI'S BIDDING. TAMAKI'S SHIEKI WAS A HUMAN BOY, SOUICHI, WHO TAMAKI EXORCISED. HE MANIFESTS AS A BUTTERFLY.

TAMAKI OTOYA: BORN TO SOUETSU, THE PREVIOUS HEAD OF THE OTOYA FAMILY, AND KANAME, A WOMAN TRAINED AS A JAHOUTSUKAI OF THE GEKKA FAMILY, TAMAKI IS YOUNG, BUT POWERFUL. RESENTED BY THE SPRAWLING OTOYA CLAN FOR HIS SUPPOSEDLY "TAINTED" BLOODLINE, HE IS TORN BETWEEN HIS DUTY TO PROTECT PEOPLE FROM BECOMING JAKI, AND HIS FRUSTRATION AT NEVER BEING ABLE TO STOP TERRIBLE THINGS BEFORE THEY HAPPEN--ONLY CLEAN UP THE DAMAGE.

ASAHI: TAMAKI'S FRIEND AND LOVER, ASAHI IS SWEET AND CHEERFUL IN SPITE OF A TROUBLED CHILDHOOD. TRAGICALLY, SHE IS ALSO THE REINCARNATION OF SUIGEKKA, AND HAS RECENTLY CHOSEN TO RETURN TO KING HIRA'S SIDE, FIGHTING AGAINST TAMAKI.

EIJI: A YOUNG JAHOUTSUKAI, WORKING FOR HIRA'S RESURRECTION AND THE CREATION OF HIS IDEAL WORLD. TORMENTED, AND POSSIBLY SLOWLY DYING, EIJI HAS A TWISTED MIX OF LOVE AND RESPECT FOR TAMAKI, IN SPITE OF THEIR OPPOSING GOALS. KAGEHA, A CAT DEMON, IS EIJI'S PROTECTOR AND SOLE FRIEND.

HIDERI: A BRASH YOUNG MAN FROM THE EASTERN OTOYA BRANCH FAMILY. ONE OF TAMAKI'S DESIGNATED PROTECTORS ("HIGOSHI"), HE OFTEN ACTS MORE LIKE AN OLDER BROTHER THAN A GUARDIAN. HE HAD A CRUSH ON TAMAKI'S MOTHER.

MIGIRI: THE SECOND OF THE OTOYA HIGOSHI, SHE IS GENERALLY QUIET, BUT HAS QUITE A TEMPER WHEN PROVOKED. HIDERI IS HER BIG BROTHER, AND SHE ADDRESSES HIM AS "ANIUE."

TOKIWA: TWO YEARS YOUNGER THAN TAMAKI, TOKIWA IS THE THIRD OTOYA HIGOSHI. HE SEES TAMAKI AS AN OLDER BROTHER FIGURE, AND ADDRESSES HIM AS SUCH, CALLING HIM "NII-SAN."

Table of Contents

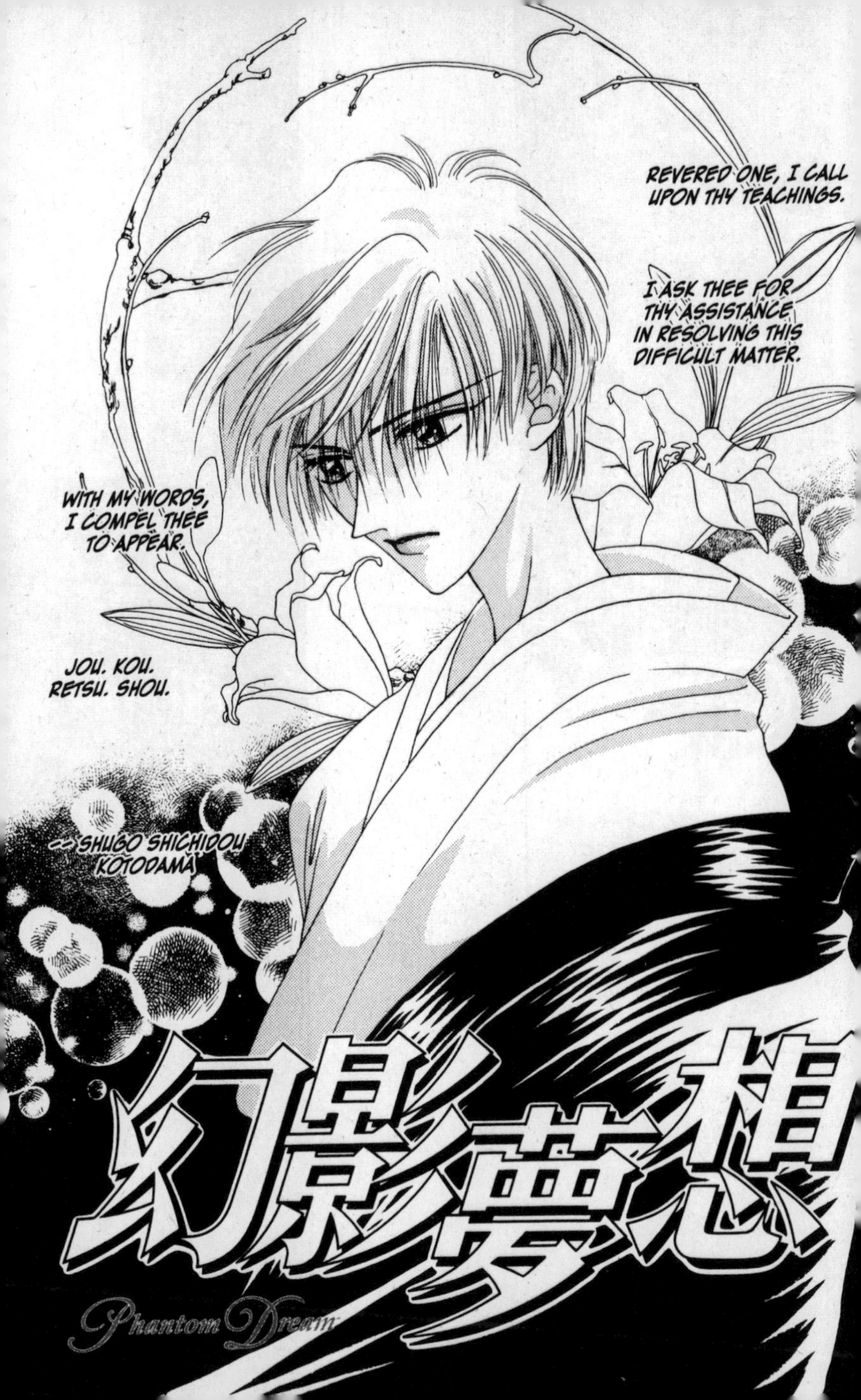
REVERED ONE, I CALL UPON THY TEACHINGS.
I ASK THEE FOR THY ASSISTANCE IN RESOLVING THIS DIFFICULT MATTER.
WITH MY WORDS, I COMPEL THEE TO APPEAR.
JOU. KOU. RETSU. SHOU.
-- SHUGO SHICHIDOU KOTODAMA
幻影夢想
Phantom Dream

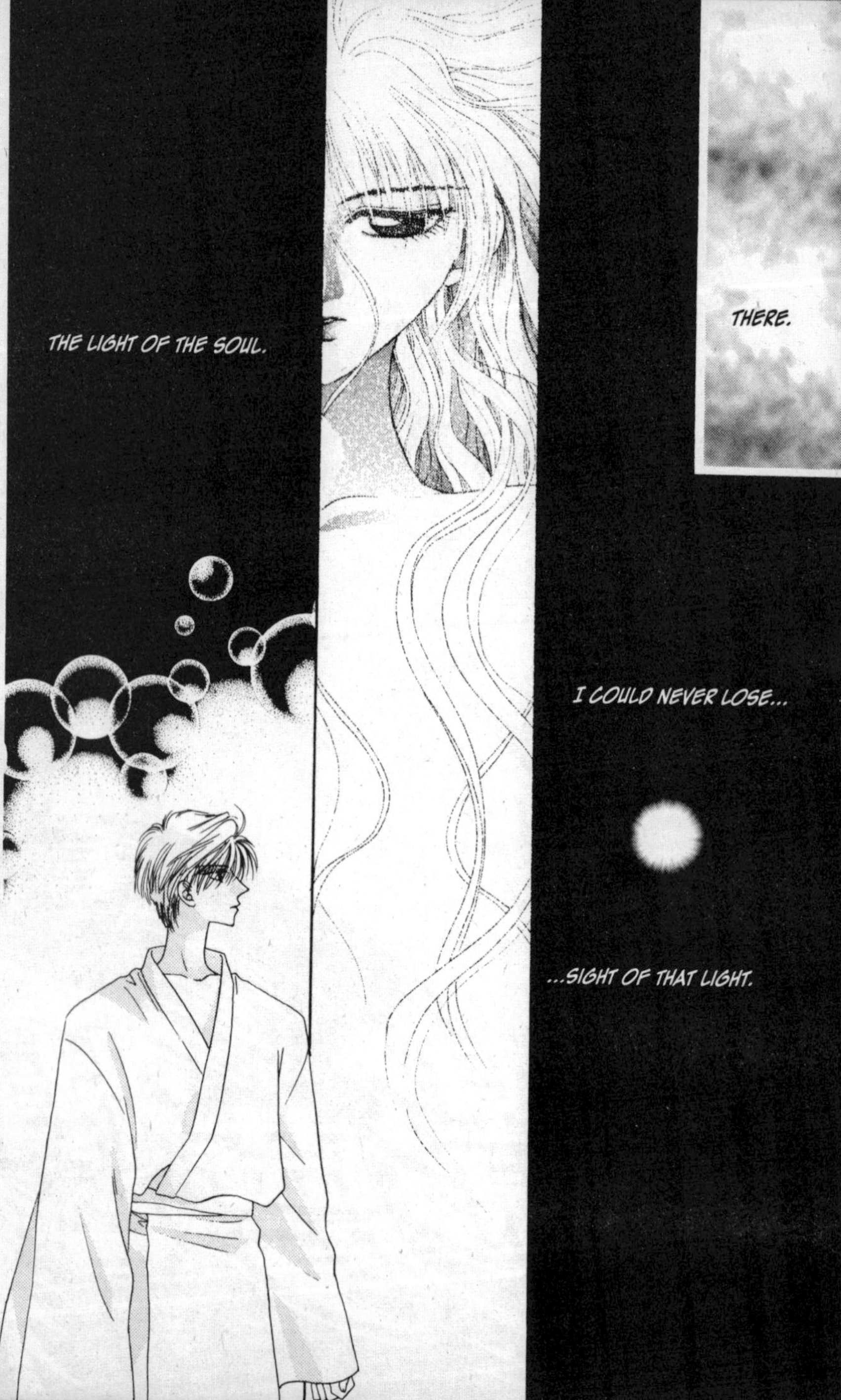
THERE.
I COULD NEVER LOSE...
...SIGHT OF THAT LIGHT.
THE LIGHT OF THE SOUL.

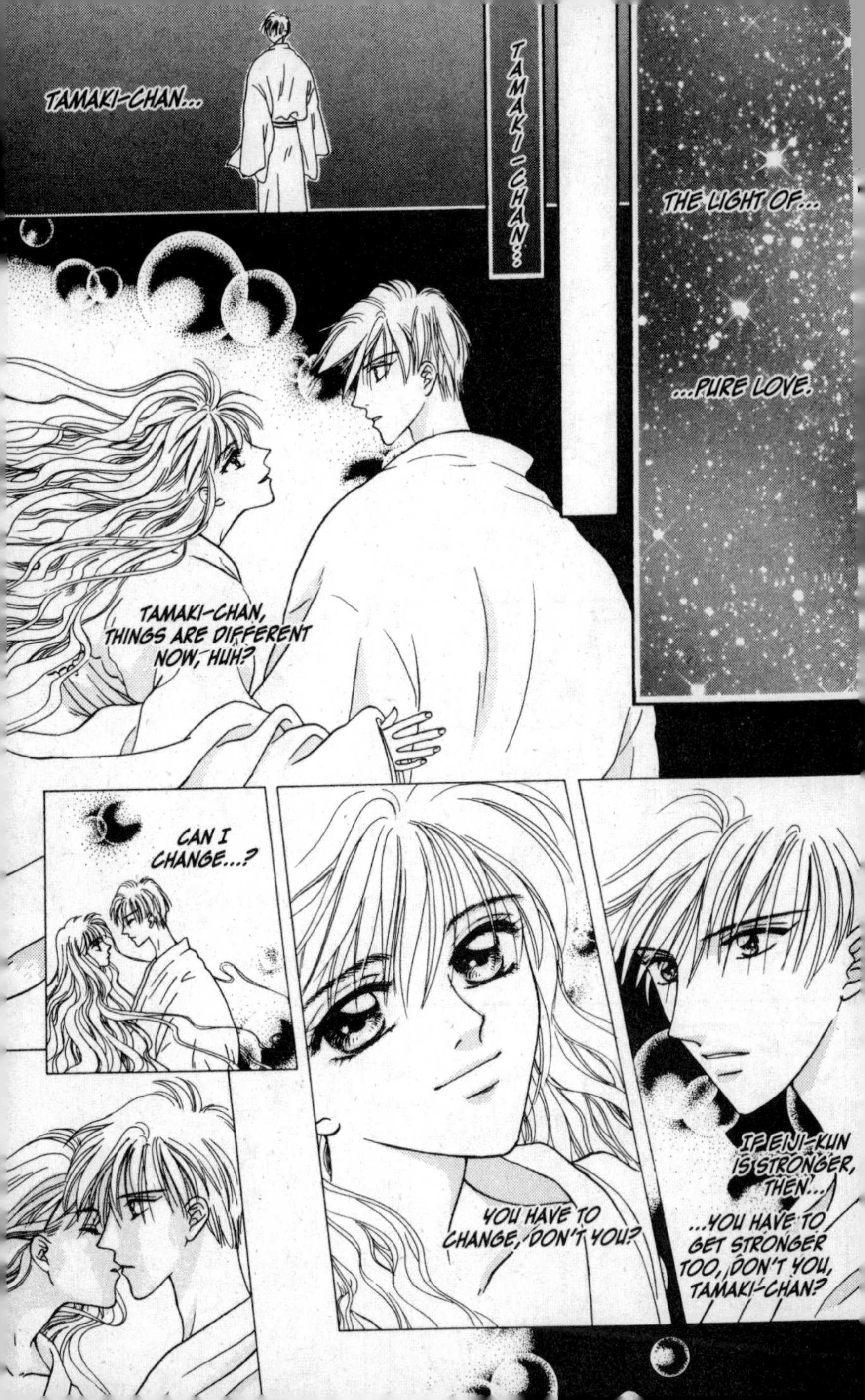
THE LIGHT OF...
...PURE LOVE.
TAMAKI-CHAN...
TAMAKI-CHAN...
TAMAKI-CHAN, THINGS ARE DIFFERENT NOW, HUH?
IF EIJI-KUN IS STRONGER, THEN...
...YOU HAVE TO GET STRONGER TOO, DON'T YOU, TAMAKI-CHAN?
YOU HAVE TO CHANGE, DON'T YOU?
CAN I CHANGE...?

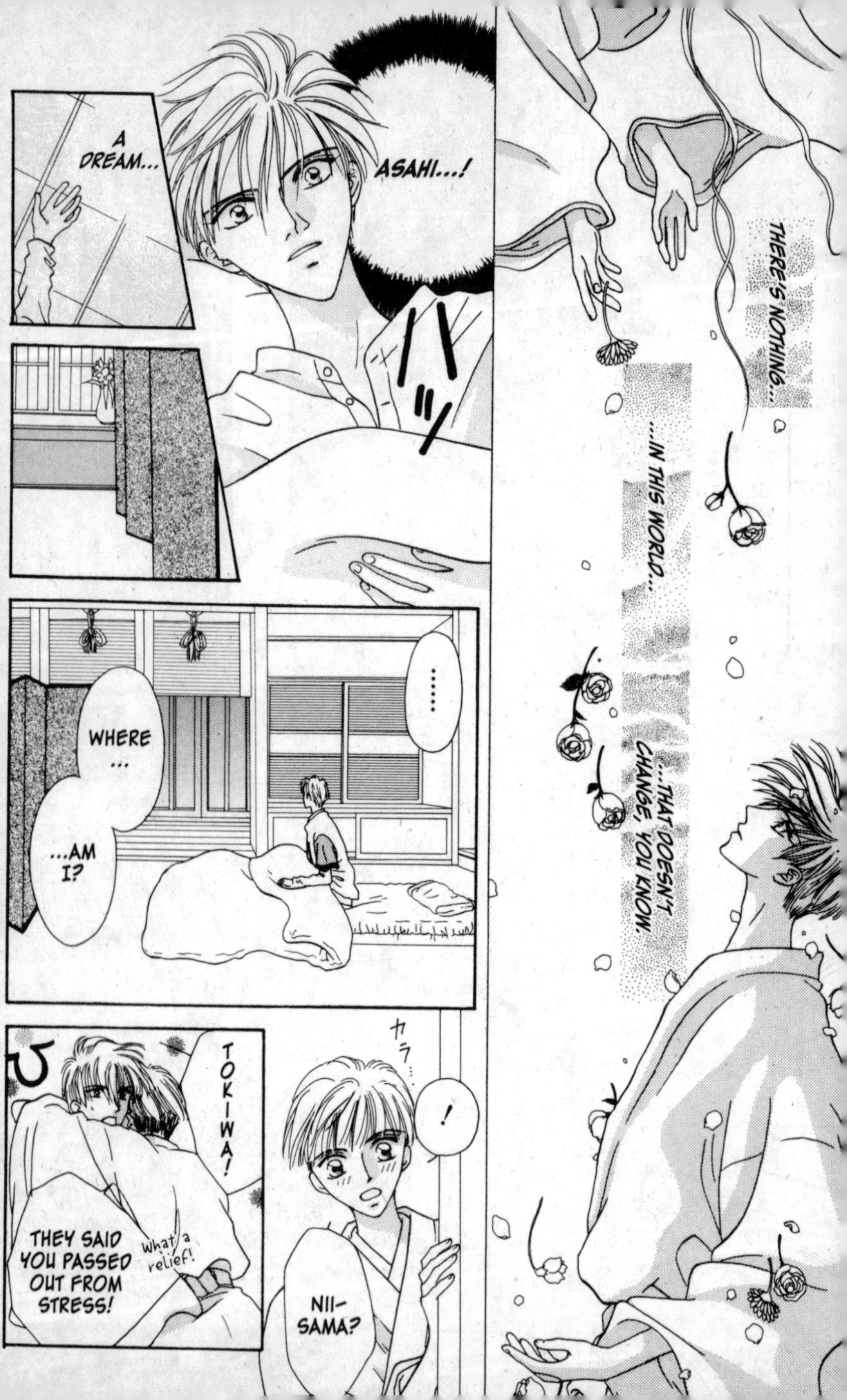
THERE'S NOTHING...
...IN THIS WORLD...
...THAT DOESN'T CHANGE, YOU KNOW.
ASAHI...!
A DREAM...
......
WHERE...
...AM I?
カラ...
!
NII-SAMA?
TOKIWA!
THEY SAID YOU PASSED OUT FROM STRESS!
What a relief!

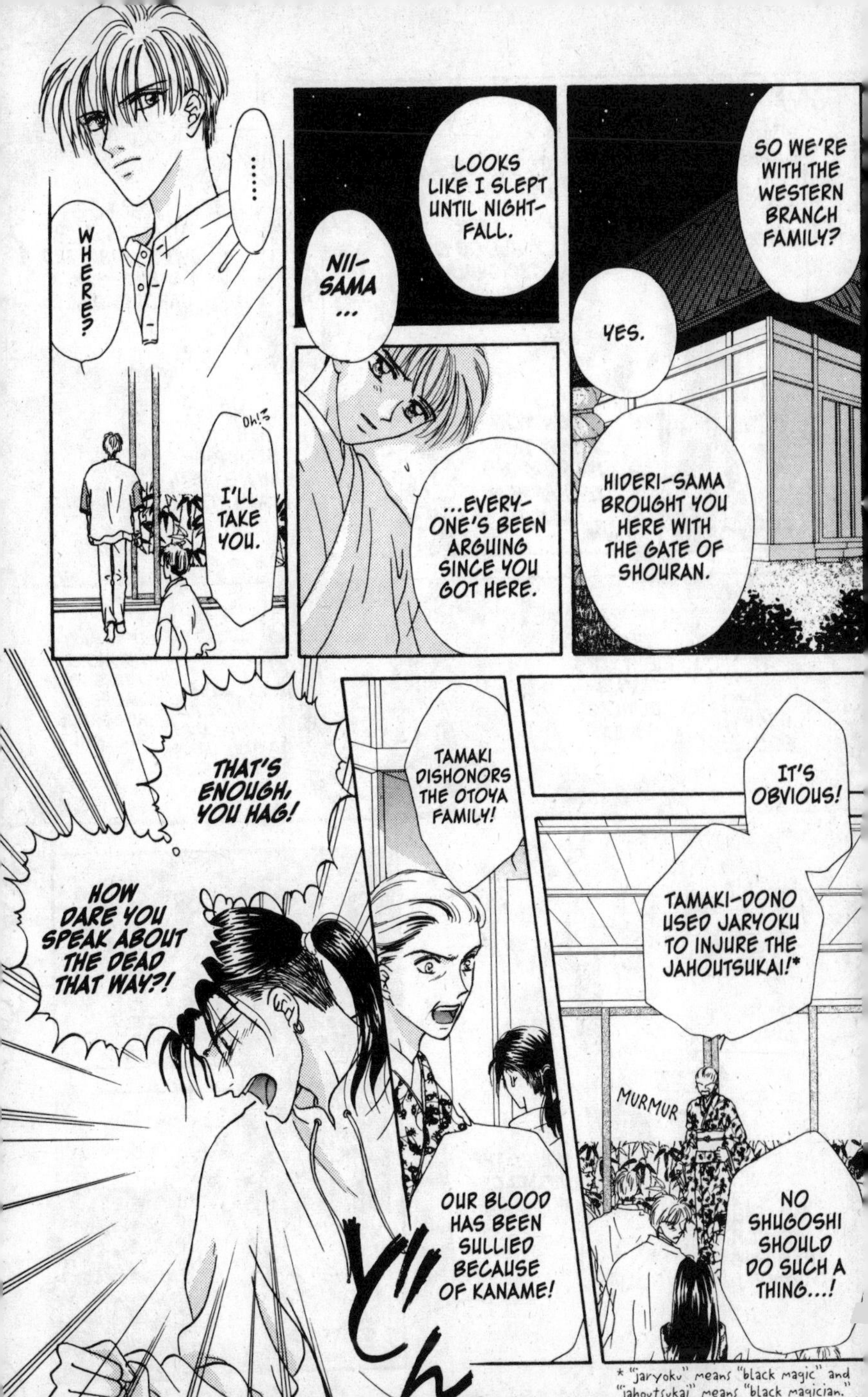
SO WE'RE WITH THE WESTERN BRANCH FAMILY?
YES.
HIDERI-SAMA BROUGHT YOU HERE WITH THE GATE OF SHOURAN.
LOOKS LIKE I SLEPT UNTIL NIGHT-FALL.
NII-SAMA ...
...EVERY-ONE'S BEEN ARGUING SINCE YOU GOT HERE.
......
WHERE?
Oh!?
I'LL TAKE YOU.
IT'S OBVIOUS!
TAMAKI-DONO USED JARYOKU TO INJURE THE JAHOUTSUKAI!*
MURMUR
NO SHUGOSHI SHOULD DO SUCH A THING...!
TAMAKI DISHONORS THE OTOYA FAMILY!
OUR BLOOD HAS BEEN SULLIED BECAUSE OF KANAME!
THAT'S ENOUGH, YOU HAG!
HOW DARE YOU SPEAK ABOUT THE DEAD THAT WAY?!

* "jaryoku" means "black magic" and "jahoutsukai" means "black magician."

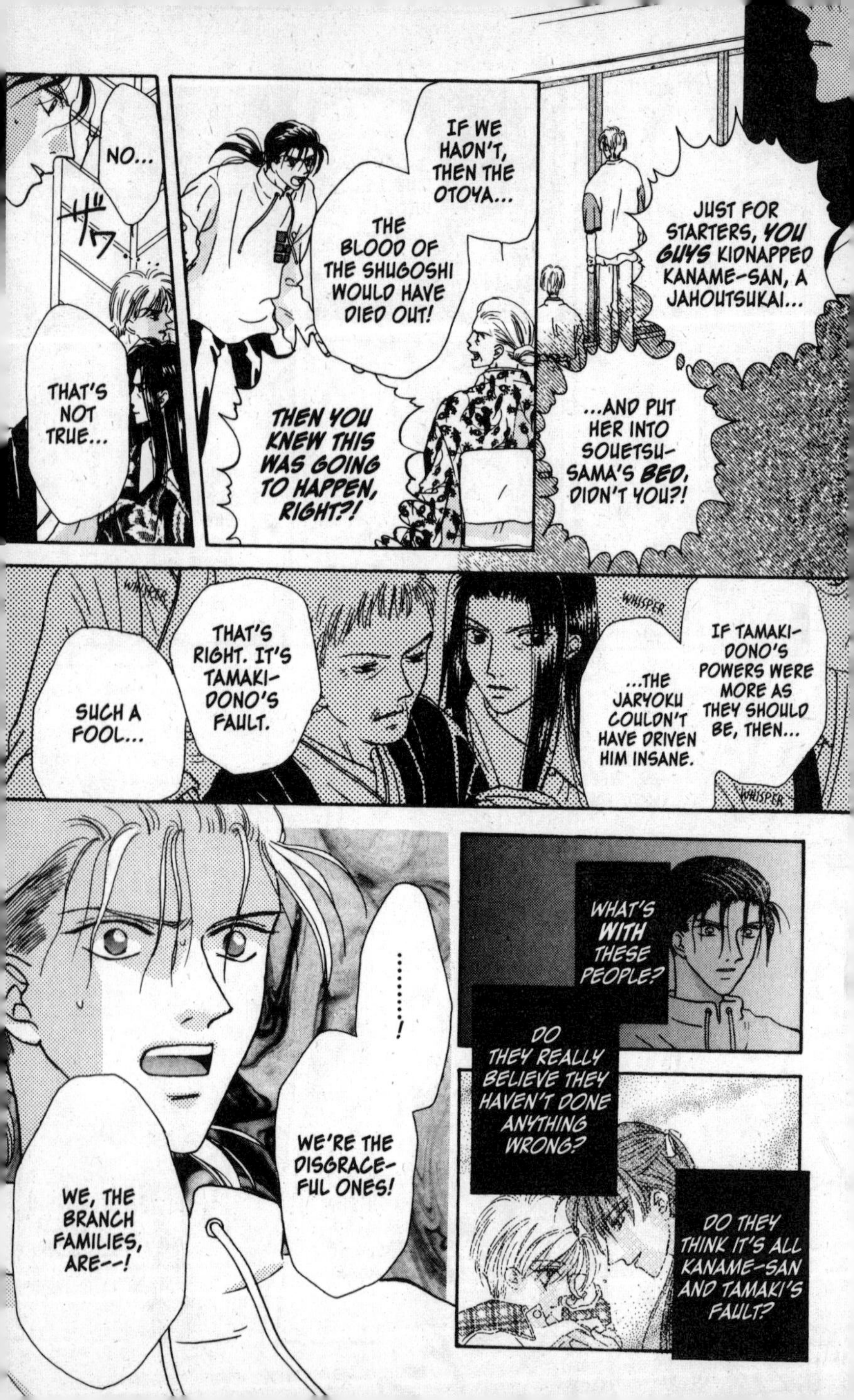
JUST FOR STARTERS, YOU GUYS KIDNAPPED KANAME-SAN, A JAHOUTSUKAI...
...AND PUT HER INTO SOUETSU-SAMA'S BED, DIDN'T YOU?!
IF WE HADN'T, THEN THE OTOYA...
THE BLOOD OF THE SHUGOSHI WOULD HAVE DIED OUT!
THEN YOU KNEW THIS WAS GOING TO HAPPEN, RIGHT?!
NO...
ザワ
THAT'S NOT TRUE...
WHISPER
IF TAMAKI-DONO'S POWERS WERE MORE AS THEY SHOULD BE, THEN...
...THE JARYOKU COULDN'T HAVE DRIVEN HIM INSANE.
WHISPER
WHISPER
THAT'S RIGHT. IT'S TAMAKI-DONO'S FAULT.
SUCH A FOOL...
WHAT'S WITH THESE PEOPLE?
DO THEY REALLY BELIEVE THEY HAVEN'T DONE ANYTHING WRONG?
DO THEY THINK IT'S ALL KANAME-SAN AND TAMAKI'S FAULT?
........!
WE'RE THE DISGRACE-FUL ONES!
WE, THE BRANCH FAMILIES, ARE--!

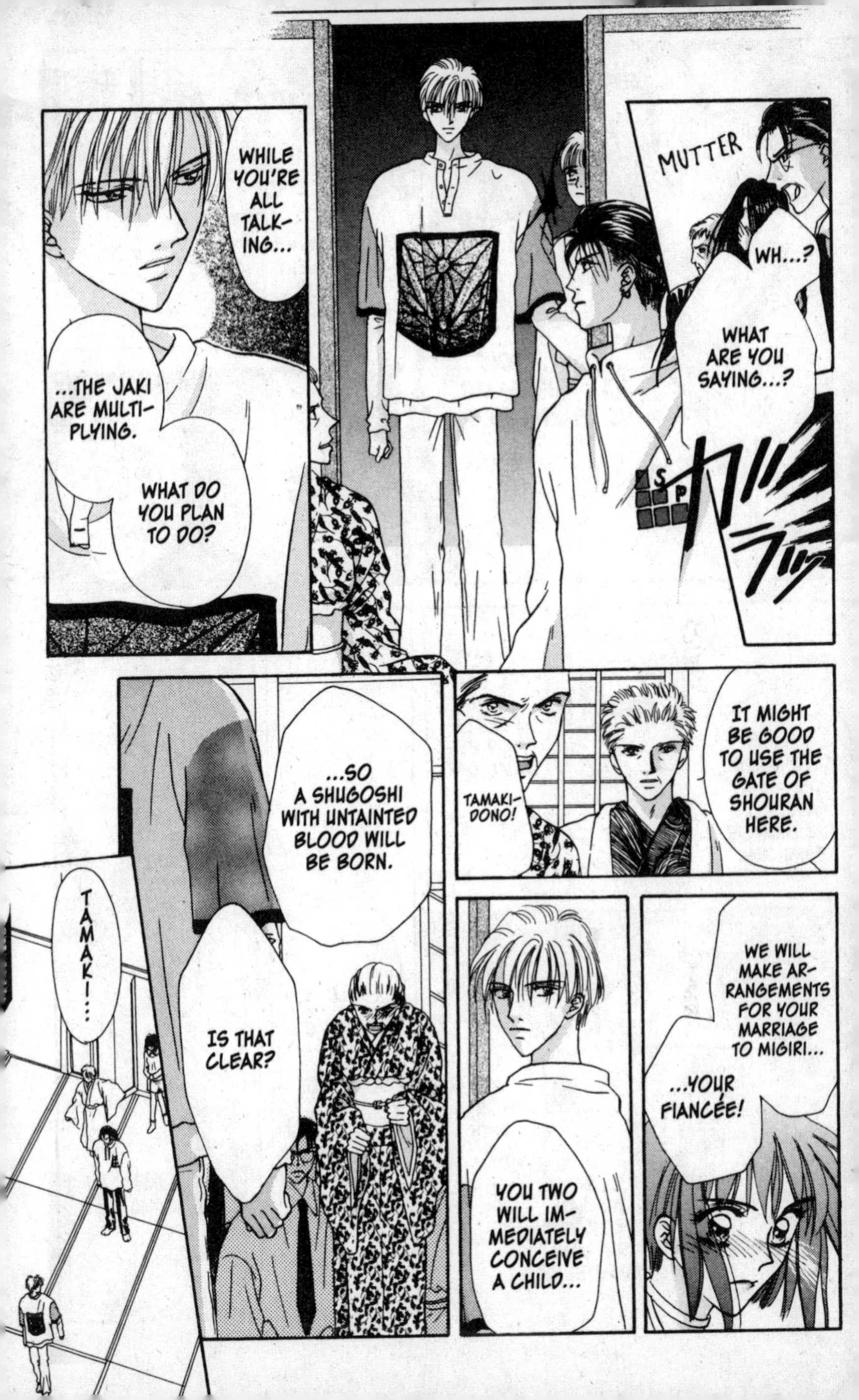
MUTTER
WH...?
WHAT ARE YOU SAYING...?
WHILE YOU'RE ALL TALKING...
...THE JAKI ARE MULTIPLYING.
WHAT DO YOU PLAN TO DO?
IT MIGHT BE GOOD TO USE THE GATE OF SHOURAN HERE.
TAMAKI-DONO!
WE WILL MAKE ARRANGEMENTS FOR YOUR MARRIAGE TO MIGIRI...
...YOUR FIANCÉE!
YOU TWO WILL IMMEDIATELY CONCEIVE A CHILD...
...SO A SHUGOSHI WITH UNTAINTED BLOOD WILL BE BORN.
IS THAT CLEAR?
TAMAKI...

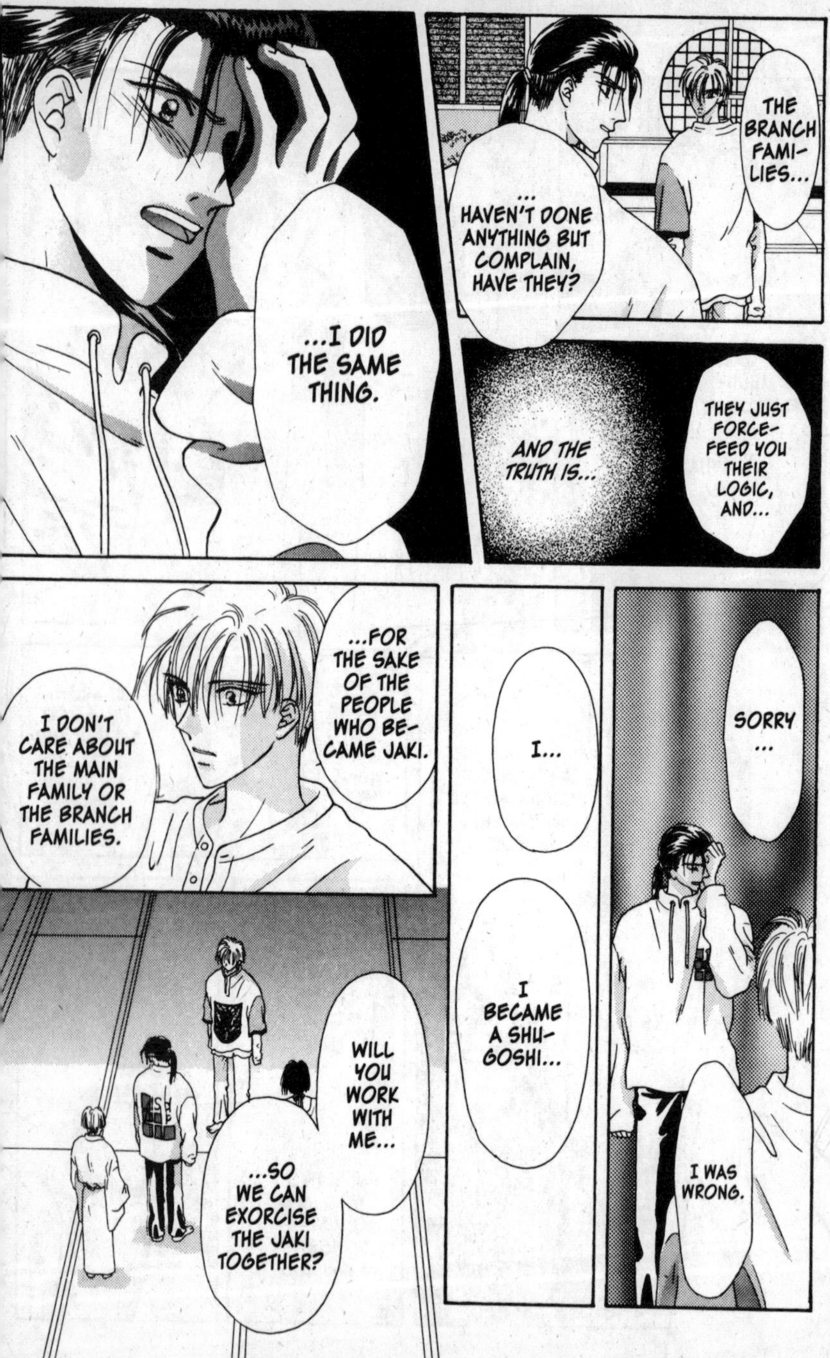
THE BRANCH FAMI-LIES...
...HAVEN'T DONE ANYTHING BUT COMPLAIN, HAVE THEY?
THEY JUST FORCE-FEED YOU THEIR LOGIC, AND...
AND THE TRUTH IS...
...I DID THE SAME THING.
SORRY...
I WAS WRONG.
I...
I BECAME A SHU-GOSHI...
...FOR THE SAKE OF THE PEOPLE WHO BE-CAME JAKI.
I DON'T CARE ABOUT THE MAIN FAMILY OR THE BRANCH FAMILIES.
WILL YOU WORK WITH ME...
...SO WE CAN EXORCISE THE JAKI TOGETHER?

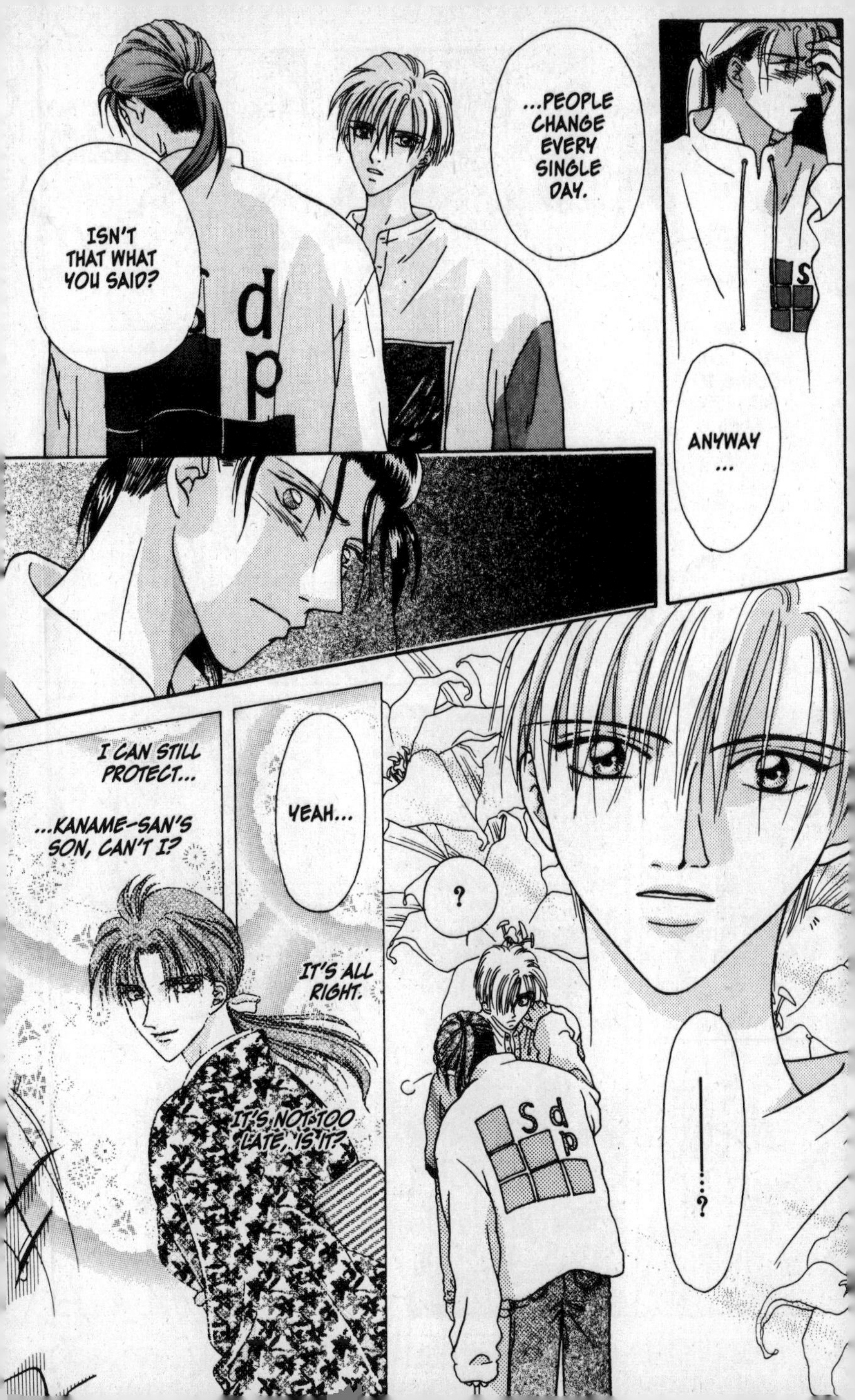
ANYWAY...
...PEOPLE CHANGE EVERY SINGLE DAY.
ISN'T THAT WHAT YOU SAID?
?
—...?
YEAH...
IT'S ALL RIGHT.
IT'S NOT TOO LATE, IS IT?
I CAN STILL PROTECT...
...KANAME-SAN'S SON, CAN'T I?

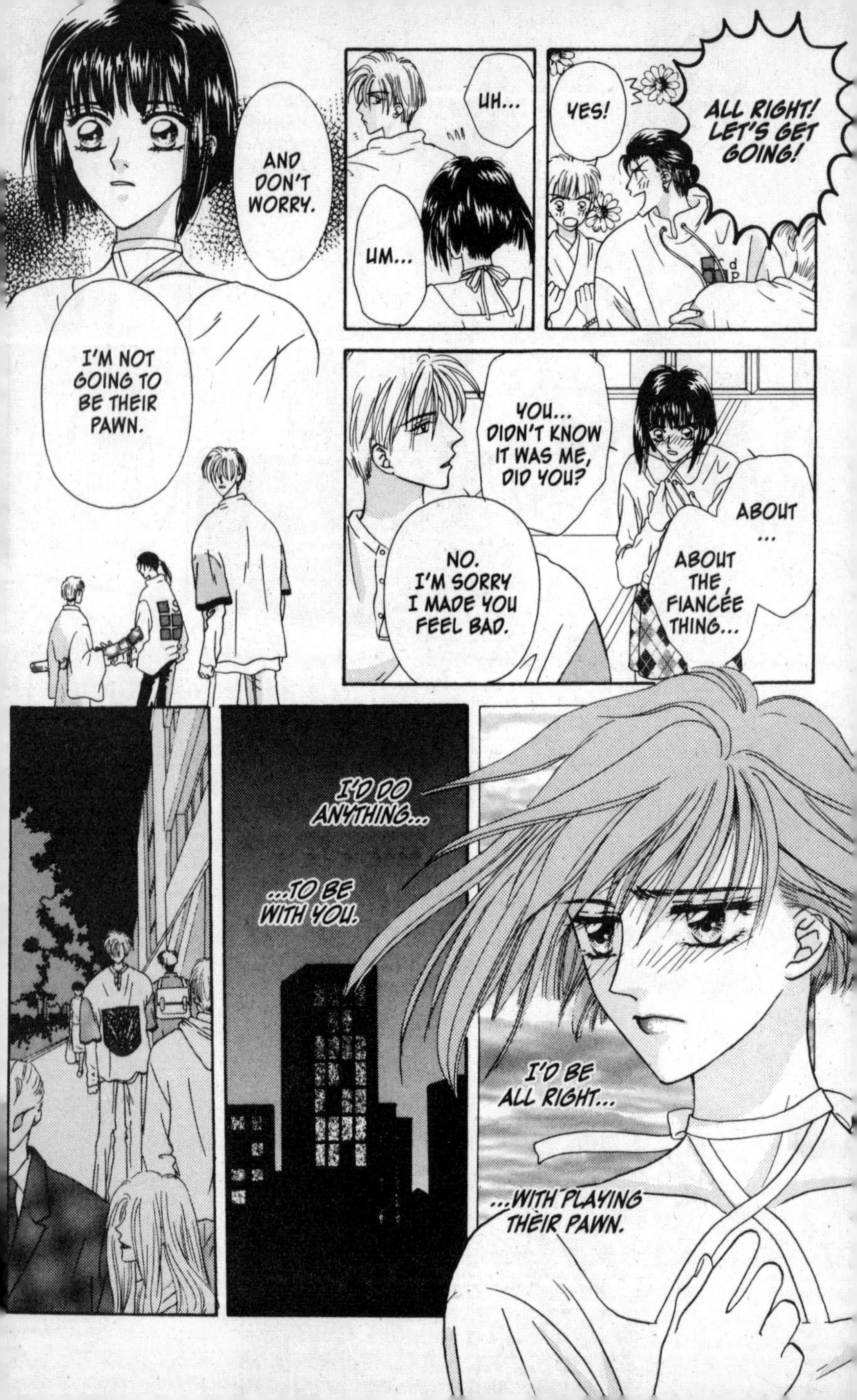
ALL RIGHT! LET'S GET GOING!
YES!
UH...
UM...
ABOUT...
YOU... DIDN'T KNOW IT WAS ME, DID YOU?
ABOUT THE FIANCÉE THING...
NO. I'M SORRY I MADE YOU FEEL BAD.
AND DON'T WORRY.
I'M NOT GOING TO BE THEIR PAWN.
I'D BE ALL RIGHT...
...WITH PLAYING THEIR PAWN.
I'D DO ANYTHING...
...TO BE WITH YOU.

Phantom Dream

Scroll One

Nice to meet you! Or maybe I should say, "Hello, this is Takaya."

It's pretty much a given that you never know what'll happen in life.

This is volume three. Volume three! That's why Eiji is on the cover.

I was told it's unusual for a supporting character to grace the cover, but that's okay. They're all main characters in a way (laughs).

Now that we've come this far, you might have realized that the covers are all very uniform... I'm making them do that. It's because my blood type is A, but I guess that really has nothing to do with it. Doesn't it feel nice when everything matches, though? Like, when you have them all lined up together? Oh...I guess you can only see the spines when you line them up, huh? Ooops. My bad!

Well, anyhow, this is the third volume. Thank you!

Please enjoy it!

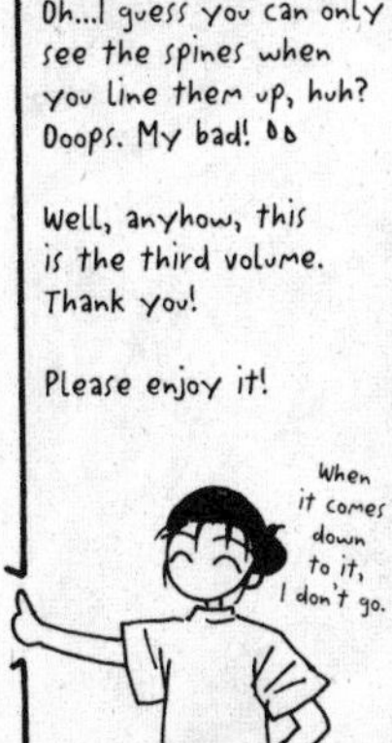
When it comes down to it, I don't go.

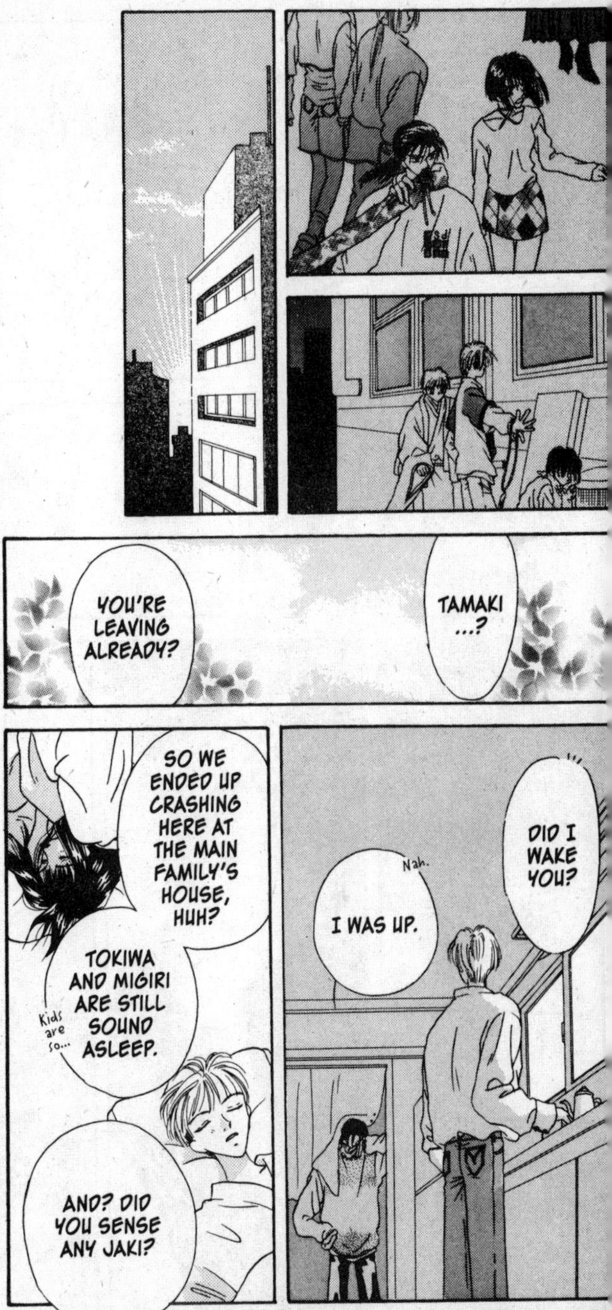
TAMAKI ...?
YOU'RE LEAVING ALREADY?
DID I WAKE YOU?
Nah.
I WAS UP.
SO WE ENDED UP CRASHING HERE AT THE MAIN FAMILY'S HOUSE, HUH?
TOKIWA AND MIGIRI ARE STILL SOUND ASLEEP.
Kids are so...
AND? DID YOU SENSE ANY JAKI?

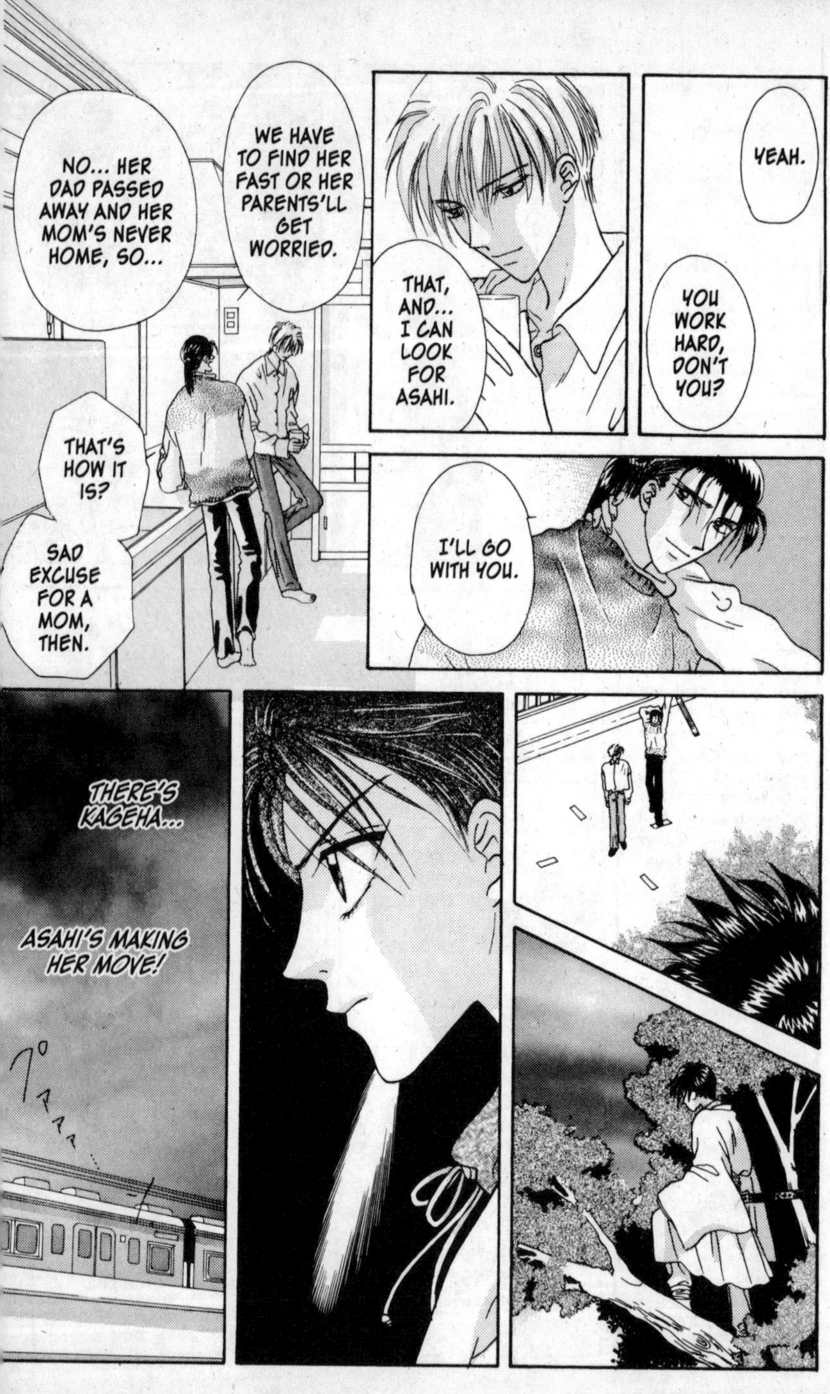
WE HAVE TO FIND HER FAST OR HER PARENTS'LL GET WORRIED.
NO... HER DAD PASSED AWAY AND HER MOM'S NEVER HOME, SO...
THAT'S HOW IT IS?
SAD EXCUSE FOR A MOM, THEN.
THAT, AND... I CAN LOOK FOR ASAHI.
YEAH.
YOU WORK HARD, DON'T YOU?
I'LL GO WITH YOU.
THERE'S KAGEHA...
ASAHI'S MAKING HER MOVE!
プァァァ

Scroll Two

Lately, I haven't really been able to play games (So I say, but it's my own fault...). I haven't even finished Dai 4 Ji Super Robot Taisen S. (I did finish the SFC version!)

But! Right before my eyes, the ultimate piece of software appeared! It's...Fire Emblem <Seisen no Keifu>! The game before it, FE (Fire Emblem) entertained me right down to my bones. It's got that commercial that goes, "I wanted to see you, Marth!" It's like Marth doesn't make an appearance, but... (laughs) That's right, huh? Or wrong? It's fine that I ordered it two days before it came out, but I haven't even touched it (so why did I order it early?). Nae Yuuki was cute. I like her. She's...well, I'll get back on topic.

It's different from the previous one in a lot of ways. Like, the map is huge and looks like it's worth playing; I seriously want to play FE!!! That's how it is. I want to play! Ooh, I want to play...! (laughs) But in December there's Final Fantasy, and when BioHazard 2 comes out I want to play that too, and...and... games, you're so mean...!!! (laughs)

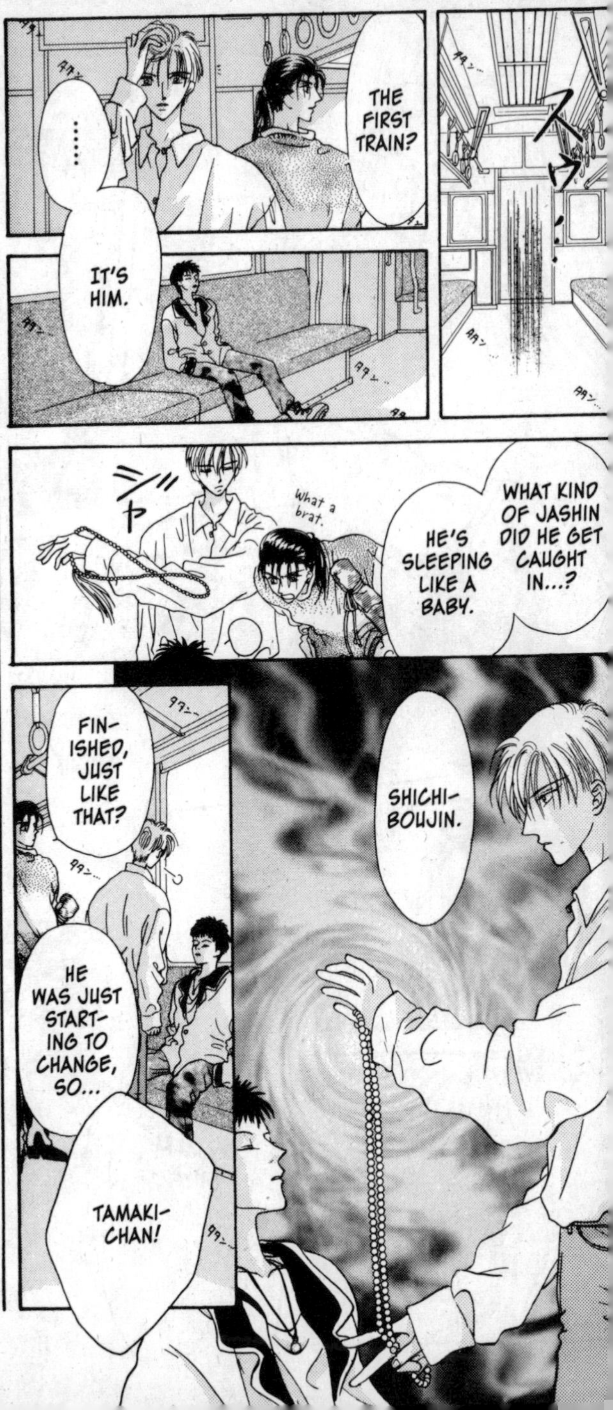
THE FIRST TRAIN?
......
IT'S HIM.
WHAT KIND OF JASHIN DID HE GET CAUGHT IN...?
HE'S SLEEPING LIKE A BABY.
What a brat.
SHICHI-BOUJIN.
FIN-ISHED, JUST LIKE THAT?
HE WAS JUST STARTING TO CHANGE, SO...
TAMAKI-CHAN!

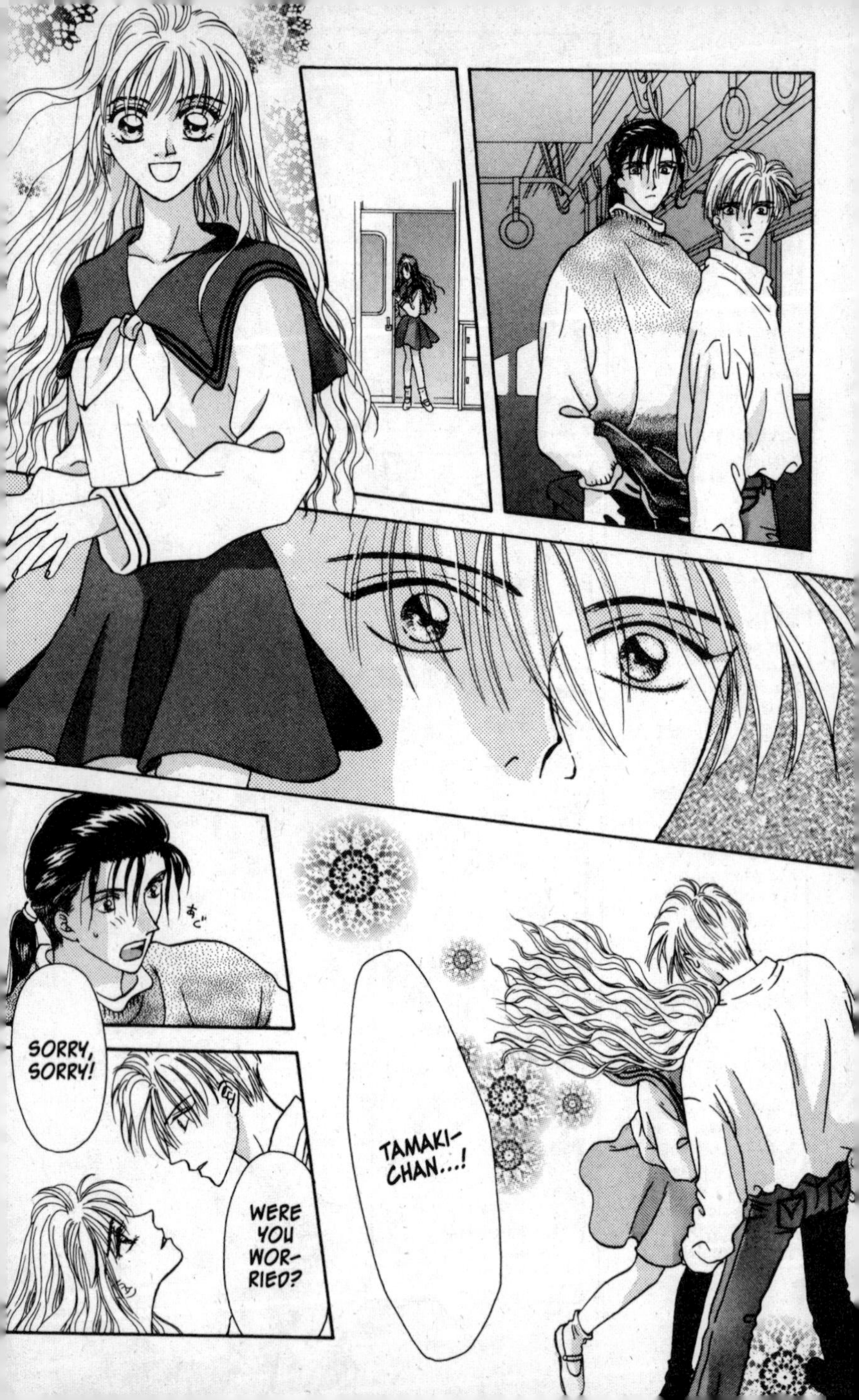
TAMAKI-CHAN...!
SORRY, SORRY!
WERE YOU WORRIED?

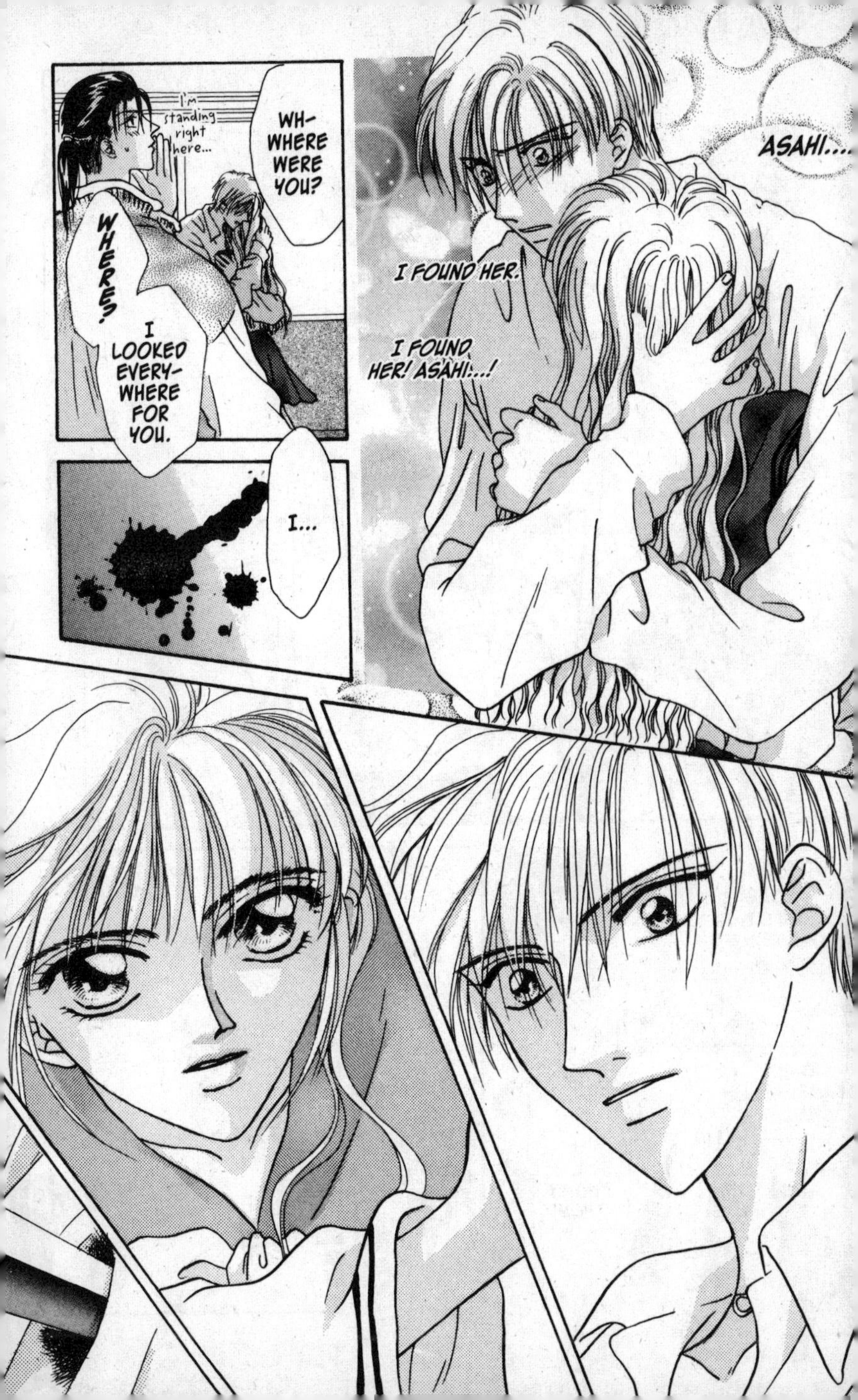

ASAHI....
I FOUND HER.
I FOUND HER! ASAHI...!
WH-WHERE WERE YOU?
I'm standing right here...
WHERE?
I LOOKED EVERY-WHERE FOR YOU.
I...

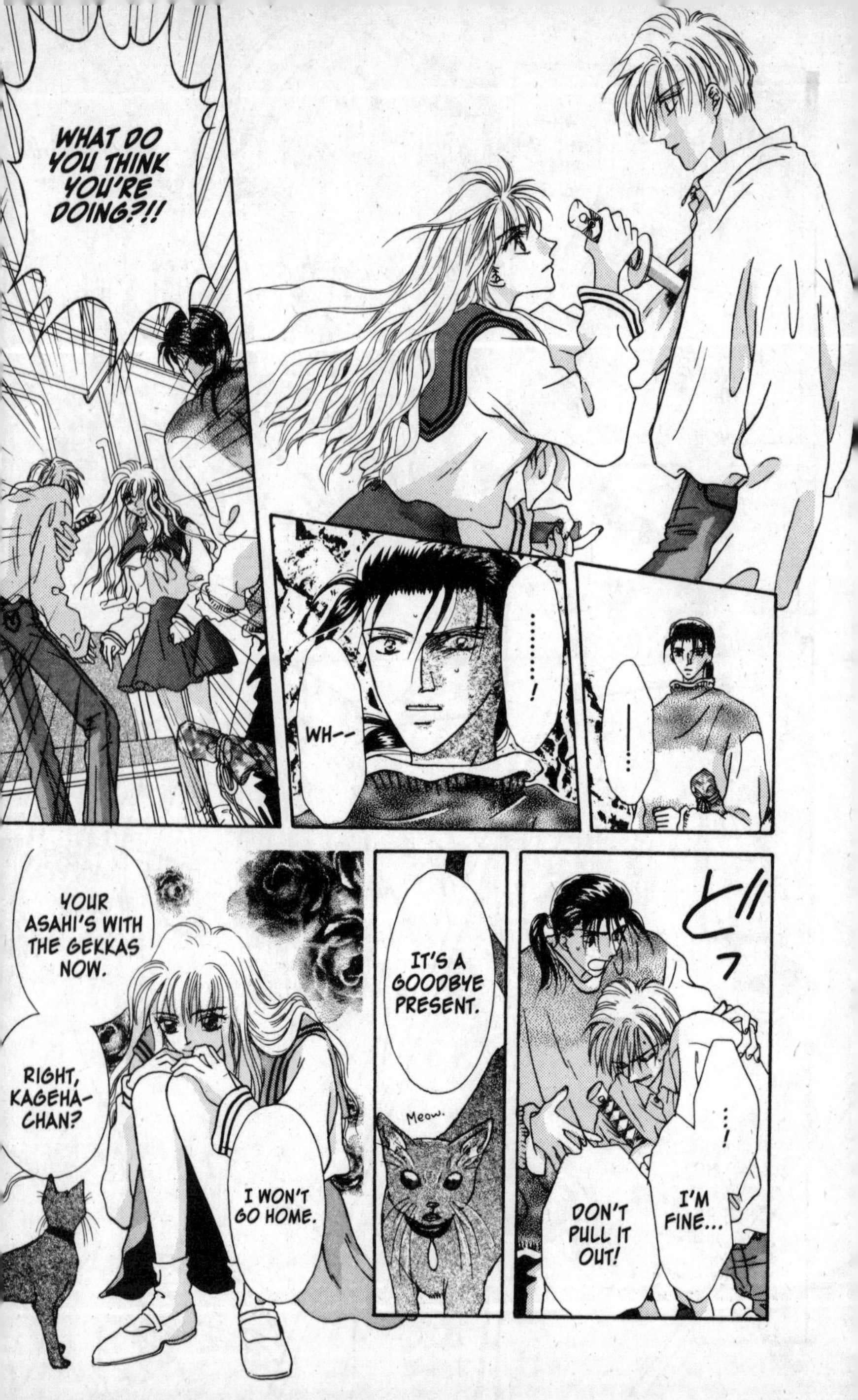

—......
......!
WH--
WHAT DO YOU THINK YOU'RE DOING?!!
どッ
...!
I'M FINE...
DON'T PULL IT OUT!
IT'S A GOODBYE PRESENT.
Meow.
YOUR ASAHI'S WITH THE GEKKAS NOW.
RIGHT, KAGEHA-CHAN?
I WON'T GO HOME.

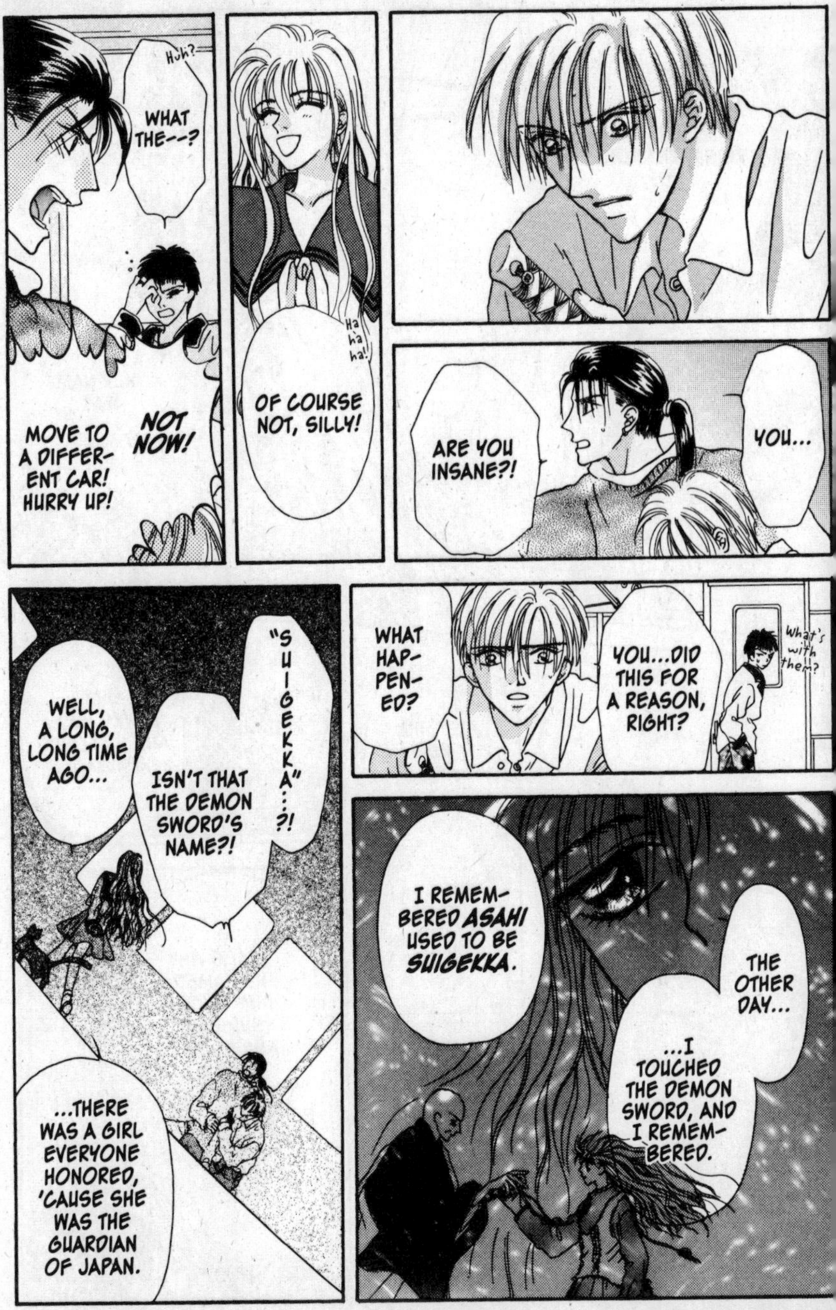
YOU...
ARE YOU INSANE?!
Ha ha ha!
OF COURSE NOT, SILLY!
Huh?
WHAT THE--?
NOT NOW!
MOVE TO A DIFFER-ENT CAR! HURRY UP!
What's with them?
YOU...DID THIS FOR A REASON, RIGHT?
WHAT HAP-PEN-ED?
THE OTHER DAY...
...I TOUCHED THE DEMON SWORD, AND I REMEM-BERED.
I REMEM-BERED ASAHI USED TO BE SUIGEKKA.
"SUIGEKKA"...?!
ISN'T THAT THE DEMON SWORD'S NAME?!
WELL, A LONG, LONG TIME AGO...
...THERE WAS A GIRL EVERYONE HONORED, 'CAUSE SHE WAS THE GUARDIAN OF JAPAN.

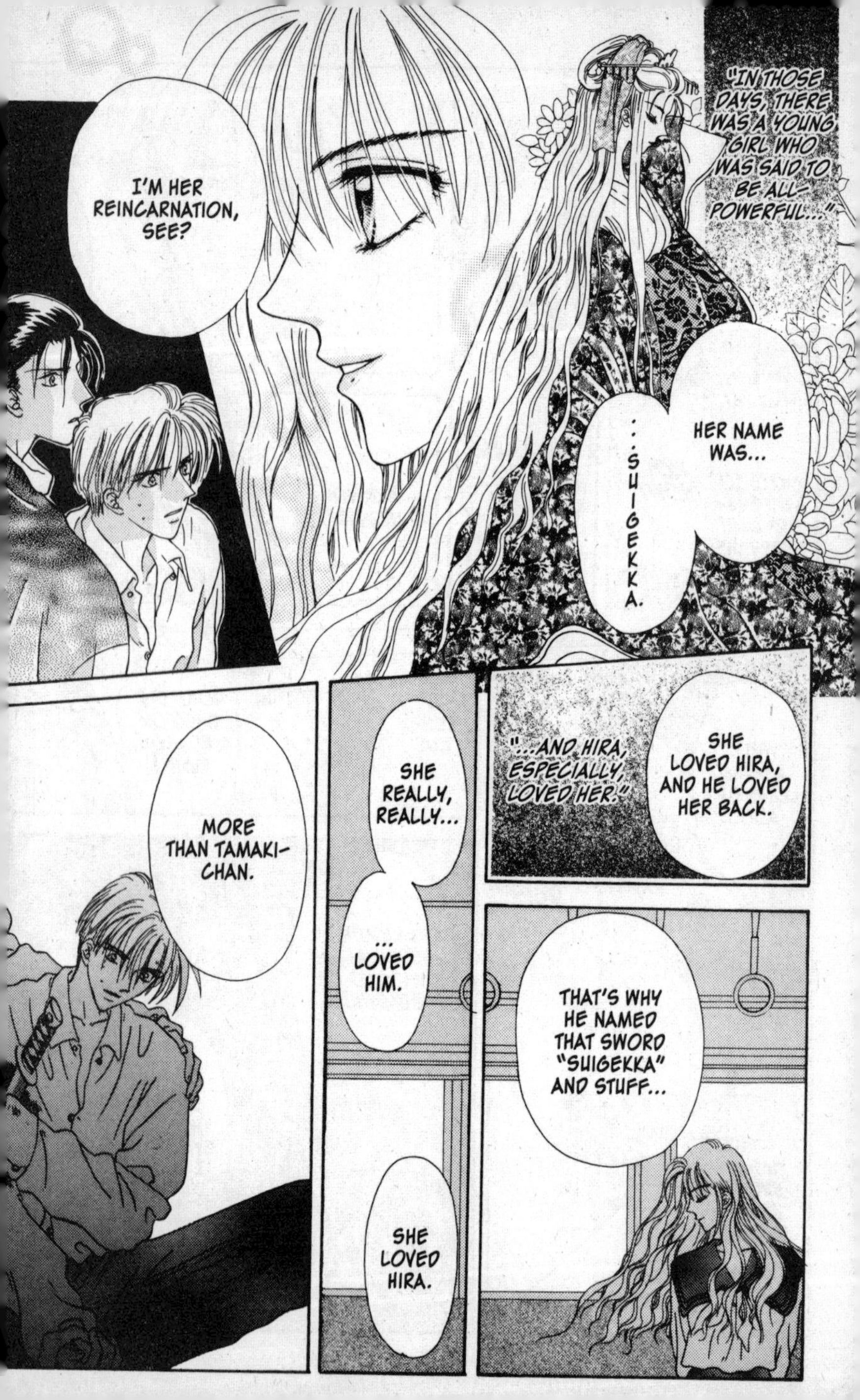
"IN THOSE DAYS, THERE WAS A YOUNG GIRL WHO WAS SAID TO BE ALL-POWERFUL..."
HER NAME WAS...
...SUIGEKKA.
I'M HER REINCARNATION, SEE?
SHE LOVED HIRA, AND HE LOVED HER BACK.
"...AND HIRA, ESPECIALLY, LOVED HER."
THAT'S WHY HE NAMED THAT SWORD "SUIGEKKA" AND STUFF...
SHE REALLY, REALLY...
...LOVED HIM.
SHE LOVED HIRA.
MORE THAN TAMAKI-CHAN.

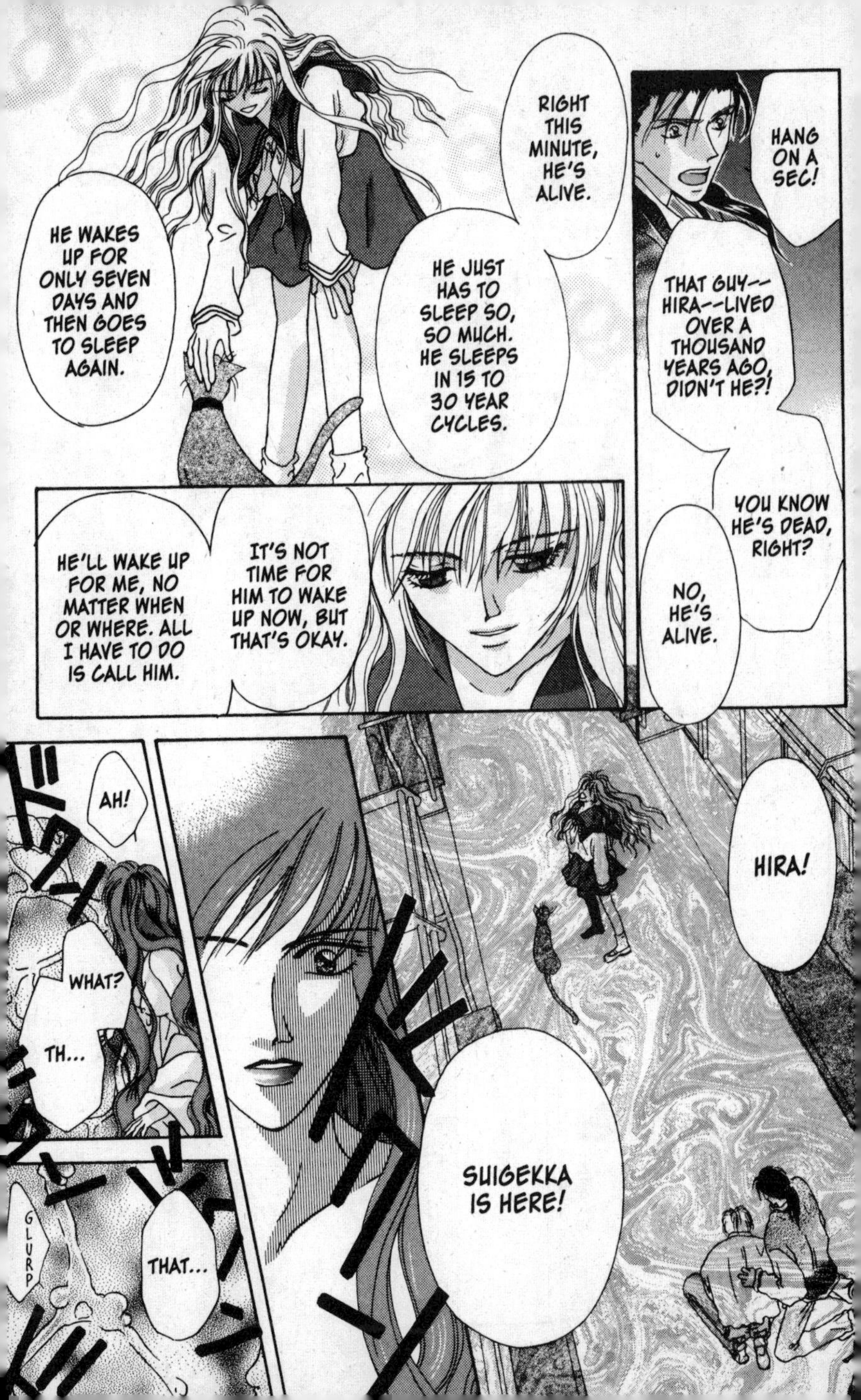
HANG ON A SEC!
THAT GUY--HIRA--LIVED OVER A THOUSAND YEARS AGO, DIDN'T HE?!
YOU KNOW HE'S DEAD, RIGHT?
NO, HE'S ALIVE.
RIGHT THIS MINUTE, HE'S ALIVE.
HE JUST HAS TO SLEEP SO, SO MUCH. HE SLEEPS IN 15 TO 30 YEAR CYCLES.
HE WAKES UP FOR ONLY SEVEN DAYS AND THEN GOES TO SLEEP AGAIN.
IT'S NOT TIME FOR HIM TO WAKE UP NOW, BUT THAT'S OKAY.
HE'LL WAKE UP FOR ME, NO MATTER WHEN OR WHERE. ALL I HAVE TO DO IS CALL HIM.
HIRA!
SUIGEKKA IS HERE!
AH!
WHAT?
TH...
THAT...
GLURP

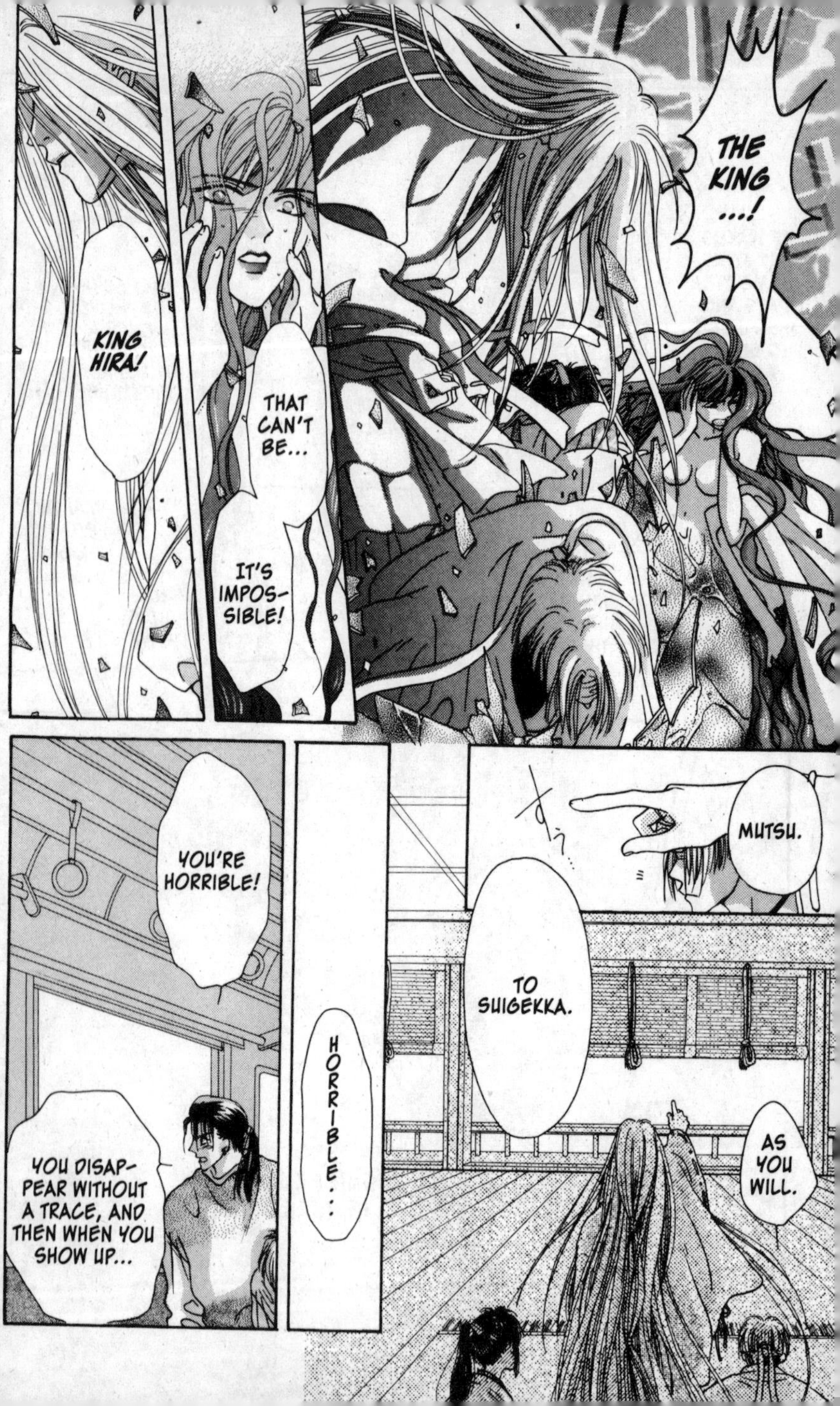
THE KING ...!
THAT CAN'T BE...
IT'S IMPOS-SIBLE!
KING HIRA!
MUTSU.
TO SUIGEKKA.
AS YOU WILL.
HORRIBLE...
YOU'RE HORRIBLE!
YOU DISAP-PEAR WITHOUT A TRACE, AND THEN WHEN YOU SHOW UP...

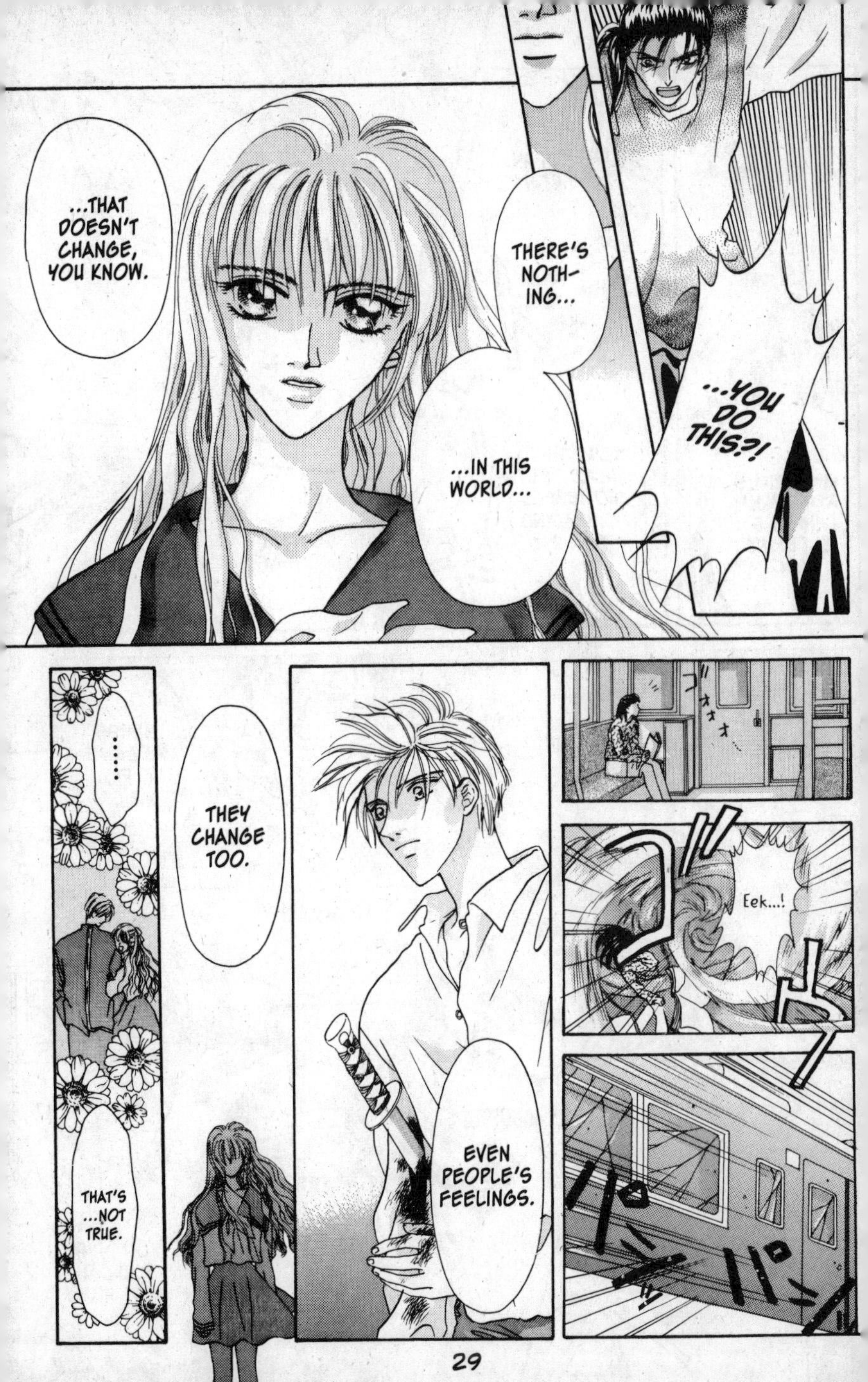
...YOU DO THIS?!
THERE'S NOTHING...
...IN THIS WORLD...
...THAT DOESN'T CHANGE, YOU KNOW.
Eek...!
THEY CHANGE TOO.
EVEN PEOPLE'S FEELINGS.
......
THAT'S ...NOT TRUE.

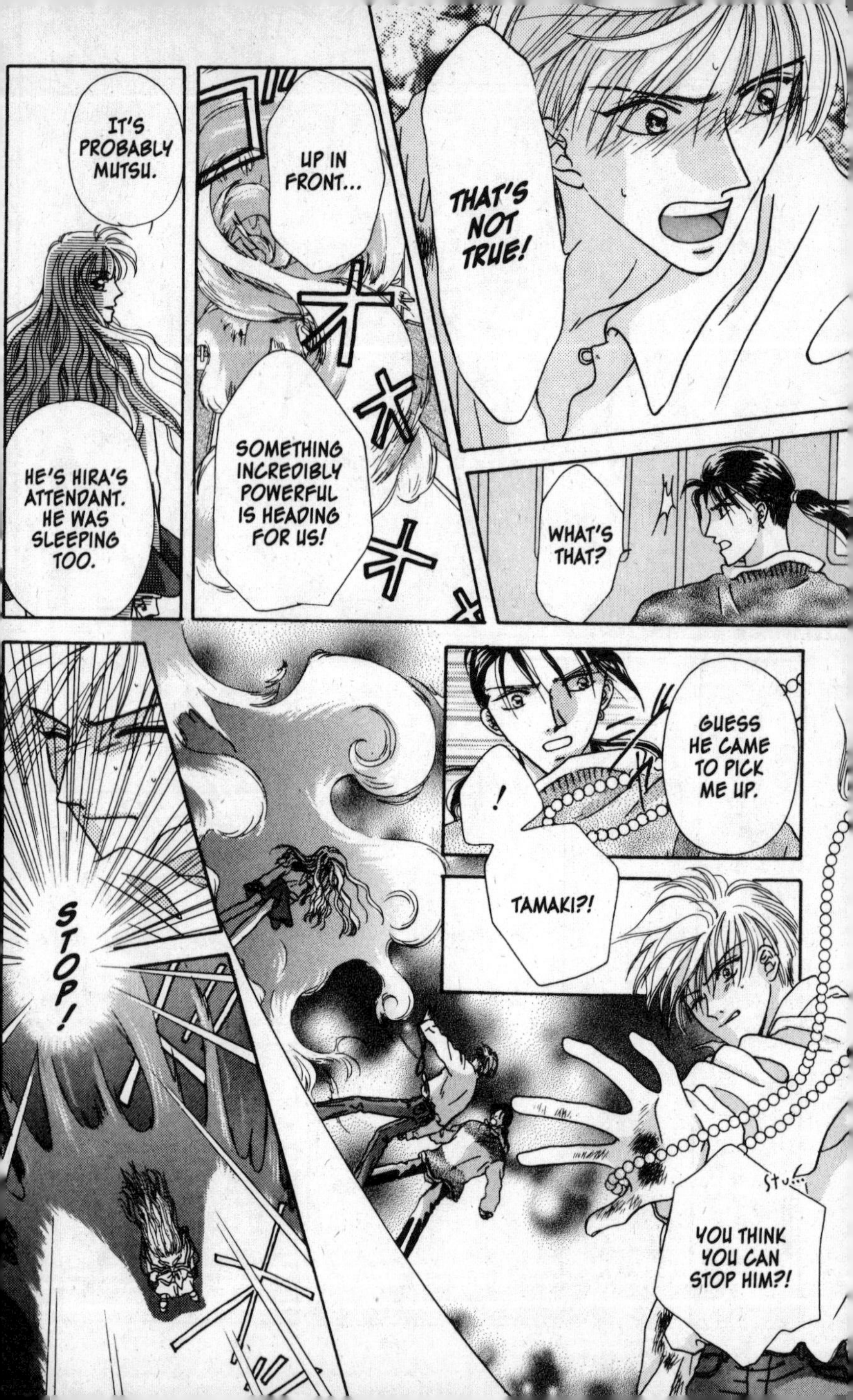

THAT'S NOT TRUE!
WHAT'S THAT?
UP IN FRONT...
SOMETHING INCREDIBLY POWERFUL IS HEADING FOR US!
IT'S PROBABLY MUTSU.
HE'S HIRA'S ATTENDANT. HE WAS SLEEPING TOO.
GUESS HE CAME TO PICK ME UP.
!
TAMAKI?!
Stu...
YOU THINK YOU CAN STOP HIM?!
STOP!

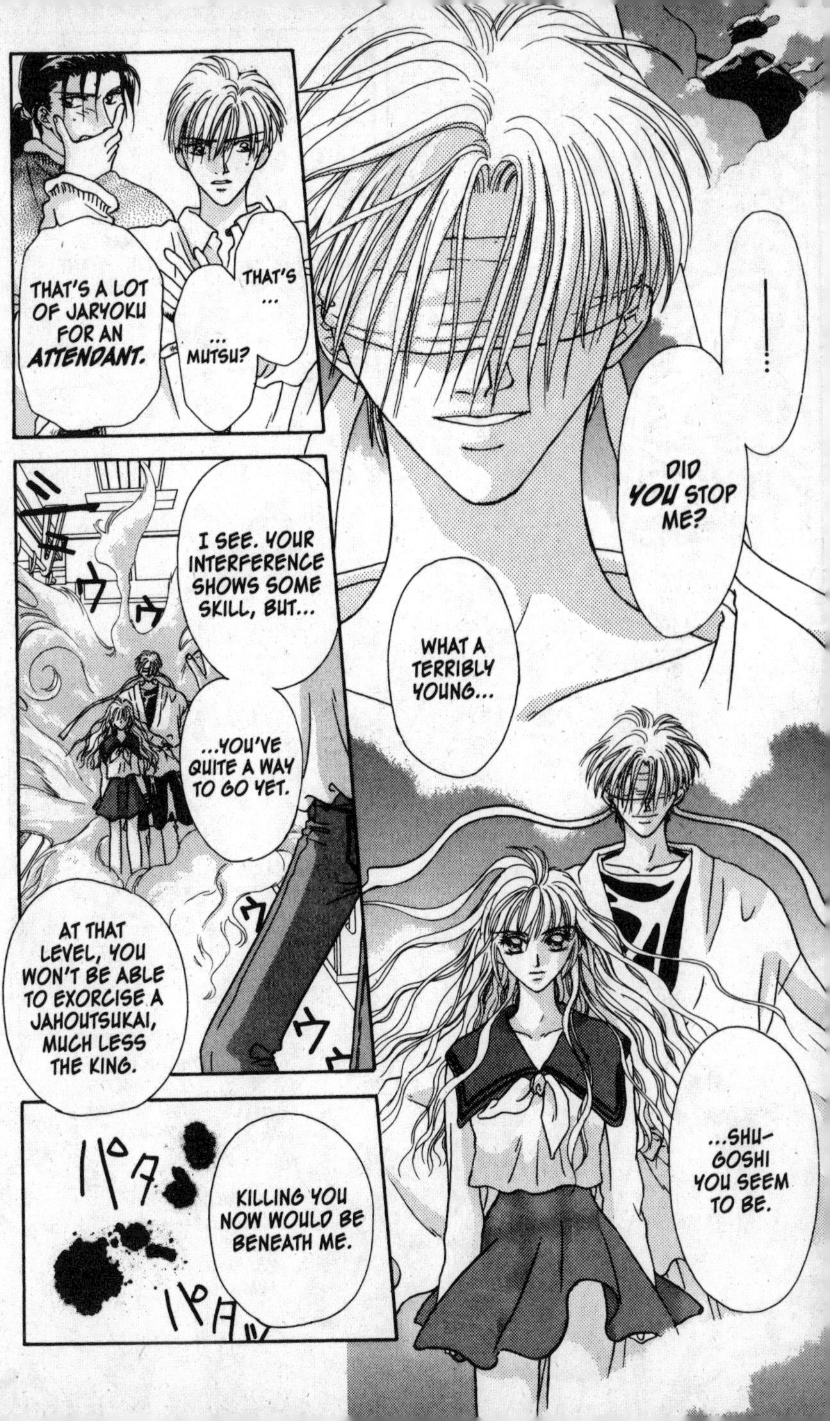

…!
DID *YOU* STOP ME?
WHAT A TERRIBLY YOUNG...
...SHU-GOSHI YOU SEEM TO BE.
THAT'S ... ... MUTSU?
THAT'S A LOT OF JARYOKU FOR AN *ATTENDANT.*
I SEE. YOUR INTERFERENCE SHOWS SOME SKILL, BUT...
...YOU'VE QUITE A WAY TO GO YET.
AT THAT LEVEL, YOU WON'T BE ABLE TO EXORCISE A JAHOUTSUKAI, MUCH LESS THE KING.
KILLING YOU NOW WOULD BE BENEATH ME.
パタ
パタッ

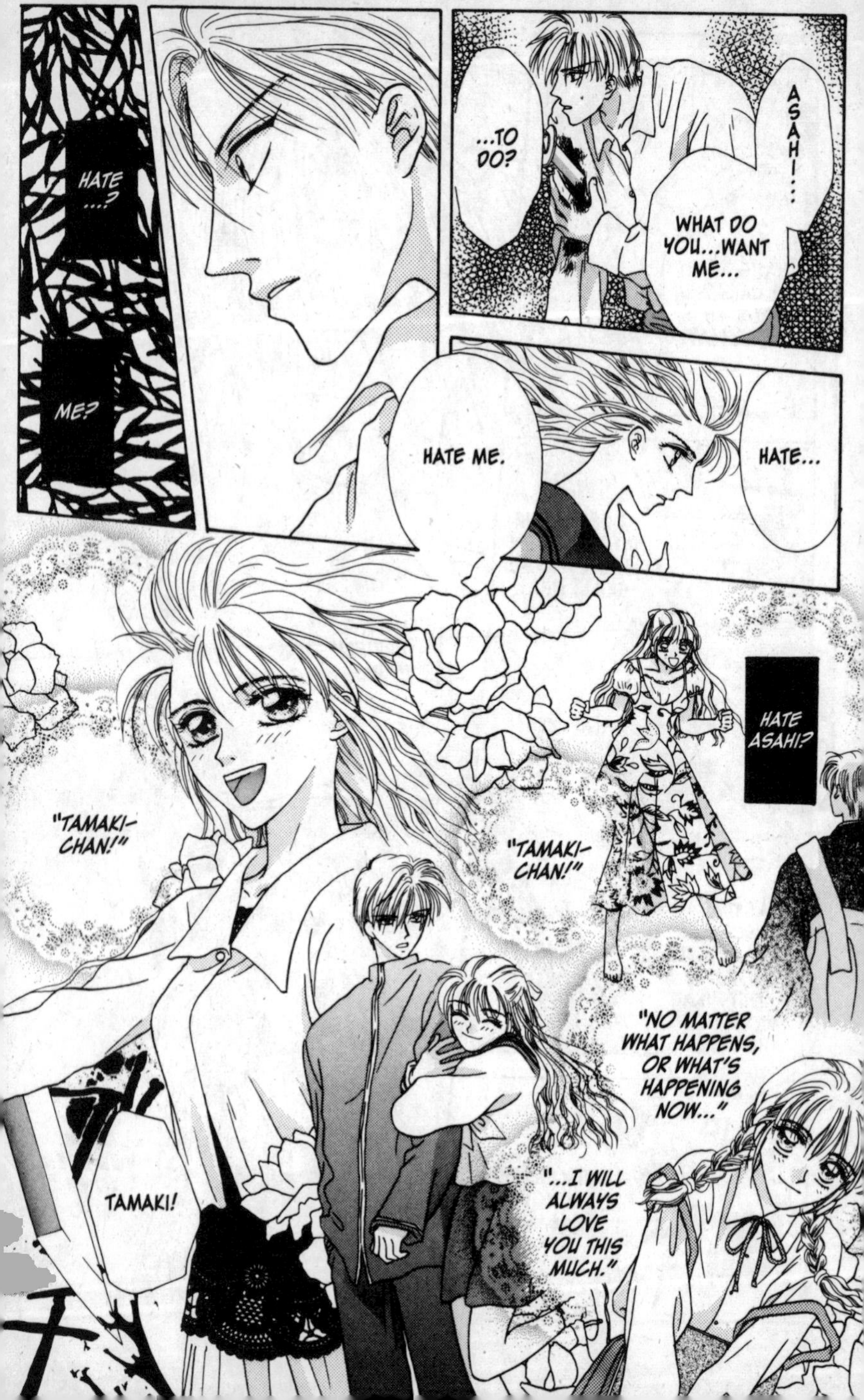
ASAHI...
WHAT DO YOU...WANT ME...
...TO DO?
HATE...
HATE ME.
HATE ...?
ME?
HATE ASAHI?
"TAMAKI-CHAN!"
"TAMAKI-CHAN!"
"NO MATTER WHAT HAPPENS, OR WHAT'S HAPPENING NOW..."
"...I WILL ALWAYS LOVE YOU THIS MUCH."
TAMAKI!

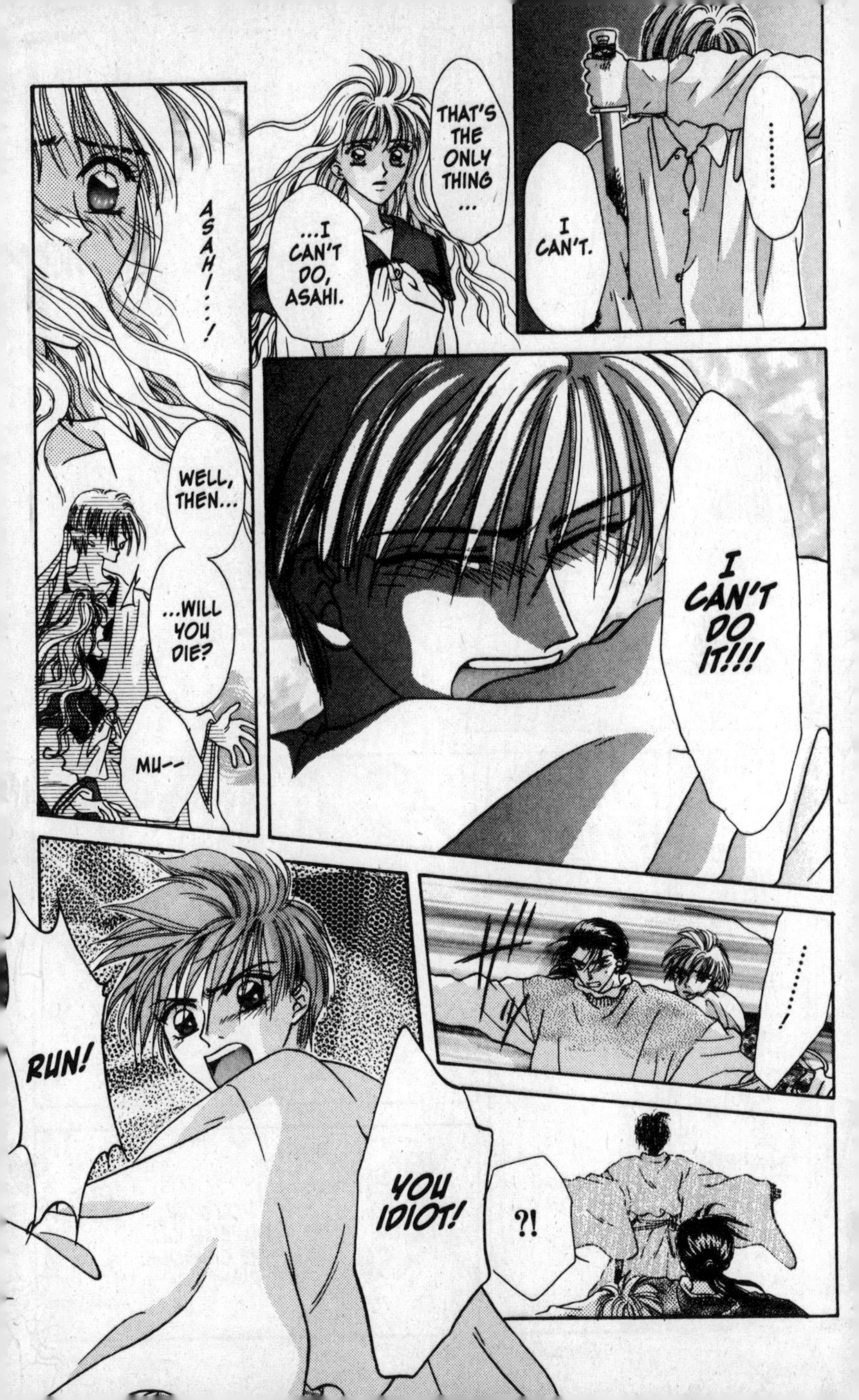

......
I CAN'T.
THAT'S THE ONLY THING...
...I CAN'T DO, ASAHI.
I CAN'T DO IT!!!
ASAHI...!
WELL, THEN...
...WILL YOU DIE?
MU--
......!
?!
RUN!
YOU IDIOT!

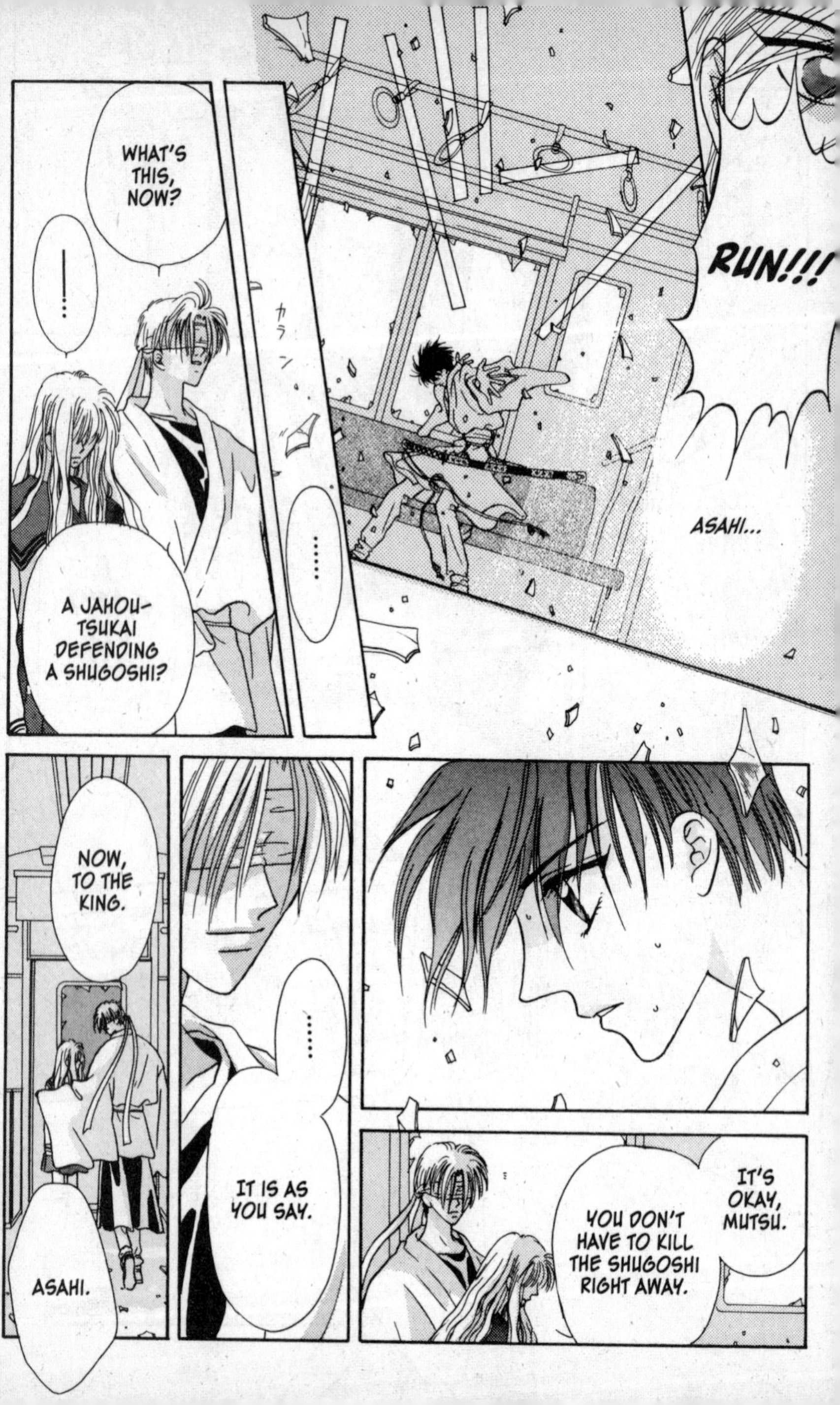
RUN!!!
カラン
ASAHI...
......
WHAT'S THIS, NOW?
!......
A JAHOU-TSUKAI DEFENDING A SHUGOSHI?
IT'S OKAY, MUTSU.
YOU DON'T HAVE TO KILL THE SHUGOSHI RIGHT AWAY.
......
IT IS AS YOU SAY.
NOW, TO THE KING.
ASAHI.

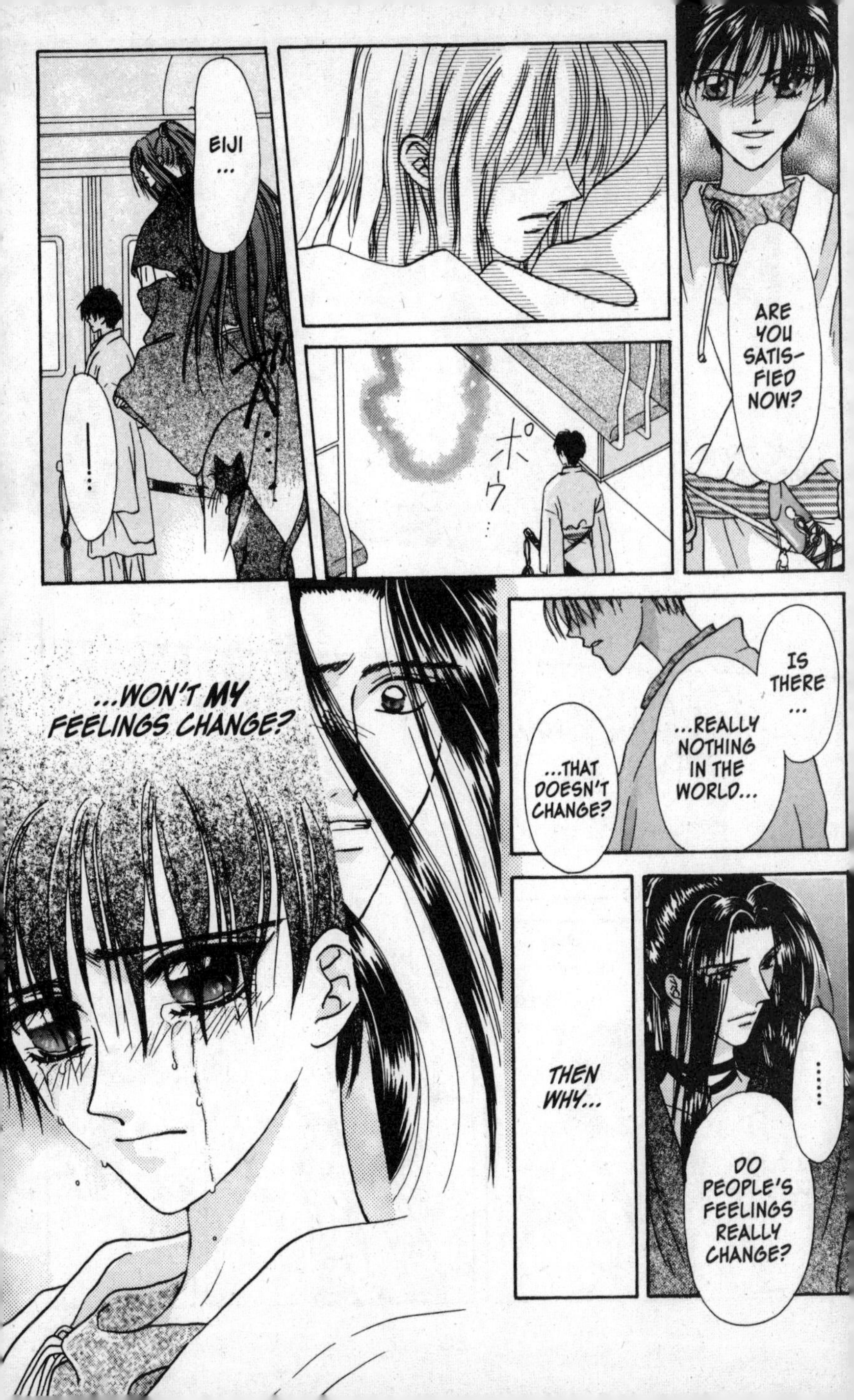
ARE YOU SATIS-FIED NOW?
ポゥ...
EIJI ...
—...
IS THERE ...
...REALLY NOTHING IN THE WORLD...
...THAT DOESN'T CHANGE?
......
DO PEOPLE'S FEELINGS REALLY CHANGE?
THEN WHY...
...WON'T MY FEELINGS CHANGE?

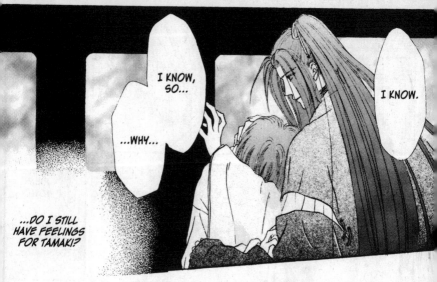

I KNOW, SO...

...WHY...

I KNOW.

...DO I STILL HAVE FEELINGS FOR TAMAKI?

ROKA'S...

...AWAKE TOO, HUH?

YES.

I SLEPT ALONGSIDE THE KING.

36

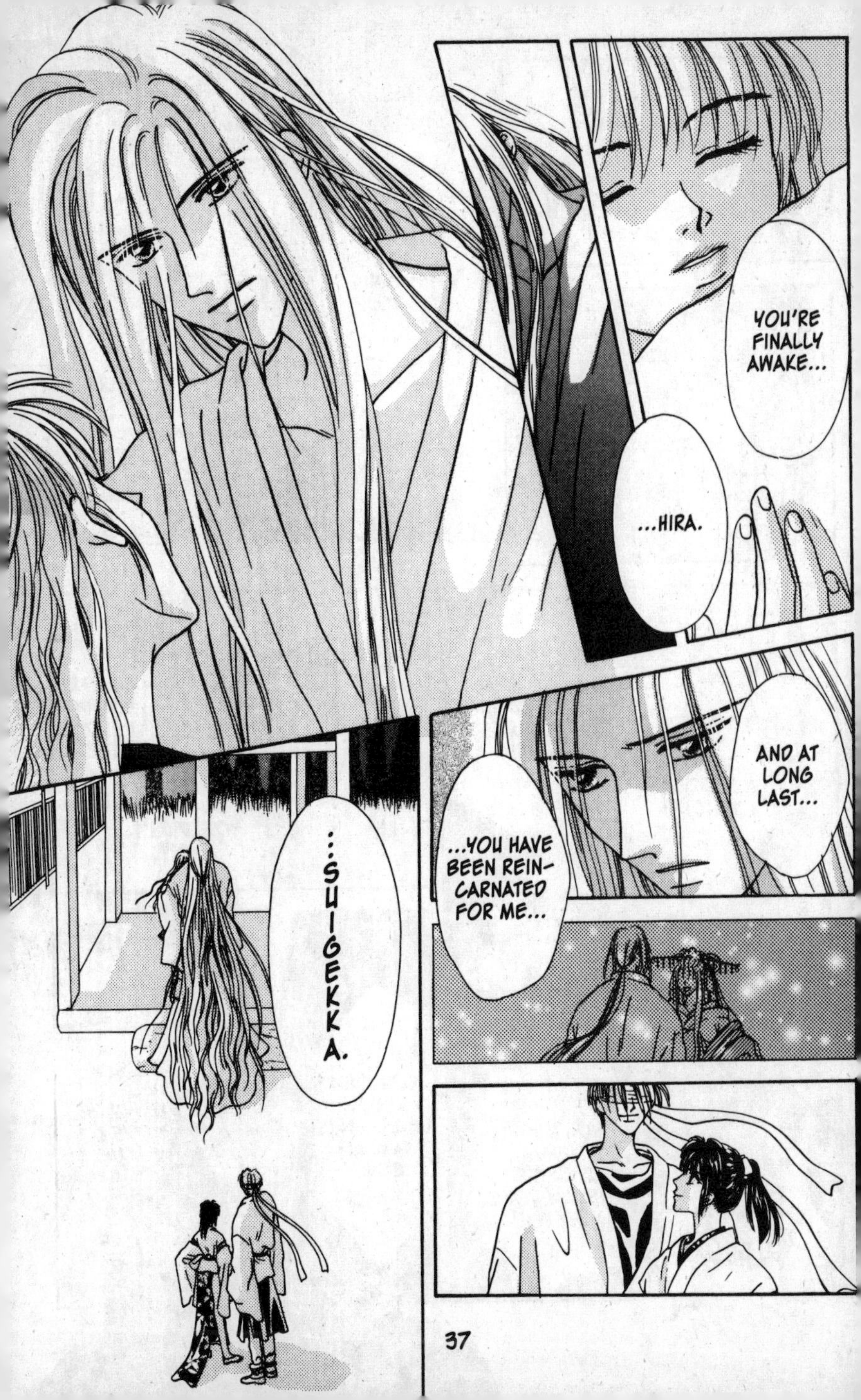
YOU'RE FINALLY AWAKE...
...HIRA.
AND AT LONG LAST...
...YOU HAVE BEEN REIN-CARNATED FOR ME...
...SHIGEKKA.

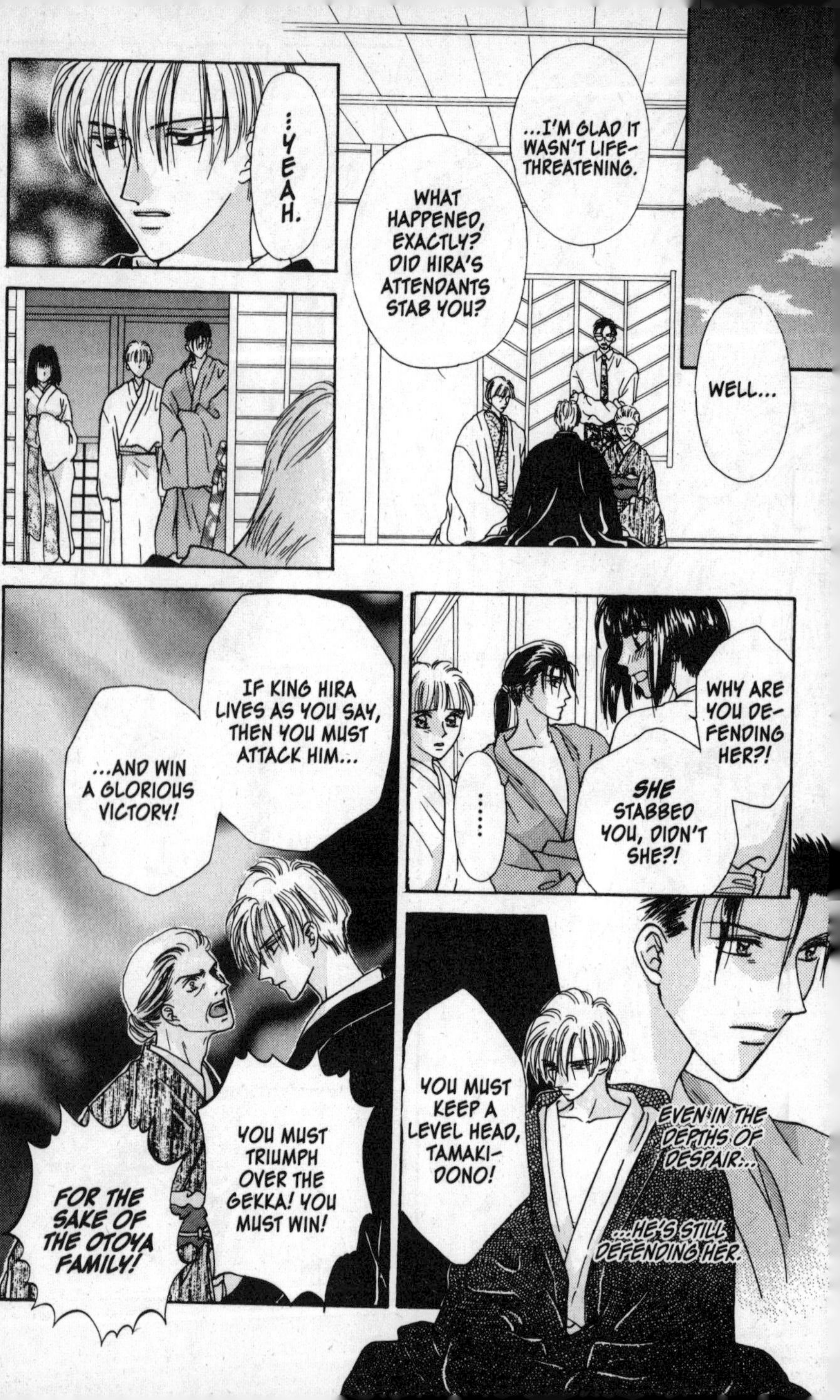
...I'M GLAD IT WASN'T LIFE-THREATENING.
WHAT HAPPENED, EXACTLY? DID HIRA'S ATTENDANTS STAB YOU?
WELL...
...YEAH.
WHY ARE YOU DEFENDING HER?!
SHE STABBED YOU, DIDN'T SHE?!
.....
YOU MUST KEEP A LEVEL HEAD, TAMAKI-DONO!
EVEN IN THE DEPTHS OF DESPAIR...
...HE'S STILL DEFENDING HER.
IF KING HIRA LIVES AS YOU SAY, THEN YOU MUST ATTACK HIM...
...AND WIN A GLORIOUS VICTORY!
YOU MUST TRIUMPH OVER THE GEKKA! YOU MUST WIN!
FOR THE SAKE OF THE OTOYA FAMILY!

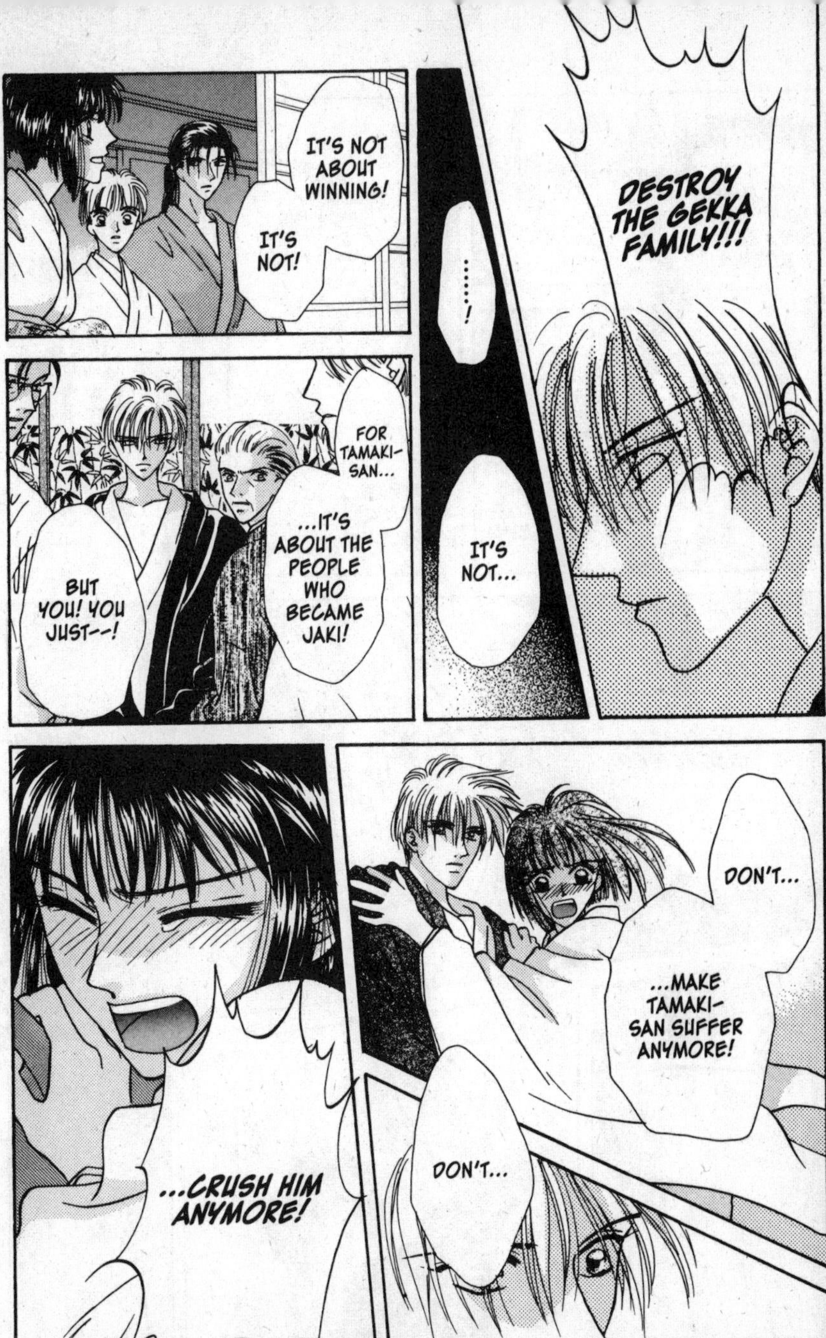
DESTROY THE GEKKA FAMILY!!!
......!
IT'S NOT...
IT'S NOT ABOUT WINNING!
IT'S NOT!
FOR TAMAKI-SAN...
...IT'S ABOUT THE PEOPLE WHO BECAME JAKI!
BUT YOU! YOU JUST--!
DON'T...
...MAKE TAMAKI-SAN SUFFER ANYMORE!
DON'T...
...CRUSH HIM ANYMORE!

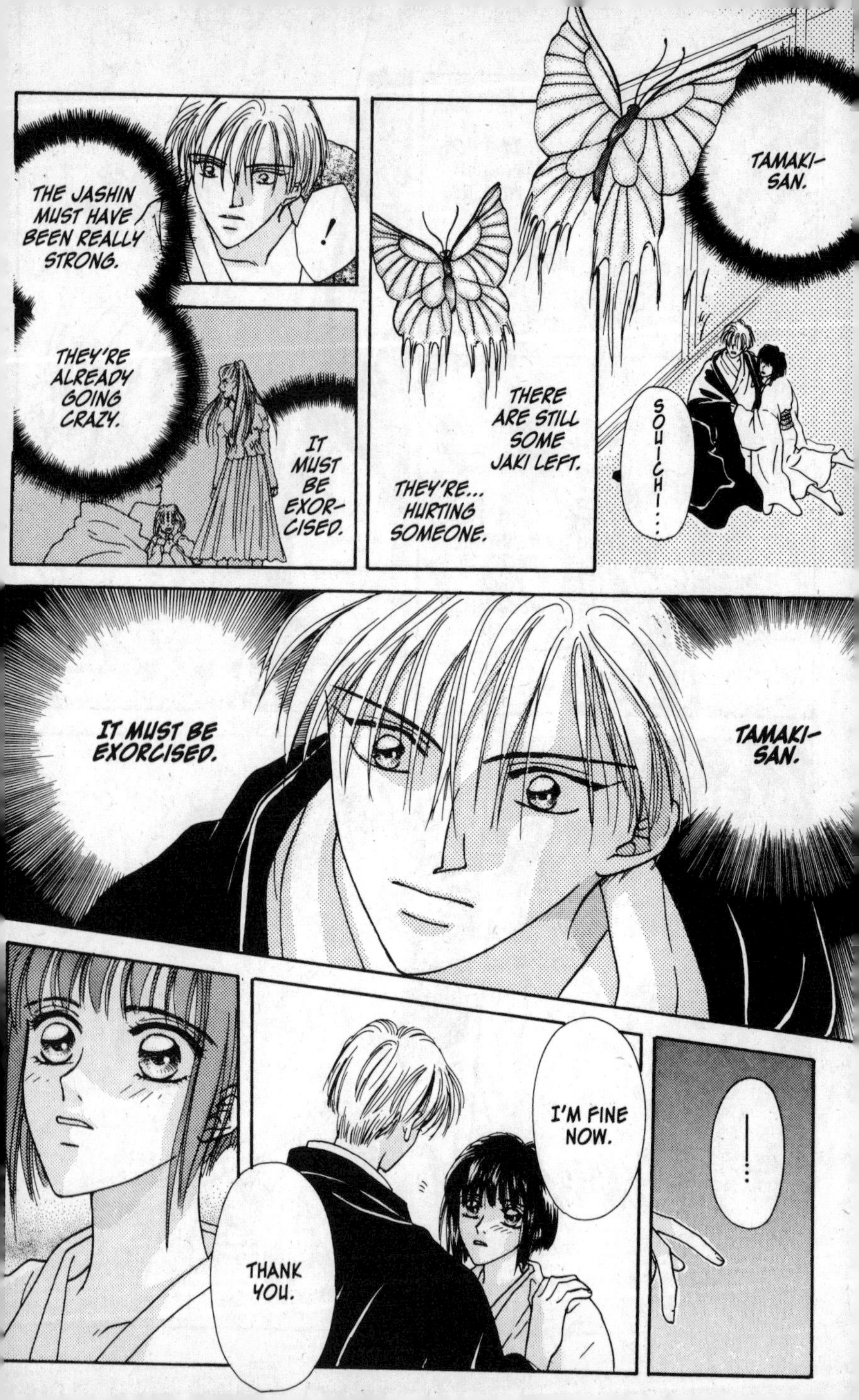
TAMAKI-SAN.
SOUICHI...
THERE ARE STILL SOME JAKI LEFT.
THEY'RE... HURTING SOMEONE.
THE JASHIN MUST HAVE BEEN REALLY STRONG.
!
THEY'RE ALREADY GOING CRAZY.
IT MUST BE EXORCISED.
TAMAKI-SAN.
IT MUST BE EXORCISED.
!...
I'M FINE NOW.
THANK YOU.

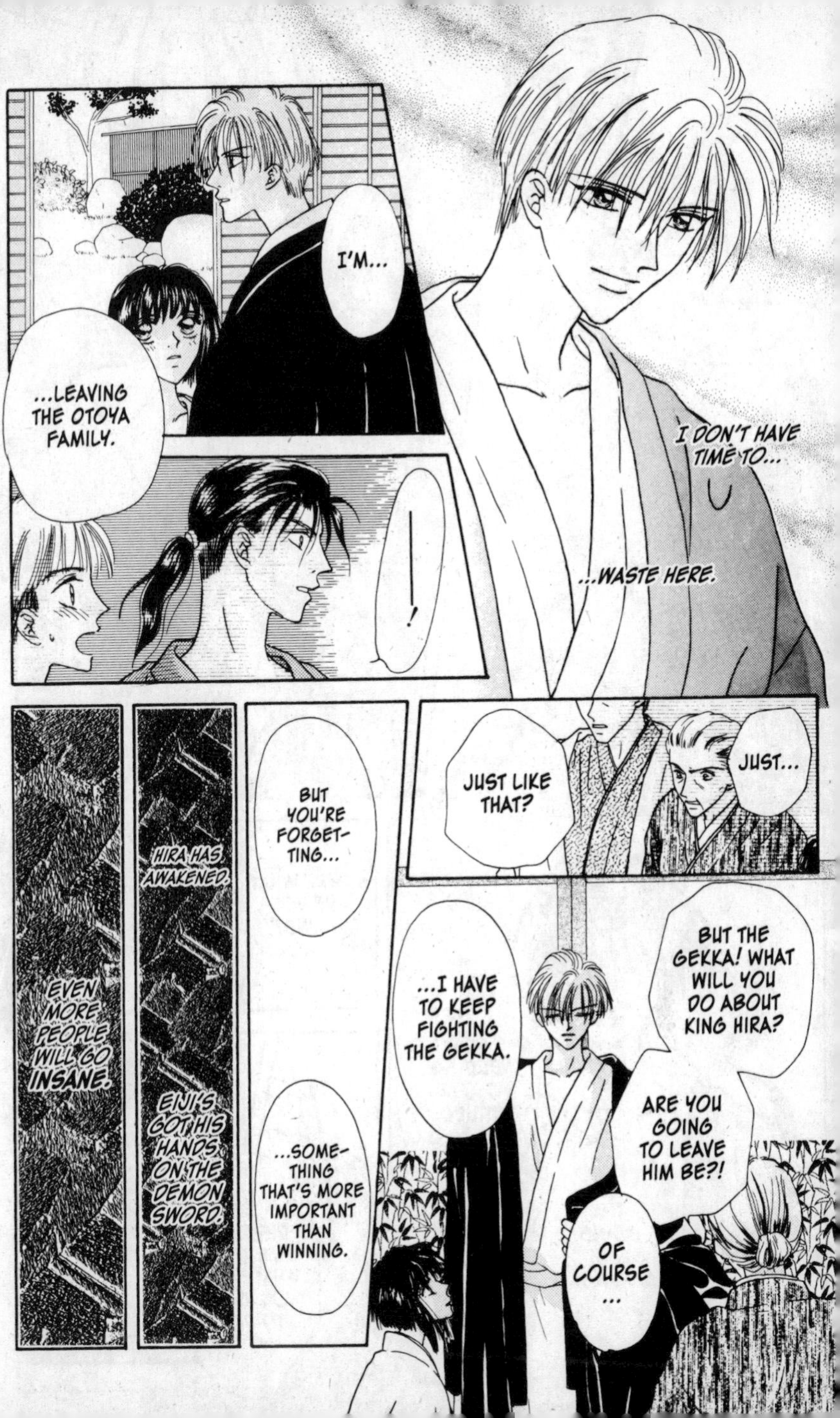
I DON'T HAVE TIME TO...
...WASTE HERE.
I'M...
...LEAVING THE OTOYA FAMILY.
!
JUST...
JUST LIKE THAT?
BUT THE GEKKA! WHAT WILL YOU DO ABOUT KING HIRA?
ARE YOU GOING TO LEAVE HIM BE?!
OF COURSE...
...I HAVE TO KEEP FIGHTING THE GEKKA.
BUT YOU'RE FORGET-TING...
...SOME-THING THAT'S MORE IMPORTANT THAN WINNING.
HIRA HAS AWAKENED.
EIJI'S GOT HIS HANDS ON THE DEMON SWORD.
EVEN MORE PEOPLE WILL GO INSANE.

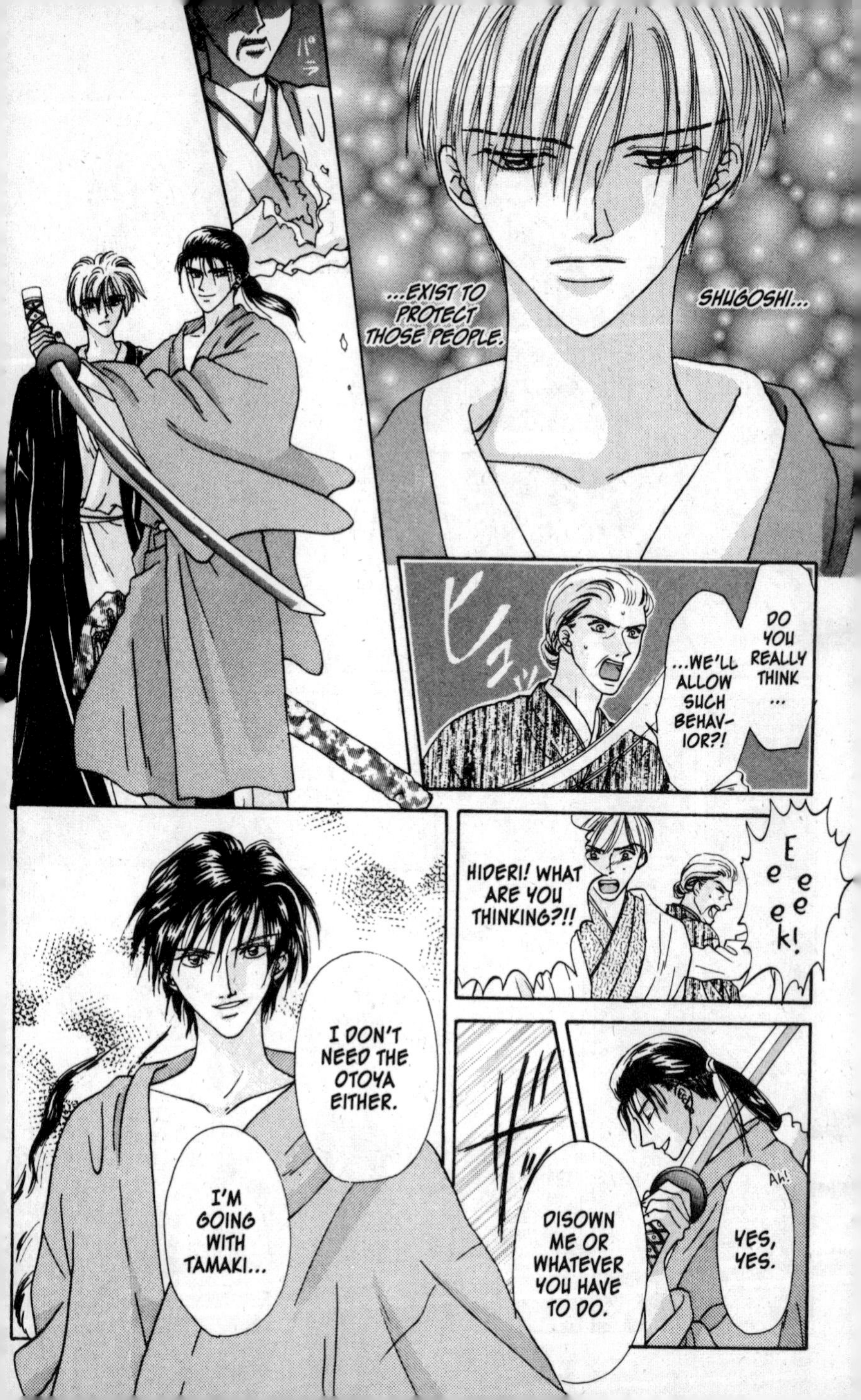
SHUGOSHI...
...EXIST TO PROTECT THOSE PEOPLE.
DO YOU REALLY THINK...
...WE'LL ALLOW SUCH BEHAVIOR?!
HIDERI! WHAT ARE YOU THINKING?!!
Eeeeek!
Ah!
YES, YES.
DISOWN ME OR WHATEVER YOU HAVE TO DO.
I DON'T NEED THE OTOYA EITHER.
I'M GOING WITH TAMAKI...

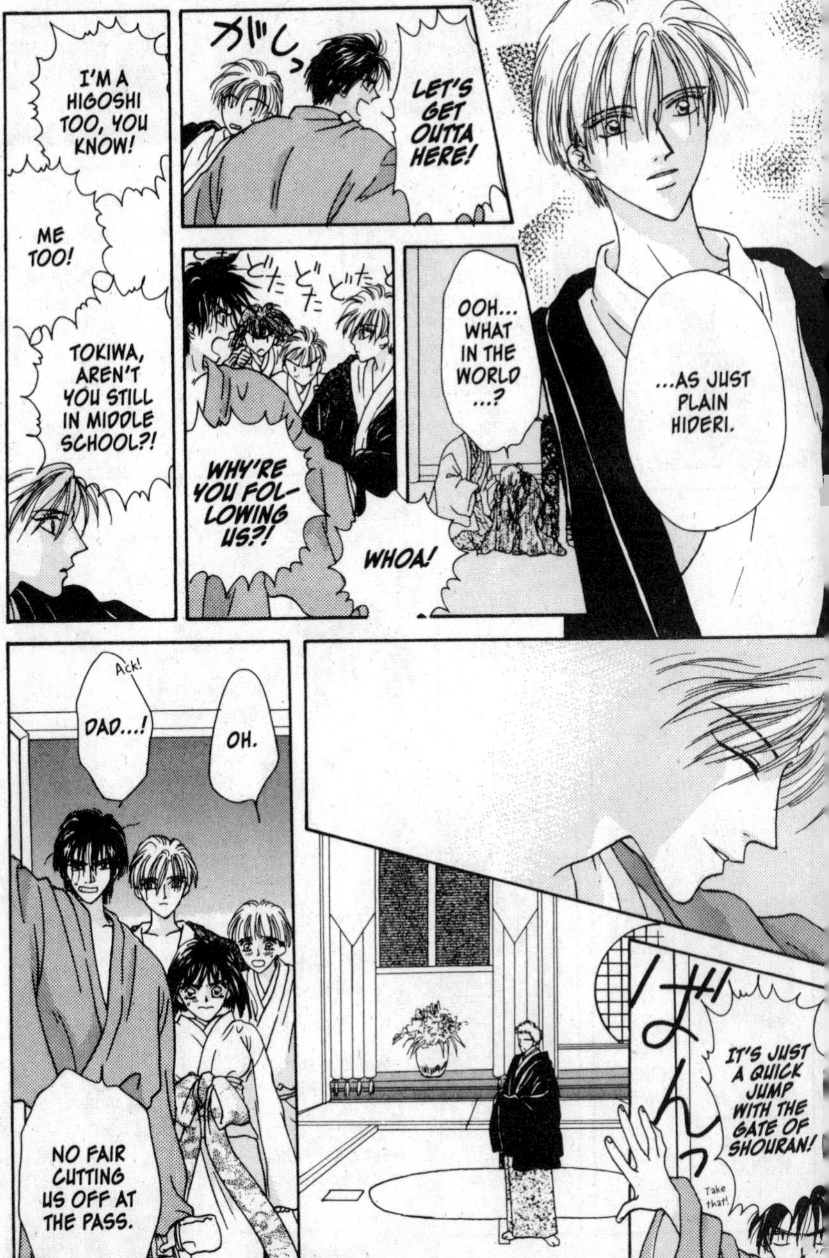
...AS JUST PLAIN HIDERI.
がしっ
LET'S GET OUTTA HERE!
OOH... WHAT IN THE WORLD ...?
どたどたどたどた
WHY'RE YOU FOL-LOWING US?!
WHOA!
I'M A HIGOSHI TOO, YOU KNOW!
ME TOO!
TOKIWA, AREN'T YOU STILL IN MIDDLE SCHOOL?!
ばんっ
IT'S JUST A QUICK JUMP WITH THE GATE OF SHOURAN!
Take that!
Ack!
DAD...!
OH.
NO FAIR CUTTING US OFF AT THE PASS.

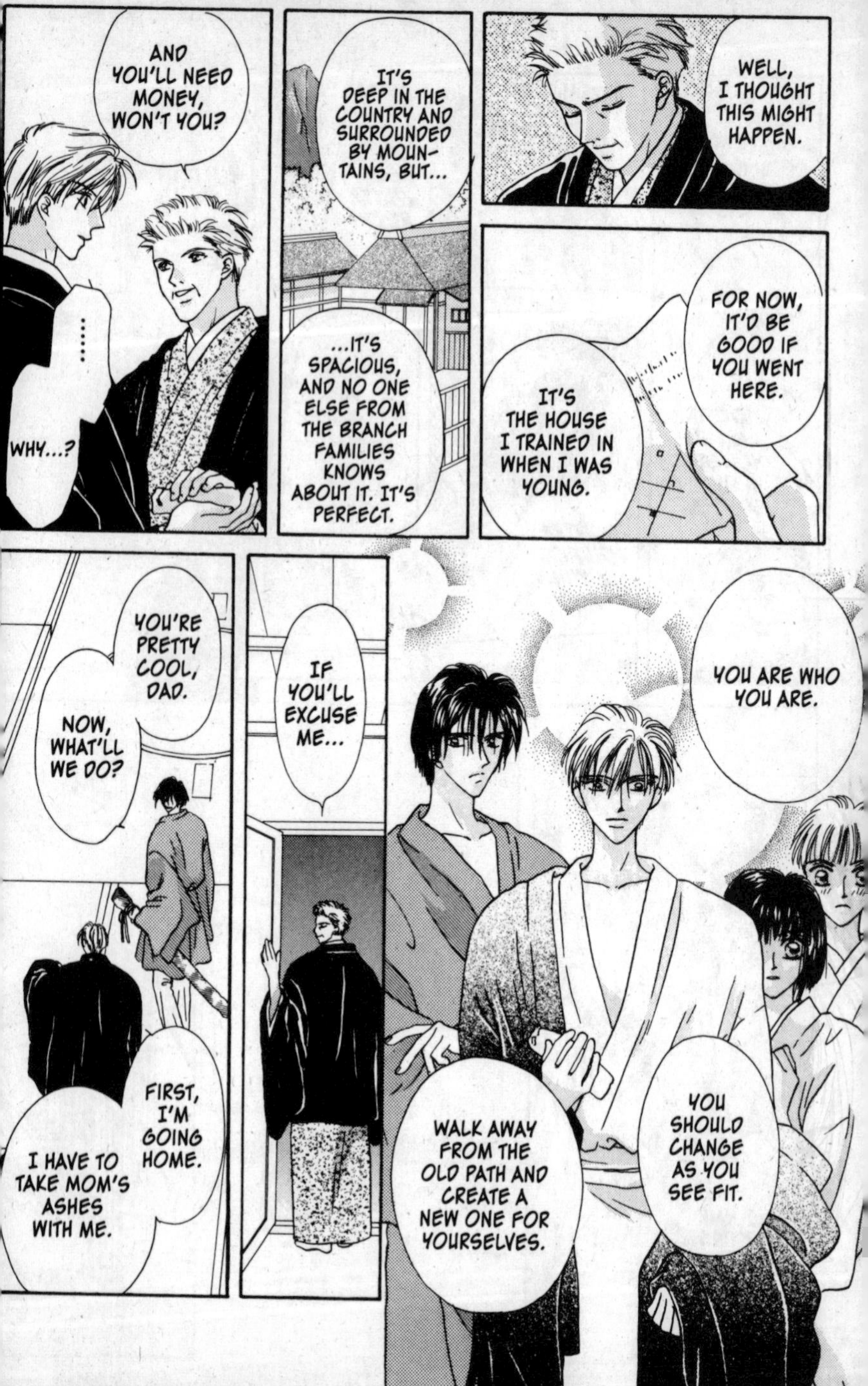
WELL, I THOUGHT THIS MIGHT HAPPEN.
FOR NOW, IT'D BE GOOD IF YOU WENT HERE.
IT'S THE HOUSE I TRAINED IN WHEN I WAS YOUNG.
IT'S DEEP IN THE COUNTRY AND SURROUNDED BY MOUNTAINS, BUT...
...IT'S SPACIOUS, AND NO ONE ELSE FROM THE BRANCH FAMILIES KNOWS ABOUT IT. IT'S PERFECT.
AND YOU'LL NEED MONEY, WON'T YOU?
......
WHY...?
YOU ARE WHO YOU ARE.
YOU SHOULD CHANGE AS YOU SEE FIT.
WALK AWAY FROM THE OLD PATH AND CREATE A NEW ONE FOR YOURSELVES.
IF YOU'LL EXCUSE ME...
YOU'RE PRETTY COOL, DAD.
NOW, WHAT'LL WE DO?
FIRST, I'M GOING HOME.
I HAVE TO TAKE MOM'S ASHES WITH ME.

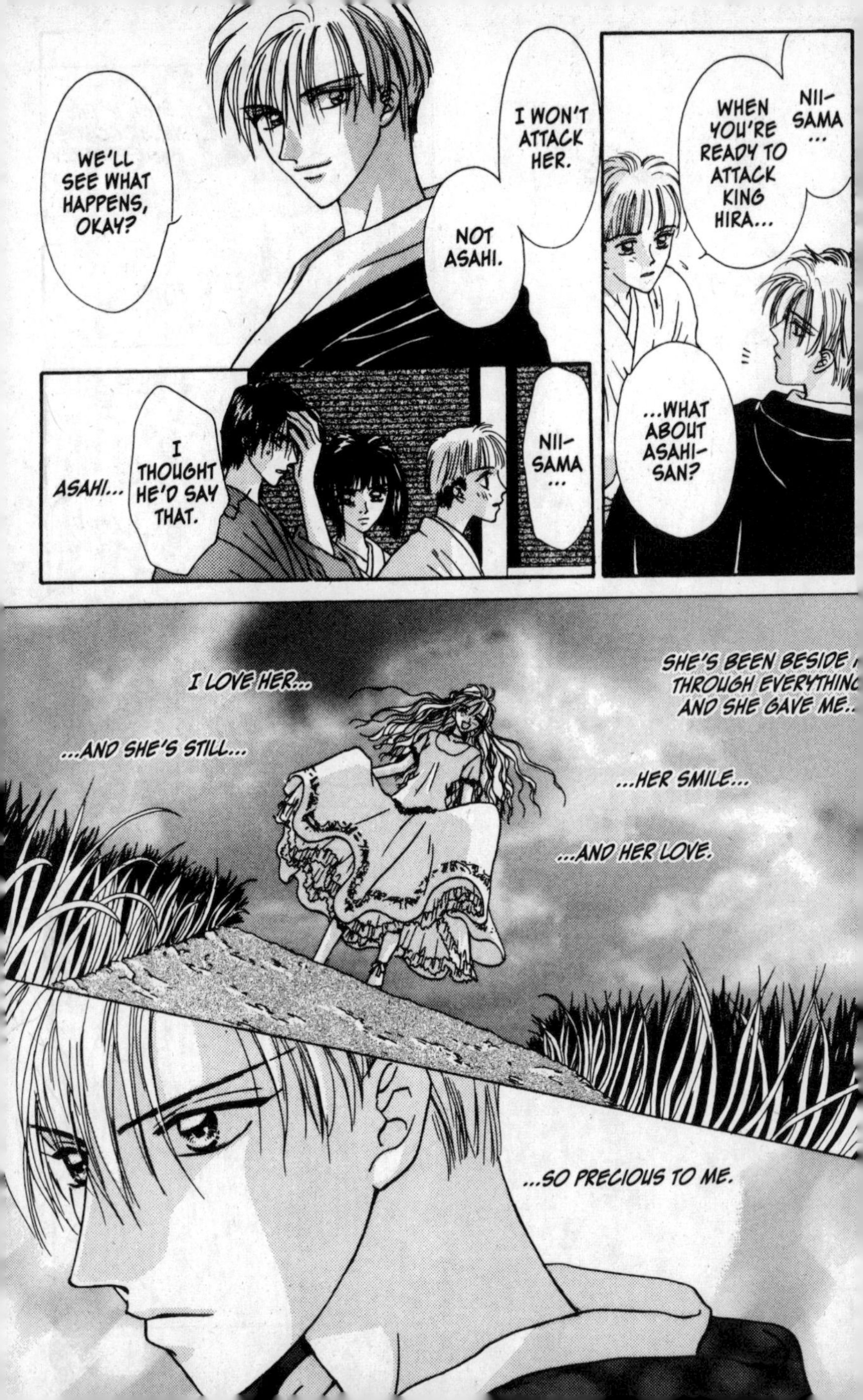
NII-SAMA...
WHEN YOU'RE READY TO ATTACK KING HIRA...
...WHAT ABOUT ASAHI-SAN?
I WON'T ATTACK HER.
NOT ASAHI.
WE'LL SEE WHAT HAPPENS, OKAY?
NII-SAMA...
I THOUGHT HE'D SAY THAT.
ASAHI...
SHE'S BEEN BESIDE
THROUGH EVERYTHIN
AND SHE GAVE ME...
...HER SMILE...
...AND HER LOVE.
I LOVE HER...
...AND SHE'S STILL...
...SO PRECIOUS TO ME.

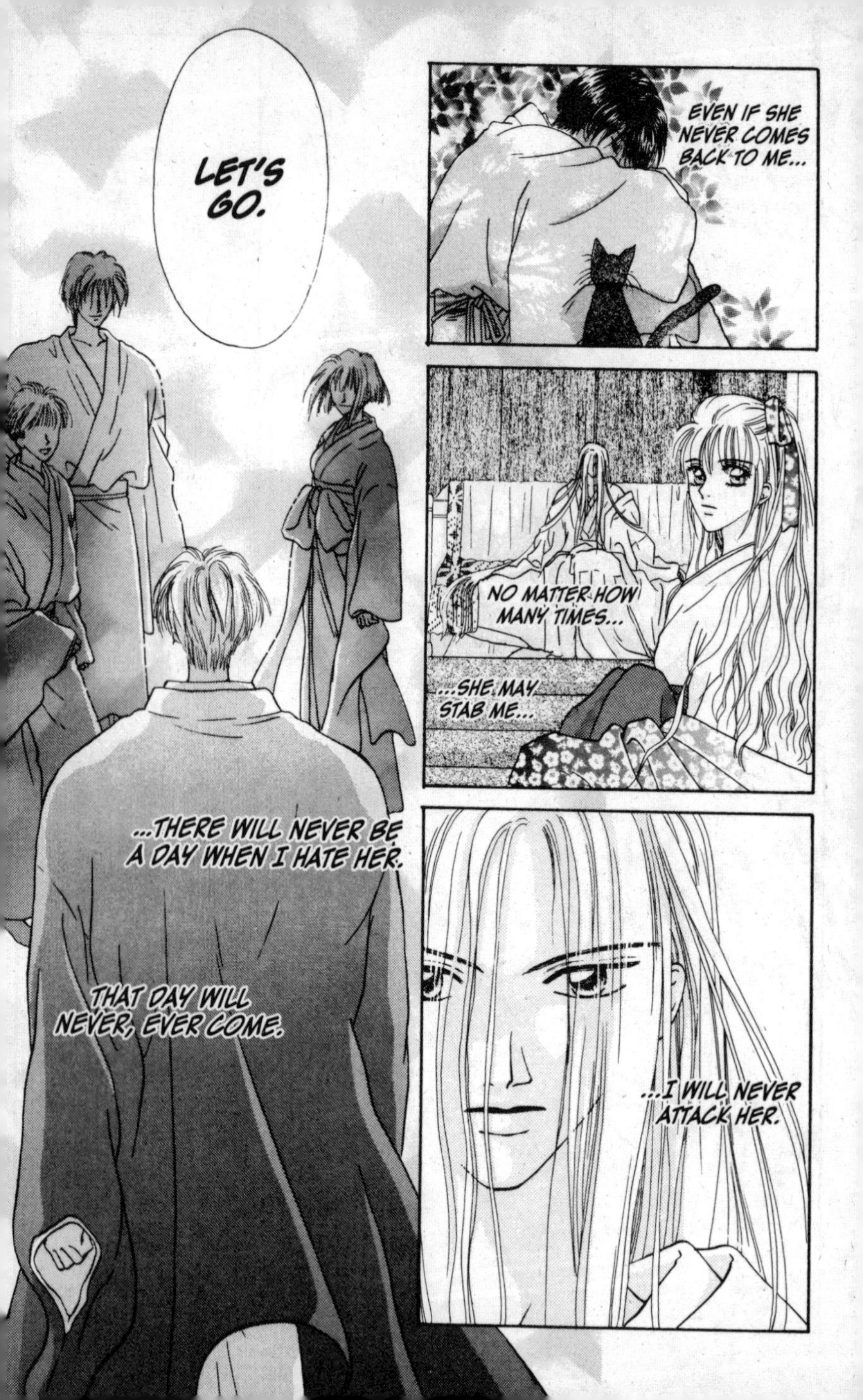
EVEN IF SHE NEVER COMES BACK TO ME...
NO MATTER HOW MANY TIMES...
...SHE MAY STAB ME...
...I WILL NEVER ATTACK HER.
LET'S GO.
...THERE WILL NEVER BE A DAY WHEN I HATE HER.
THAT DAY WILL NEVER, EVER COME.

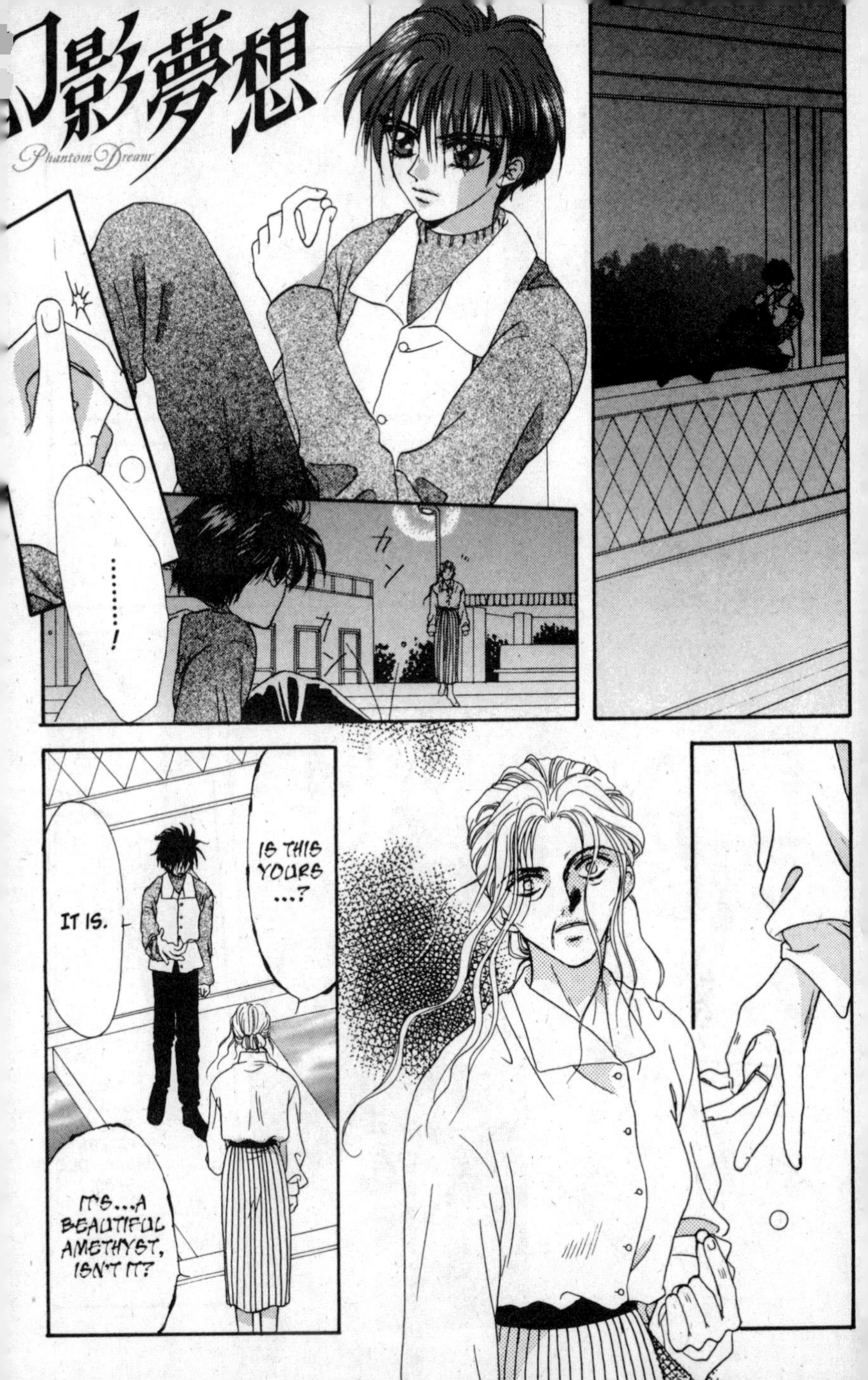
幻影夢想
Phantom Dream
.........!
カン
カン
IS THIS YOURS ...?
IT IS.
IT'S...A BEAUTIFUL AMETHYST, ISN'T IT?

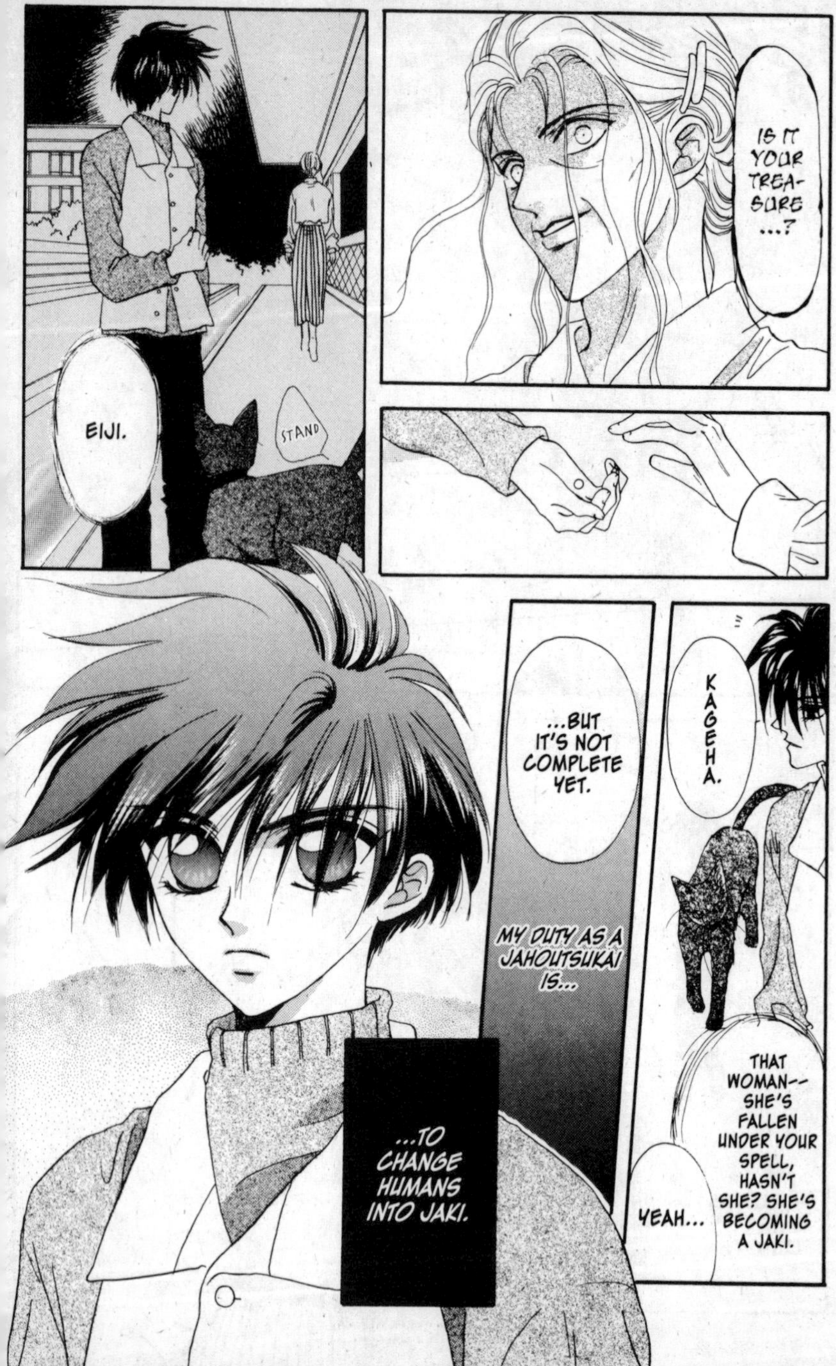
IS IT YOUR TREASURE ...?
EIJI.
STAND
KAGEHA.
THAT WOMAN-- SHE'S FALLEN UNDER YOUR SPELL, HASN'T SHE? SHE'S BECOMING A JAKI.
YEAH...
...BUT IT'S NOT COMPLETE YET.
MY DUTY AS A JAHOUTSUKAI IS...
...TO CHANGE HUMANS INTO JAKI.

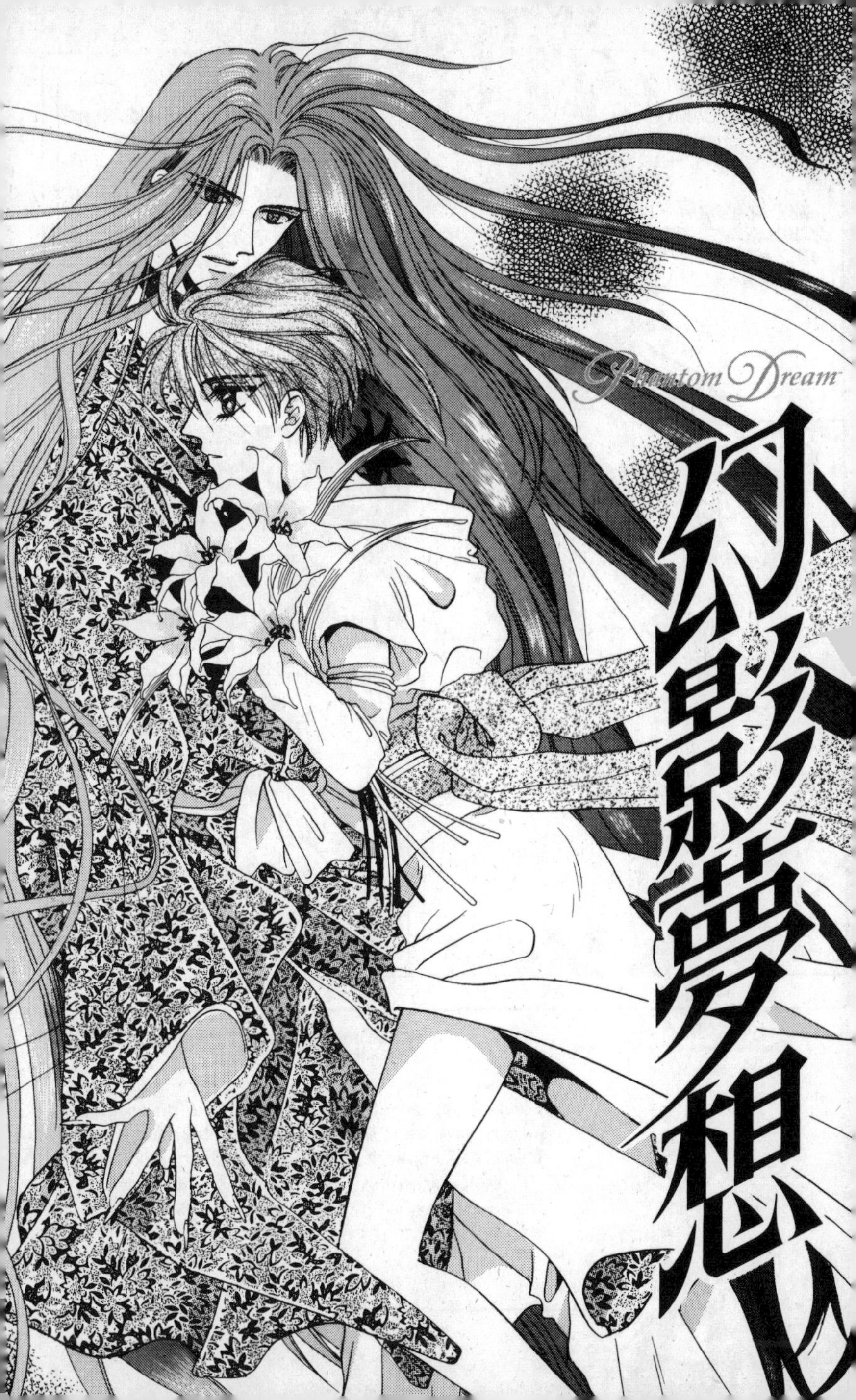
Phantom Dream
幻影夢想

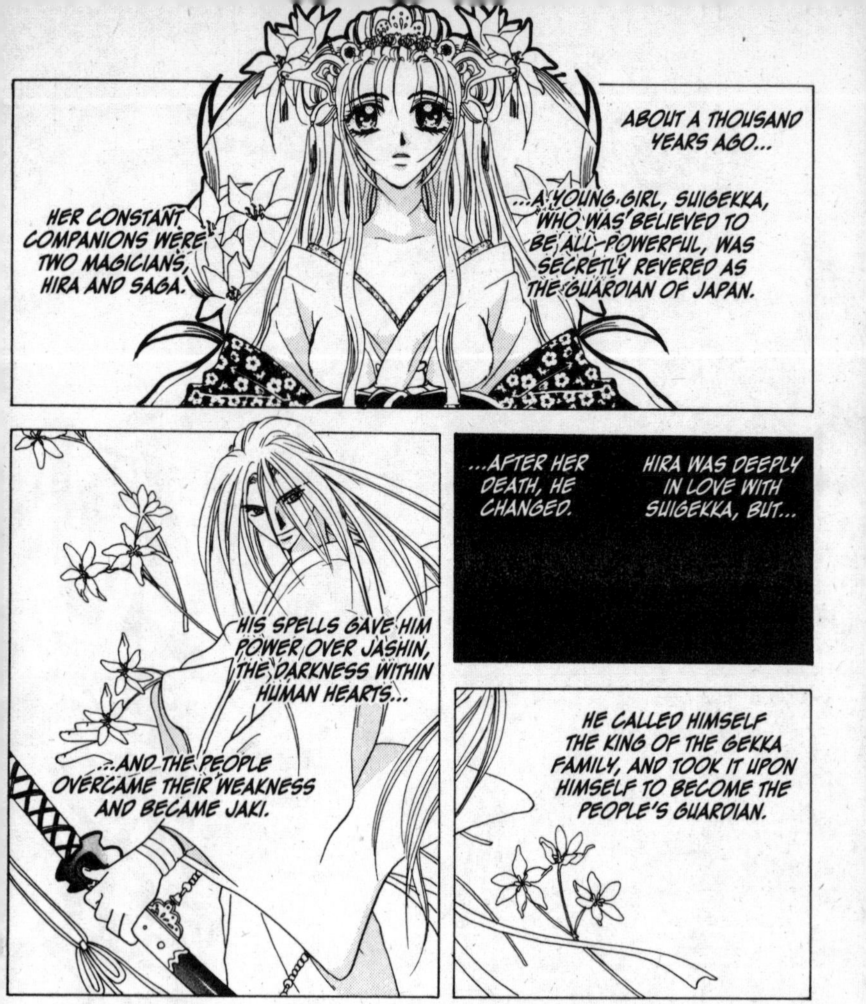
ABOUT A THOUSAND YEARS AGO...
...A YOUNG GIRL, SUIGEKKA, WHO WAS BELIEVED TO BE ALL-POWERFUL, WAS SECRETLY REVERED AS THE GUARDIAN OF JAPAN.
HER CONSTANT COMPANIONS WERE TWO MAGICIANS, HIRA AND SAGA.
HIRA WAS DEEPLY IN LOVE WITH SUIGEKKA, BUT...
...AFTER HER DEATH, HE CHANGED.
HE CALLED HIMSELF THE KING OF THE GEKKA FAMILY, AND TOOK IT UPON HIMSELF TO BECOME THE PEOPLE'S GUARDIAN.
HIS SPELLS GAVE HIM POWER OVER JASHIN, THE DARKNESS WITHIN HUMAN HEARTS...
...AND THE PEOPLE OVERCAME THEIR WEAKNESS AND BECAME JAKI.

ULTRA SPECIAL ***THINGS THAT DON'T MATTER I***
(YOU'RE DOING THIS AGAIN?)

Kageha's cat form has a model--it's a breed called the Russian Blue. When I was drawing him and thinking it'd be nice to have a cat like him, my big sister bought a Russian Blue out of nowhere. I was surprised! It's sooo cute. ♥ It's really friendly, and it sulks if you don't pet it. I'm a dog lover, but this is a lovely cat that makes me (me!) think that cats might be nice too.

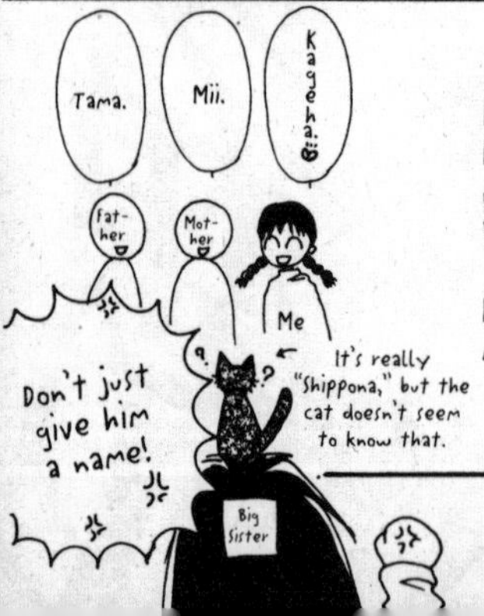
Kageha.♥
Mii.
Tama.
Father
Mother
Me
It's really "Shippona," but the cat doesn't seem to know that.
Don't just give him a name!
Big Sister

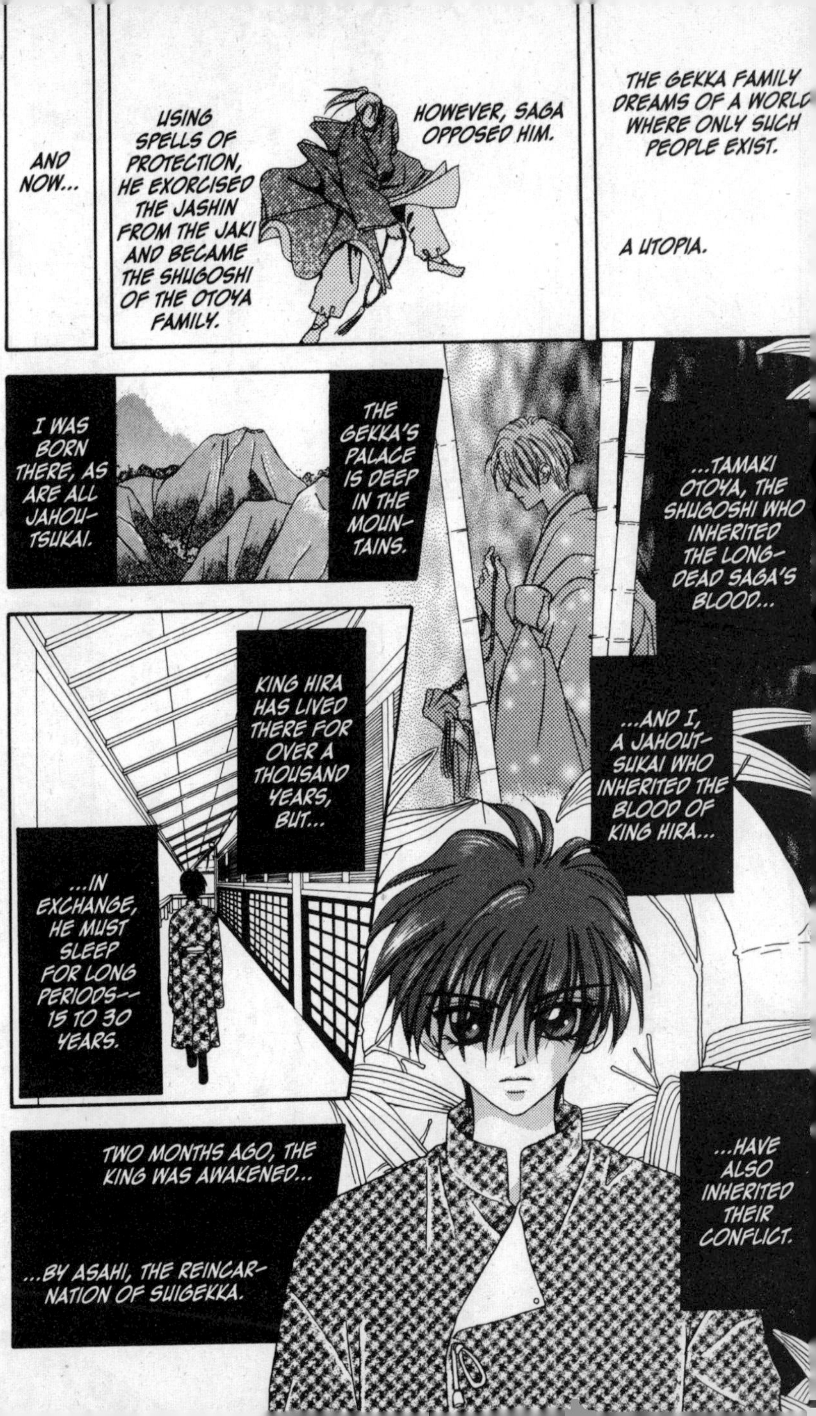
THE GEKKA FAMILY DREAMS OF A WORLD WHERE ONLY SUCH PEOPLE EXIST.
A UTOPIA.
HOWEVER, SAGA OPPOSED HIM.
USING SPELLS OF PROTECTION, HE EXORCISED THE JASHIN FROM THE JAKI AND BECAME THE SHUGOSHI OF THE OTOYA FAMILY.
AND NOW...
...TAMAKI OTOYA, THE SHUGOSHI WHO INHERITED THE LONG-DEAD SAGA'S BLOOD...
...AND I, A JAHOUT-SUKAI WHO INHERITED THE BLOOD OF KING HIRA...
...HAVE ALSO INHERITED THEIR CONFLICT.
THE GEKKA'S PALACE IS DEEP IN THE MOUN-TAINS.
I WAS BORN THERE, AS ARE ALL JAHOU-TSUKAI.
KING HIRA HAS LIVED THERE FOR OVER A THOUSAND YEARS, BUT...
...IN EXCHANGE, HE MUST SLEEP FOR LONG PERIODS--15 TO 30 YEARS.
TWO MONTHS AGO, THE KING WAS AWAKENED...
...BY ASAHI, THE REINCAR-NATION OF SUIGEKKA.

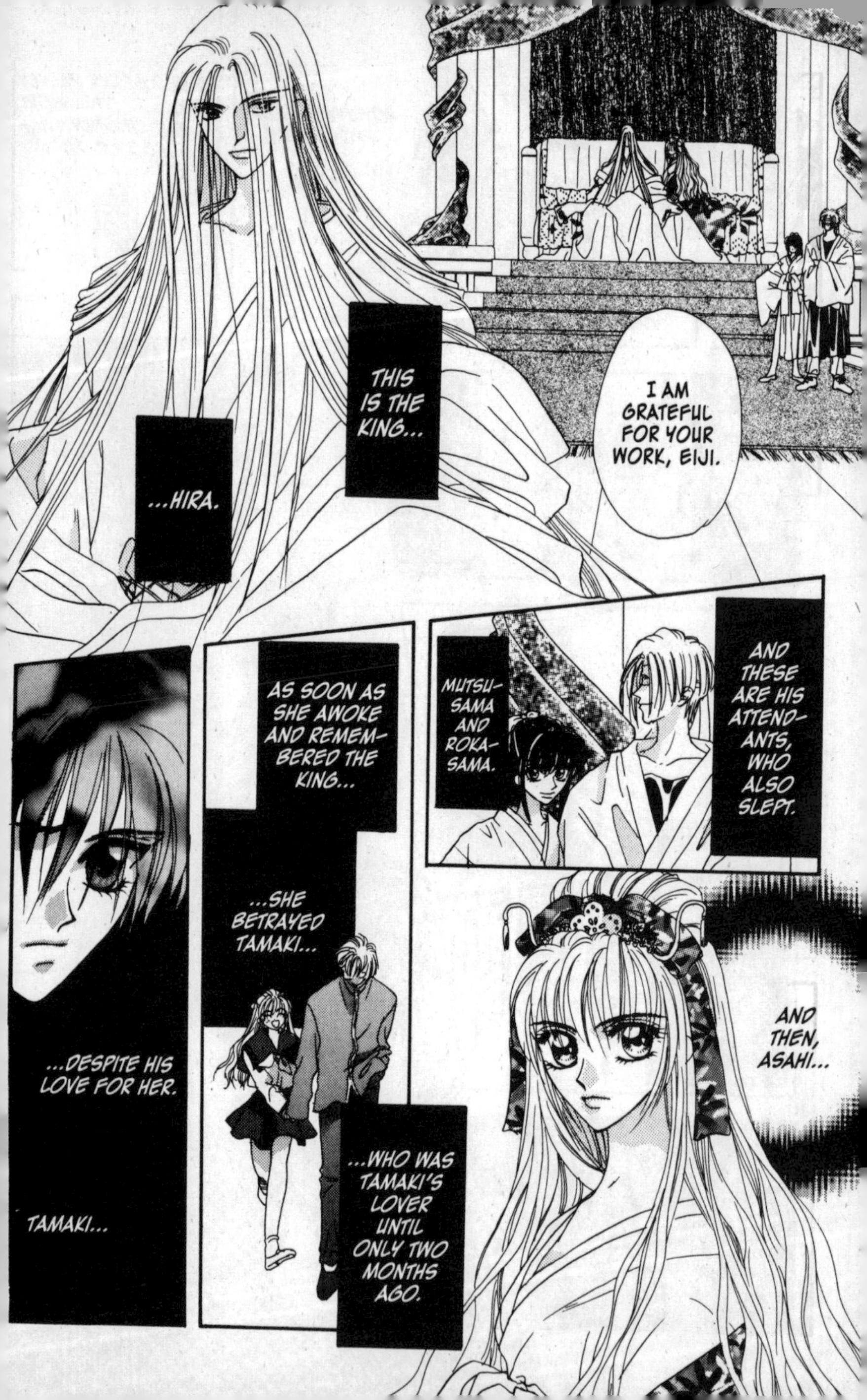
I AM GRATEFUL FOR YOUR WORK, EIJI.
THIS IS THE KING...
...HIRA.
AND THESE ARE HIS ATTENDANTS, WHO ALSO SLEPT.
MUTSU-SAMA AND ROKA-SAMA.
AND THEN, ASAHI...
...WHO WAS TAMAKI'S LOVER UNTIL ONLY TWO MONTHS AGO.
AS SOON AS SHE AWOKE AND REMEMBERED THE KING...
...SHE BETRAYED TAMAKI...
...DESPITE HIS LOVE FOR HER.
TAMAKI...

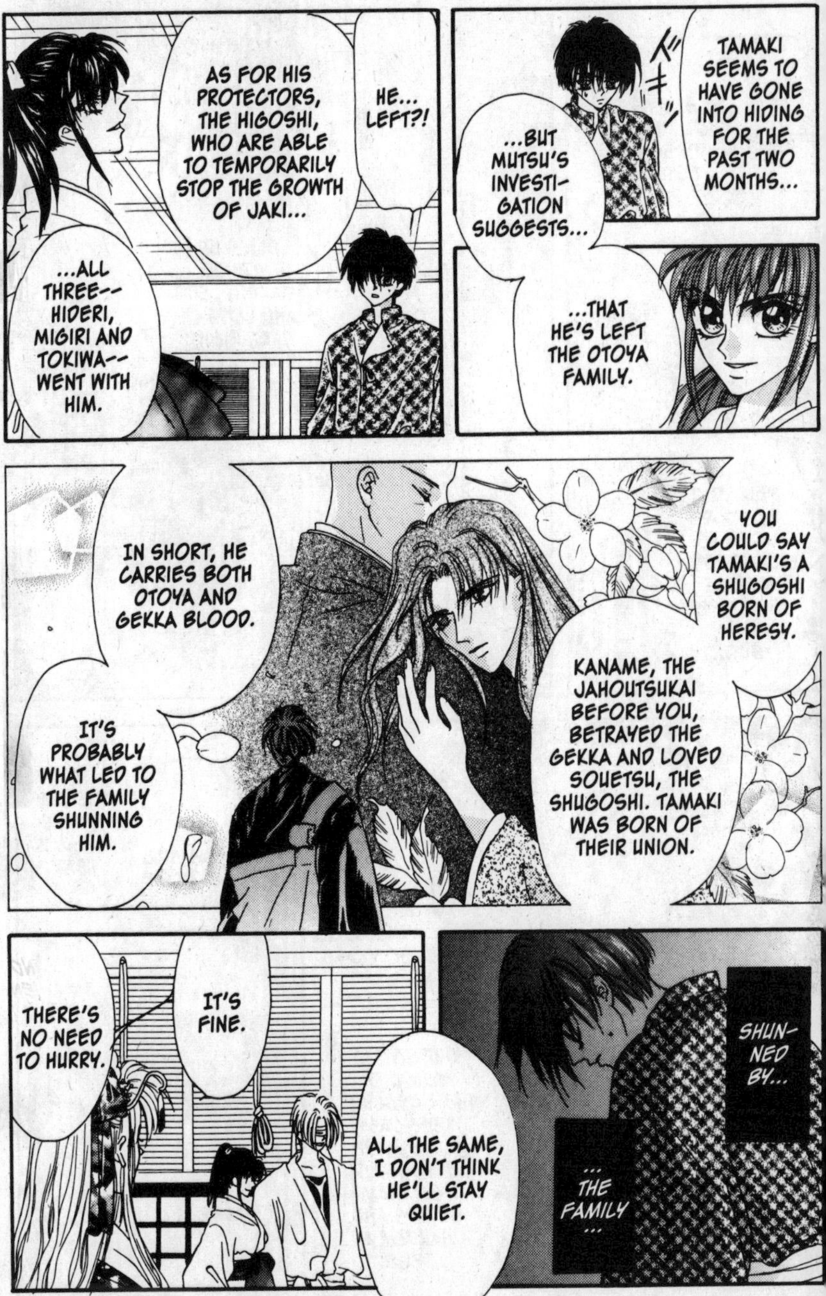
TAMAKI SEEMS TO HAVE GONE INTO HIDING FOR THE PAST TWO MONTHS...
ドキッ
...BUT MUTSU'S INVESTI-GATION SUGGESTS...
...THAT HE'S LEFT THE OTOYA FAMILY.
HE... LEFT?!
AS FOR HIS PROTECTORS, THE HIGOSHI, WHO ARE ABLE TO TEMPORARILY STOP THE GROWTH OF JAKI...
...ALL THREE--HIDERI, MIGIRI AND TOKIWA--WENT WITH HIM.
YOU COULD SAY TAMAKI'S A SHUGOSHI BORN OF HERESY.
KANAME, THE JAHOUTSUKAI BEFORE YOU, BETRAYED THE GEKKA AND LOVED SOUETSU, THE SHUGOSHI. TAMAKI WAS BORN OF THEIR UNION.
IN SHORT, HE CARRIES BOTH OTOYA AND GEKKA BLOOD.
IT'S PROBABLY WHAT LED TO THE FAMILY SHUNNING HIM.
SHUN-NED BY...
...THE FAMILY...
IT'S FINE.
THERE'S NO NEED TO HURRY.
ALL THE SAME, I DON'T THINK HE'LL STAY QUIET.

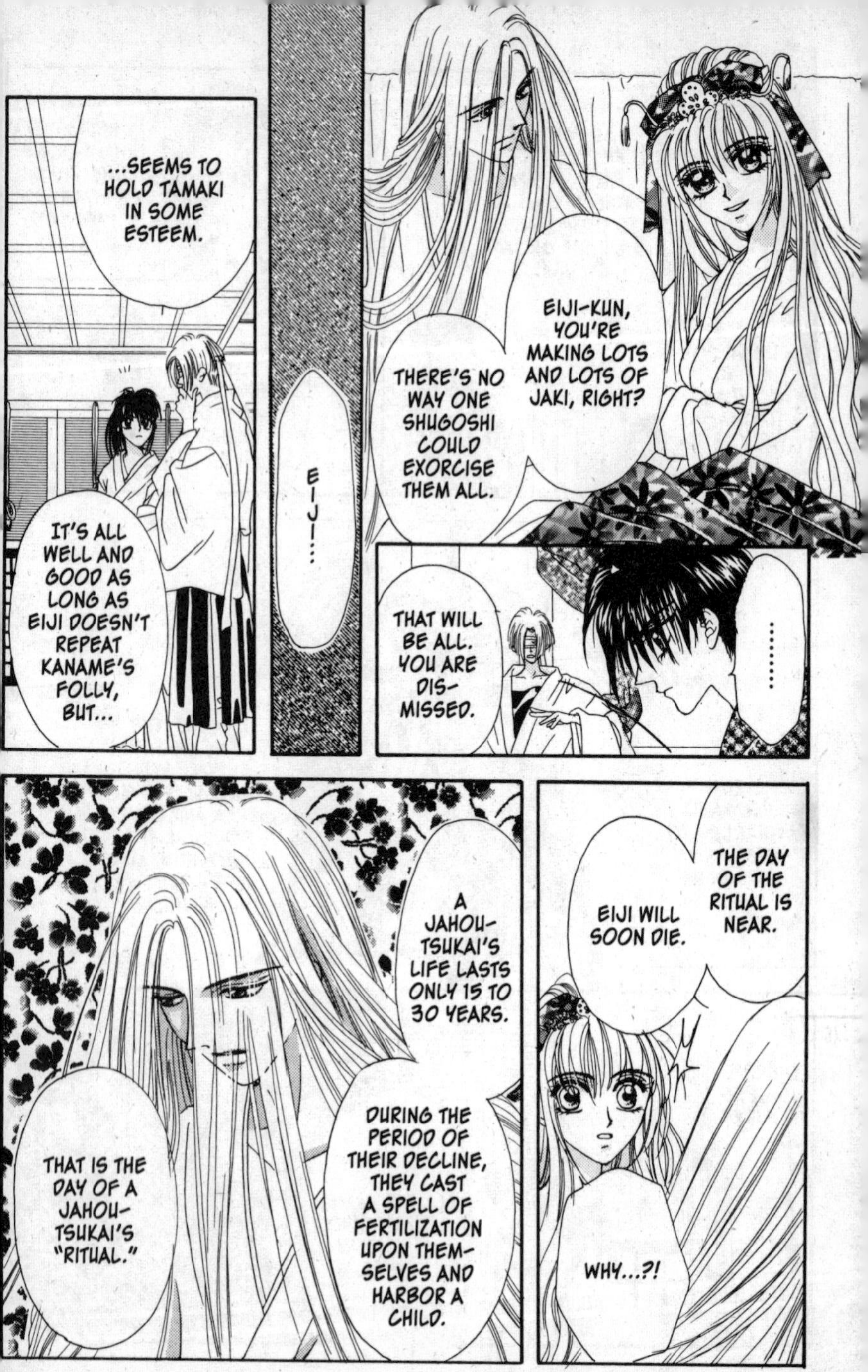
EIJI-KUN, YOU'RE MAKING LOTS AND LOTS OF JAKI, RIGHT?
THERE'S NO WAY ONE SHUGOSHI COULD EXORCISE THEM ALL.
......
THAT WILL BE ALL. YOU ARE DIS-MISSED.
EIJI...
...SEEMS TO HOLD TAMAKI IN SOME ESTEEM.
IT'S ALL WELL AND GOOD AS LONG AS EIJI DOESN'T REPEAT KANAME'S FOLLY, BUT...
THE DAY OF THE RITUAL IS NEAR.
EIJI WILL SOON DIE.
WHY...?!
A JAHOU-TSUKAI'S LIFE LASTS ONLY 15 TO 30 YEARS.
DURING THE PERIOD OF THEIR DECLINE, THEY CAST A SPELL OF FERTILIZATION UPON THEM-SELVES AND HARBOR A CHILD.
THAT IS THE DAY OF A JAHOU-TSUKAI'S "RITUAL."

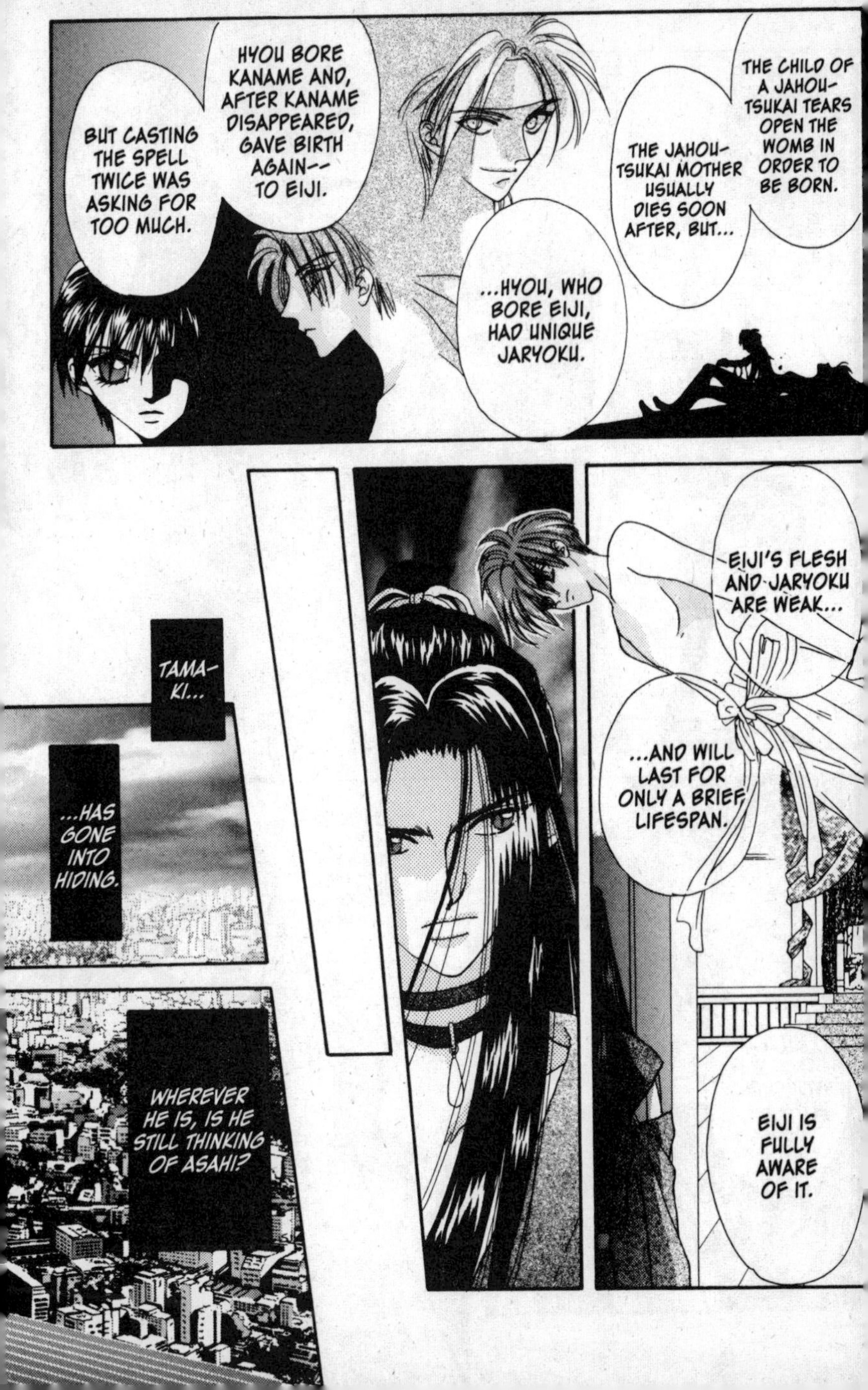
THE CHILD OF A JAHOU-TSUKAI TEARS OPEN THE WOMB IN ORDER TO BE BORN.
THE JAHOU-TSUKAI MOTHER USUALLY DIES SOON AFTER, BUT...
...HYOU, WHO BORE EIJI, HAD UNIQUE JARYOKU.
HYOU BORE KANAME AND, AFTER KANAME DISAPPEARED, GAVE BIRTH AGAIN-- TO EIJI.
BUT CASTING THE SPELL TWICE WAS ASKING FOR TOO MUCH.
EIJI'S FLESH AND JARYOKU ARE WEAK...
...AND WILL LAST FOR ONLY A BRIEF LIFESPAN.
EIJI IS FULLY AWARE OF IT.
TAMAKI...
...HAS GONE INTO HIDING.
WHEREVER HE IS, IS HE STILL THINKING OF ASAHI?

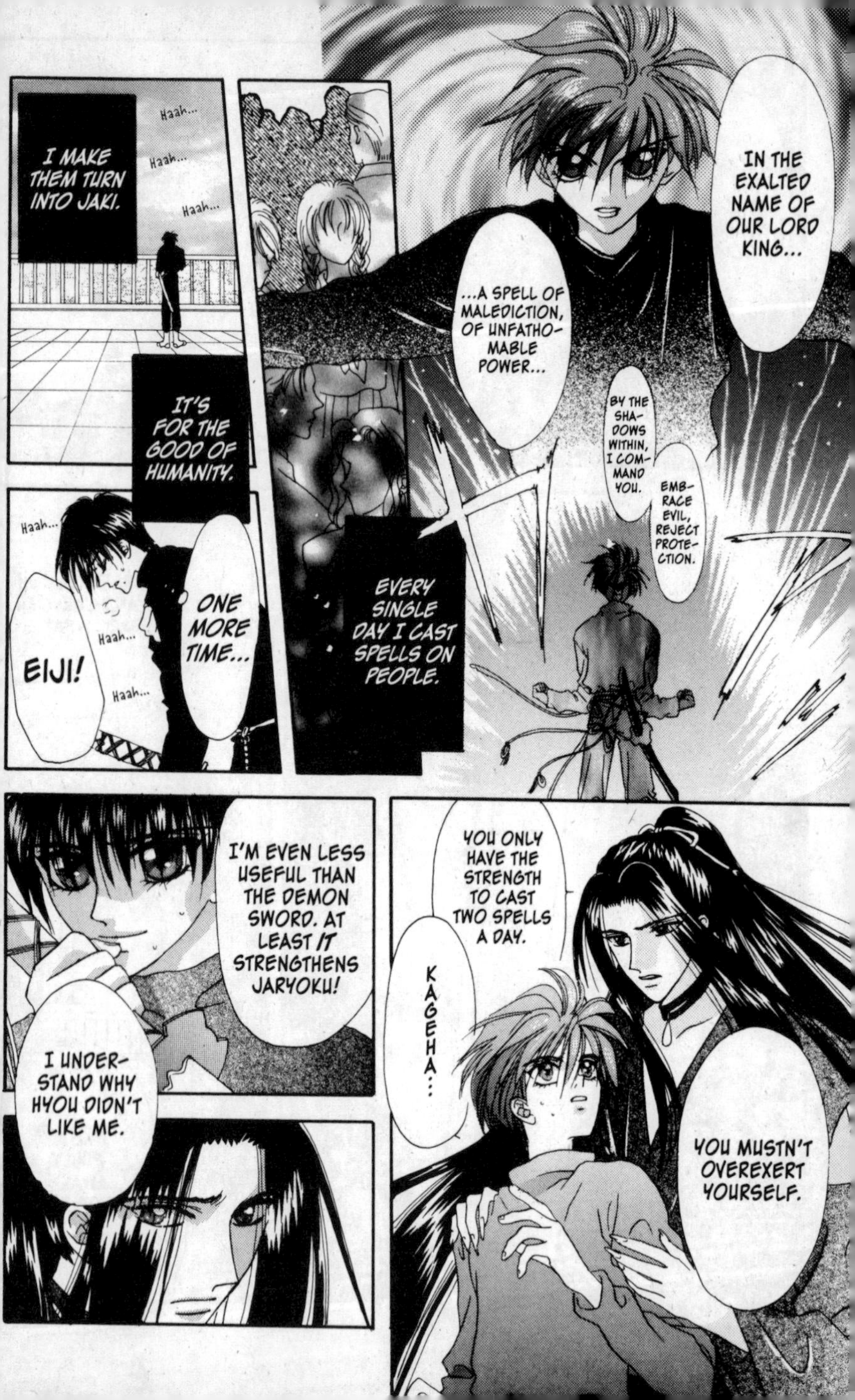
IN THE EXALTED NAME OF OUR LORD KING...
...A SPELL OF MALEDICTION, OF UNFATHOMABLE POWER...
BY THE SHADOWS WITHIN, I COMMAND YOU.
EMBRACE EVIL, REJECT PROTECTION.
EVERY SINGLE DAY I CAST SPELLS ON PEOPLE.
Haah...
Haah...
Haah...
I MAKE THEM TURN INTO JAKI.
IT'S FOR THE GOOD OF HUMANITY.
Haah...
ONE MORE TIME...
Haah...
Haah...
EIJI!
YOU ONLY HAVE THE STRENGTH TO CAST TWO SPELLS A DAY.
KAGEHA...
YOU MUSTN'T OVEREXERT YOURSELF.
I'M EVEN LESS USEFUL THAN THE DEMON SWORD. AT LEAST IT STRENGTHENS JARYOKU!
I UNDERSTAND WHY HYOU DIDN'T LIKE ME.

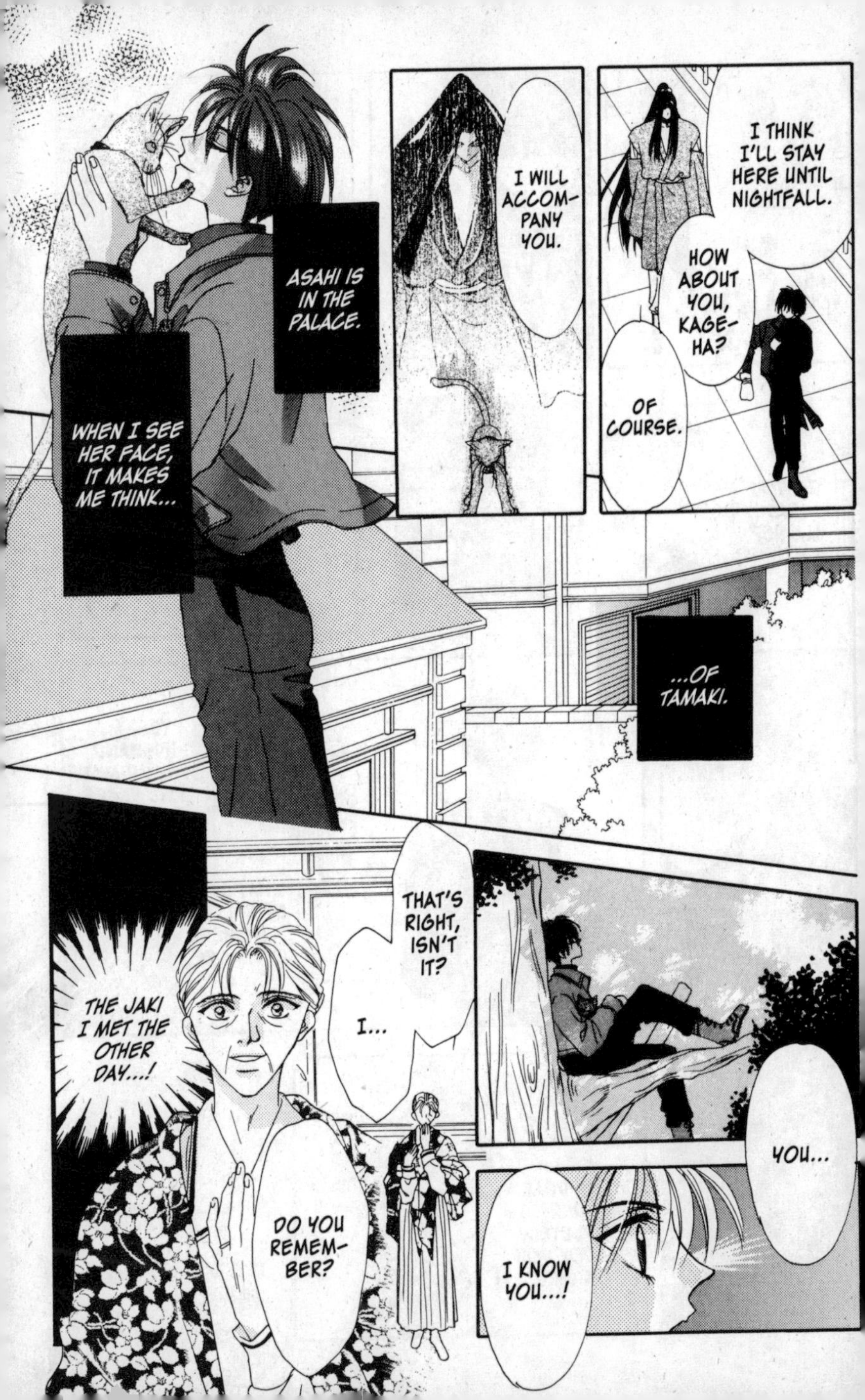
I THINK I'LL STAY HERE UNTIL NIGHTFALL.
HOW ABOUT YOU, KAGE-HA?
OF COURSE.
I WILL ACCOMPANY YOU.
ASAHI IS IN THE PALACE.
WHEN I SEE HER FACE, IT MAKES ME THINK...
...OF TAMAKI.
YOU...
I KNOW YOU...!
THAT'S RIGHT, ISN'T IT?
I...
THE JAKI I MET THE OTHER DAY...!
DO YOU REMEMBER?

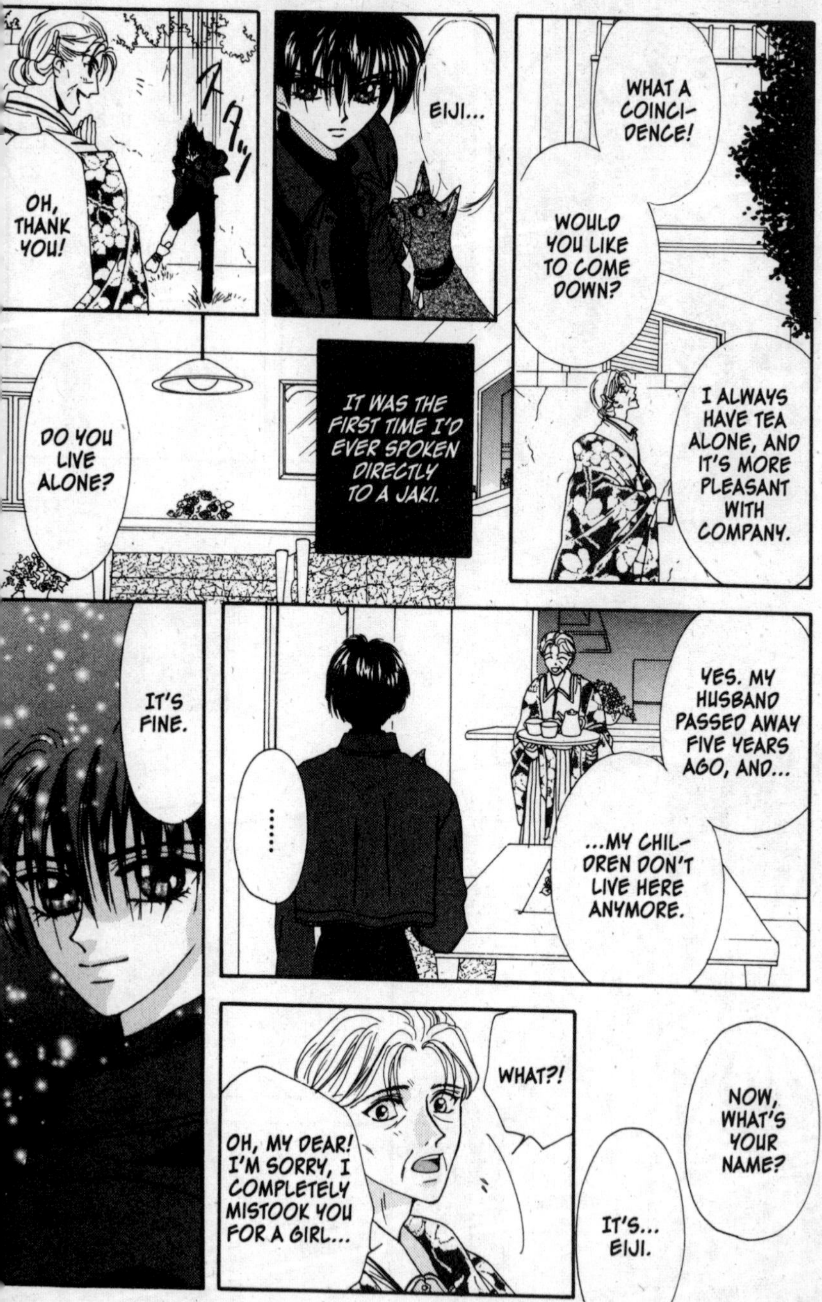
WHAT A COINCIDENCE!
WOULD YOU LIKE TO COME DOWN?
I ALWAYS HAVE TEA ALONE, AND IT'S MORE PLEASANT WITH COMPANY.
EIJI...
OH, THANK YOU!
IT WAS THE FIRST TIME I'D EVER SPOKEN DIRECTLY TO A JAKI.
DO YOU LIVE ALONE?
YES. MY HUSBAND PASSED AWAY FIVE YEARS AGO, AND...
...MY CHILDREN DON'T LIVE HERE ANYMORE.
......
NOW, WHAT'S YOUR NAME?
IT'S... EIJI.
WHAT?!
OH, MY DEAR! I'M SORRY, I COMPLETELY MISTOOK YOU FOR A GIRL...
IT'S FINE.

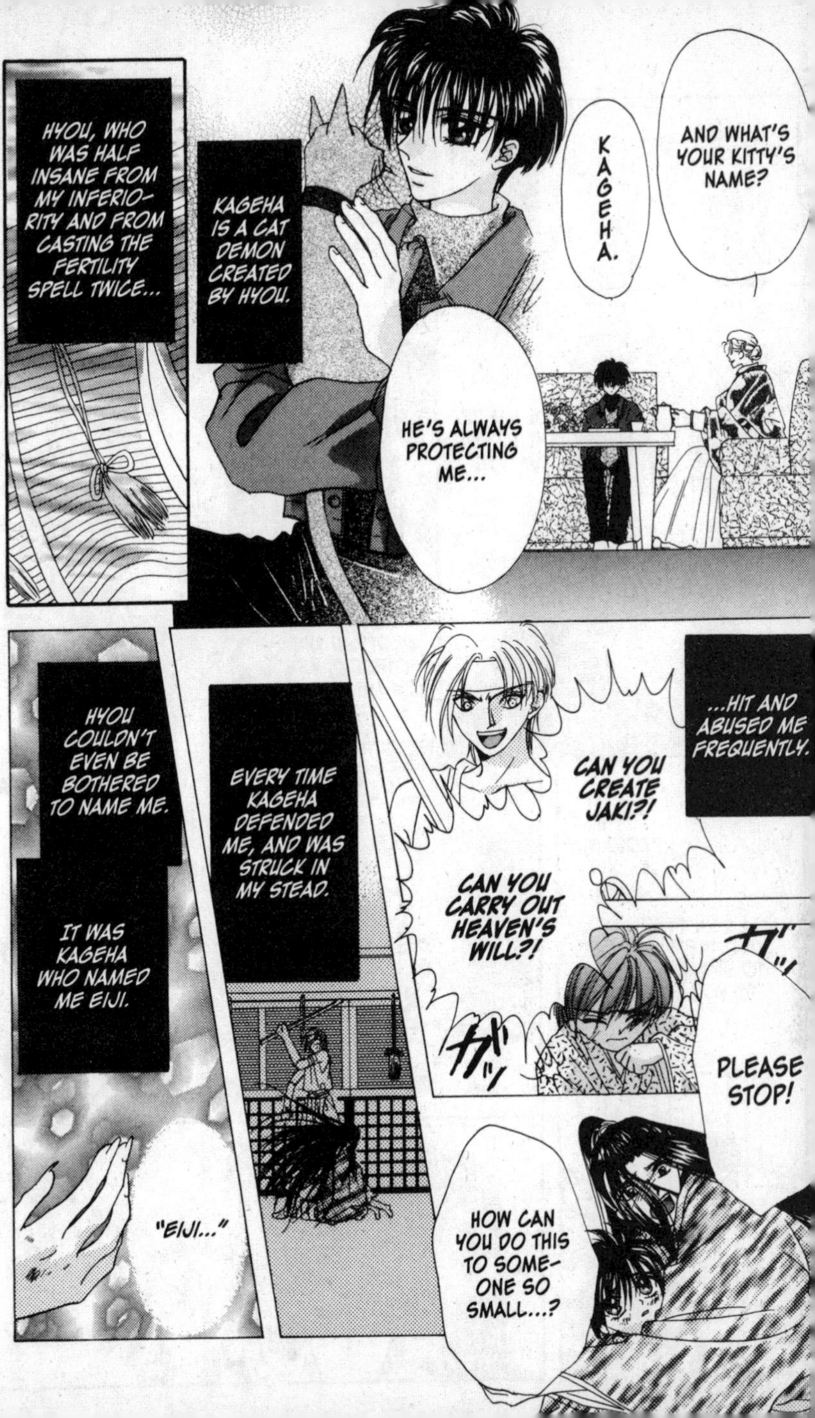
AND WHAT'S YOUR KITTY'S NAME?
KAGEHA.
HE'S ALWAYS PROTECTING ME...
KAGEHA IS A CAT DEMON CREATED BY HYOU.
HYOU, WHO WAS HALF INSANE FROM MY INFERIORITY AND FROM CASTING THE FERTILITY SPELL TWICE...
...HIT AND ABUSED ME FREQUENTLY.
CAN YOU CREATE JAKI?!
CAN YOU CARRY OUT HEAVEN'S WILL?!
PLEASE STOP!
HOW CAN YOU DO THIS TO SOME-ONE SO SMALL...?
EVERY TIME KAGEHA DEFENDED ME, AND WAS STRUCK IN MY STEAD.
HYOU COULDN'T EVEN BE BOTHERED TO NAME ME.
IT WAS KAGEHA WHO NAMED ME EIJI.
"EIJI..."

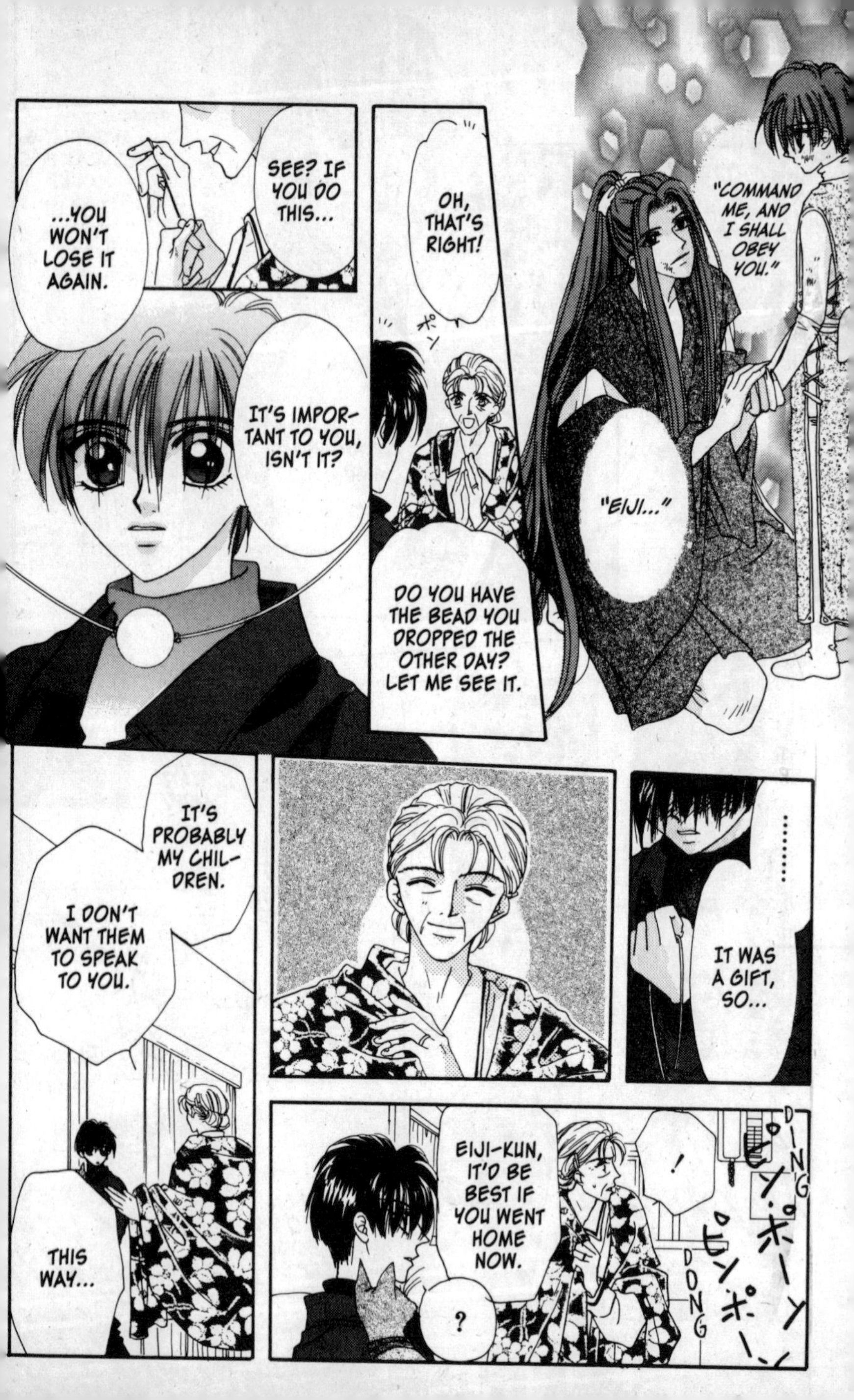
"COMMAND ME, AND I SHALL OBEY YOU."
"EIJI..."
OH, THAT'S RIGHT!
ポン
DO YOU HAVE THE BEAD YOU DROPPED THE OTHER DAY? LET ME SEE IT.
SEE? IF YOU DO THIS...
...YOU WON'T LOSE IT AGAIN.
IT'S IMPORTANT TO YOU, ISN'T IT?
......
IT WAS A GIFT, SO...
DING DONG
ピンポーン ピンポーン
!
EIJI-KUN, IT'D BE BEST IF YOU WENT HOME NOW.
?
IT'S PROBABLY MY CHILDREN.
I DON'T WANT THEM TO SPEAK TO YOU.
THIS WAY...

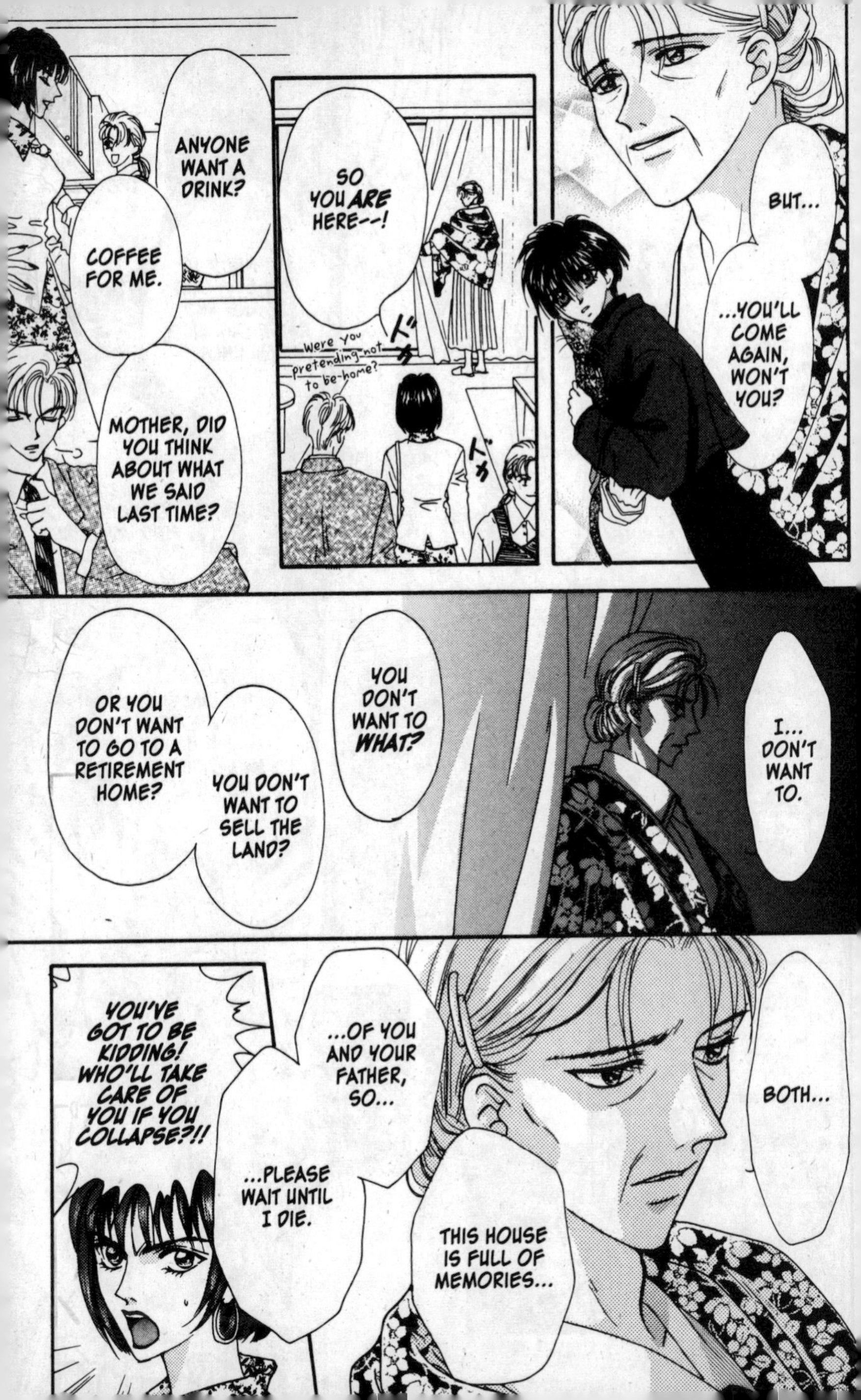
BUT...
...YOU'LL COME AGAIN, WON'T YOU?
SO YOU **ARE** HERE--!
ドカ
ドカ
Were you pretending not to be home?
ANYONE WANT A DRINK?
COFFEE FOR ME.
MOTHER, DID YOU THINK ABOUT WHAT WE SAID LAST TIME?
I... DON'T WANT TO.
YOU DON'T WANT TO *WHAT?*
YOU DON'T WANT TO SELL THE LAND?
OR YOU DON'T WANT TO GO TO A RETIREMENT HOME?
BOTH...
THIS HOUSE IS FULL OF MEMORIES...
...OF YOU AND YOUR FATHER, SO...
...PLEASE WAIT UNTIL I DIE.
YOU'VE GOT TO BE KIDDING! WHO'LL TAKE CARE OF YOU IF YOU COLLAPSE?!!

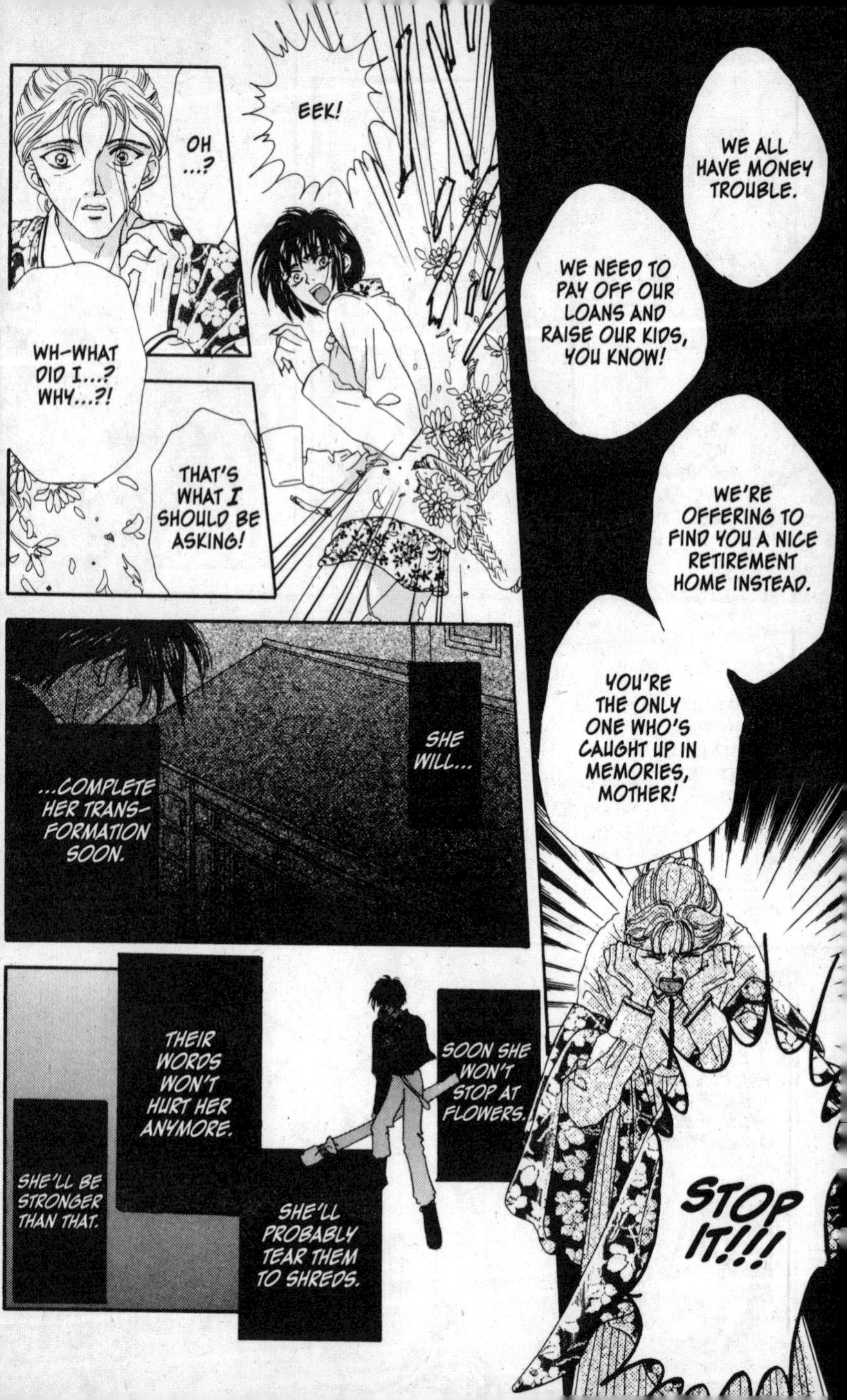
WE ALL HAVE MONEY TROUBLE.
WE NEED TO PAY OFF OUR LOANS AND RAISE OUR KIDS, YOU KNOW!
WE'RE OFFERING TO FIND YOU A NICE RETIREMENT HOME INSTEAD.
YOU'RE THE ONLY ONE WHO'S CAUGHT UP IN MEMORIES, MOTHER!
STOP IT!!!
EEK!
OH ...?
WH-WHAT DID I...? WHY...?!
THAT'S WHAT I SHOULD BE ASKING!
SHE WILL...
...COMPLETE HER TRANS-FORMATION SOON.
SOON SHE WON'T STOP AT FLOWERS.
SHE'LL PROBABLY TEAR THEM TO SHREDS.
THEIR WORDS WON'T HURT HER ANYMORE.
SHE'LL BE STRONGER THAN THAT.

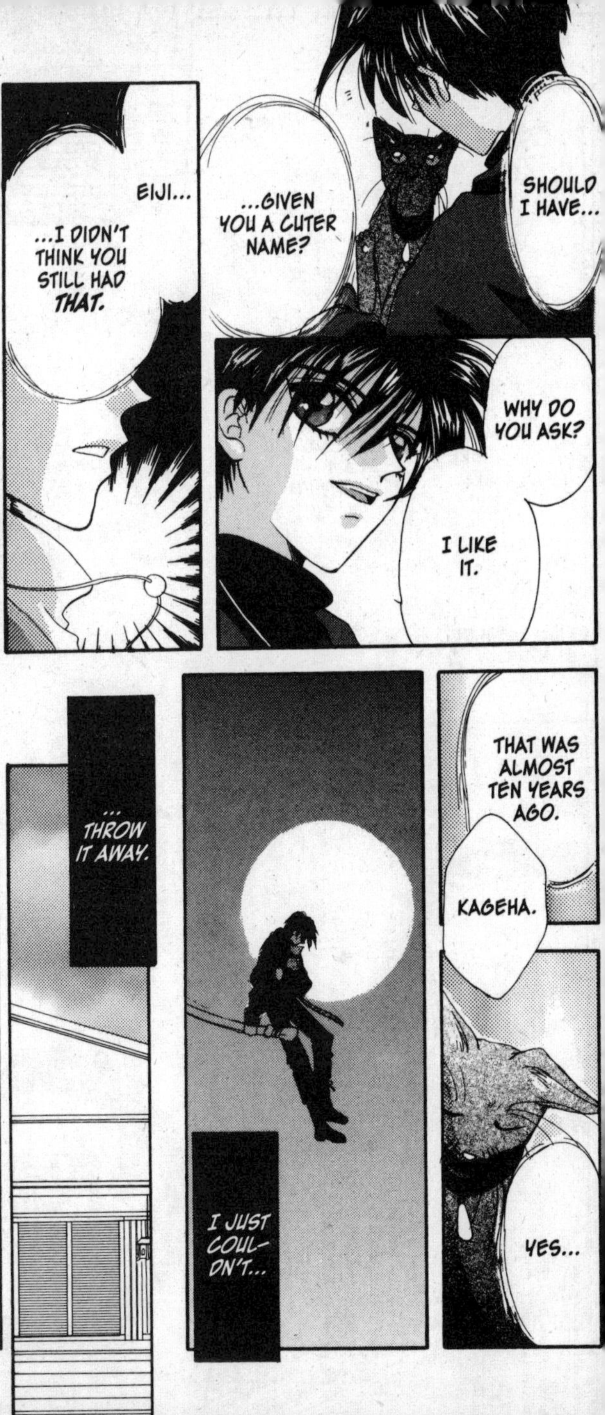
SHOULD I HAVE...
...GIVEN YOU A CUTER NAME?
WHY DO YOU ASK?
I LIKE IT.
EIJI...
...I DIDN'T THINK YOU STILL HAD *THAT.*
THAT WAS ALMOST TEN YEARS AGO.
KAGEHA.
YES...
I JUST COUL-DN'T...
... THROW IT AWAY.

Scroll Three

Yes, that's it, huh? Have you all played Biohazard? It was fun, don't you think? It was creepy, though... It's like a nightmare I had a lot when I was a kid. It really is. (Except there was a mannequin in my dream.) ಠಠ Ever since I got a rocket launcher, which has unlimited ammo, I've just been shooting everything in sight (from really far away, too). Hurry up and get used to it, me! I want to hurry and see the cruel ending... Please let me have seen it by the time this book comes out. Please, please? Anyway...

There's a bad guy in Biohazard, and even before I started playing I was all, "This one! This one's definitely the traitor! You can tell by the way s/he looks!" So I laughed a little when I found out s/he really was the traitor. What do you think? I'm a good judge of people, huh?

But it's like, anyone can figure it out. After all, s/he totally looks the part, right? (laughs) Oh, but can you believe they don't have a left-handed controller? I've gotten used to it, but it's still hard when you have to fire all the time, you know? I wonder what everyone else does...

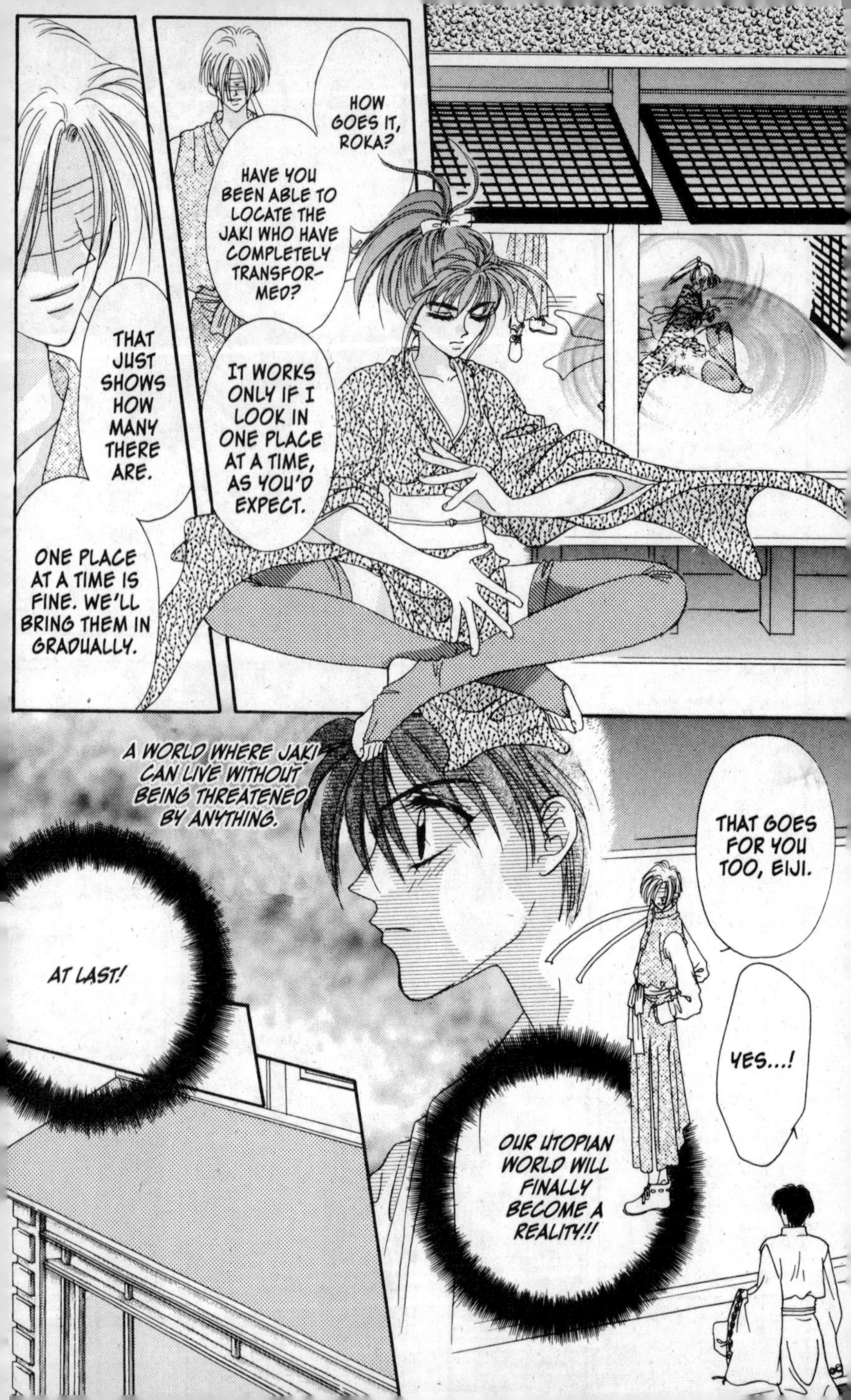
HOW GOES IT, ROKA?
HAVE YOU BEEN ABLE TO LOCATE THE JAKI WHO HAVE COMPLETELY TRANSFOR-MED?
IT WORKS ONLY IF I LOOK IN ONE PLACE AT A TIME, AS YOU'D EXPECT.
THAT JUST SHOWS HOW MANY THERE ARE.
ONE PLACE AT A TIME IS FINE. WE'LL BRING THEM IN GRADUALLY.
THAT GOES FOR YOU TOO, EIJI.
YES...!
A WORLD WHERE JAKI CAN LIVE WITHOUT BEING THREATENED BY ANYTHING.
AT LAST!
OUR UTOPIAN WORLD WILL FINALLY BECOME A REALITY!!

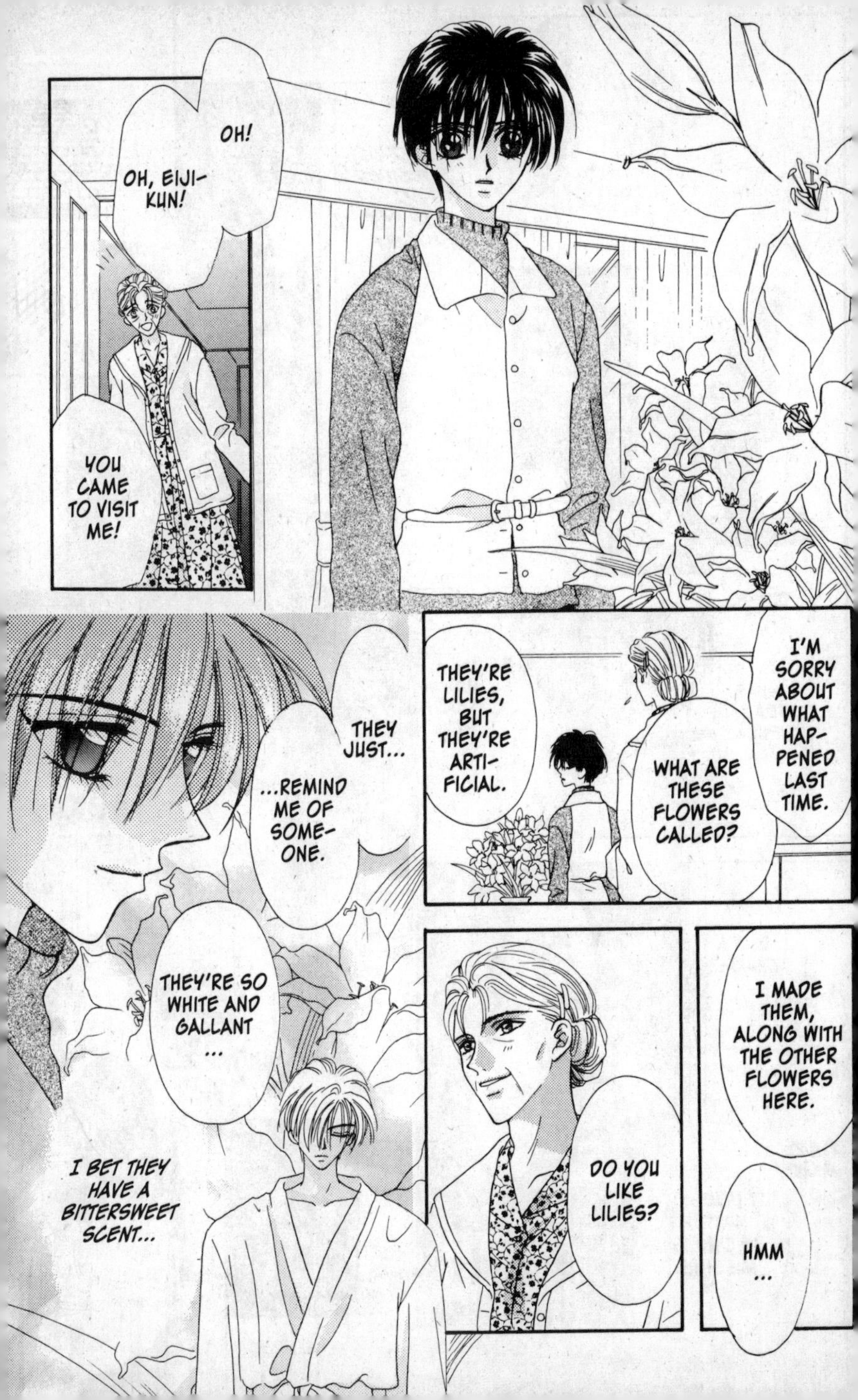
OH!
OH, EIJI-KUN!
YOU CAME TO VISIT ME!
I'M SORRY ABOUT WHAT HAPPENED LAST TIME.
WHAT ARE THESE FLOWERS CALLED?
THEY'RE LILIES, BUT THEY'RE ARTIFICIAL.
I MADE THEM, ALONG WITH THE OTHER FLOWERS HERE.
HMM...
DO YOU LIKE LILIES?
THEY JUST...
...REMIND ME OF SOMEONE.
THEY'RE SO WHITE AND GALLANT...
I BET THEY HAVE A BITTERSWEET SCENT...

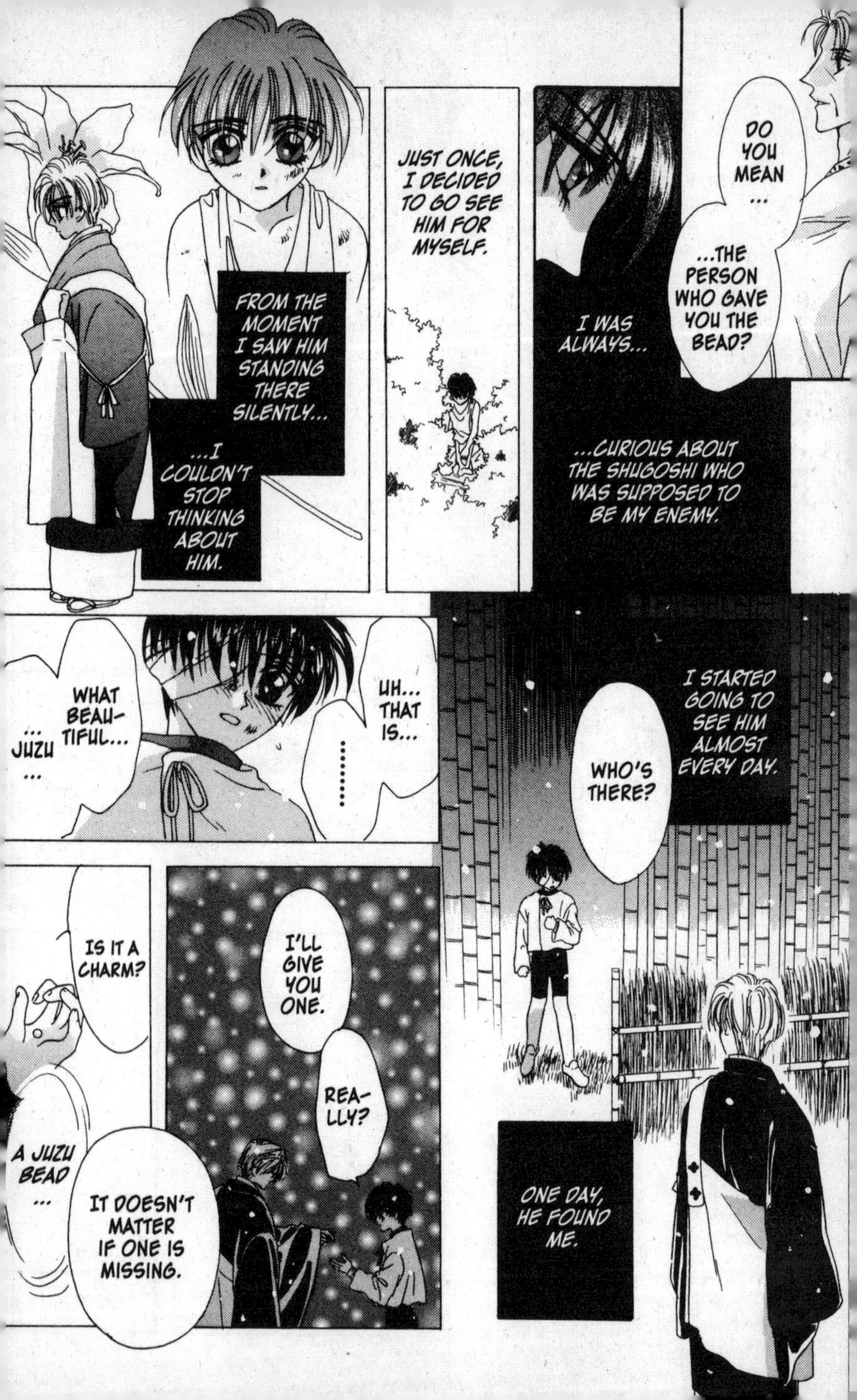
DO YOU MEAN ...
...THE PERSON WHO GAVE YOU THE BEAD?
I WAS ALWAYS...
...CURIOUS ABOUT THE SHUGOSHI WHO WAS SUPPOSED TO BE MY ENEMY.
JUST ONCE, I DECIDED TO GO SEE HIM FOR MYSELF.
FROM THE MOMENT I SAW HIM STANDING THERE SILENTLY...
...I COULDN'T STOP THINKING ABOUT HIM.
I STARTED GOING TO SEE HIM ALMOST EVERY DAY.
WHO'S THERE?
ONE DAY, HE FOUND ME.
UH... THAT IS...
......
WHAT BEAU-TIFUL...
...JUZU...
I'LL GIVE YOU ONE.
REA-LLY?
IT DOESN'T MATTER IF ONE IS MISSING.
IS IT A CHARM?
A JUZU BEAD ...

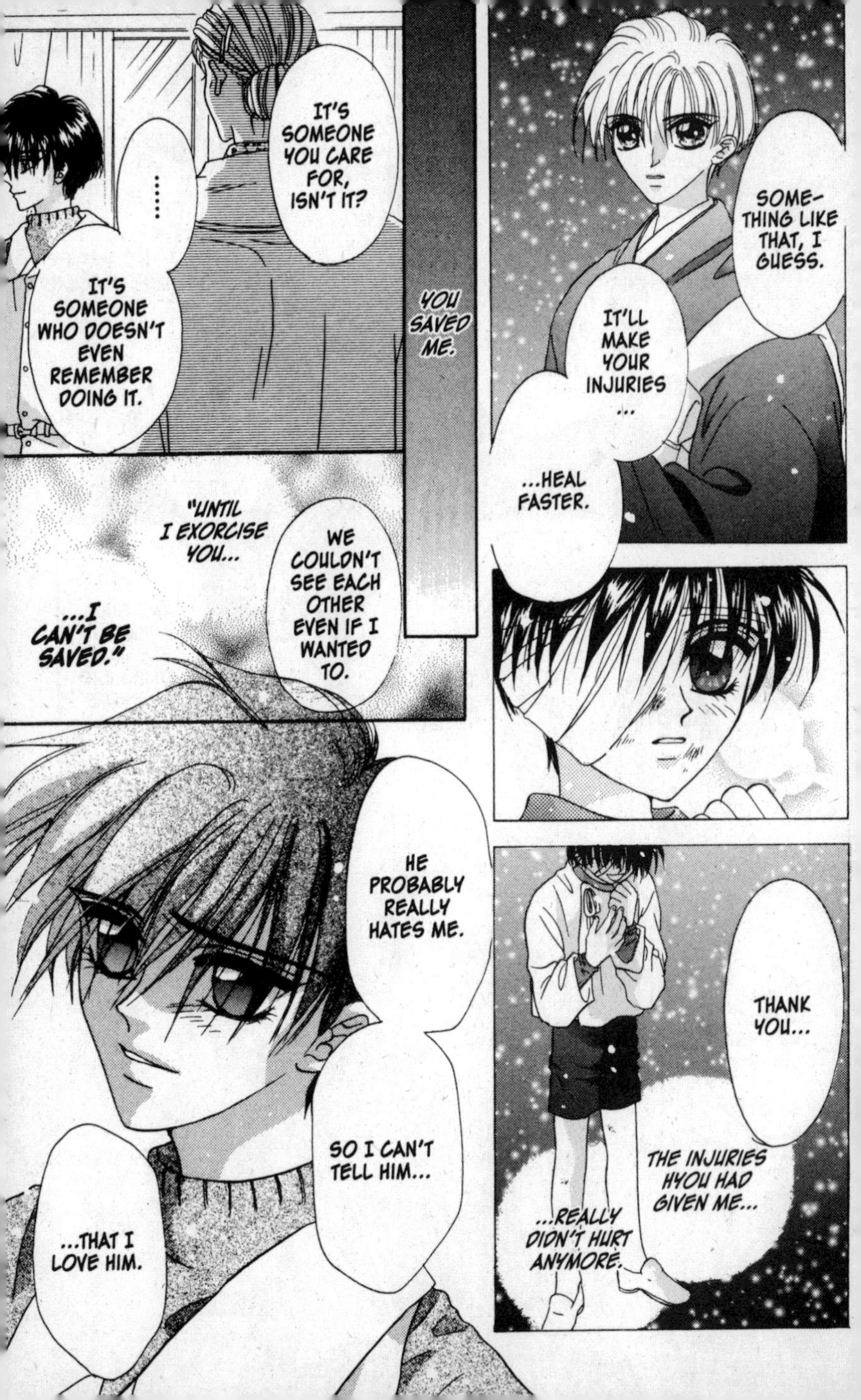
SOME-THING LIKE THAT, I GUESS.
IT'LL MAKE YOUR INJURIES ...
...HEAL FASTER.
IT'S SOMEONE YOU CARE FOR, ISN'T IT?
......
IT'S SOMEONE WHO DOESN'T EVEN REMEMBER DOING IT.
YOU SAVED ME.
WE COULDN'T SEE EACH OTHER EVEN IF I WANTED TO.
"UNTIL I EXORCISE YOU...
...I CAN'T BE SAVED."
THANK YOU...
THE INJURIES HYOU HAD GIVEN ME...
...REALLY DIDN'T HURT ANYMORE.
HE PROBABLY REALLY HATES ME.
SO I CAN'T TELL HIM...
...THAT I LOVE HIM.

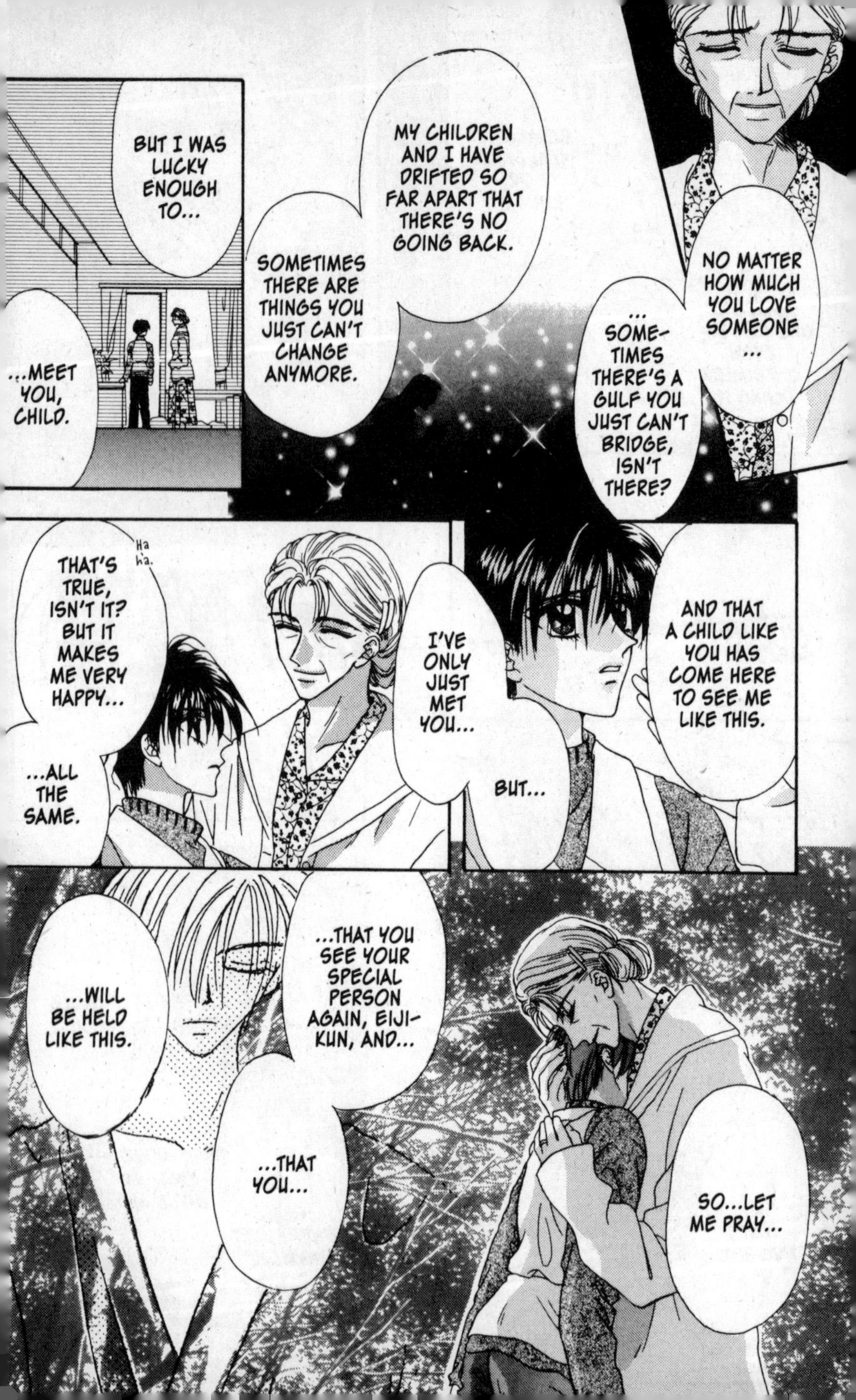
NO MATTER HOW MUCH YOU LOVE SOMEONE...
...SOMETIMES THERE'S A GULF YOU JUST CAN'T BRIDGE, ISN'T THERE?
MY CHILDREN AND I HAVE DRIFTED SO FAR APART THAT THERE'S NO GOING BACK.
SOMETIMES THERE ARE THINGS YOU JUST CAN'T CHANGE ANYMORE.
BUT I WAS LUCKY ENOUGH TO...
...MEET YOU, CHILD.
AND THAT A CHILD LIKE YOU HAS COME HERE TO SEE ME LIKE THIS.
I'VE ONLY JUST MET YOU...
BUT...
Ha ha.
THAT'S TRUE, ISN'T IT? BUT IT MAKES ME VERY HAPPY...
...ALL THE SAME.
SO...LET ME PRAY...
...THAT YOU SEE YOUR SPECIAL PERSON AGAIN, EIJI-KUN, AND...
...THAT YOU...
...WILL BE HELD LIKE THIS.

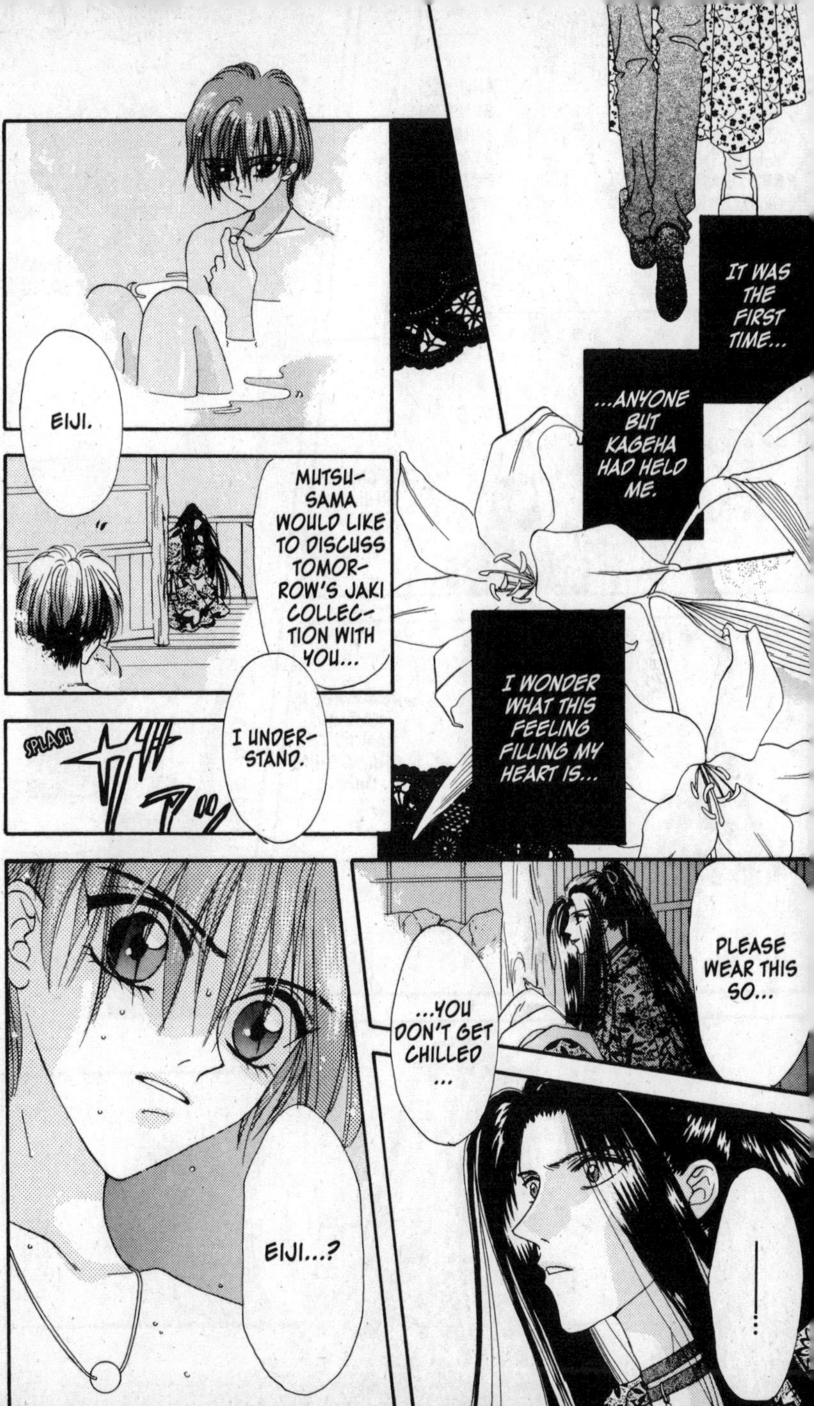
IT WAS THE FIRST TIME...
...ANYONE BUT KAGEHA HAD HELD ME.
I WONDER WHAT THIS FEELING FILLING MY HEART IS...
EIJI.
MUTSU-SAMA WOULD LIKE TO DISCUSS TOMORROW'S JAKI COLLECTION WITH YOU...
I UNDERSTAND.
SPLASH
PLEASE WEAR THIS SO...
...YOU DON'T GET CHILLED ...
......
EIJI...?

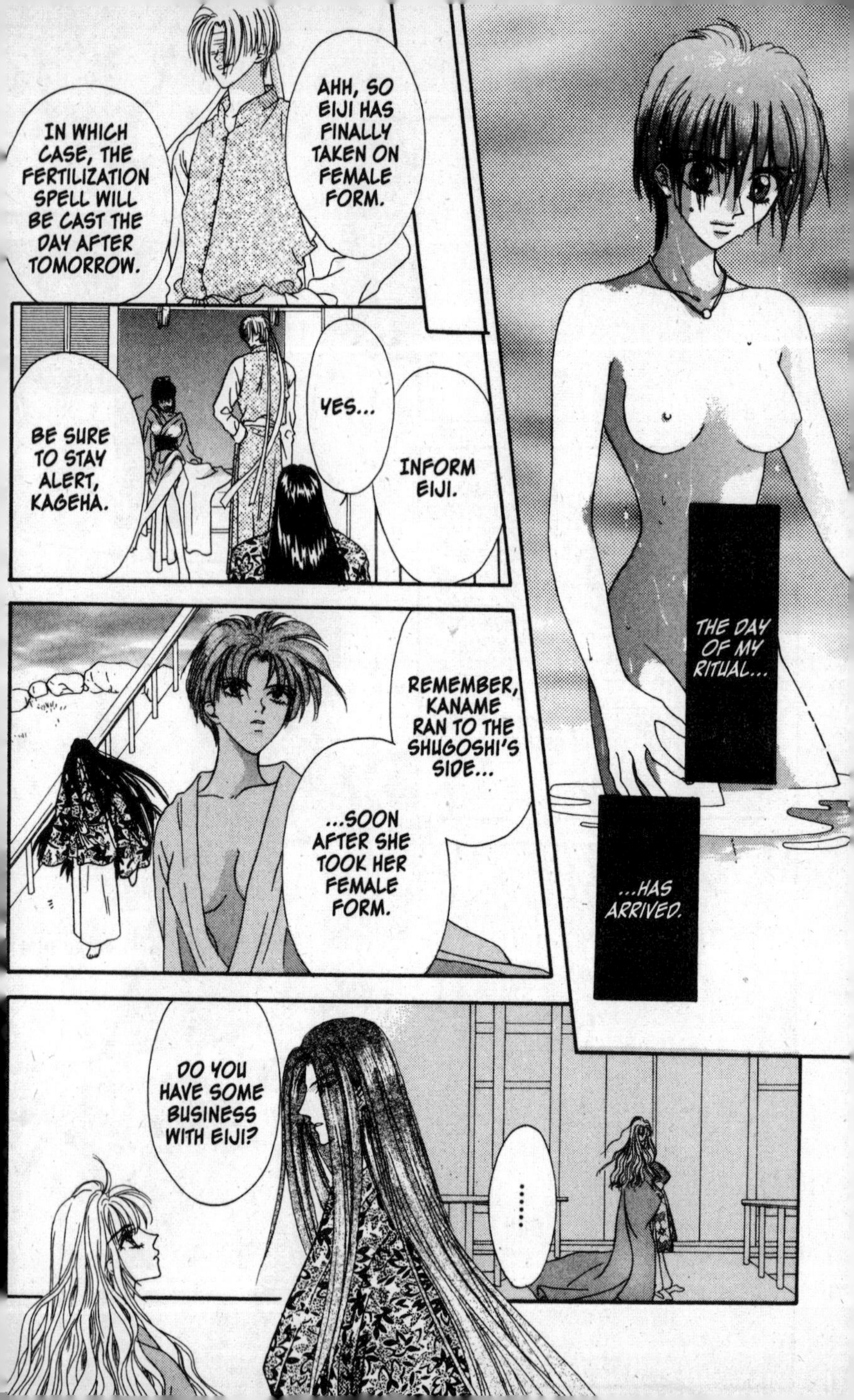
THE DAY OF MY RITUAL...
...HAS ARRIVED.
AHH, SO EIJI HAS FINALLY TAKEN ON FEMALE FORM.
IN WHICH CASE, THE FERTILIZATION SPELL WILL BE CAST THE DAY AFTER TOMORROW.
YES...
INFORM EIJI.
BE SURE TO STAY ALERT, KAGEHA.
REMEMBER, KANAME RAN TO THE SHUGOSHI'S SIDE...
...SOON AFTER SHE TOOK HER FEMALE FORM.
DO YOU HAVE SOME BUSINESS WITH EIJI?
......

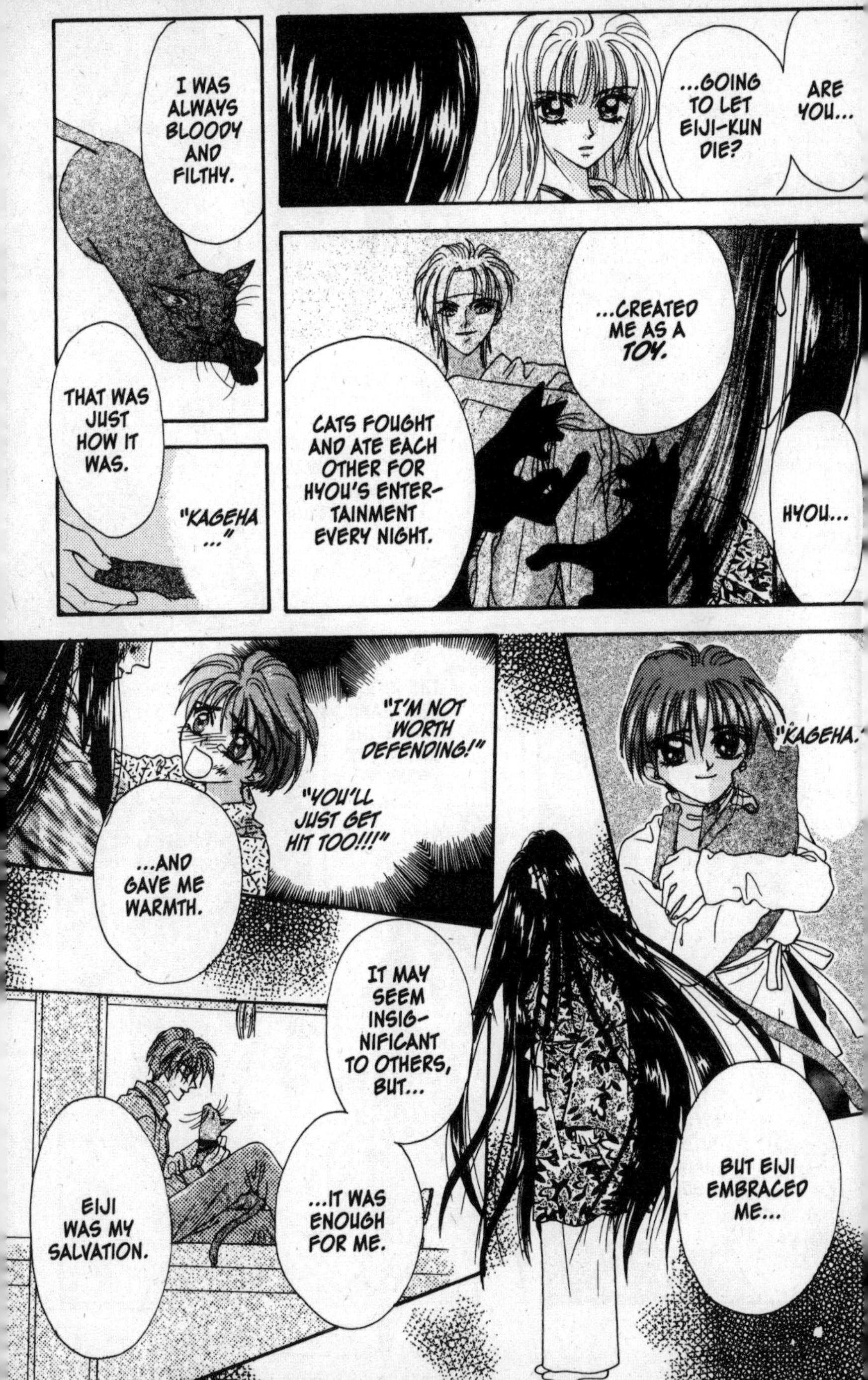
ARE YOU...
...GOING TO LET EIJI-KUN DIE?
HYOU...
...CREATED ME AS A *TOY.*
CATS FOUGHT AND ATE EACH OTHER FOR HYOU'S ENTER-TAINMENT EVERY NIGHT.
I WAS ALWAYS BLOODY AND FILTHY.
THAT WAS JUST HOW IT WAS.
"KAGEHA..."
"KAGEHA."
BUT EIJI EMBRACED ME...
"I'M NOT WORTH DEFENDING!"
"YOU'LL JUST GET HIT TOO!!!"
...AND GAVE ME WARMTH.
IT MAY SEEM INSIG-NIFICANT TO OTHERS, BUT...
...IT WAS ENOUGH FOR ME.
EIJI WAS MY SALVATION.

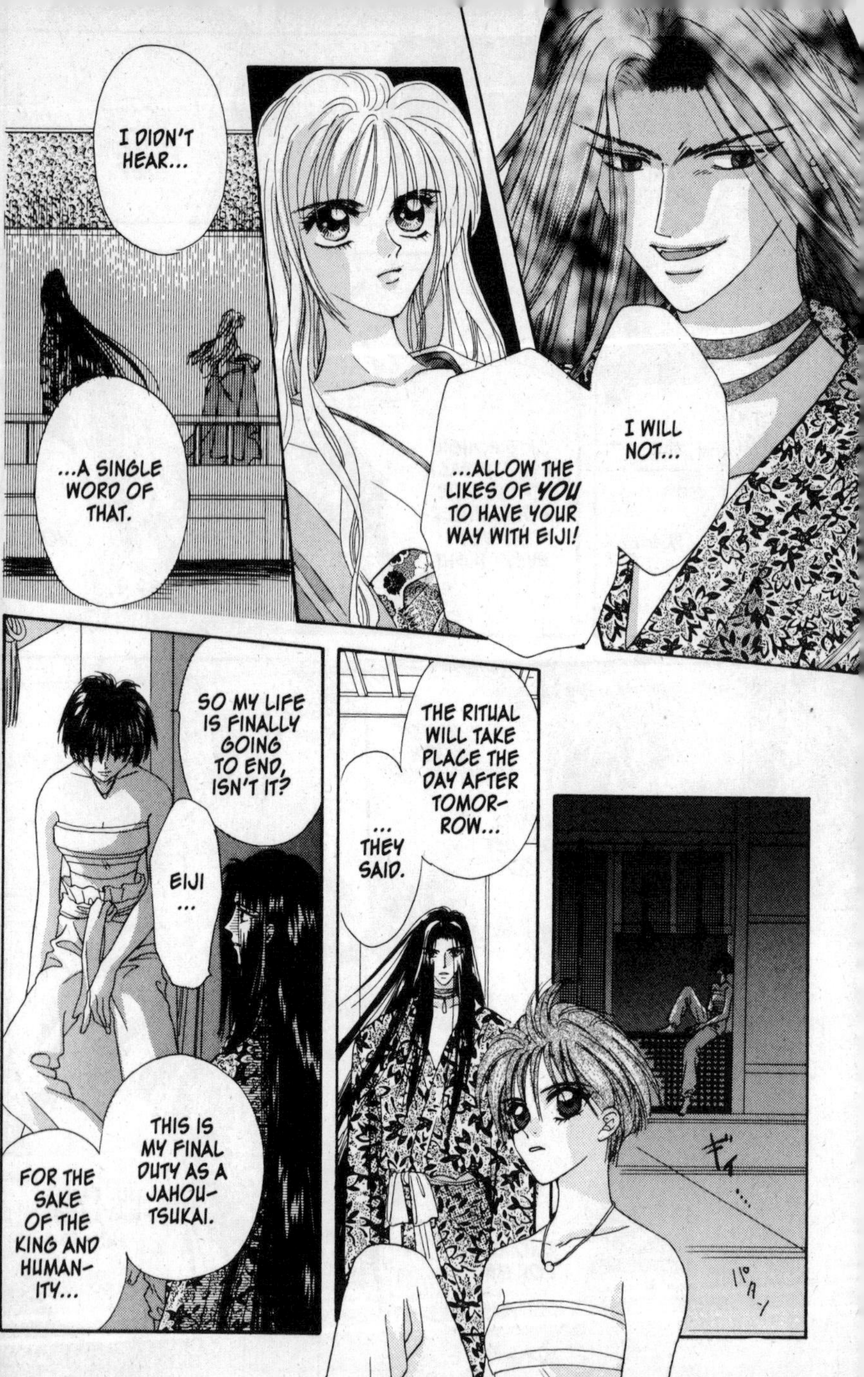
I WILL NOT...
...ALLOW THE LIKES OF YOU TO HAVE YOUR WAY WITH EIJI!
I DIDN'T HEAR...
...A SINGLE WORD OF THAT.
THE RITUAL WILL TAKE PLACE THE DAY AFTER TOMORROW...
...THEY SAID.
SO MY LIFE IS FINALLY GOING TO END, ISN'T IT?
EIJI...
THIS IS MY FINAL DUTY AS A JAHOU-TSUKAI.
FOR THE SAKE OF THE KING AND HUMANITY...

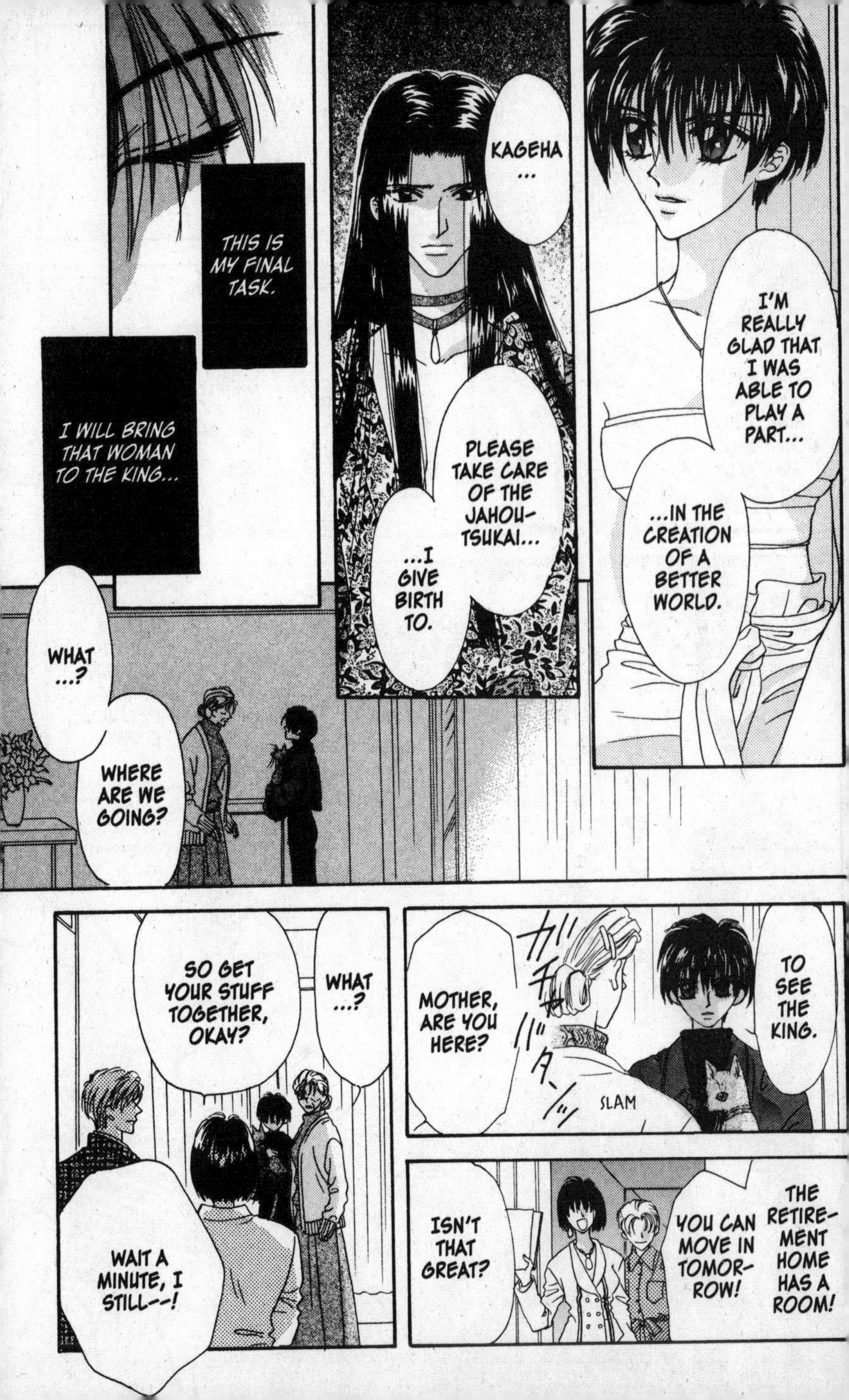
I'M REALLY GLAD THAT I WAS ABLE TO PLAY A PART...
...IN THE CREATION OF A BETTER WORLD.
KAGEHA...
PLEASE TAKE CARE OF THE JAHOU-TSUKAI...
...I GIVE BIRTH TO.
THIS IS MY FINAL TASK.
I WILL BRING THAT WOMAN TO THE KING...
WHAT...?
WHERE ARE WE GOING?
TO SEE THE KING.
MOTHER, ARE YOU HERE?
SLAM
THE RETIREMENT HOME HAS A ROOM!
YOU CAN MOVE IN TOMORROW!
ISN'T THAT GREAT?
WHAT...?
SO GET YOUR STUFF TOGETHER, OKAY?
WAIT A MINUTE, I STILL--!

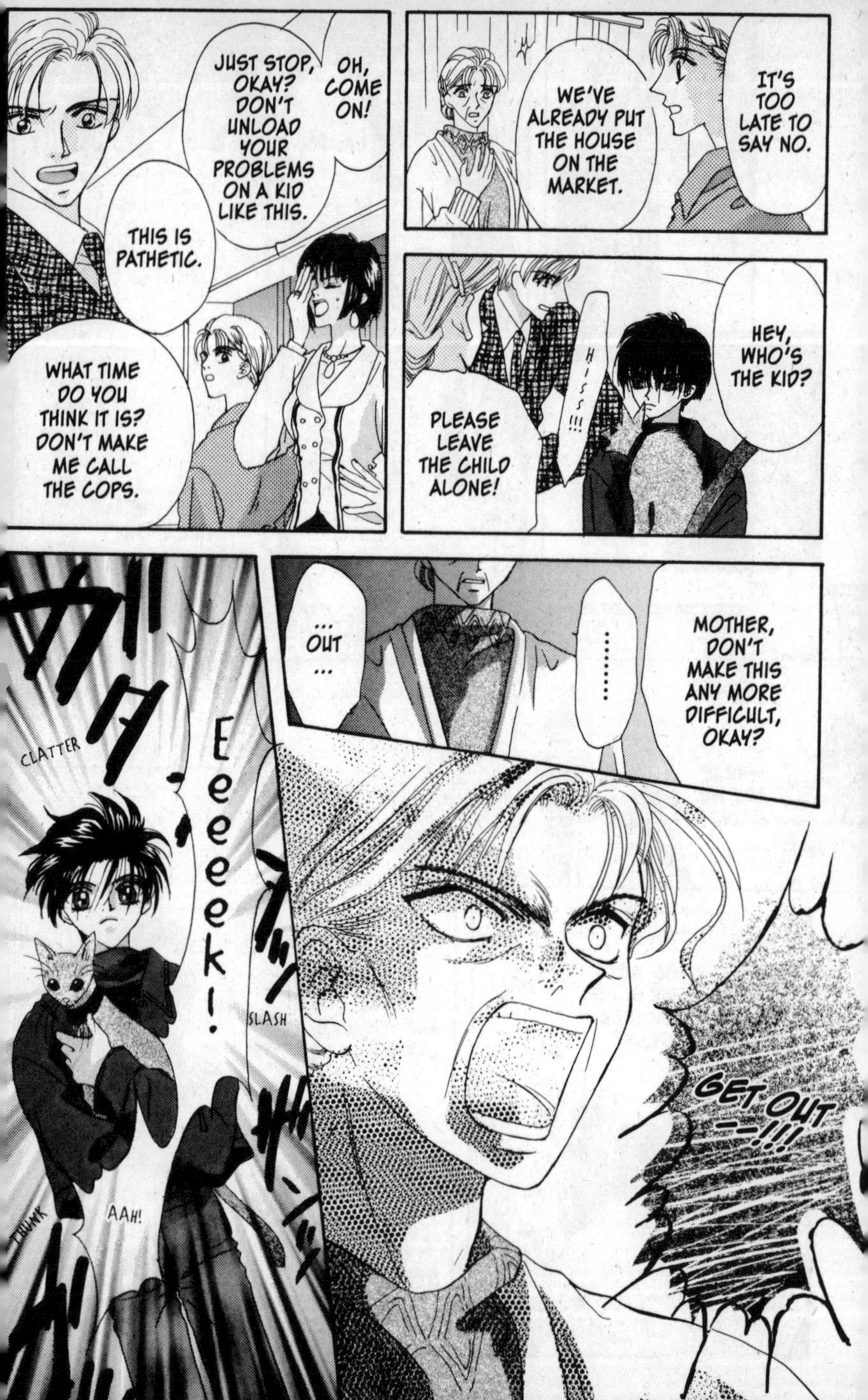
IT'S TOO LATE TO SAY NO.
WE'VE ALREADY PUT THE HOUSE ON THE MARKET.
HEY, WHO'S THE KID?
HISS!!!
PLEASE LEAVE THE CHILD ALONE!
OH, COME ON!
JUST STOP, OKAY? DON'T UNLOAD YOUR PROBLEMS ON A KID LIKE THIS.
THIS IS PATHETIC.
WHAT TIME DO YOU THINK IT IS? DON'T MAKE ME CALL THE COPS.
MOTHER, DON'T MAKE THIS ANY MORE DIFFICULT, OKAY?
......
... OUT ...
GET OUT --!!!
CLATTER
Eeeeek!
SLASH
AAH!
THUNK

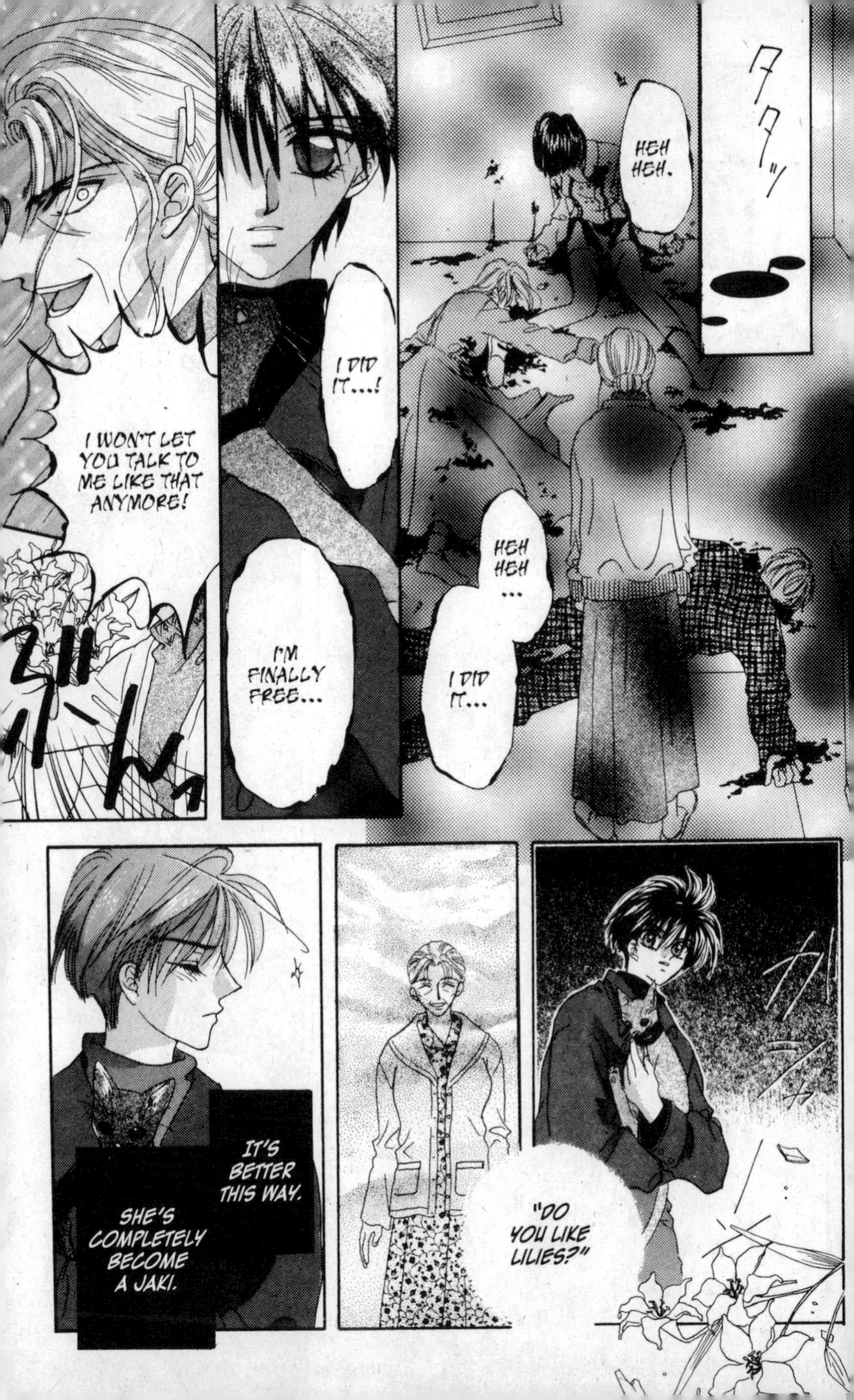
タタッ
HEH HEH.
HEH HEH...
I DID IT...
I DID IT...!
I'M FINALLY FREE...
I WON'T LET YOU TALK TO ME LIKE THAT ANYMORE!
"DO YOU LIKE LILIES?"
IT'S BETTER THIS WAY.
SHE'S COMPLETELY BECOME A JAKI.

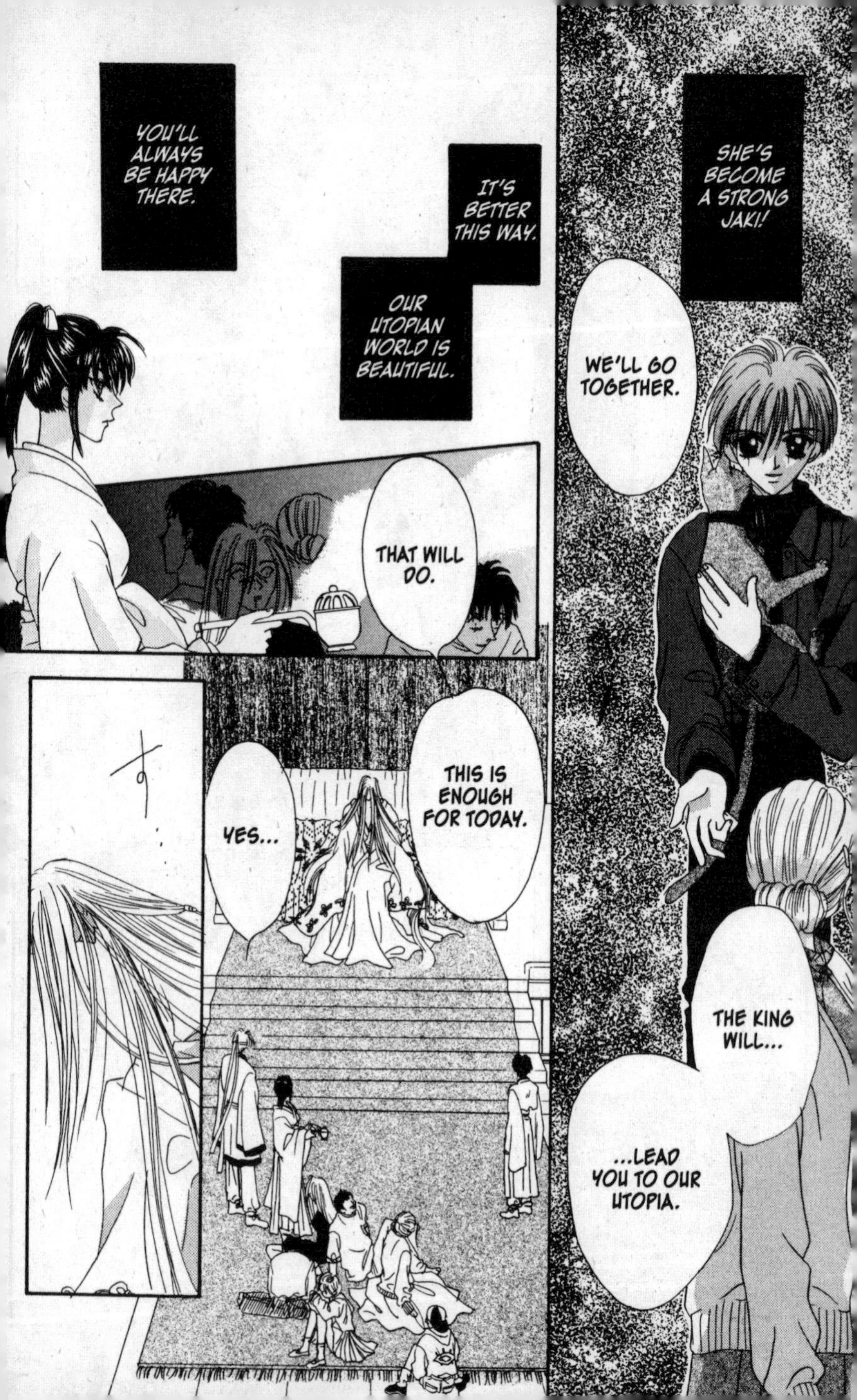
SHE'S BECOME A STRONG JAKI!
WE'LL GO TOGETHER.
THE KING WILL...
...LEAD YOU TO OUR UTOPIA.
IT'S BETTER THIS WAY.
OUR UTOPIAN WORLD IS BEAUTIFUL.
YOU'LL ALWAYS BE HAPPY THERE.
THAT WILL DO.
THIS IS ENOUGH FOR TODAY.
YES...
す

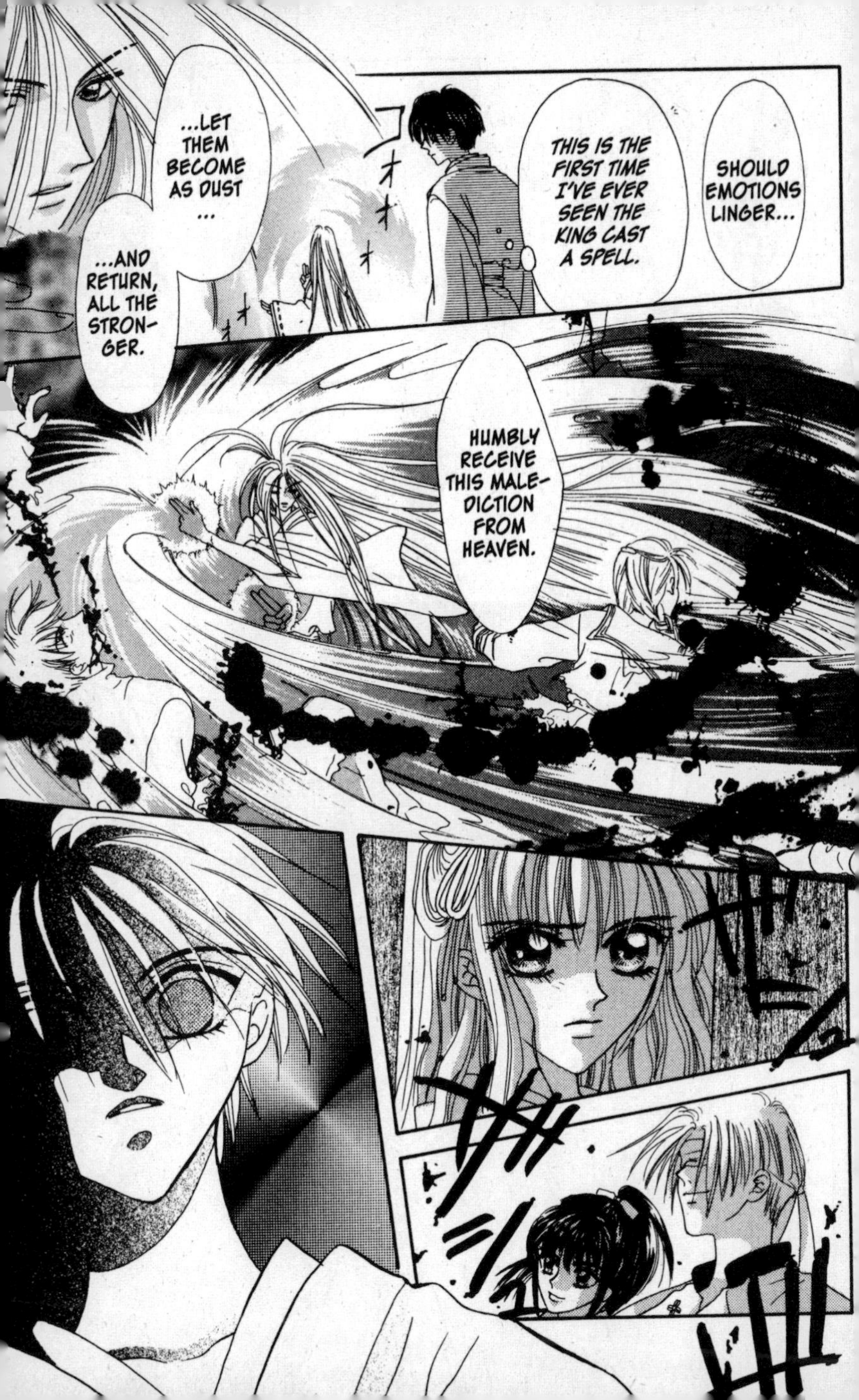
SHOULD EMOTIONS LINGER...
THIS IS THE FIRST TIME I'VE EVER SEEN THE KING CAST A SPELL.
...LET THEM BECOME AS DUST ...
...AND RETURN, ALL THE STRONGER.
HUMBLY RECEIVE THIS MALEDICTION FROM HEAVEN.

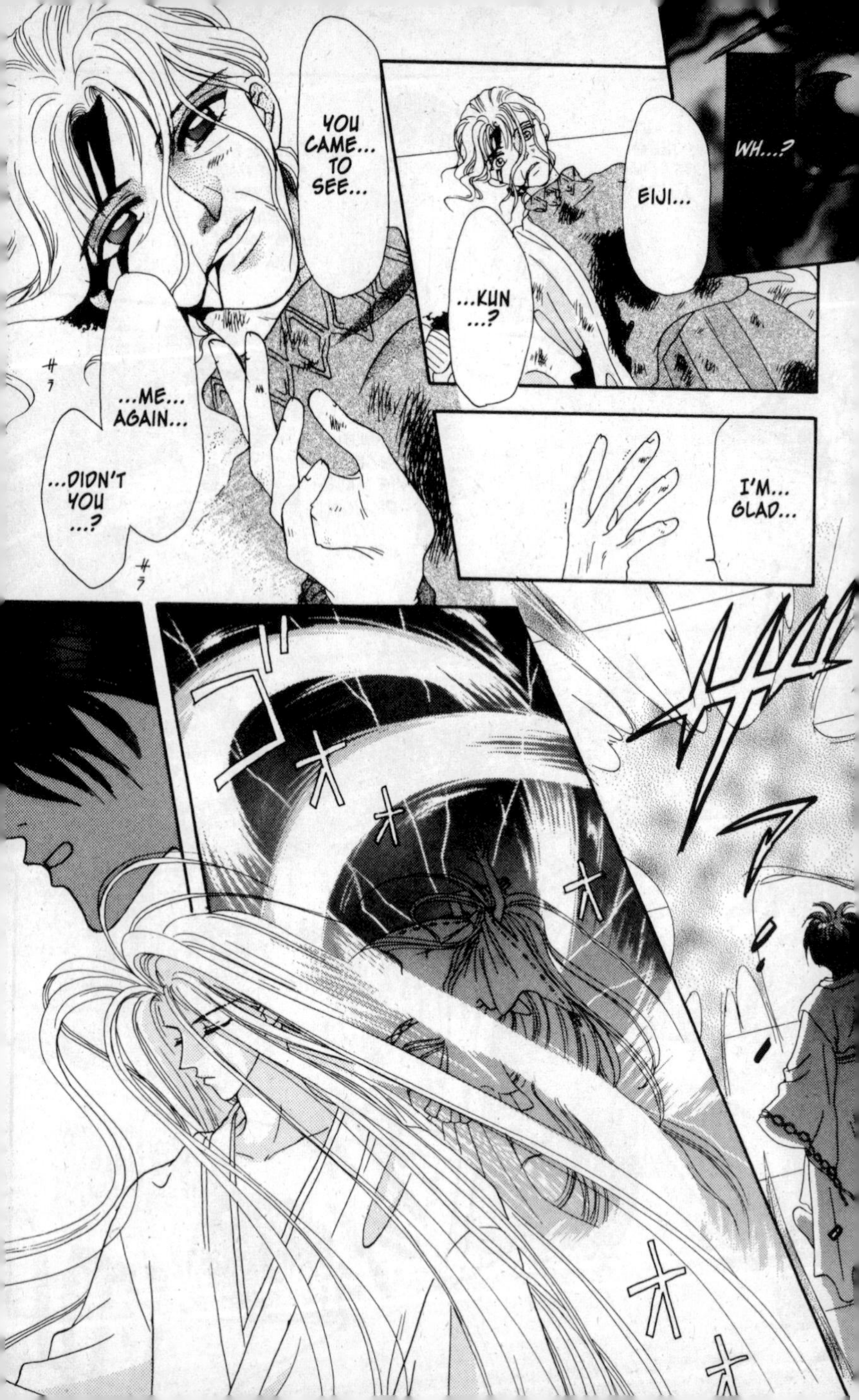
WH...?
EIJI...
...KUN ...?
I'M... GLAD...
YOU CAME... TO SEE...
...ME... AGAIN...
...DIDN'T YOU ...?
サラ
サラ

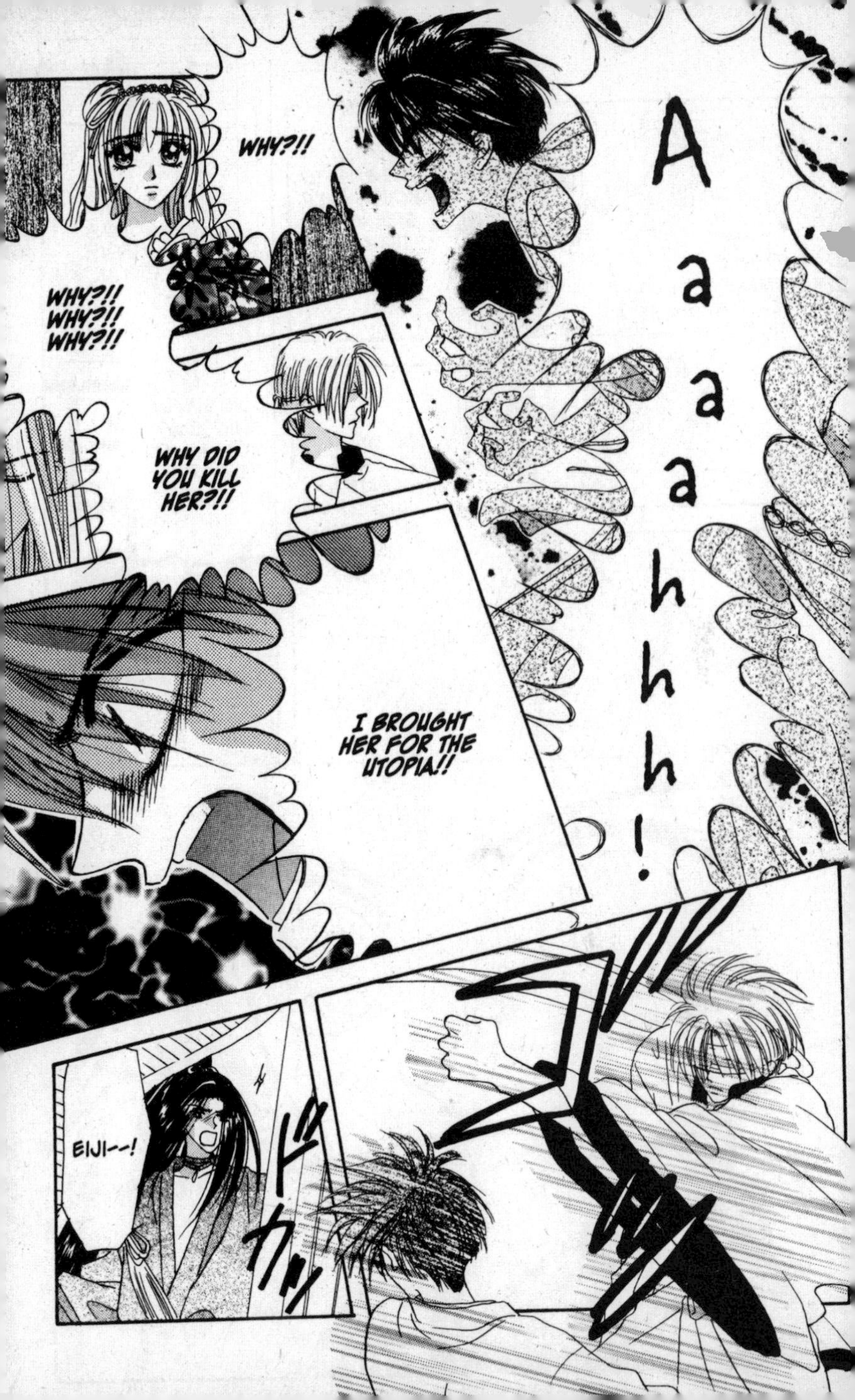
Aaaahhh!
WHY?!!
WHY?!!
WHY?!!
WHY?!!
WHY DID YOU KILL HER?!!
I BROUGHT HER FOR THE UTOPIA!!
EIJI--!

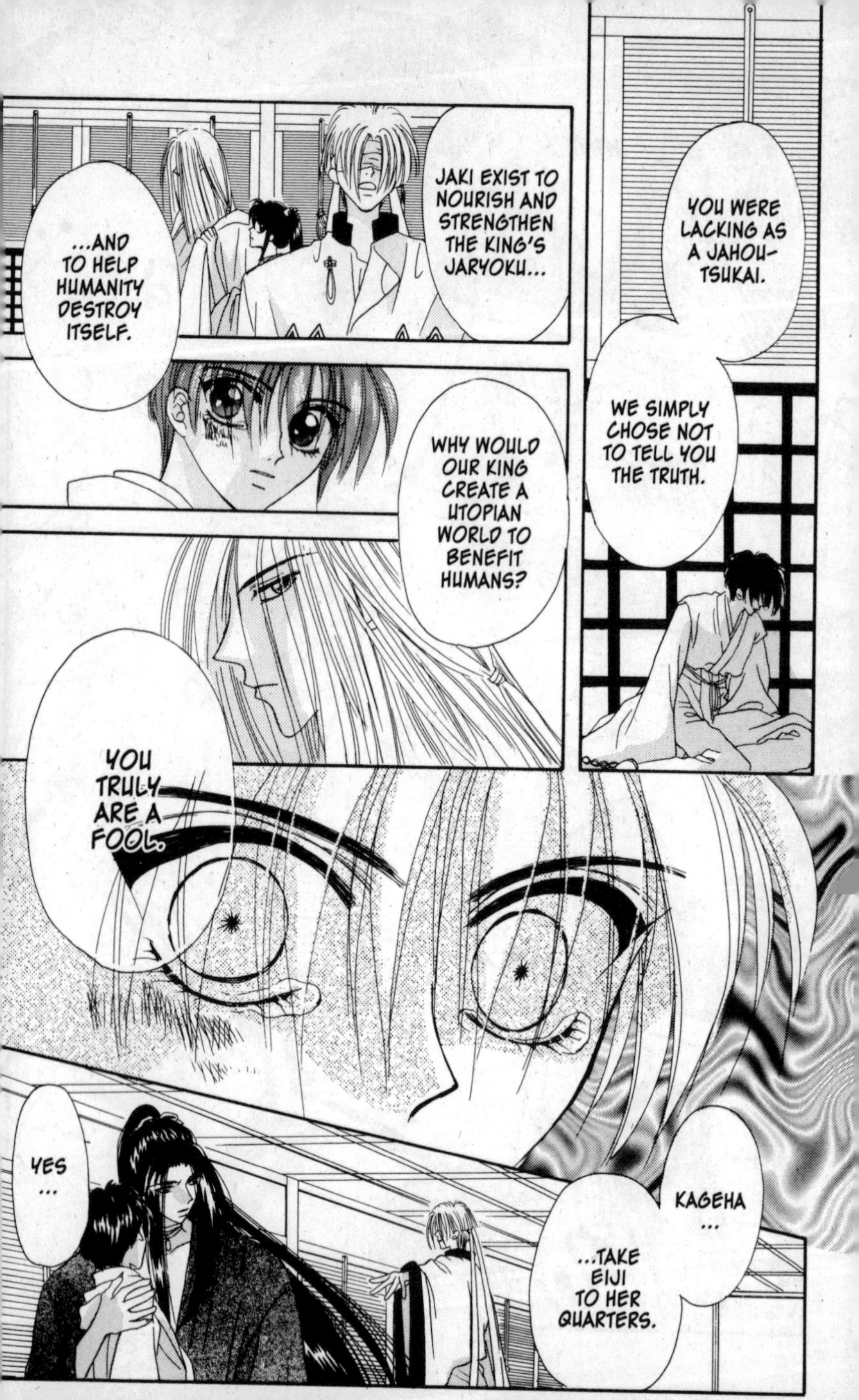
YOU WERE LACKING AS A JAHOU-TSUKAI.
WE SIMPLY CHOSE NOT TO TELL YOU THE TRUTH.
JAKI EXIST TO NOURISH AND STRENGTHEN THE KING'S JARYOKU...
...AND TO HELP HUMANITY DESTROY ITSELF.
WHY WOULD OUR KING CREATE A UTOPIAN WORLD TO BENEFIT HUMANS?
YOU TRULY ARE A FOOL.
KAGEHA ...
...TAKE EIJI TO HER QUARTERS.
YES ...

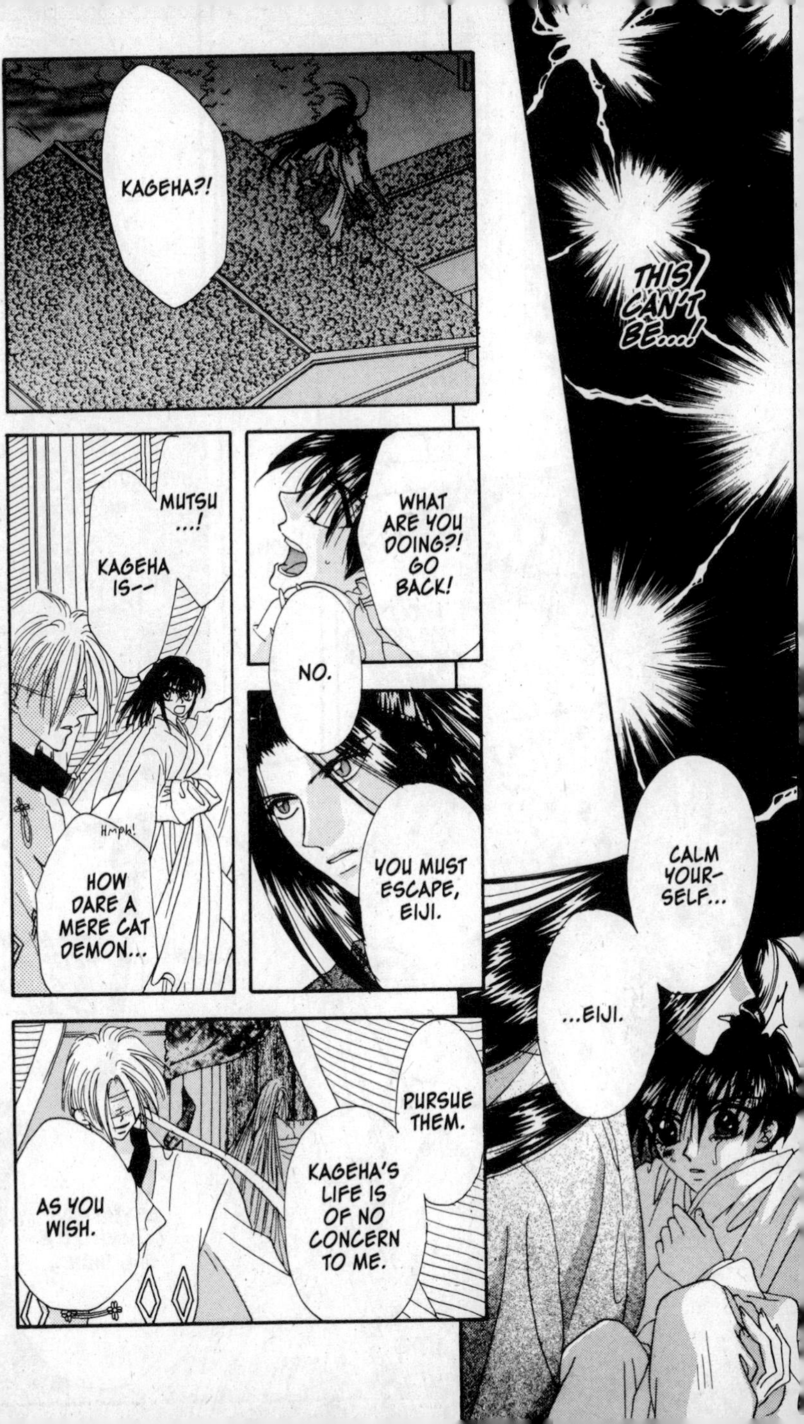
THIS CAN'T BE...!
CALM YOURSELF...
...EIJI.
KAGEHA?!
WHAT ARE YOU DOING?! GO BACK!
NO.
YOU MUST ESCAPE, EIJI.
MUTSU...!
KAGEHA IS--
Hmph!
HOW DARE A MERE CAT DEMON...
PURSUE THEM.
KAGEHA'S LIFE IS OF NO CONCERN TO ME.
AS YOU WISH.

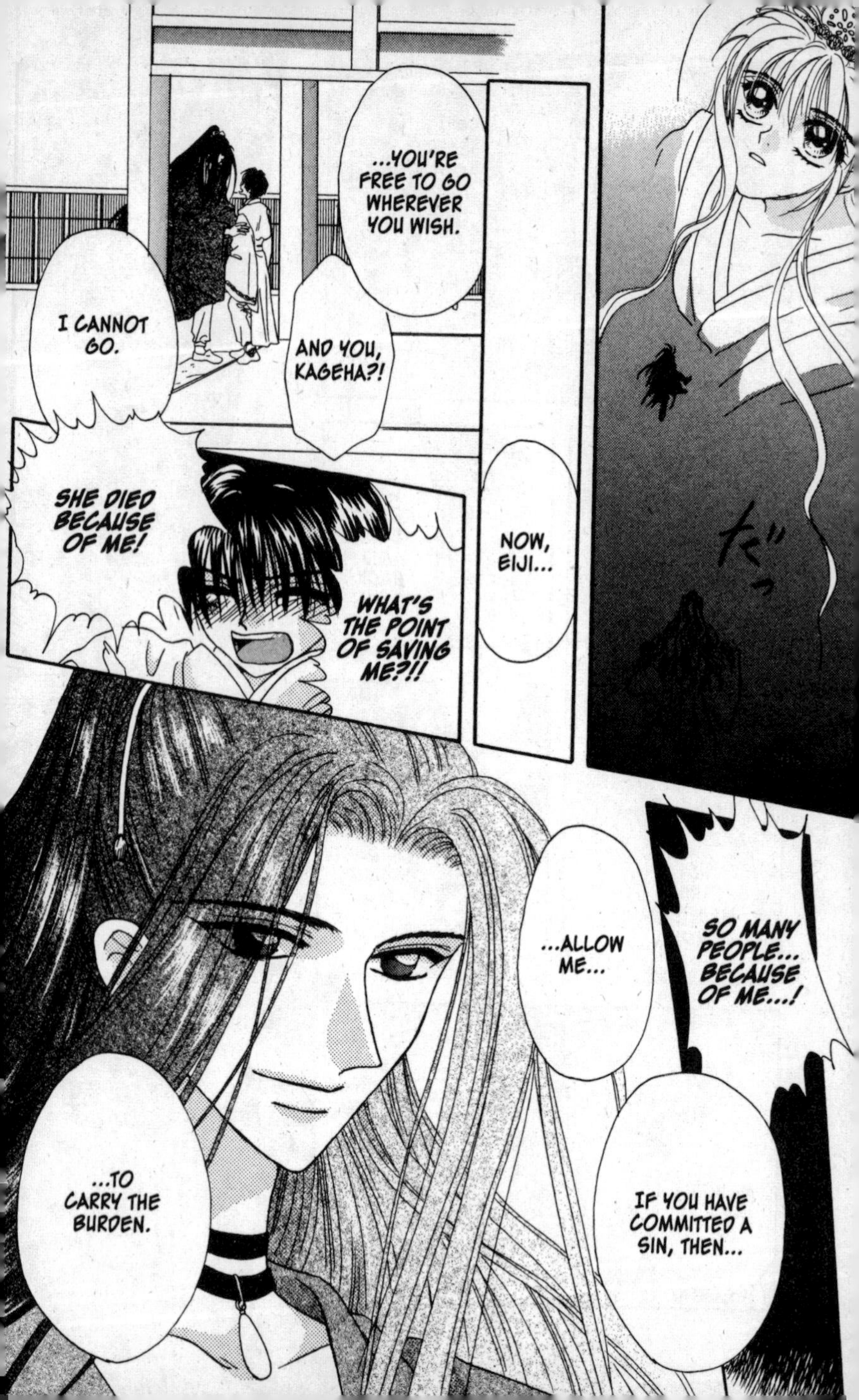
NOW, EIJI...
...YOU'RE FREE TO GO WHEREVER YOU WISH.
AND YOU, KAGEHA?!
I CANNOT GO.
SHE DIED BECAUSE OF ME!
WHAT'S THE POINT OF SAVING ME?!!
SO MANY PEOPLE... BECAUSE OF ME...!
IF YOU HAVE COMMITTED A SIN, THEN...
...ALLOW ME...
...TO CARRY THE BURDEN.

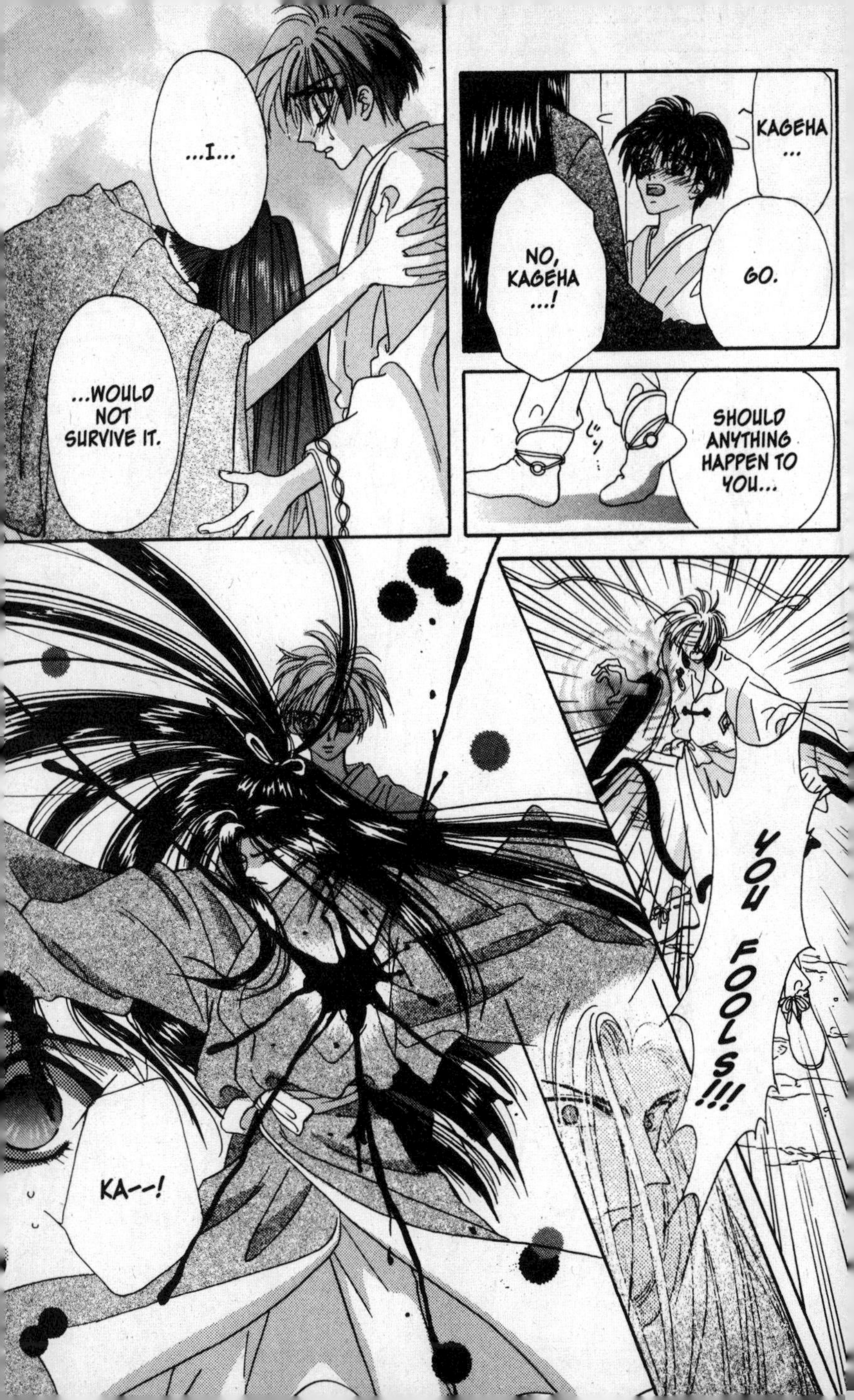
KAGEHA ...
GO.
NO, KAGEHA ...!
SHOULD ANYTHING HAPPEN TO YOU...
...I...
...WOULD NOT SURVIVE IT.
YOU FOOLS!!!
KA--!

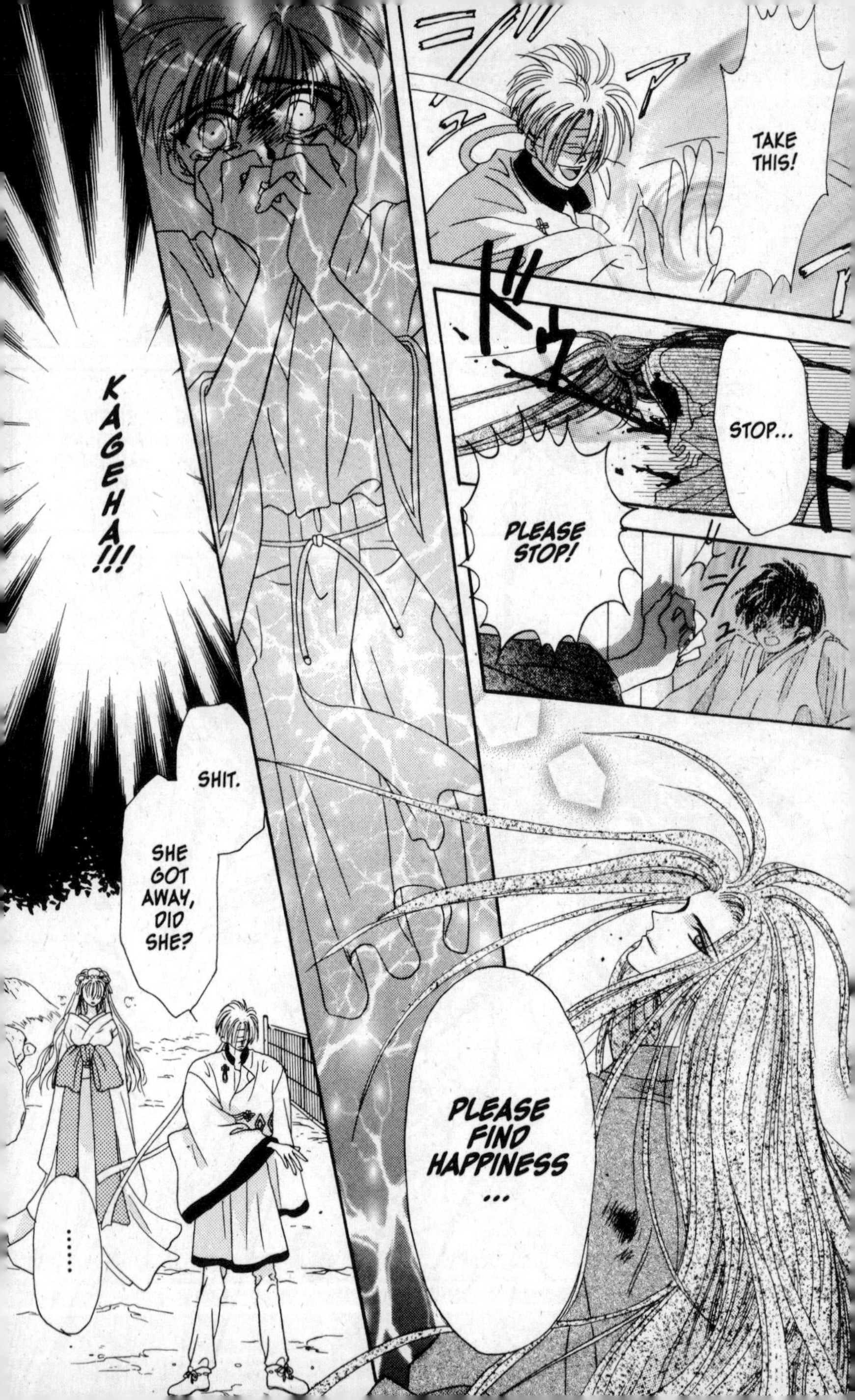
TAKE THIS!
STOP...
PLEASE STOP!
KAGEHA!!!
PLEASE FIND HAPPINESS ...
SHIT.
SHE GOT AWAY, DID SHE?
......

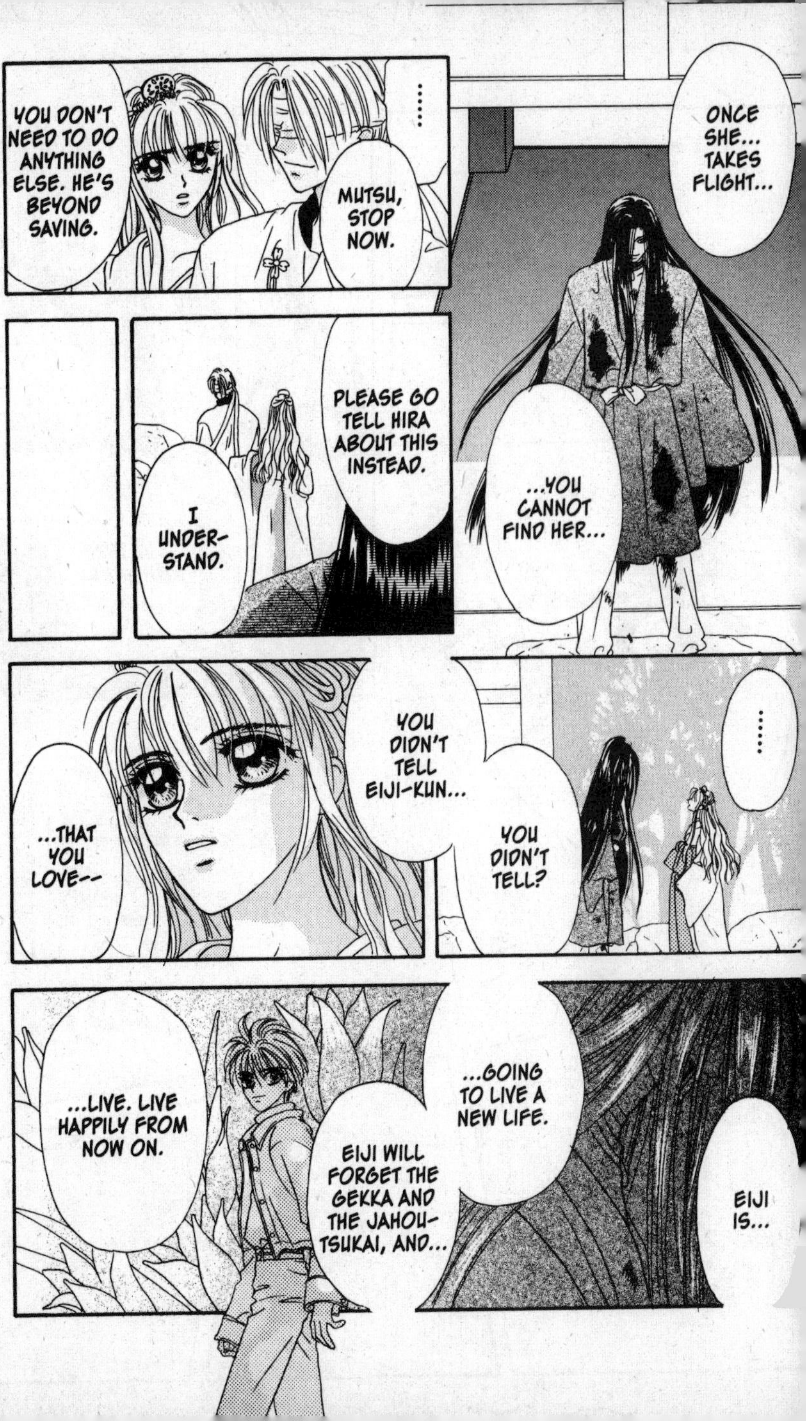
ONCE SHE... TAKES FLIGHT...
...YOU CANNOT FIND HER...
......
MUTSU, STOP NOW.
YOU DON'T NEED TO DO ANYTHING ELSE. HE'S BEYOND SAVING.
PLEASE GO TELL HIRA ABOUT THIS INSTEAD.
I UNDER-STAND.
......
YOU DIDN'T TELL?
YOU DIDN'T TELL EIJI-KUN...
...THAT YOU LOVE--
EIJI IS...
...GOING TO LIVE A NEW LIFE.
EIJI WILL FORGET THE GEKKA AND THE JAHOU-TSUKAI, AND...
...LIVE. LIVE HAPPILY FROM NOW ON.

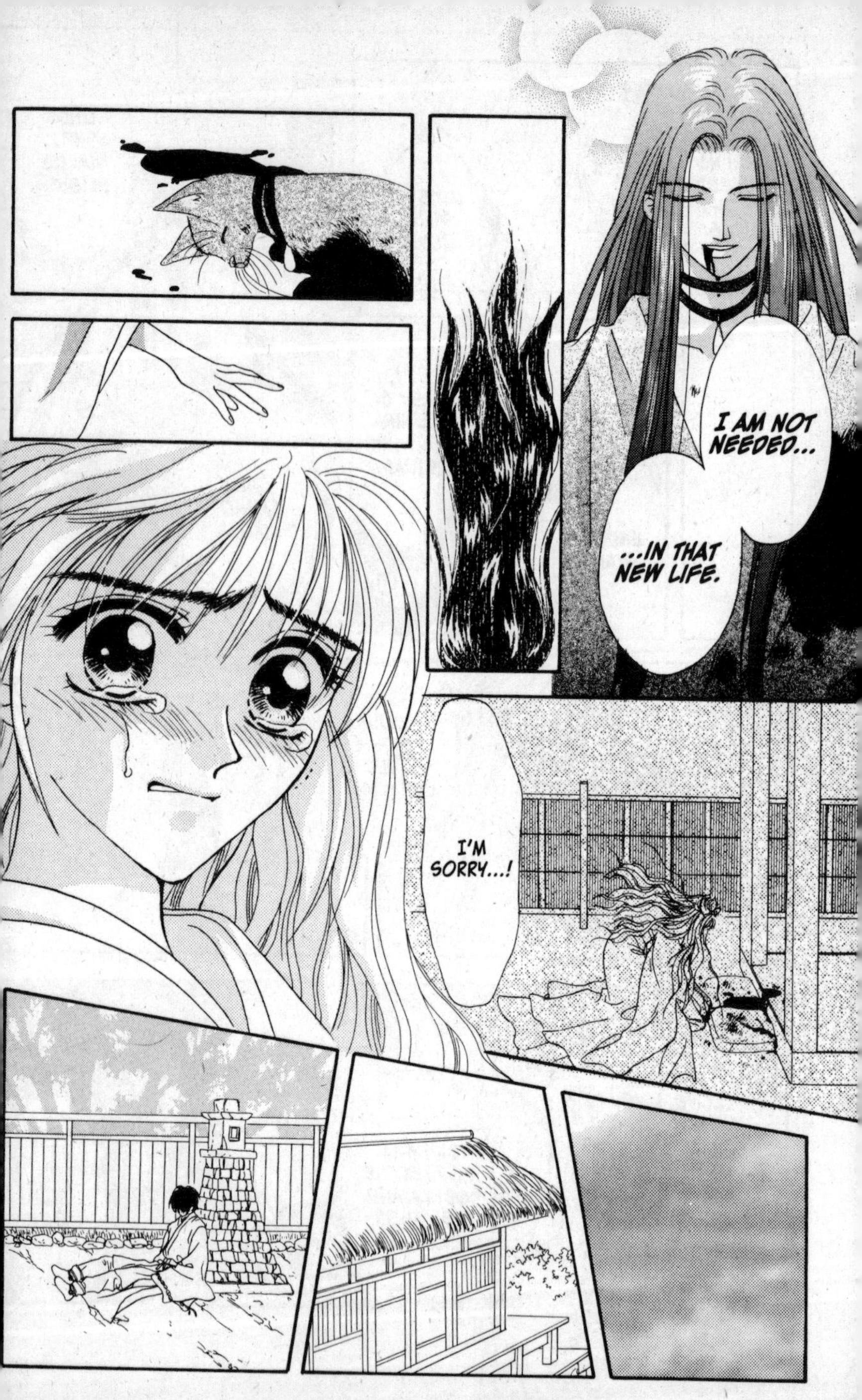
I AM NOT NEEDED...
...IN THAT NEW LIFE.
I'M SORRY...!

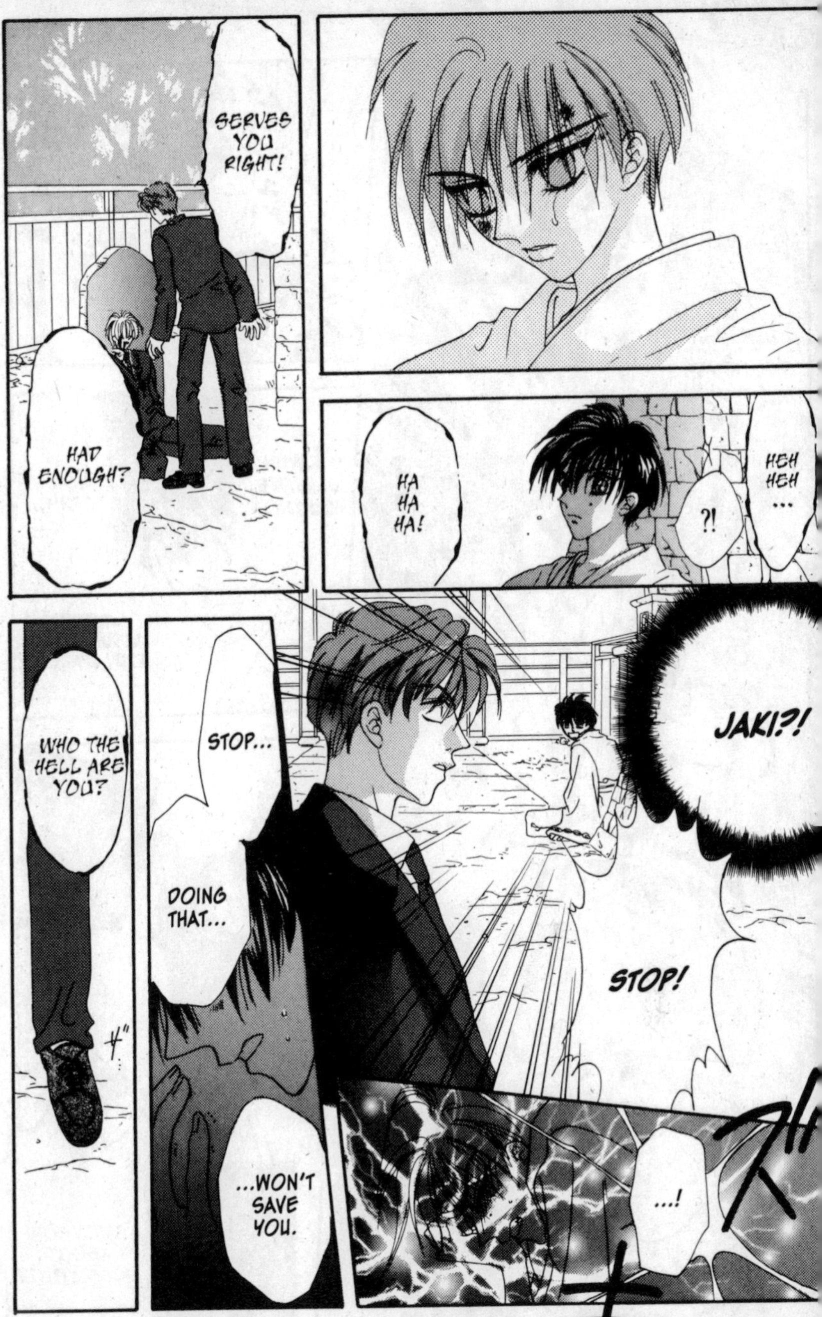
HEH HEH ...
?!
HA HA HA!
SERVES YOU RIGHT!
HAD ENOUGH?
JAKI?!
STOP!
...!
STOP...
DOING THAT...
...WON'T SAVE YOU.
WHO THE HELL ARE YOU?

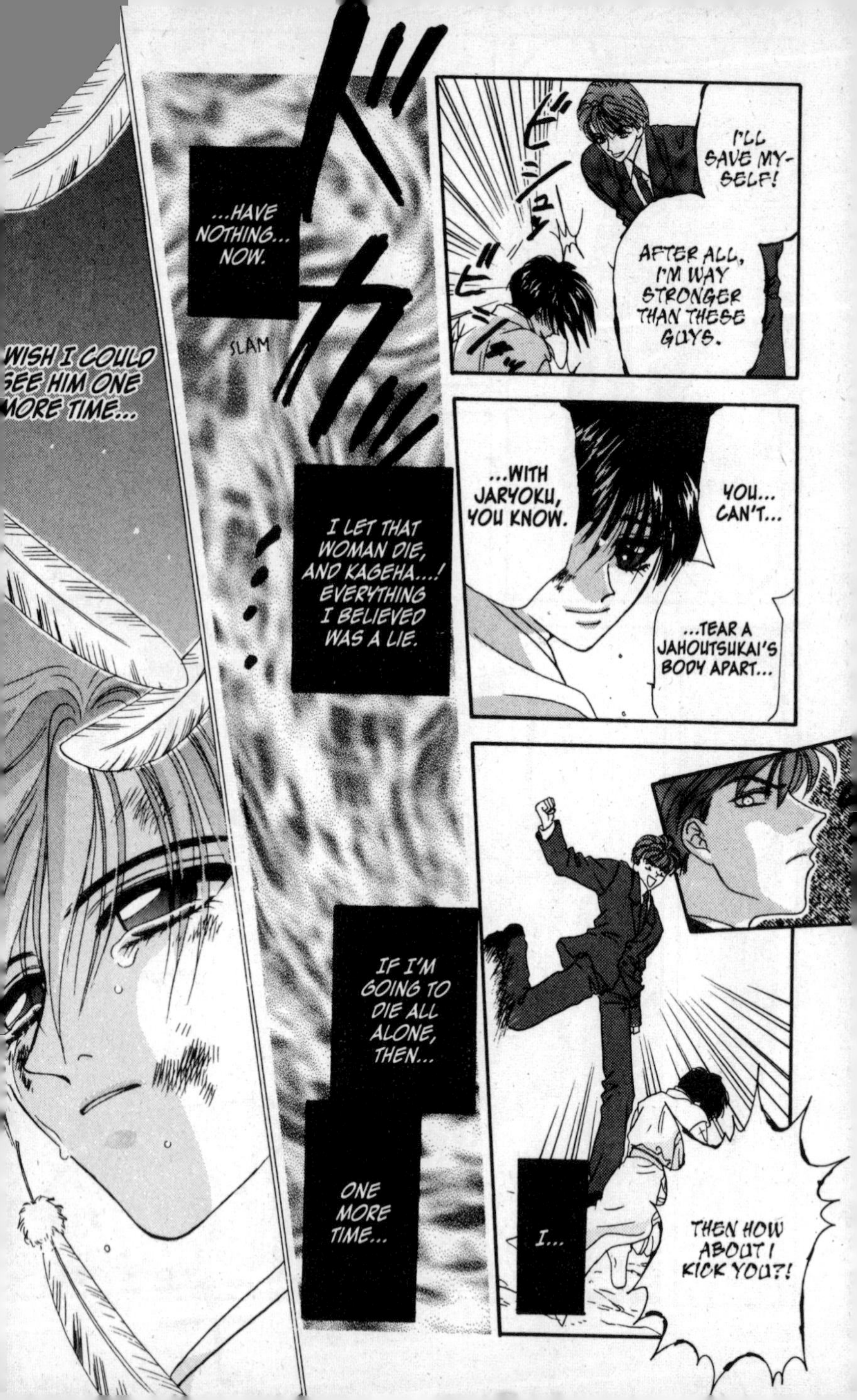
I'LL SAVE MY-SELF!
AFTER ALL, I'M WAY STRONGER THAN THESE GUYS.
YOU... CAN'T...
...TEAR A JAHOUTSUKAI'S BODY APART...
...WITH JARYOKU, YOU KNOW.
THEN HOW ABOUT I KICK YOU?!
I...
...HAVE NOTHING... NOW.
SLAM
I LET THAT WOMAN DIE, AND KAGEHA...! EVERYTHING I BELIEVED WAS A LIE.
IF I'M GOING TO DIE ALL ALONE, THEN...
ONE MORE TIME...
WISH I COULD SEE HIM ONE MORE TIME...

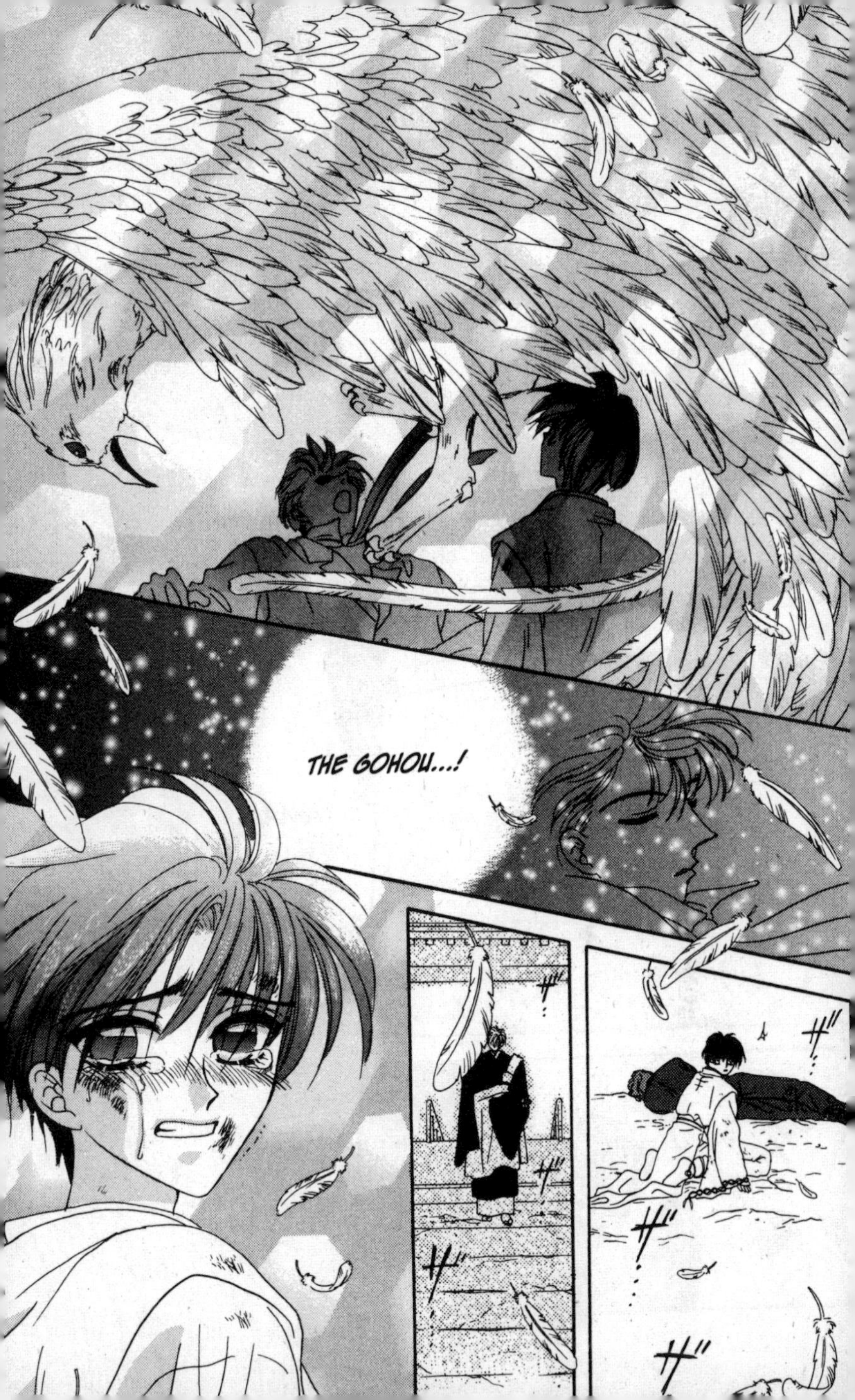
THE GOHOU...!

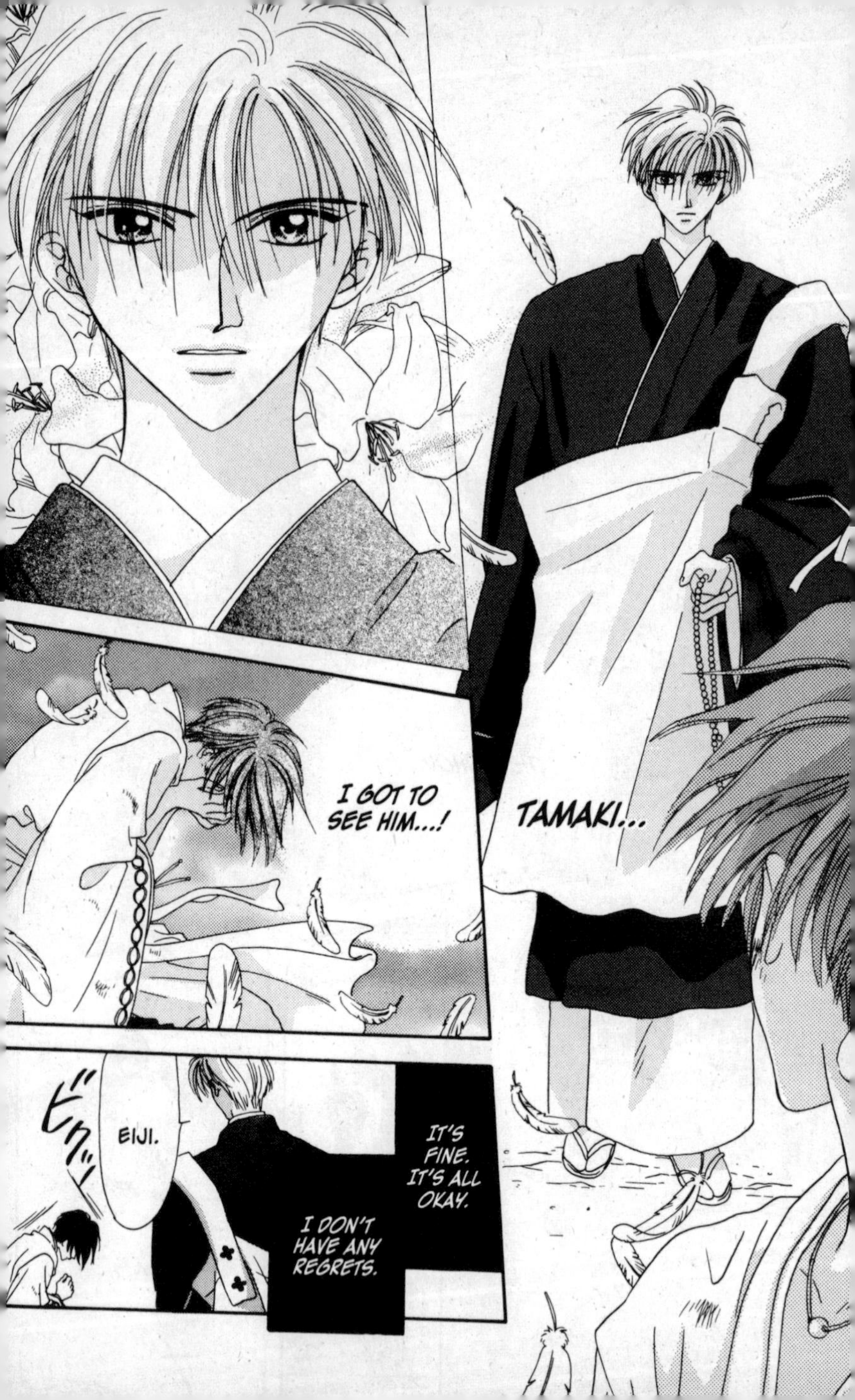
TAMAKI...
I GOT TO SEE HIM...!
IT'S FINE. IT'S ALL OKAY.
EIJI.
ビクッ
I DON'T HAVE ANY REGRETS.

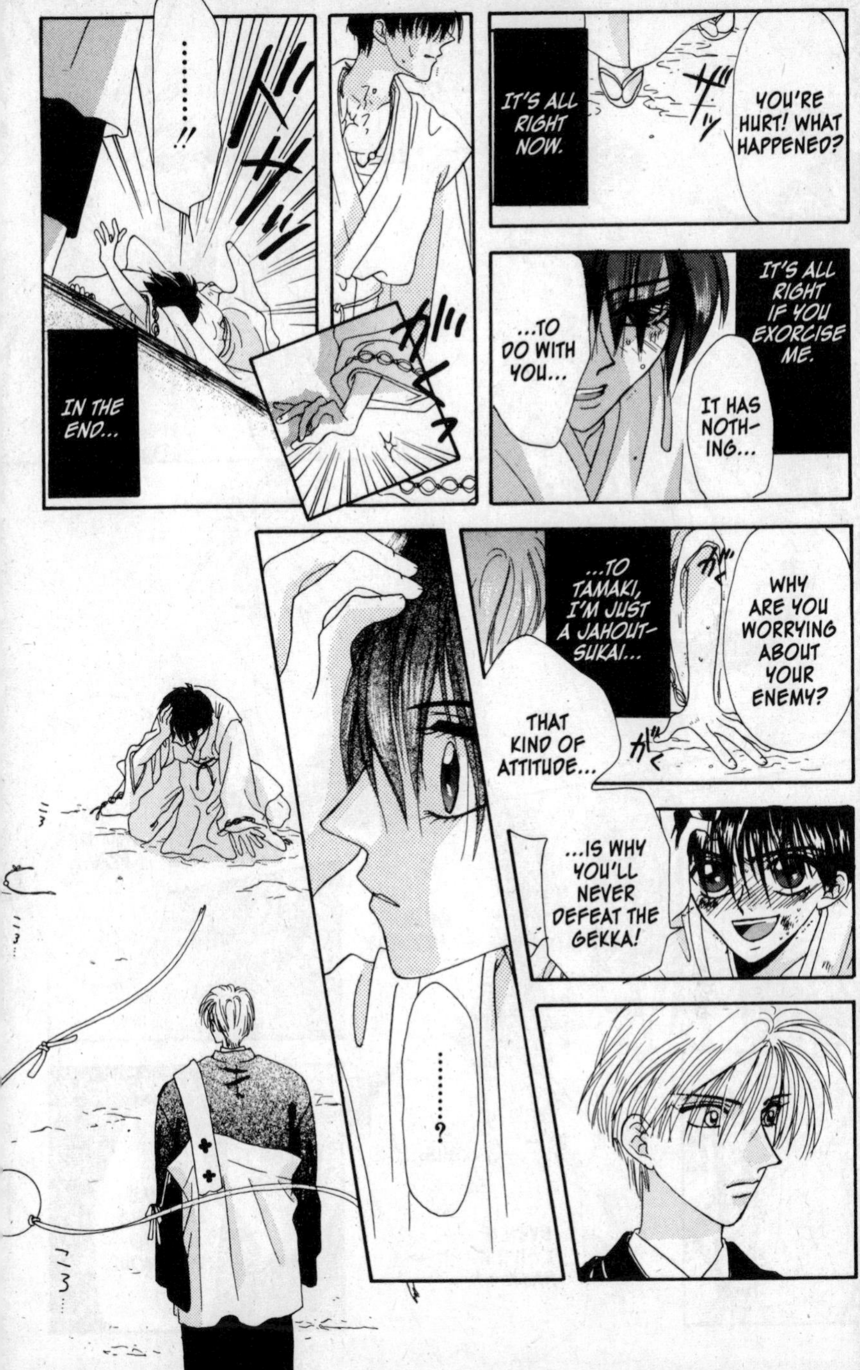
YOU'RE HURT! WHAT HAPPENED?
IT'S ALL RIGHT NOW.
IT'S ALL RIGHT IF YOU EXORCISE ME.
IT HAS NOTHING...
...TO DO WITH YOU...
......!!
IN THE END...
WHY ARE YOU WORRYING ABOUT YOUR ENEMY?
...TO TAMAKI, I'M JUST A JAHOUTSUKAI...
THAT KIND OF ATTITUDE...
...IS WHY YOU'LL NEVER DEFEAT THE GEKKA!
......?

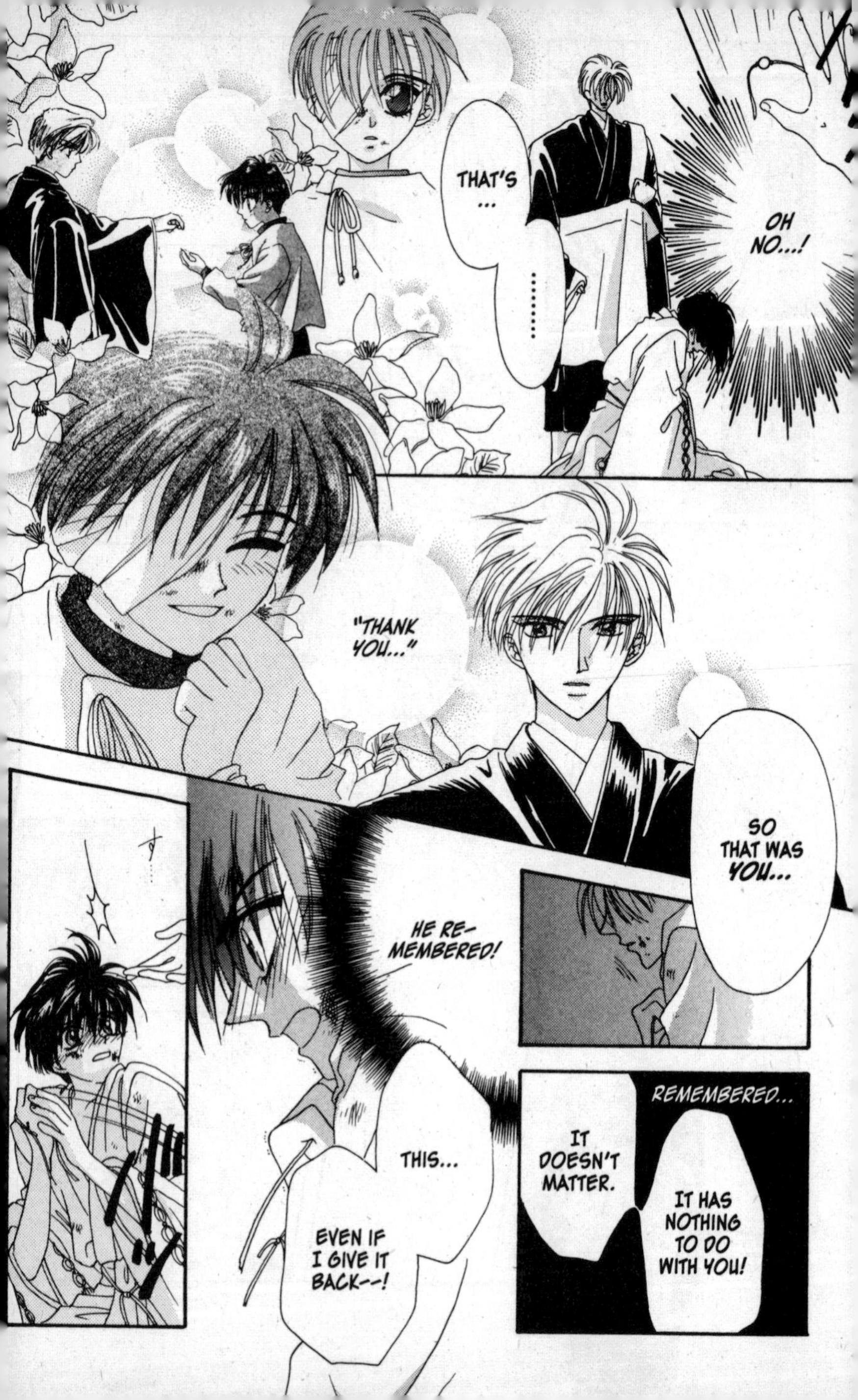
OH NO...!
THAT'S ...
......
"THANK YOU..."
SO THAT WAS YOU...
REMEMBERED...
IT DOESN'T MATTER.
IT HAS NOTHING TO DO WITH YOU!
HE RE-MEMBERED!
THIS...
EVEN IF I GIVE IT BACK--!

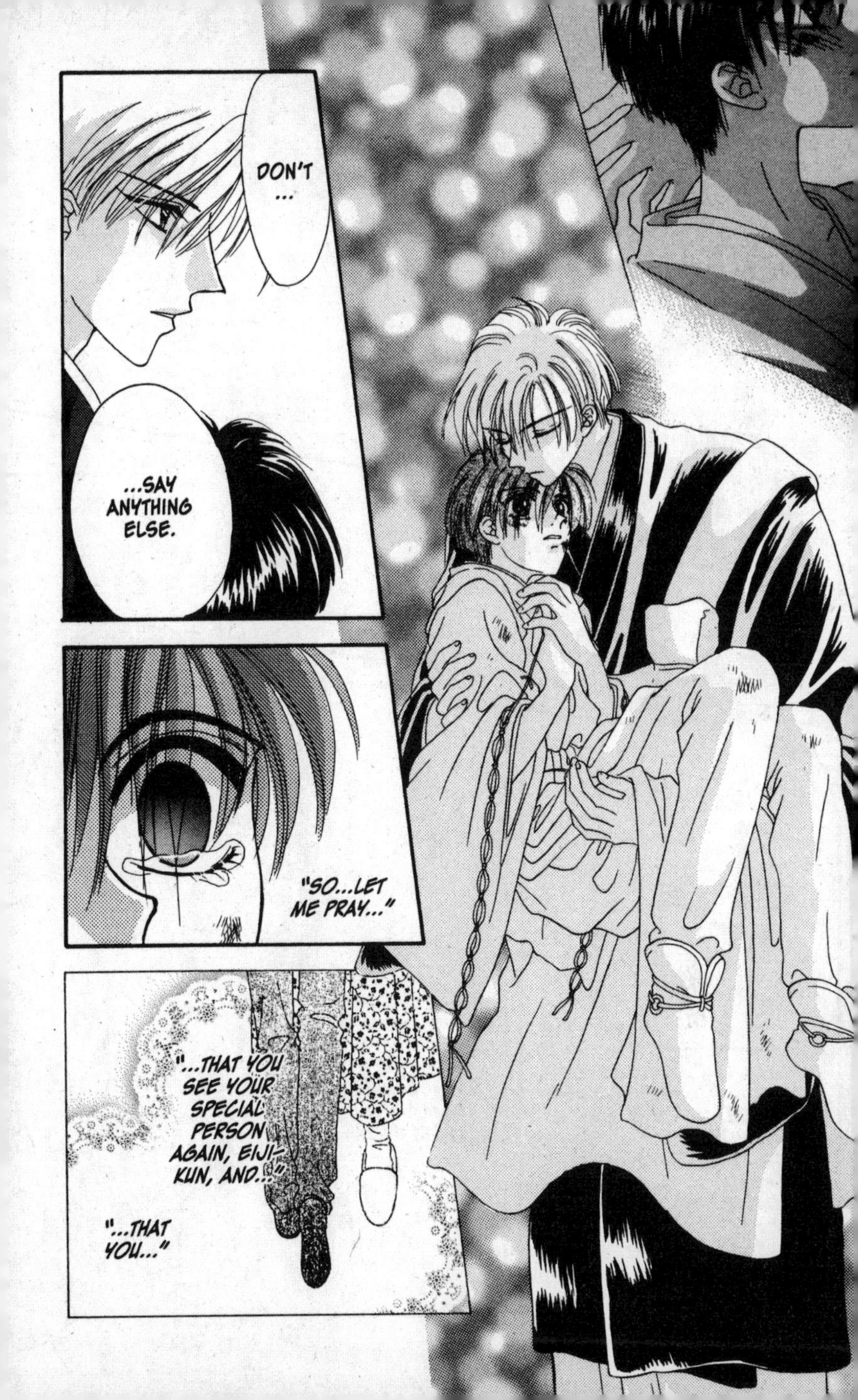
DON'T ...
...SAY ANYTHING ELSE.
"SO...LET ME PRAY..."
"...THAT YOU SEE YOUR SPECIAL PERSON AGAIN, EIJI-KUN, AND..."
"...THAT YOU..."

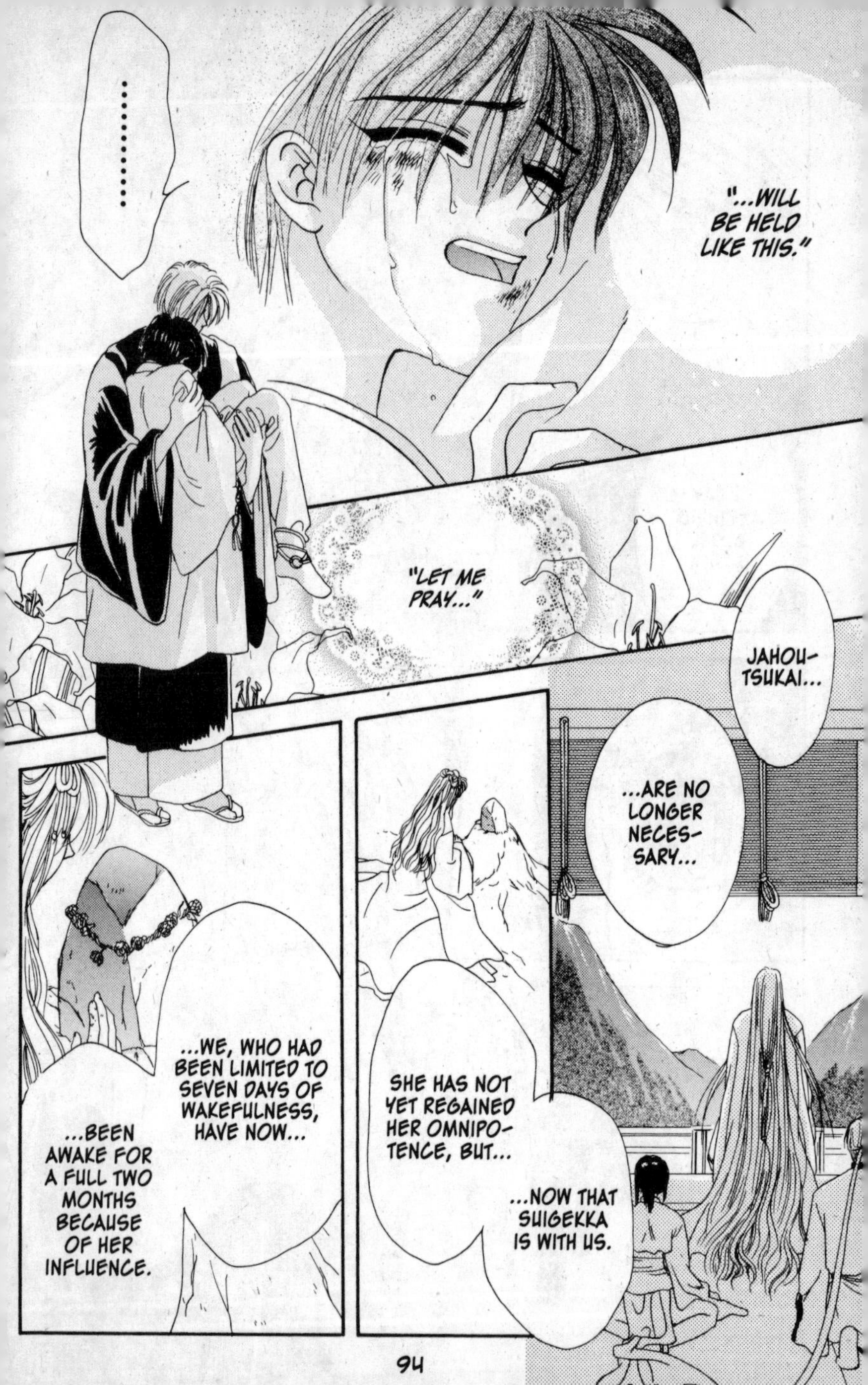
"...WILL BE HELD LIKE THIS."
......
"LET ME PRAY..."
JAHOU-TSUKAI...
...ARE NO LONGER NECES-SARY...
SHE HAS NOT YET REGAINED HER OMNIPO-TENCE, BUT...
...NOW THAT SUIGEKKA IS WITH US.
...WE, WHO HAD BEEN LIMITED TO SEVEN DAYS OF WAKEFULNESS, HAVE NOW...
...BEEN AWAKE FOR A FULL TWO MONTHS BECAUSE OF HER INFLUENCE.

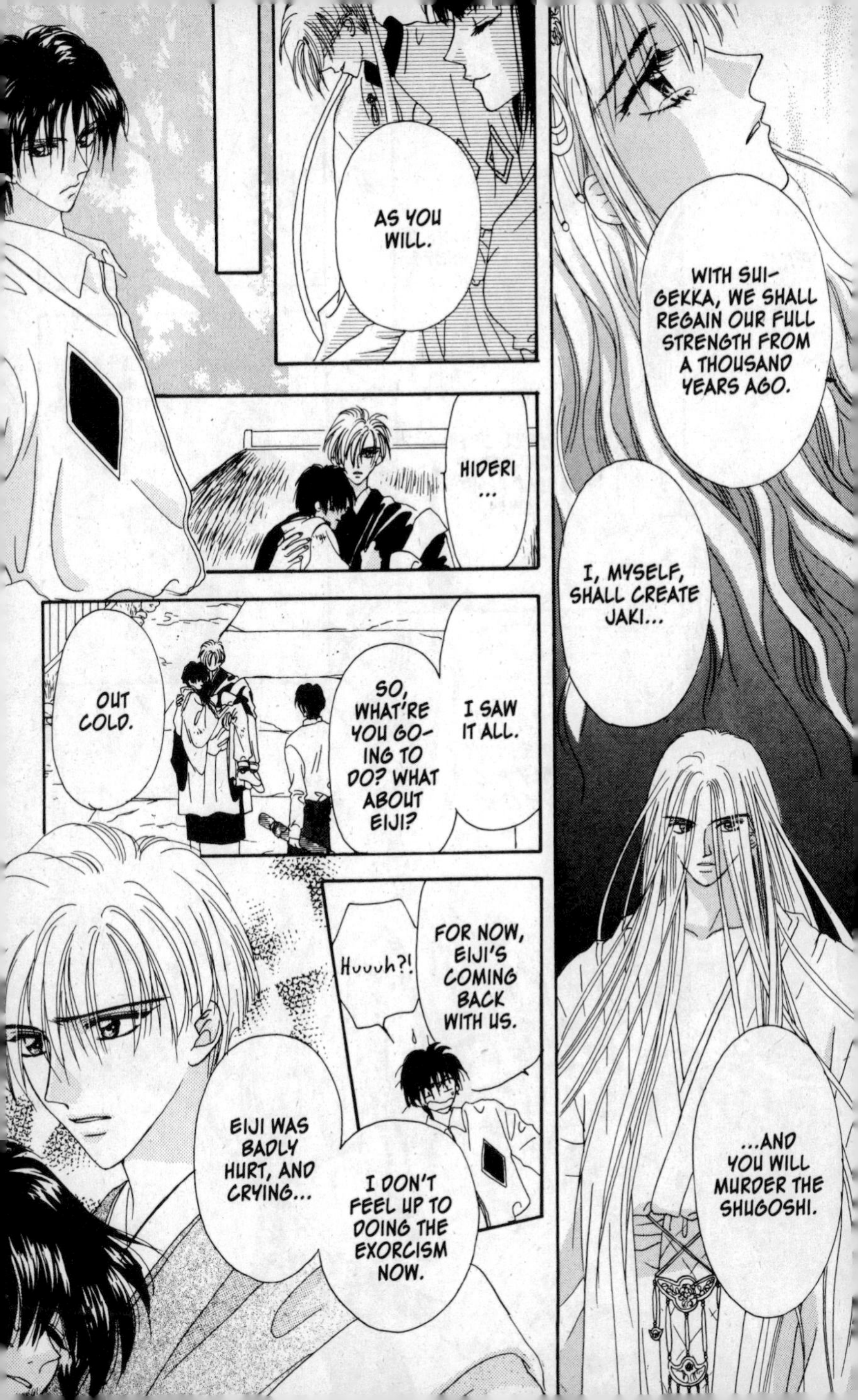
WITH SUI-GEKKA, WE SHALL REGAIN OUR FULL STRENGTH FROM A THOUSAND YEARS AGO.
I, MYSELF, SHALL CREATE JAKI...
...AND YOU WILL MURDER THE SHUGOSHI.
AS YOU WILL.
HIDERI ...
I SAW IT ALL.
SO, WHAT'RE YOU GO-ING TO DO? WHAT ABOUT EIJI?
OUT COLD.
FOR NOW, EIJI'S COMING BACK WITH US.
Huuuh?!
EIJI WAS BADLY HURT, AND CRYING...
I DON'T FEEL UP TO DOING THE EXORCISM NOW.

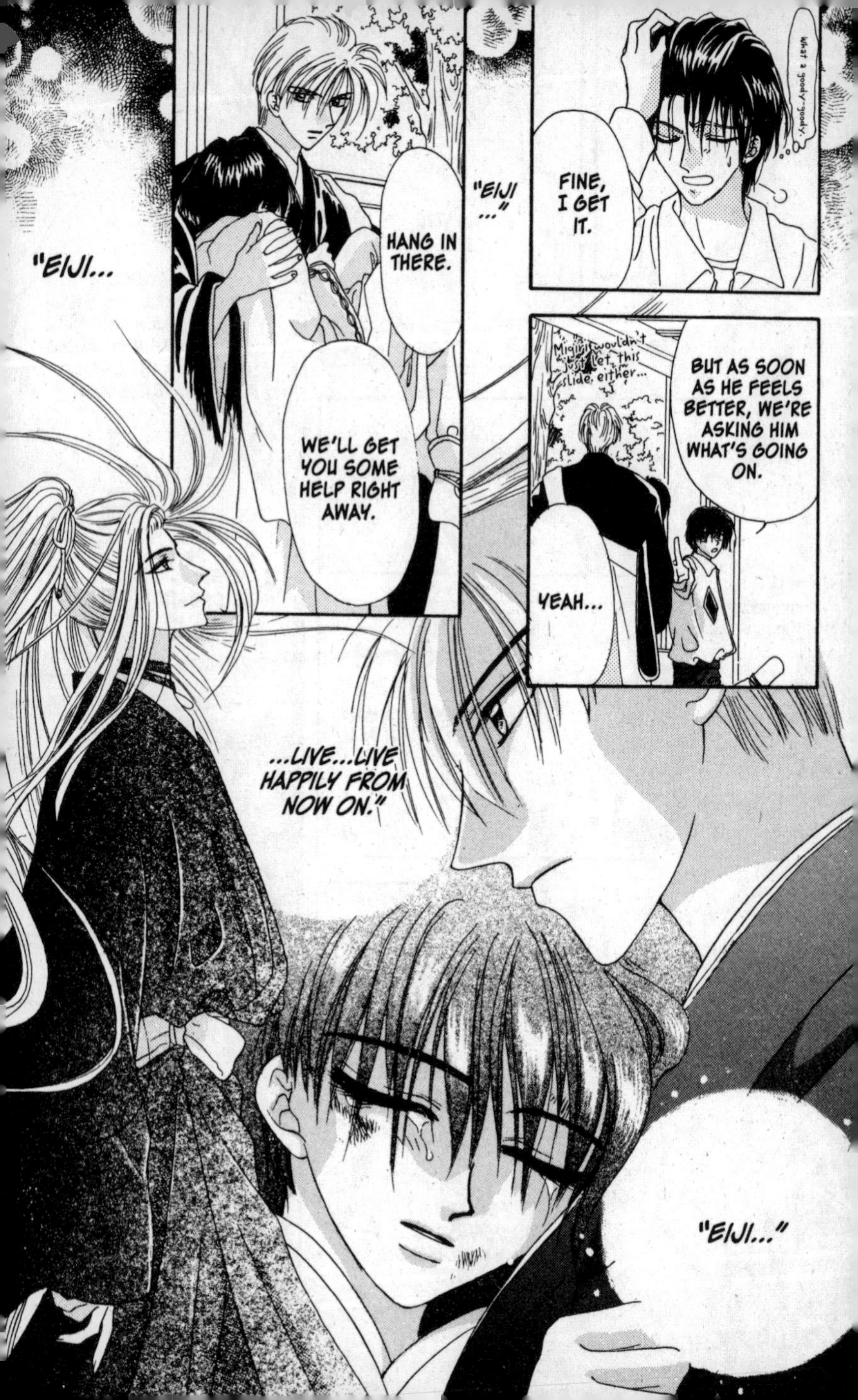
FINE, I GET IT.
what a goody-goody.
BUT AS SOON AS HE FEELS BETTER, WE'RE ASKING HIM WHAT'S GOING ON.
Migiri wouldn't just let this slide, either...
YEAH...
HANG IN THERE.
WE'LL GET YOU SOME HELP RIGHT AWAY.
"EIJI ..."
"EIJI...
...LIVE...LIVE HAPPILY FROM NOW ON."
"EIJI..."

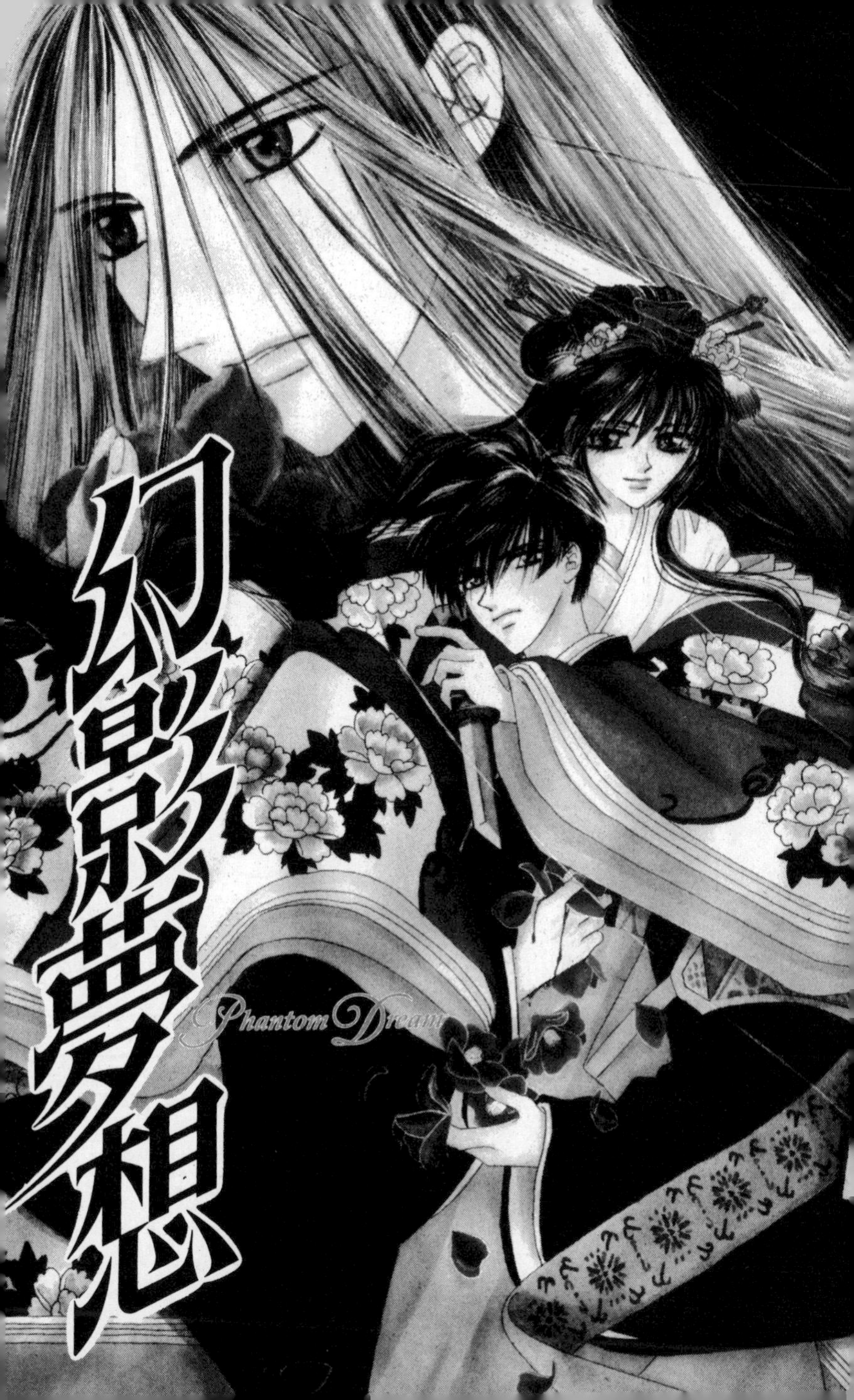
幻影夢想
Phantom Dream

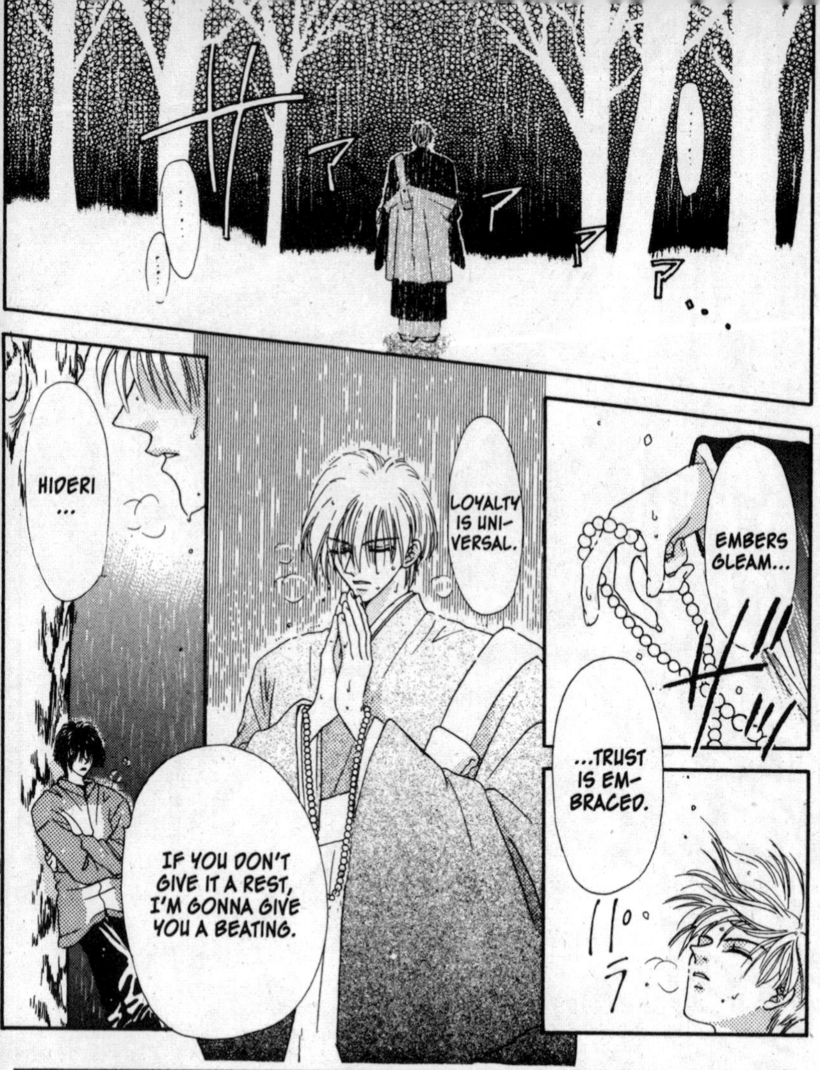
......
......
......
EMBERS GLEAM...
...TRUST IS EMBRACED.
LOYALTY IS UNIVERSAL.
HIDERI ...
IF YOU DON'T GIVE IT A REST, I'M GONNA GIVE YOU A BEATING.

ULTRA SPECIAL *THINGS THAT DON'T MATTER II.*

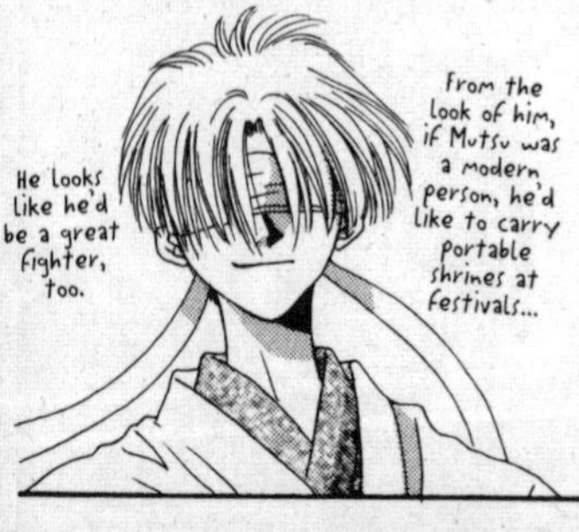
From the look of him, if Mutsu was a modern person, he'd like to carry portable shrines at festivals...
He looks like he'd be a great fighter, too.

Writing stories with spells is a lot of work, huh? There has to be something to fight, so I always wonder what I should do. If I could make it so they didn't have to fight, then... (but that's impossible). No matter how you do it, the spells are hard to understand. I thought maybe I could at least give them simple names, like "If this hits you then your bones might break! Impact Bullet!" But that might mess up the story's image, so I didn't do it. I guess that's obvious...

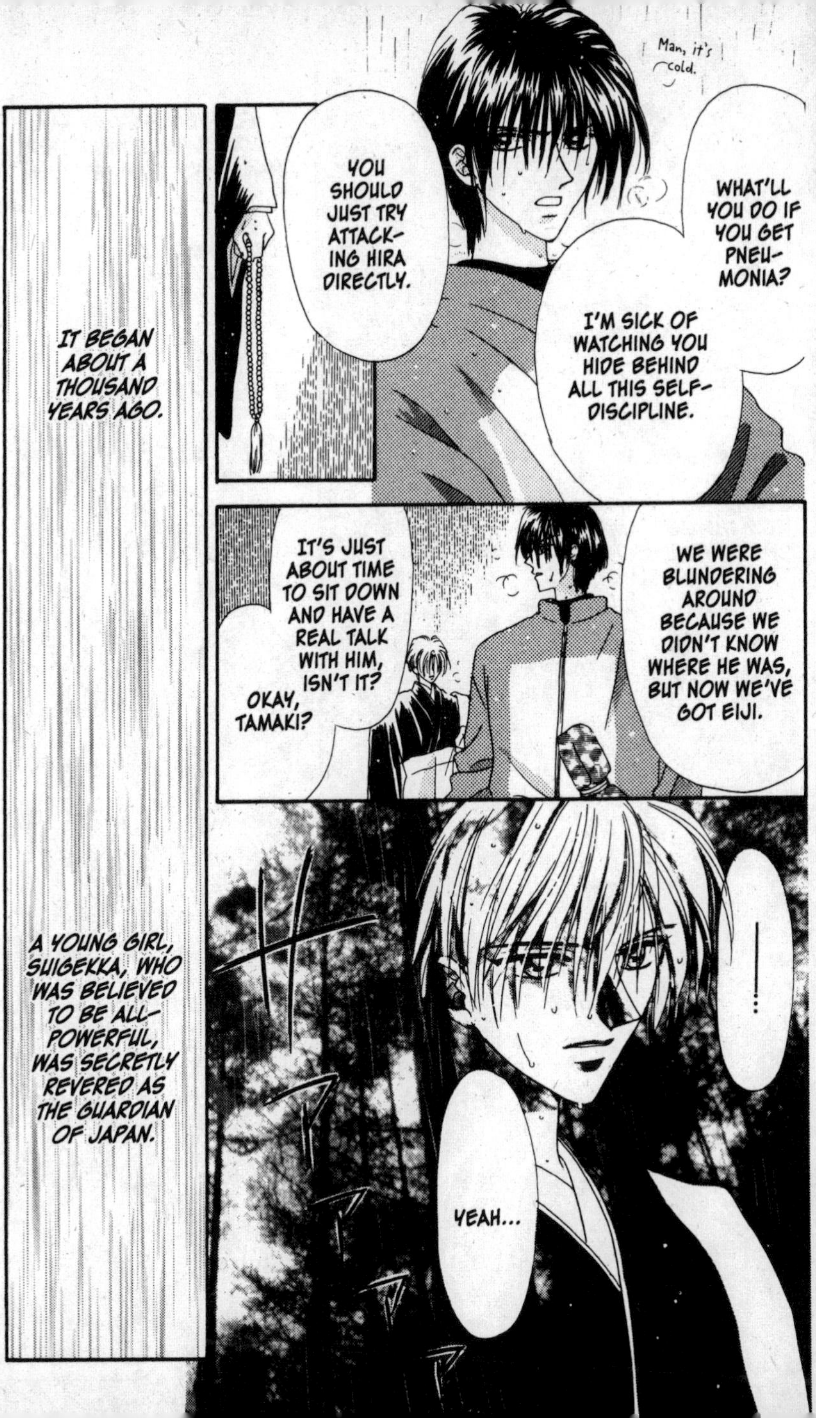
Man, it's cold.
WHAT'LL YOU DO IF YOU GET PNEU-MONIA?
I'M SICK OF WATCHING YOU HIDE BEHIND ALL THIS SELF-DISCIPLINE.
YOU SHOULD JUST TRY ATTACK-ING HIRA DIRECTLY.
WE WERE BLUNDERING AROUND BECAUSE WE DIDN'T KNOW WHERE HE WAS, BUT NOW WE'VE GOT EIJI.
IT'S JUST ABOUT TIME TO SIT DOWN AND HAVE A REAL TALK WITH HIM, ISN'T IT?
OKAY, TAMAKI?
......
YEAH...
IT BEGAN ABOUT A THOUSAND YEARS AGO.
A YOUNG GIRL, SUIGEKKA, WHO WAS BELIEVED TO BE ALL-POWERFUL, WAS SECRETLY REVERED AS THE GUARDIAN OF JAPAN.

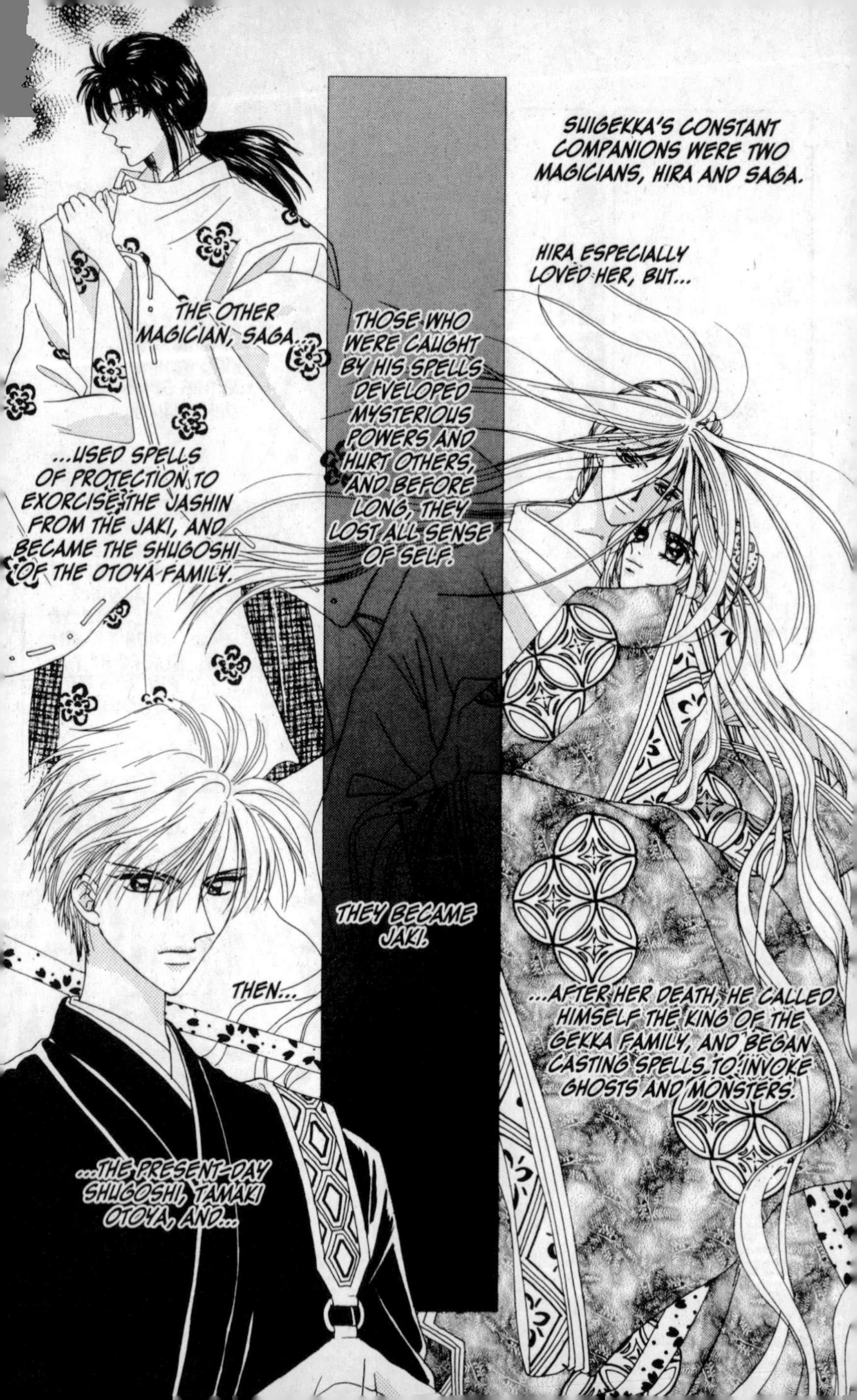
SUIGEKKA'S CONSTANT COMPANIONS WERE TWO MAGICIANS, HIRA AND SAGA.
HIRA ESPECIALLY LOVED HER, BUT...
...AFTER HER DEATH, HE CALLED HIMSELF THE KING OF THE GEKKA FAMILY, AND BEGAN CASTING SPELLS TO INVOKE GHOSTS AND MONSTERS.
THOSE WHO WERE CAUGHT BY HIS SPELLS DEVELOPED MYSTERIOUS POWERS AND HURT OTHERS, AND BEFORE LONG, THEY LOST ALL SENSE OF SELF.
THEY BECAME JAKI.
THE OTHER MAGICIAN, SAGA...
...USED SPELLS OF PROTECTION TO EXORCISE THE JASHIN FROM THE JAKI, AND BECAME THE SHUGOSHI OF THE OTOYA FAMILY.
THEN...
...THE PRESENT-DAY SHUGOSHI, TAMAKI OTOYA, AND...

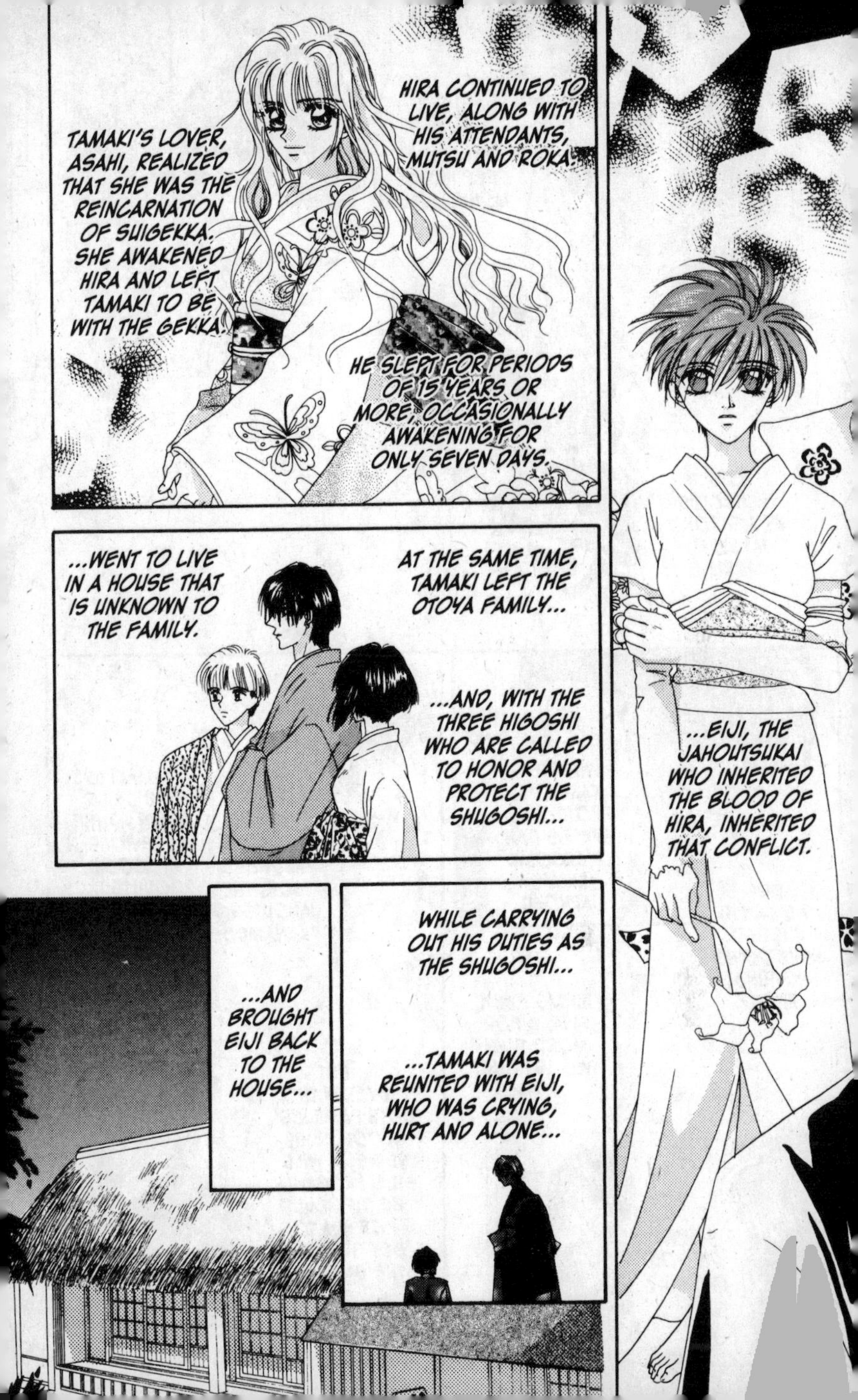
HIRA CONTINUED TO LIVE, ALONG WITH HIS ATTENDANTS, MUTSU AND ROKA.
TAMAKI'S LOVER, ASAHI, REALIZED THAT SHE WAS THE REINCARNATION OF SUIGEKKA. SHE AWAKENED HIRA AND LEFT TAMAKI TO BE WITH THE GEKKA.
HE SLEPT FOR PERIODS OF 15 YEARS OR MORE, OCCASIONALLY AWAKENING FOR ONLY SEVEN DAYS.
AT THE SAME TIME, TAMAKI LEFT THE OTOYA FAMILY...
...AND, WITH THE THREE HIGOSHI WHO ARE CALLED TO HONOR AND PROTECT THE SHUGOSHI...
...WENT TO LIVE IN A HOUSE THAT IS UNKNOWN TO THE FAMILY.
WHILE CARRYING OUT HIS DUTIES AS THE SHUGOSHI...
...TAMAKI WAS REUNITED WITH EIJI, WHO WAS CRYING, HURT AND ALONE...
...AND BROUGHT EIJI BACK TO THE HOUSE...
...EIJI, THE JAHOUTSUKAI WHO INHERITED THE BLOOD OF HIRA, INHERITED THAT CONFLICT.

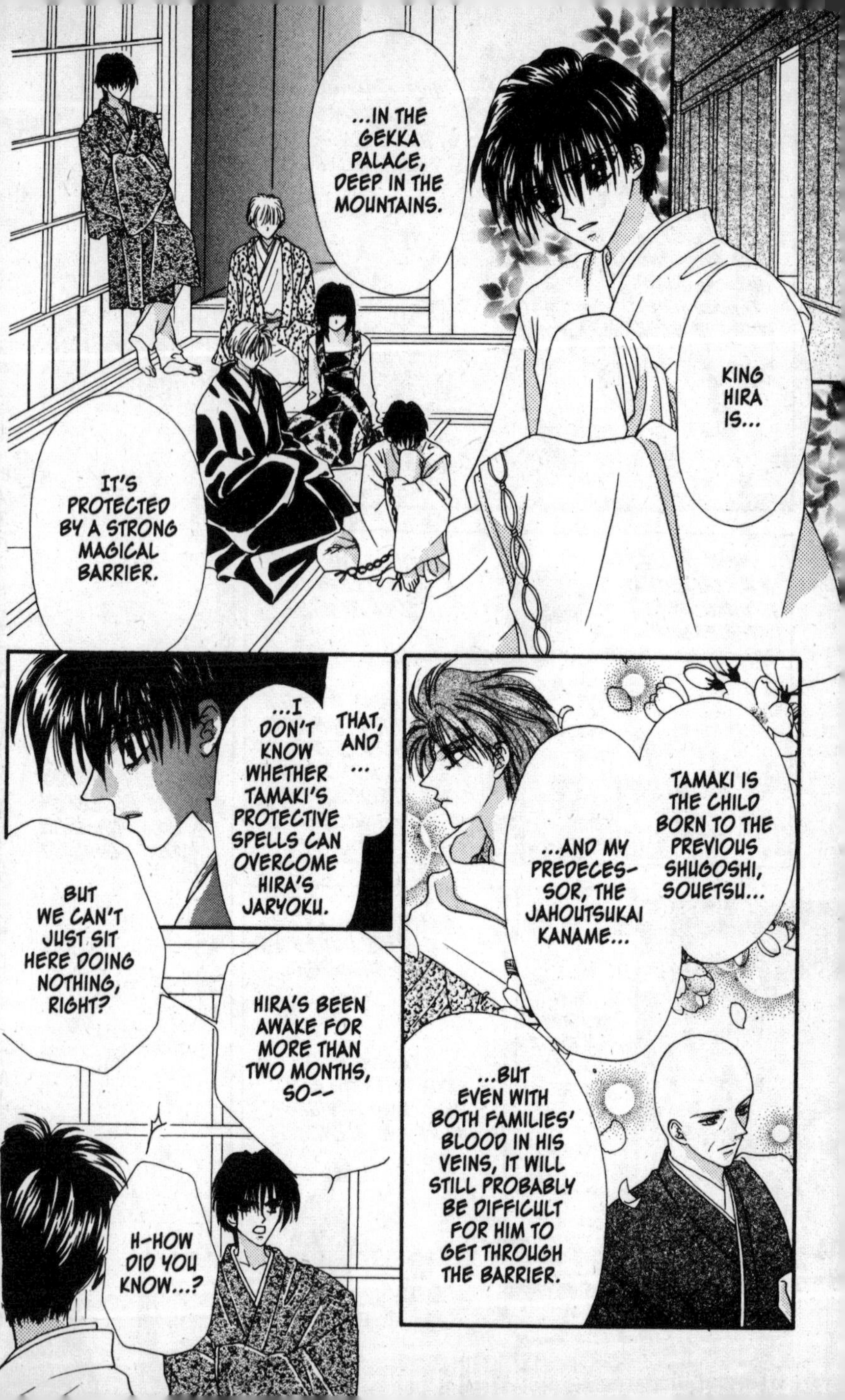
KING HIRA IS...
...IN THE GEKKA PALACE, DEEP IN THE MOUNTAINS.
IT'S PROTECTED BY A STRONG MAGICAL BARRIER.
TAMAKI IS THE CHILD BORN TO THE PREVIOUS SHUGOSHI, SOUETSU...
...AND MY PREDECES-SOR, THE JAHOUTSUKAI KANAME...
...BUT EVEN WITH BOTH FAMILIES' BLOOD IN HIS VEINS, IT WILL STILL PROBABLY BE DIFFICULT FOR HIM TO GET THROUGH THE BARRIER.
THAT, AND ...
...I DON'T KNOW WHETHER TAMAKI'S PROTECTIVE SPELLS CAN OVERCOME HIRA'S JARYOKU.
BUT WE CAN'T JUST SIT HERE DOING NOTHING, RIGHT?
HIRA'S BEEN AWAKE FOR MORE THAN TWO MONTHS, SO--
H-HOW DID YOU KNOW...?

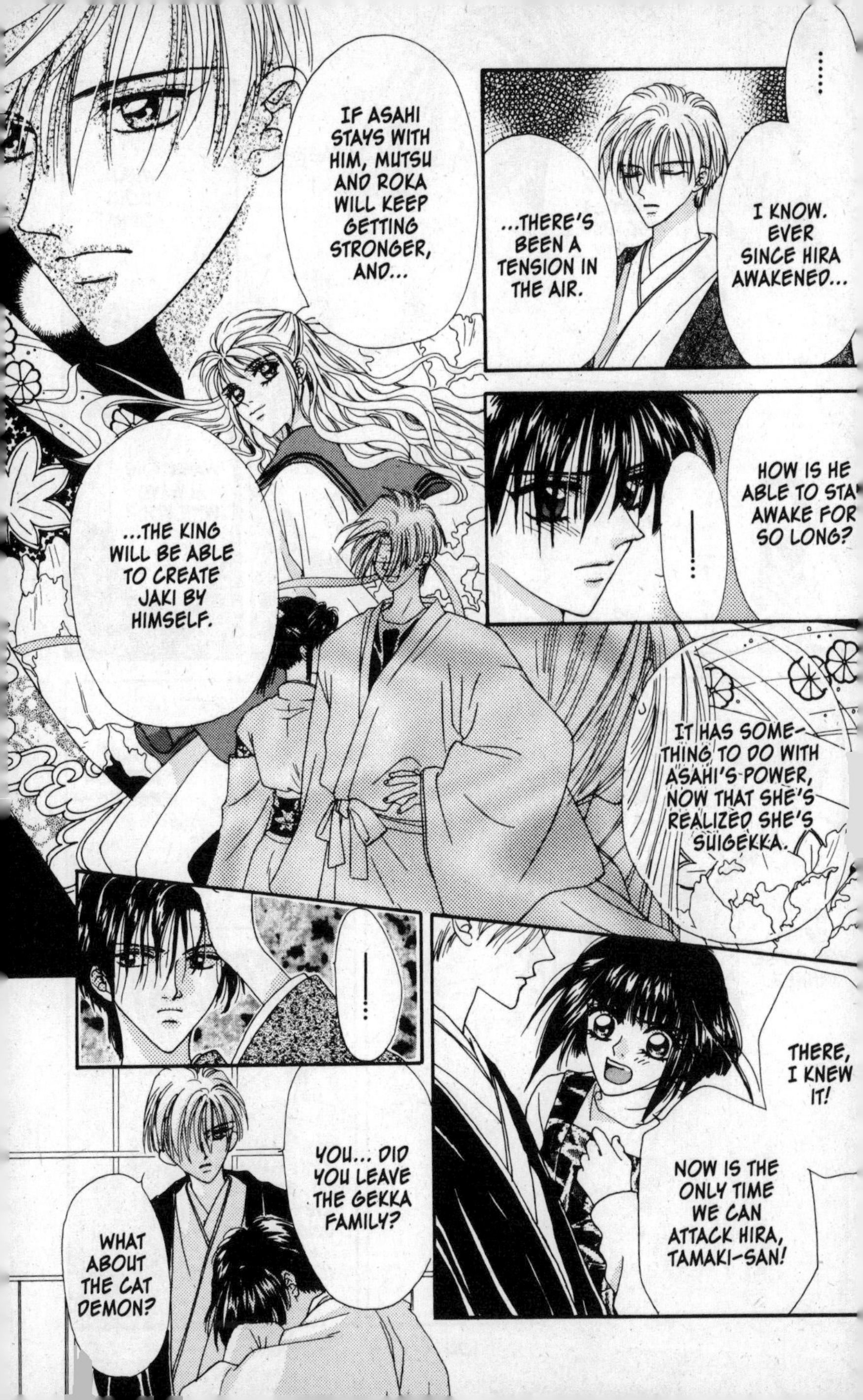
......
I KNOW. EVER SINCE HIRA AWAKENED...
...THERE'S BEEN A TENSION IN THE AIR.
HOW IS HE ABLE TO STA AWAKE FOR SO LONG?
—......
IT HAS SOME-THING TO DO WITH ASAHI'S POWER, NOW THAT SHE'S REALIZED SHE'S SUIGEKKA.
IF ASAHI STAYS WITH HIM, MUTSU AND ROKA WILL KEEP GETTING STRONGER, AND...
...THE KING WILL BE ABLE TO CREATE JAKI BY HIMSELF.
THERE, I KNEW IT!
NOW IS THE ONLY TIME WE CAN ATTACK HIRA, TAMAKI-SAN!
—......
YOU... DID YOU LEAVE THE GEKKA FAMILY?
WHAT ABOUT THE CAT DEMON?

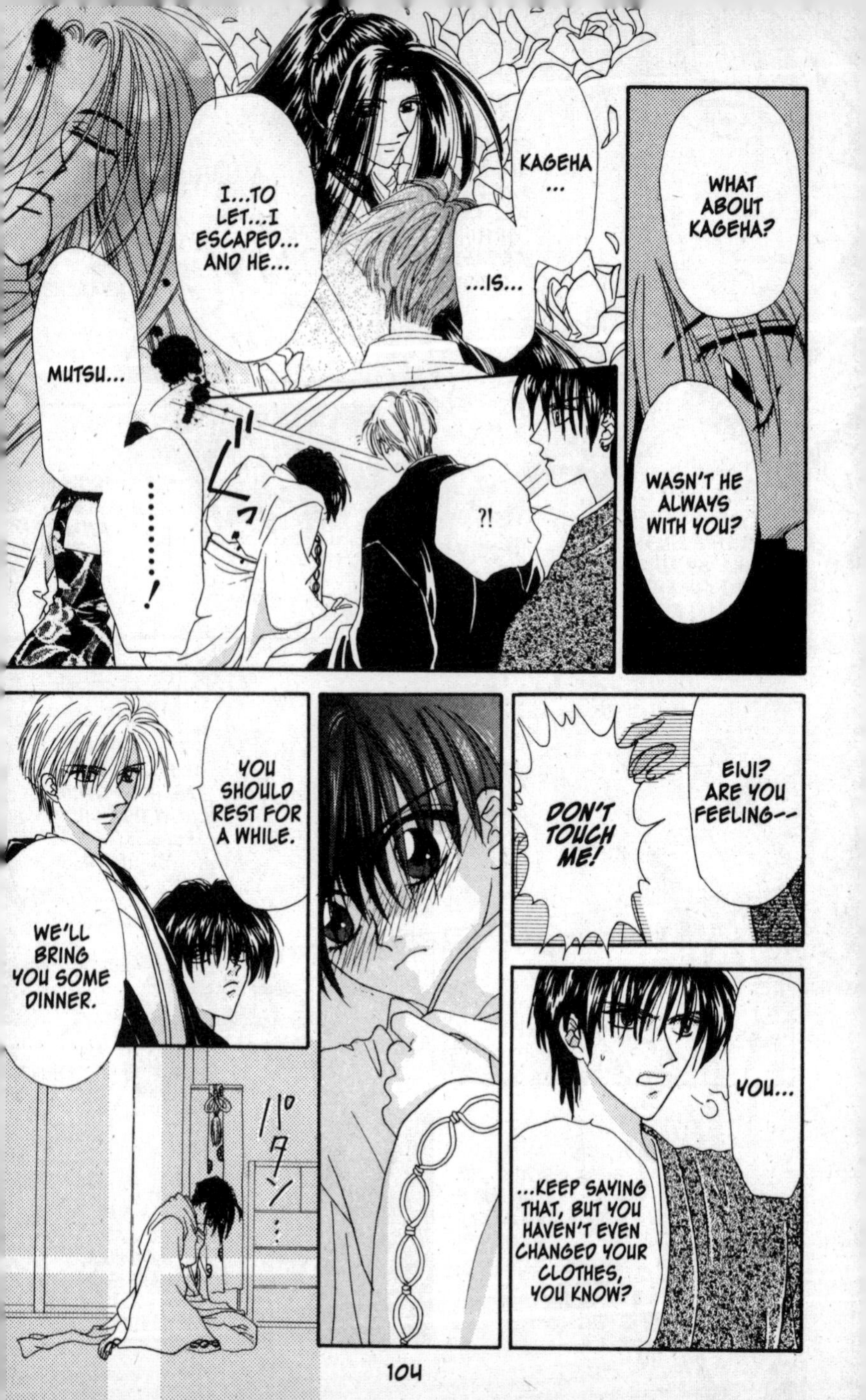
WHAT ABOUT KAGEHA?
WASN'T HE ALWAYS WITH YOU?
KAGEHA ...
...IS...
I...TO LET...I ESCAPED... AND HE...
MUTSU...
?!
......!
EIJI? ARE YOU FEELING--
DON'T TOUCH ME!
YOU...
...KEEP SAYING THAT, BUT YOU HAVEN'T EVEN CHANGED YOUR CLOTHES, YOU KNOW?
YOU SHOULD REST FOR A WHILE.
WE'LL BRING YOU SOME DINNER.
パタン…

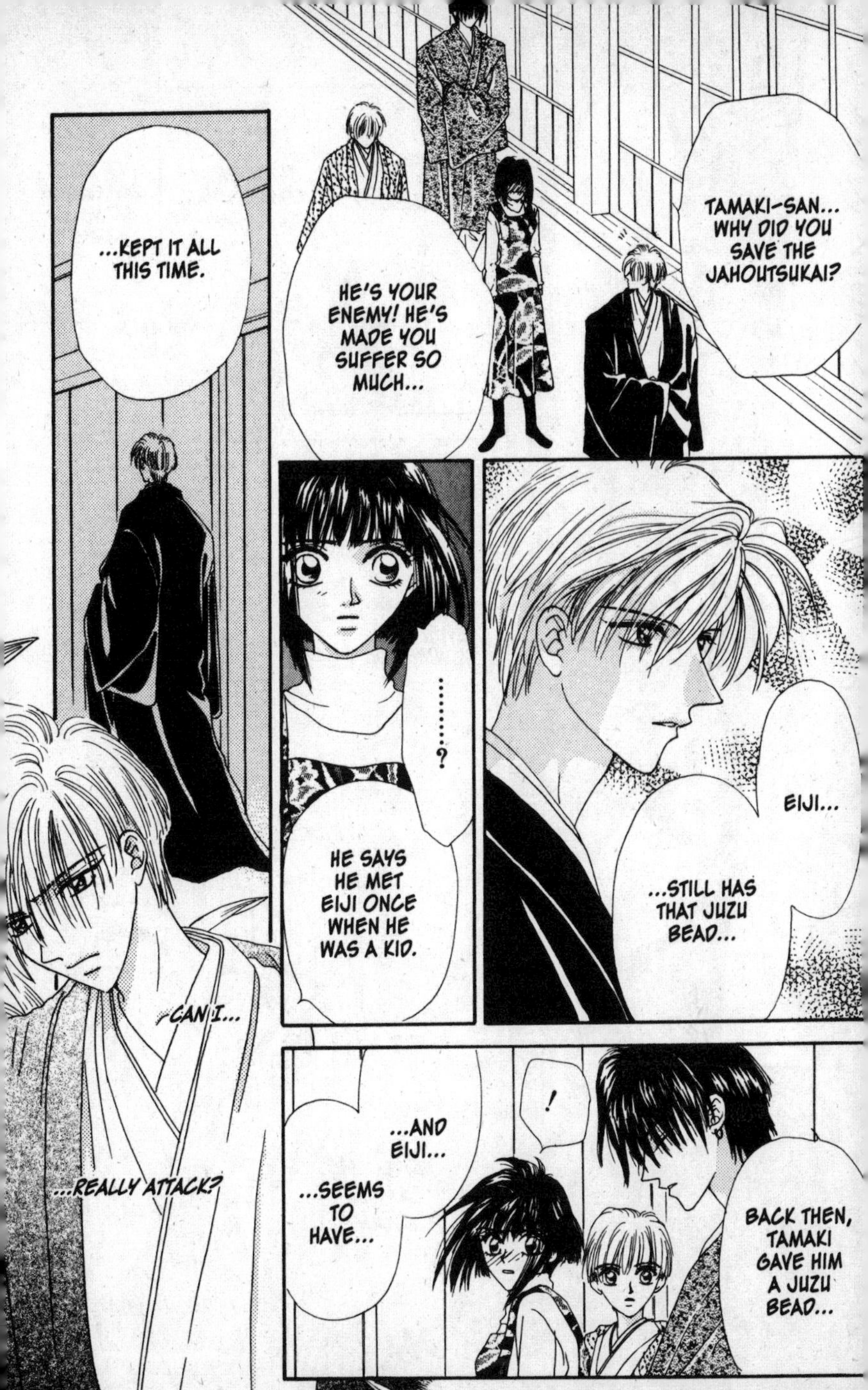
TAMAKI-SAN... WHY DID YOU SAVE THE JAHOUTSUKAI?
HE'S YOUR ENEMY! HE'S MADE YOU SUFFER SO MUCH...
EIJI...
...STILL HAS THAT JUZU BEAD...
......?
HE SAYS HE MET EIJI ONCE WHEN HE WAS A KID.
BACK THEN, TAMAKI GAVE HIM A JUZU BEAD...
!
...AND EIJI...
...SEEMS TO HAVE...
...KEPT IT ALL THIS TIME.
CAN I...
...REALLY ATTACK?

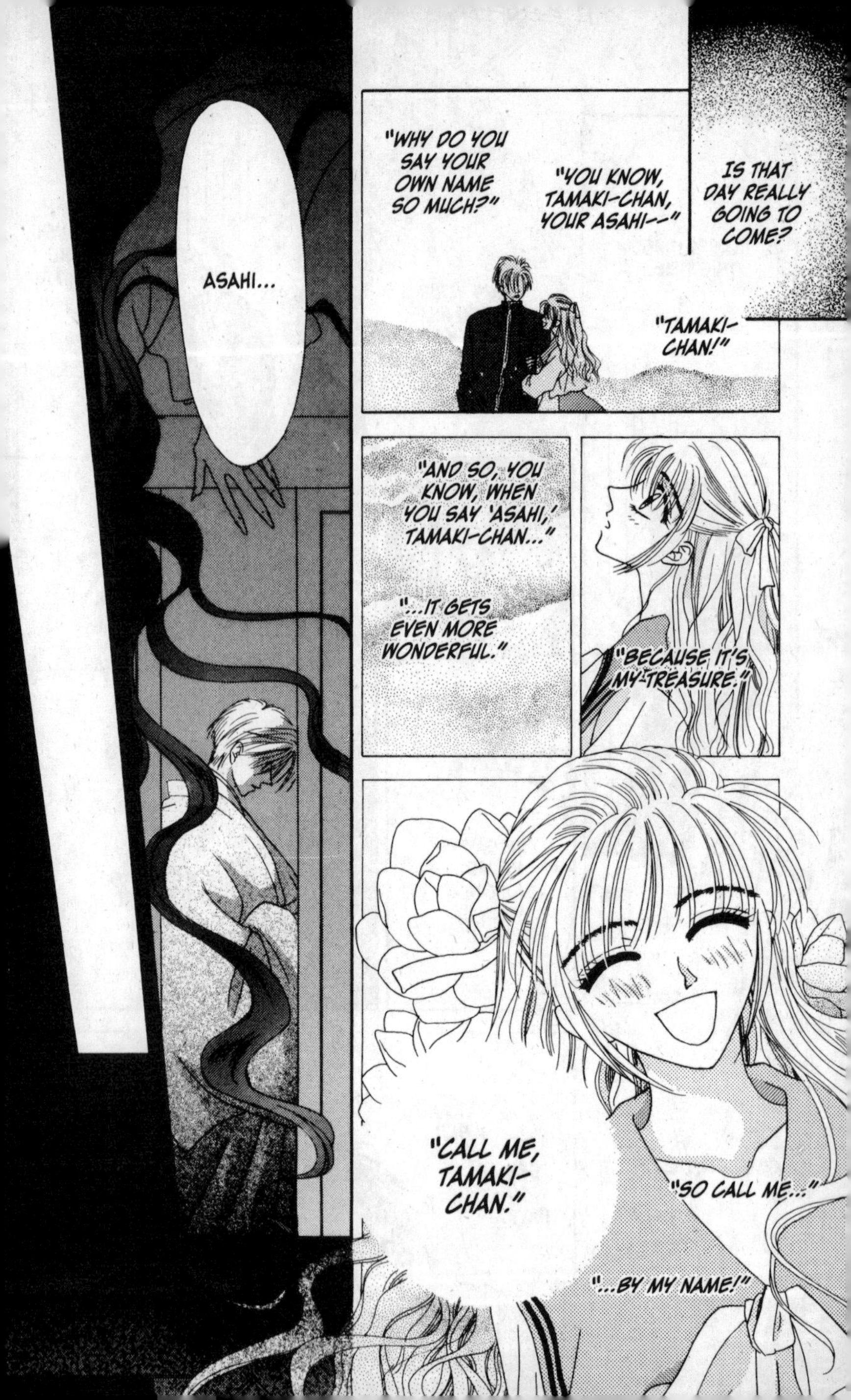
IS THAT DAY REALLY GOING TO COME?
"YOU KNOW, TAMAKI-CHAN, YOUR ASAHI--"
"WHY DO YOU SAY YOUR OWN NAME SO MUCH?"
"TAMAKI-CHAN!"
"BECAUSE IT'S MY TREASURE."
"AND SO, YOU KNOW, WHEN YOU SAY 'ASAHI,' TAMAKI-CHAN..."
"...IT GETS EVEN MORE WONDERFUL."
"SO CALL ME..."
"...BY MY NAME!"
"CALL ME, TAMAKI-CHAN."
ASAHI...

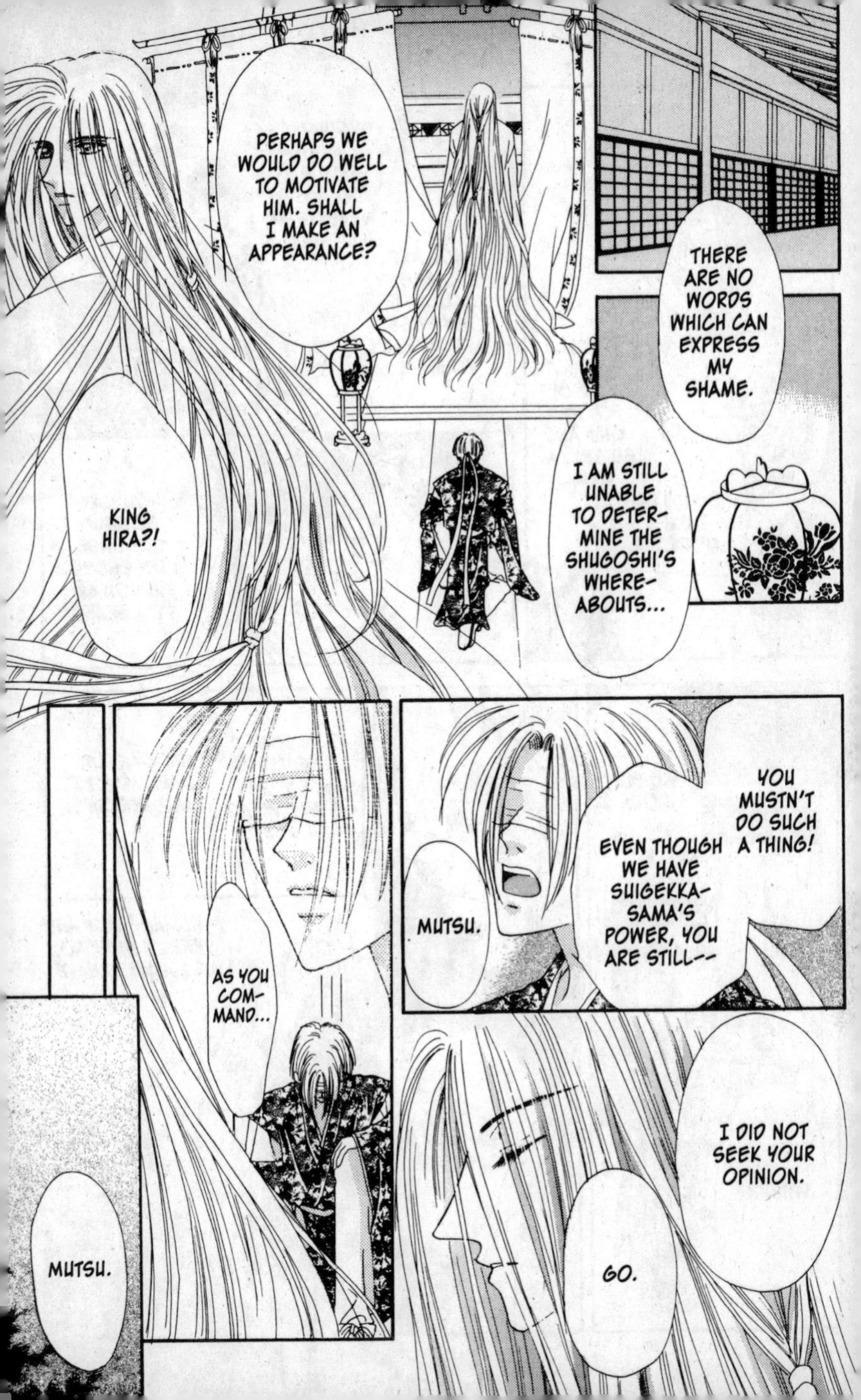
THERE ARE NO WORDS WHICH CAN EXPRESS MY SHAME.
I AM STILL UNABLE TO DETERMINE THE SHUGOSHI'S WHEREABOUTS...
PERHAPS WE WOULD DO WELL TO MOTIVATE HIM. SHALL I MAKE AN APPEARANCE?
KING HIRA?!
YOU MUSTN'T DO SUCH A THING!
EVEN THOUGH WE HAVE SUIGEKKA-SAMA'S POWER, YOU ARE STILL--
MUTSU.
I DID NOT SEEK YOUR OPINION.
GO.
AS YOU COMMAND...
MUTSU.

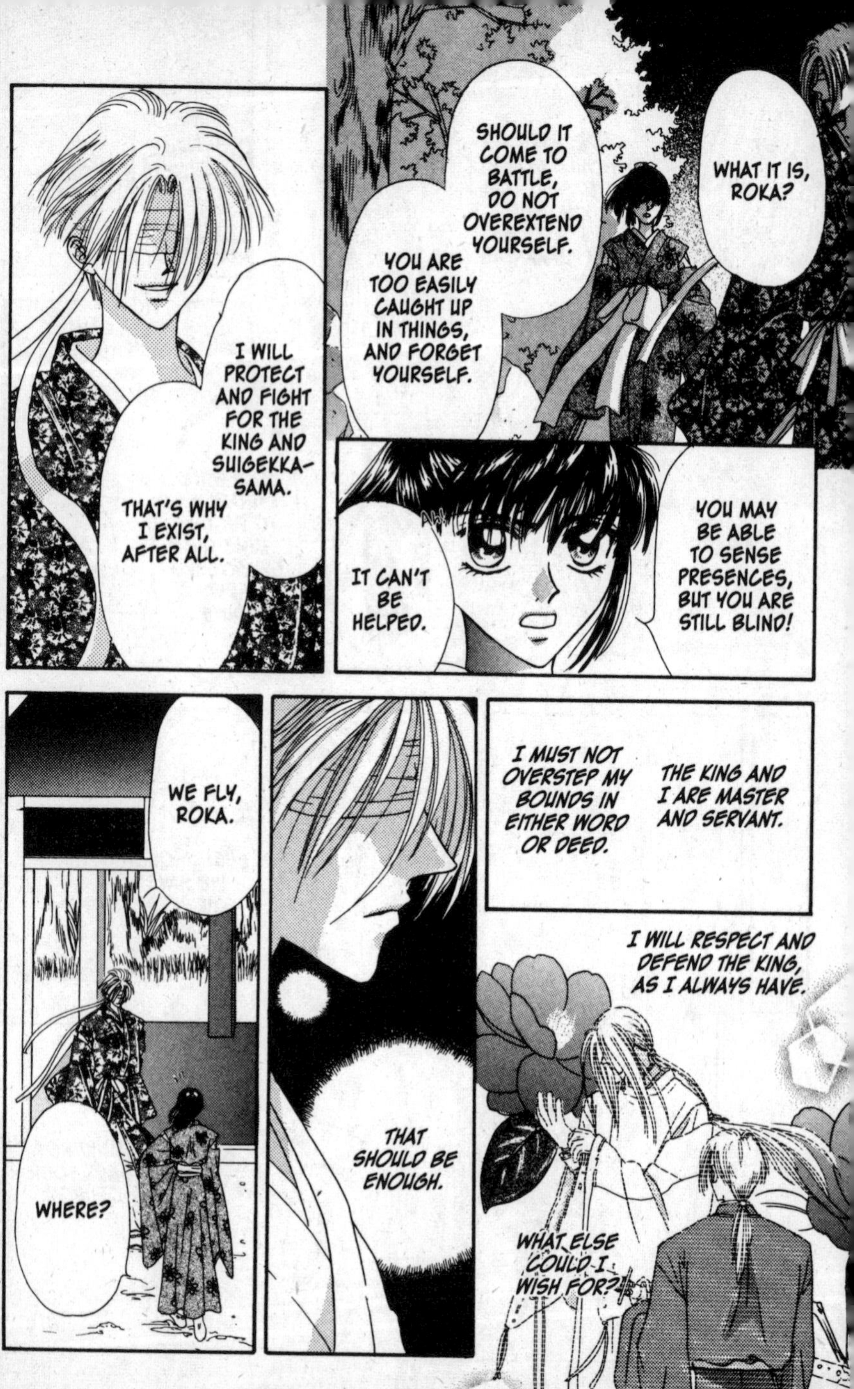
WHAT IT IS, ROKA?
SHOULD IT COME TO BATTLE, DO NOT OVEREXTEND YOURSELF.
YOU ARE TOO EASILY CAUGHT UP IN THINGS, AND FORGET YOURSELF.
YOU MAY BE ABLE TO SENSE PRESENCES, BUT YOU ARE STILL BLIND!
IT CAN'T BE HELPED.
I WILL PROTECT AND FIGHT FOR THE KING AND SUIGEKKA-SAMA.
THAT'S WHY I EXIST, AFTER ALL.
THE KING AND I ARE MASTER AND SERVANT.
I MUST NOT OVERSTEP MY BOUNDS IN EITHER WORD OR DEED.
I WILL RESPECT AND DEFEND THE KING, AS I ALWAYS HAVE.
WHAT ELSE COULD I WISH FOR?
THAT SHOULD BE ENOUGH.
WE FLY, ROKA.
WHERE?

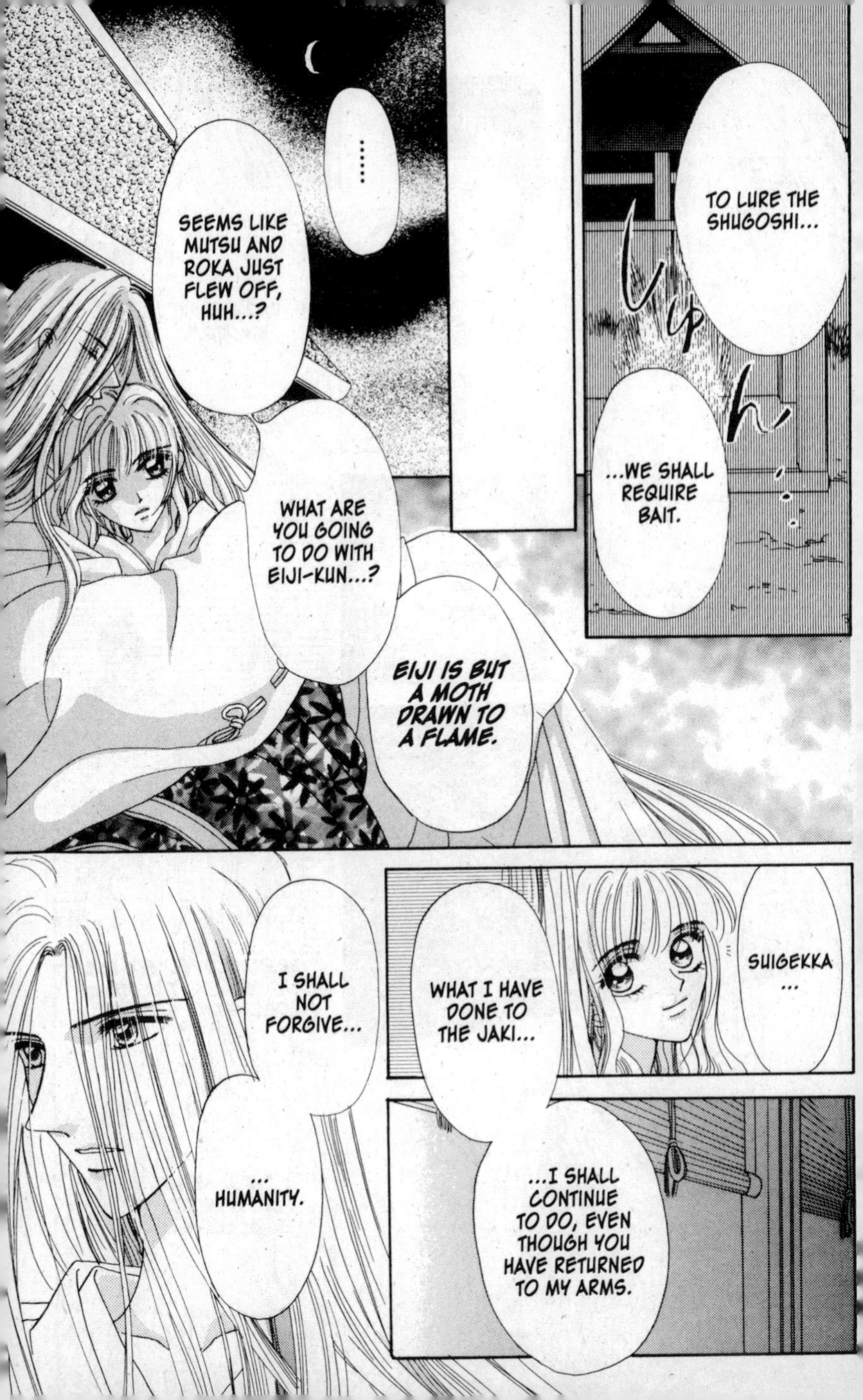

TO LURE THE SHUGOSHI...
しゅん
...WE SHALL REQUIRE BAIT.
......
SEEMS LIKE MUTSU AND ROKA JUST FLEW OFF, HUH...?
WHAT ARE YOU GOING TO DO WITH EIJI-KUN...?
EIJI IS BUT A MOTH DRAWN TO A FLAME.
SUIGEKKA...
WHAT I HAVE DONE TO THE JAKI...
...I SHALL CONTINUE TO DO, EVEN THOUGH YOU HAVE RETURNED TO MY ARMS.
I SHALL NOT FORGIVE...
...HUMANITY.

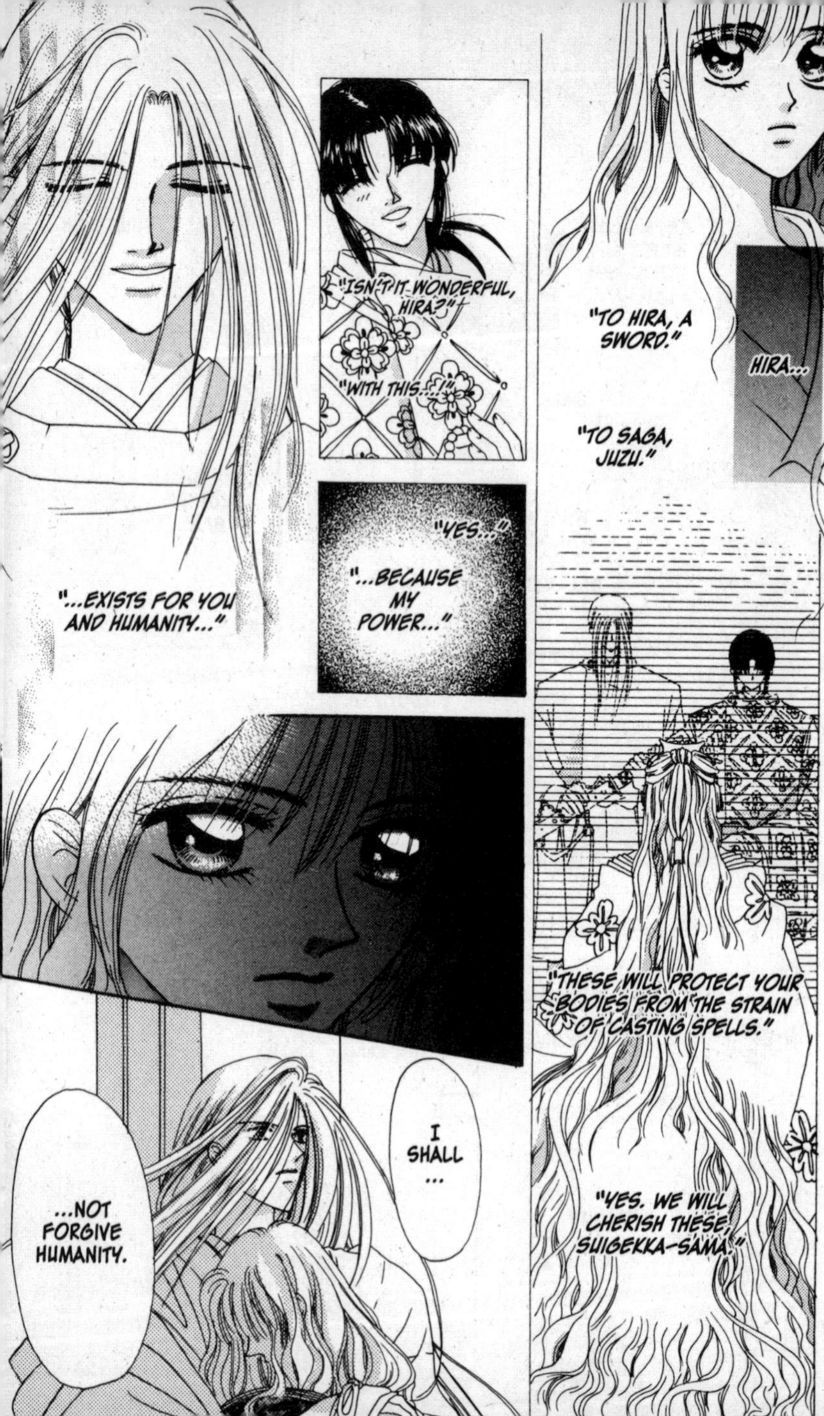
"TO HIRA, A SWORD."
"TO SAGA, JUZU."
HIRA...
"THESE WILL PROTECT YOUR BODIES FROM THE STRAIN OF CASTING SPELLS."
"YES. WE WILL CHERISH THESE, SUIGEKKA-SAMA."
"ISN'T IT WONDERFUL, HIRA?"
"WITH THIS...!!"
"YES..."
"...BECAUSE MY POWER..."
"...EXISTS FOR YOU AND HUMANITY..."
I SHALL ...
...NOT FORGIVE HUMANITY.

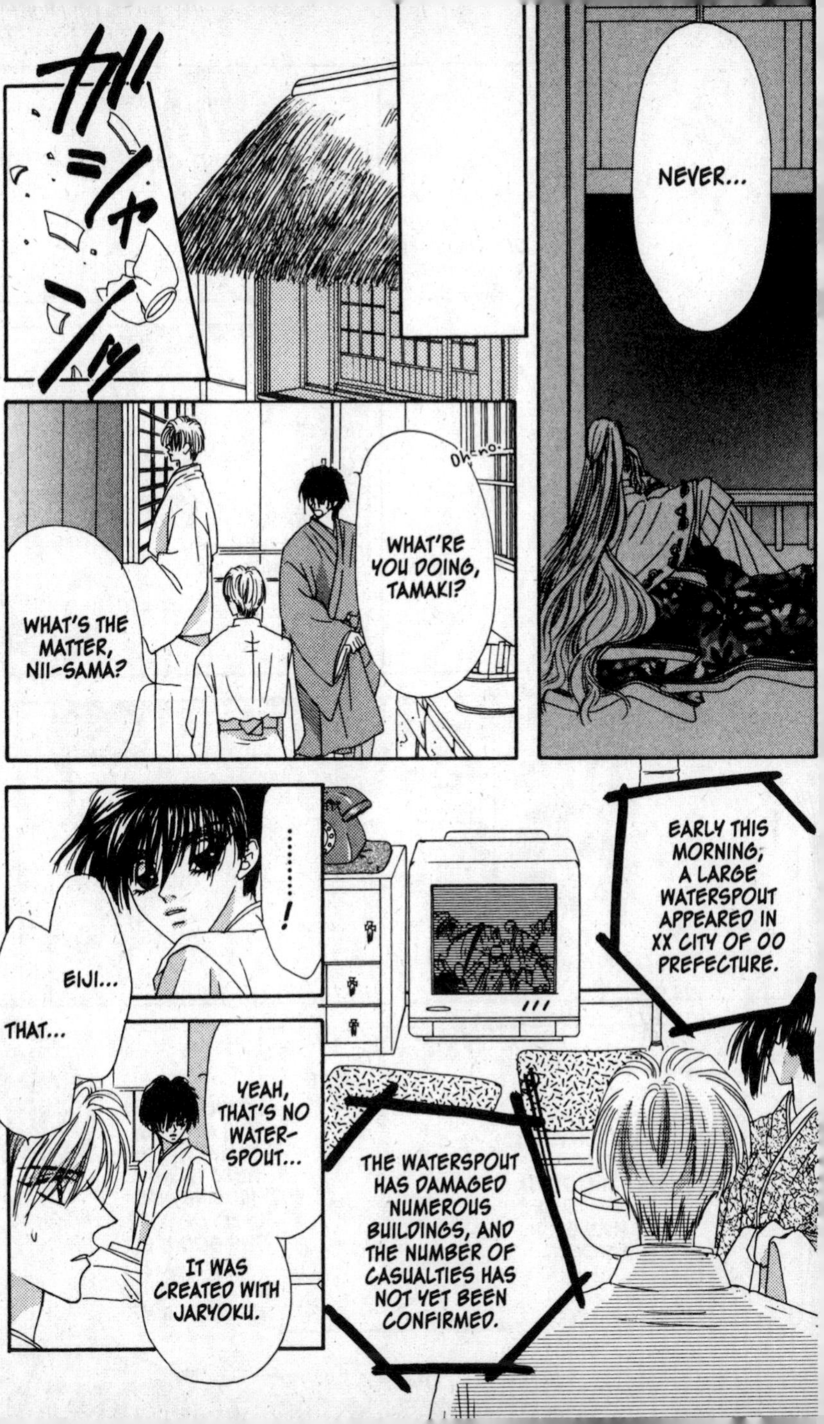

NEVER...
ガシャーンッ
Oh-no.
WHAT'RE YOU DOING, TAMAKI?
WHAT'S THE MATTER, NII-SAMA?
EARLY THIS MORNING, A LARGE WATERSPOUT APPEARED IN XX CITY OF OO PREFECTURE.
THE WATERSPOUT HAS DAMAGED NUMEROUS BUILDINGS, AND THE NUMBER OF CASUALTIES HAS NOT YET BEEN CONFIRMED.
......!
EIJI...
THAT...
YEAH, THAT'S NO WATER-SPOUT...
IT WAS CREATED WITH JARYOKU.

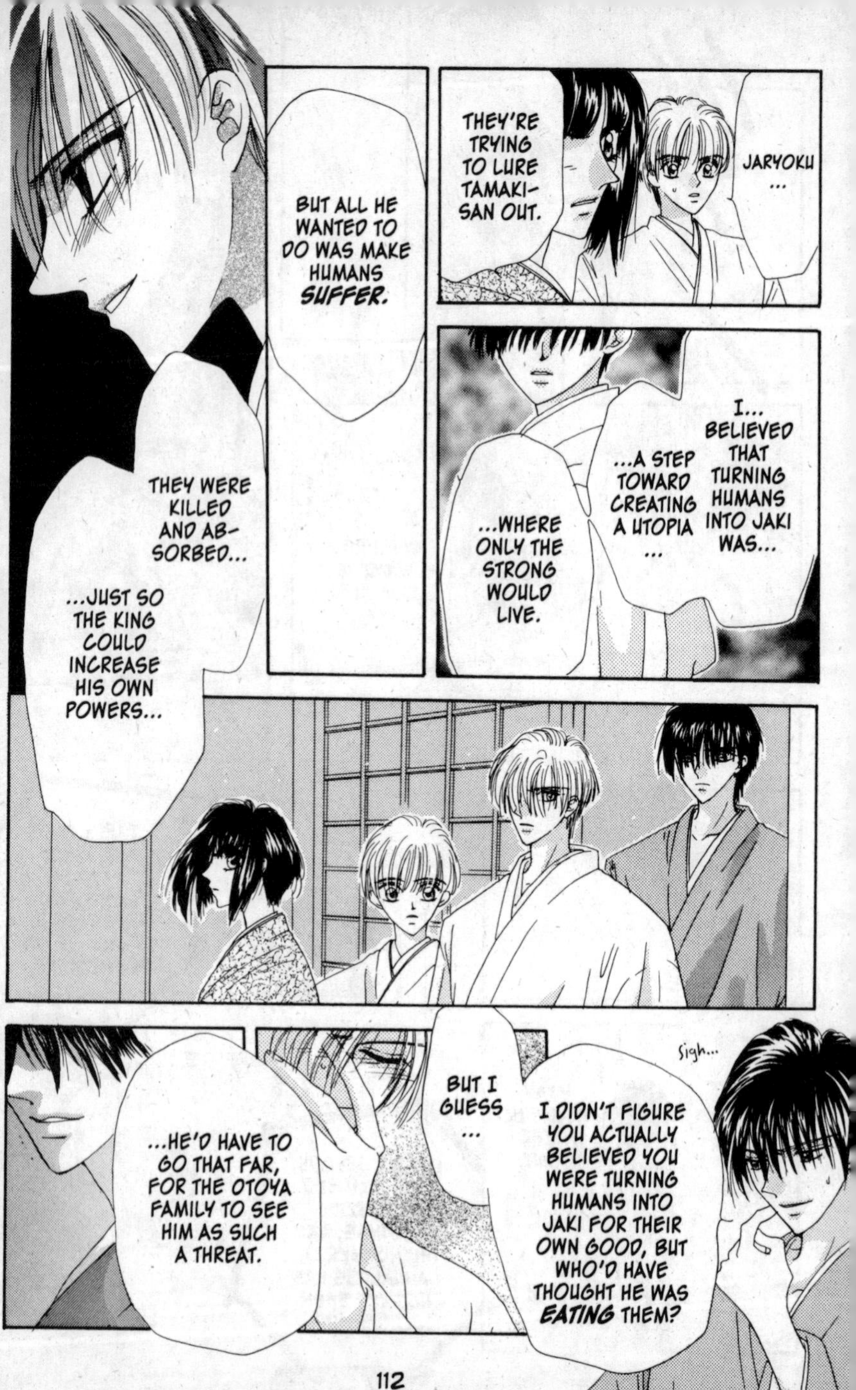
JARYOKU ...
THEY'RE TRYING TO LURE TAMAKI-SAN OUT.
I... BELIEVED THAT TURNING HUMANS INTO JAKI WAS...
...A STEP TOWARD CREATING A UTOPIA ...
...WHERE ONLY THE STRONG WOULD LIVE.
BUT ALL HE WANTED TO DO WAS MAKE HUMANS ***SUFFER.***
THEY WERE KILLED AND AB-SORBED...
...JUST SO THE KING COULD INCREASE HIS OWN POWERS...
Sigh...
I DIDN'T FIGURE YOU ACTUALLY BELIEVED YOU WERE TURNING HUMANS INTO JAKI FOR THEIR OWN GOOD, BUT WHO'D HAVE THOUGHT HE WAS ***EATING*** THEM?
BUT I GUESS ...
...HE'D HAVE TO GO THAT FAR, FOR THE OTOYA FAMILY TO SEE HIM AS SUCH A THREAT.

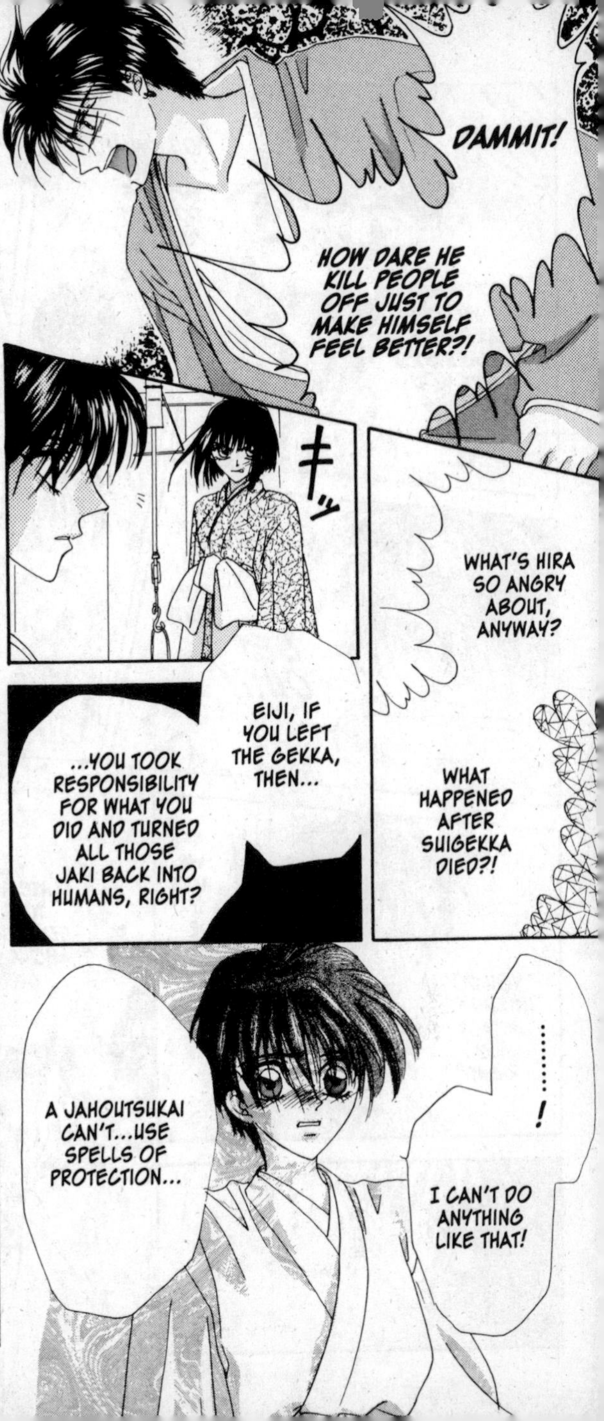
DAMMIT!
HOW DARE HE KILL PEOPLE OFF JUST TO MAKE HIMSELF FEEL BETTER?!
WHAT'S HIRA SO ANGRY ABOUT, ANYWAY?
WHAT HAPPENED AFTER SUIGEKKA DIED?!
キッ
EIJI, IF YOU LEFT THE GEKKA, THEN...
...YOU TOOK RESPONSIBILITY FOR WHAT YOU DID AND TURNED ALL THOSE JAKI BACK INTO HUMANS, RIGHT?
......!
I CAN'T DO ANYTHING LIKE THAT!
A JAHOUTSUKAI CAN'T...USE SPELLS OF PROTECTION...

Scroll Four

I listen to music for more than half of the day, so my CD players wear out pretty fast. I decided to buy a new one to celebrate this comic coming out. (Finally!) But it's a Mini Compo. (laughs) For its sake I have to throw out all of my audio components that don't work, and clean up my room...so I figure I'll wait until I have a break from work to buy one. In the meantime, I went out and bought headphones.

Headphones are nice, aren't they? The sound's different. Totally different! I didn't know it was putting out such great audio. It's like, I feel sorry now. If I buy a new Mini Compo then the sound will be really happy, right?

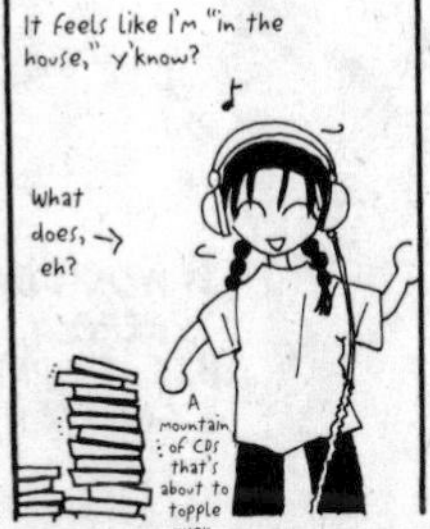
It feels like I'm "in the house," y'know?
What does, →
eh?
A mountain of CDs that's about to topple over.

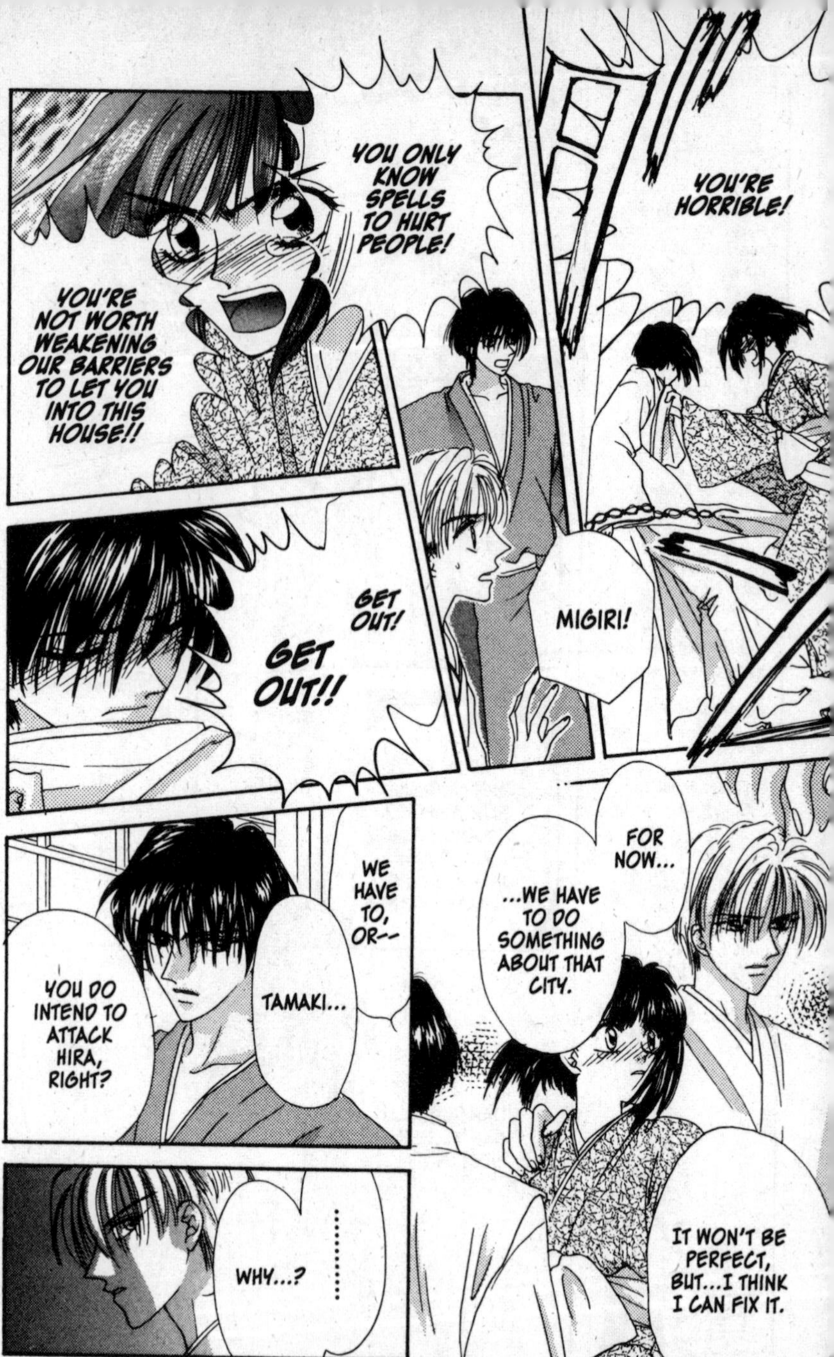
YOU'RE HORRIBLE!
MIGIRI!
YOU ONLY KNOW SPELLS TO HURT PEOPLE!
YOU'RE NOT WORTH WEAKENING OUR BARRIERS TO LET YOU INTO THIS HOUSE!!
GET OUT!
GET OUT!!
FOR NOW...
...WE HAVE TO DO SOMETHING ABOUT THAT CITY.
IT WON'T BE PERFECT, BUT...I THINK I CAN FIX IT.
WE HAVE TO, OR--
TAMAKI...
YOU DO INTEND TO ATTACK HIRA, RIGHT?
......
WHY...?

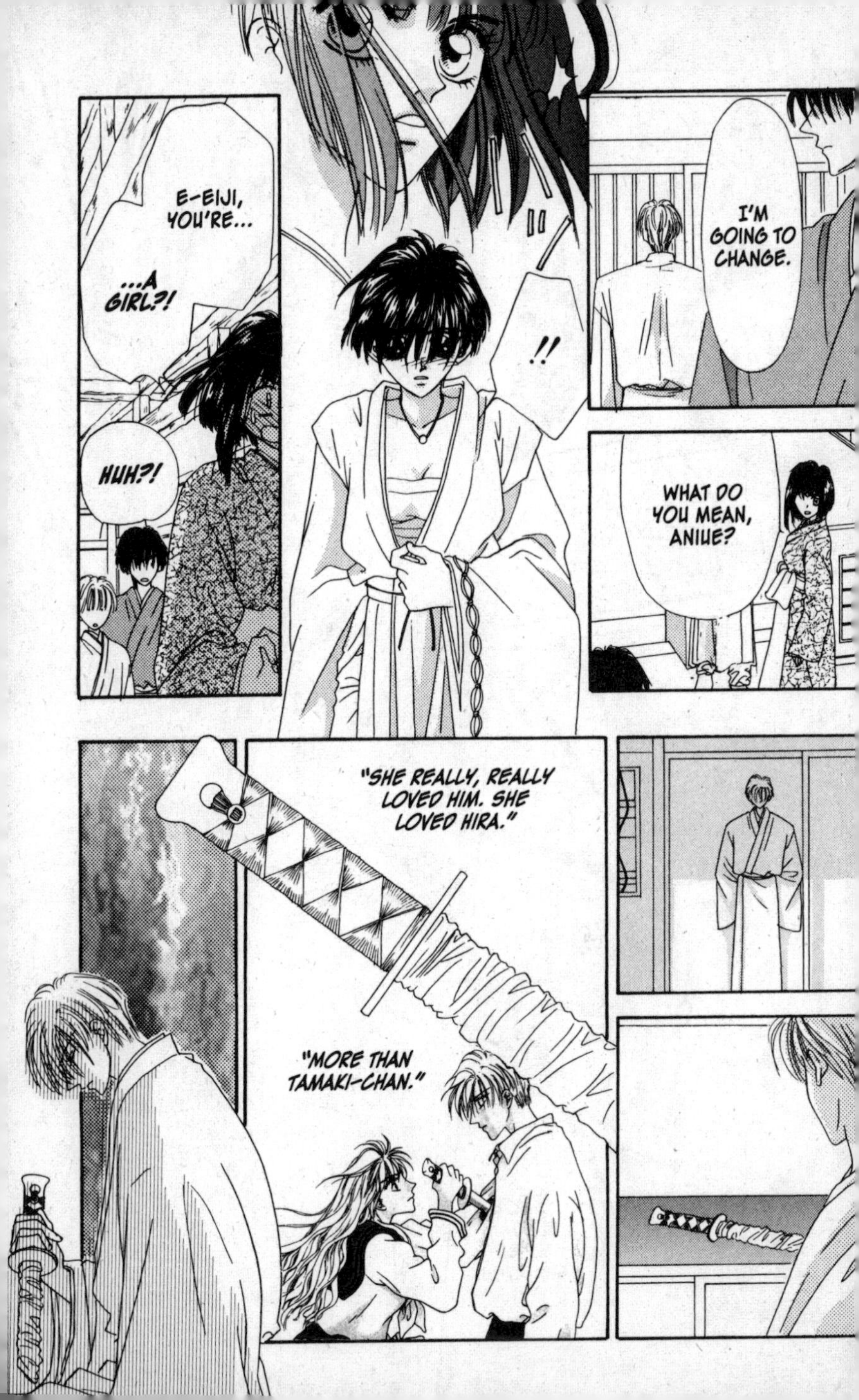
I'M GOING TO CHANGE.
WHAT DO YOU MEAN, ANIUE?
!!
E-EIJI, YOU'RE...
...A GIRL?!
HUH?!
"SHE REALLY, REALLY LOVED HIM. SHE LOVED HIRA."
"MORE THAN TAMAKI-CHAN."

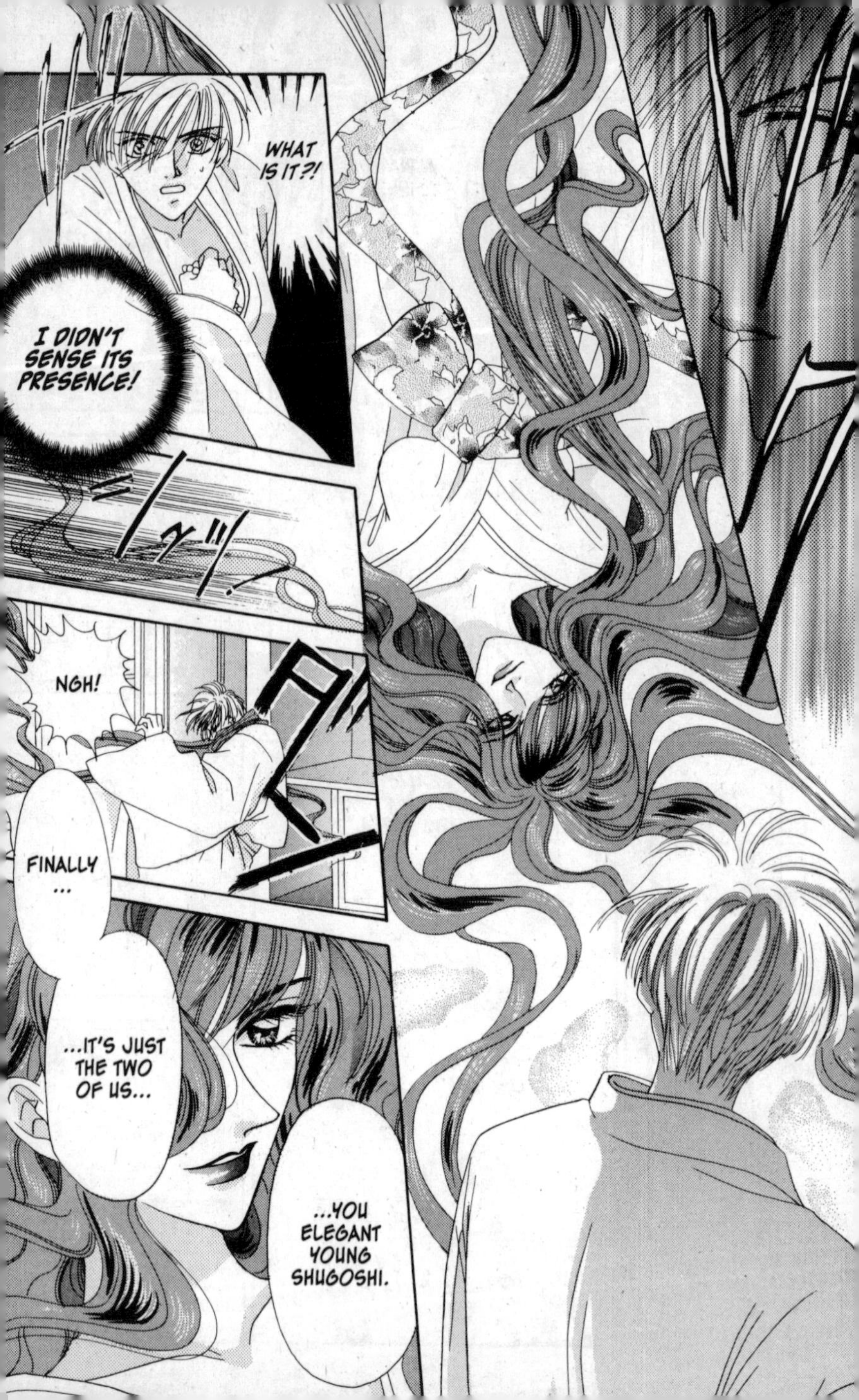
WHAT IS IT?!
I DIDN'T SENSE ITS PRESENCE!
NGH!
FINALLY ...
...IT'S JUST THE TWO OF US...
...YOU ELEGANT YOUNG SHUGOSHI.

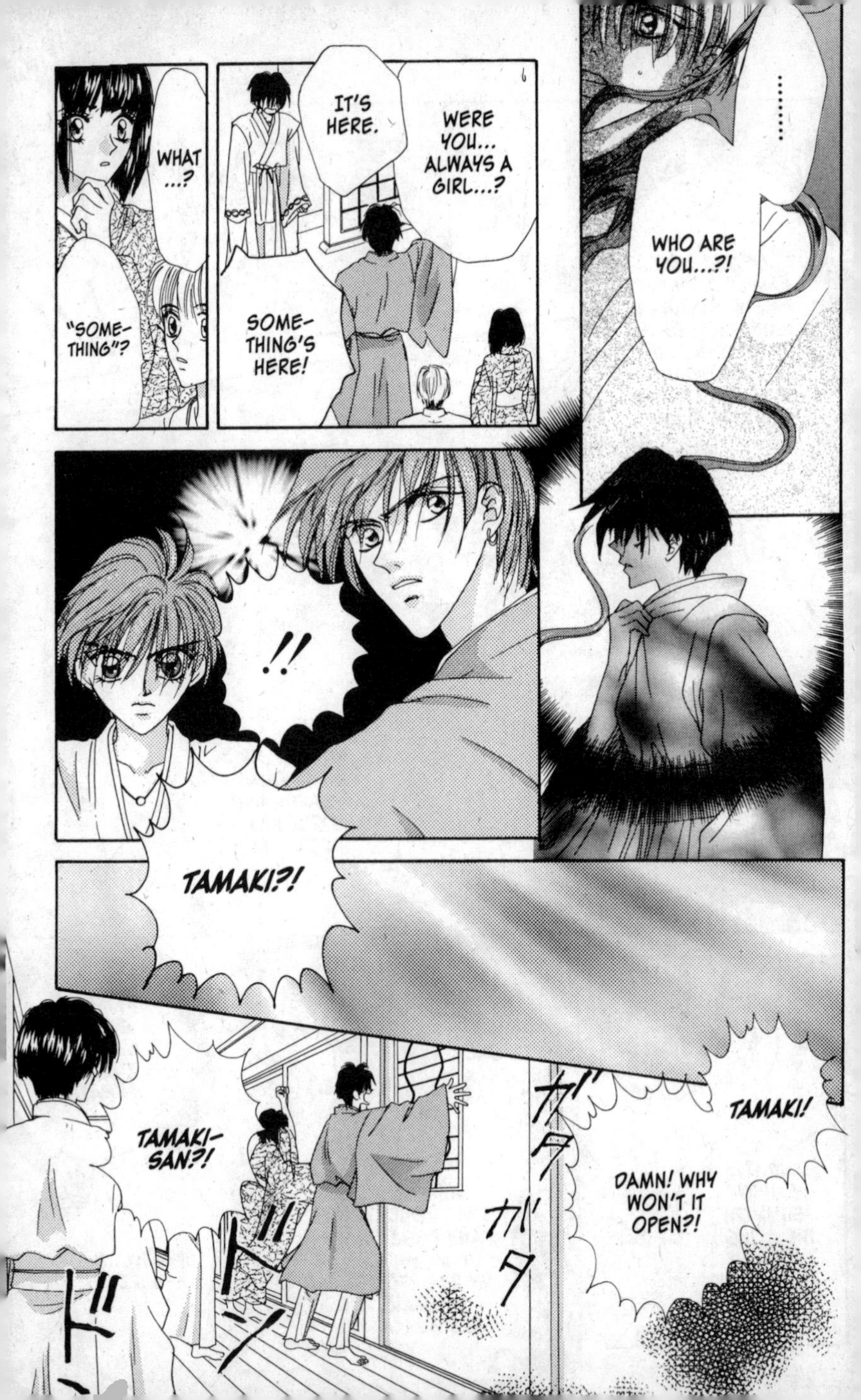
......
WHO ARE YOU...?!
IT'S HERE.
WERE YOU... ALWAYS A GIRL...?
SOMETHING'S HERE!
WHAT ...?
"SOMETHING"?
!!
TAMAKI?!
TAMAKI!
DAMN! WHY WON'T IT OPEN?!
ガタ ガタ
TAMAKI-SAN?!

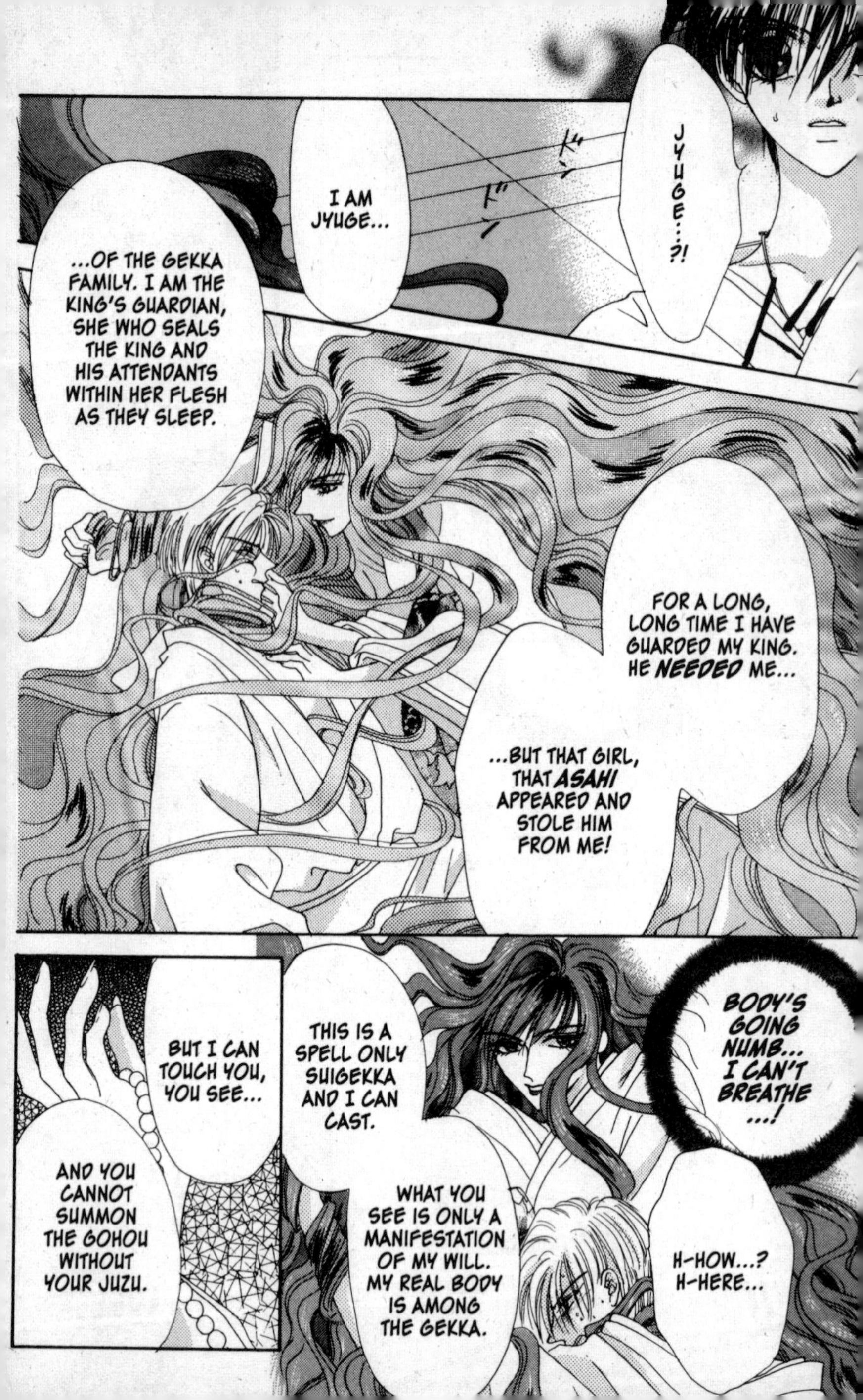
JYUGE...?!
ドン
ドン
I AM JYUGE...
...OF THE GEKKA FAMILY. I AM THE KING'S GUARDIAN, SHE WHO SEALS THE KING AND HIS ATTENDANTS WITHIN HER FLESH AS THEY SLEEP.
FOR A LONG, LONG TIME I HAVE GUARDED MY KING. HE NEEDED ME...
...BUT THAT GIRL, THAT ASAHI APPEARED AND STOLE HIM FROM ME!
BODY'S GOING NUMB... I CAN'T BREATHE ...!
H-HOW...? H-HERE...
THIS IS A SPELL ONLY SUIGEKKA AND I CAN CAST.
WHAT YOU SEE IS ONLY A MANIFESTATION OF MY WILL. MY REAL BODY IS AMONG THE GEKKA.
BUT I CAN TOUCH YOU, YOU SEE...
AND YOU CANNOT SUMMON THE GOHOU WITHOUT YOUR JUZU.

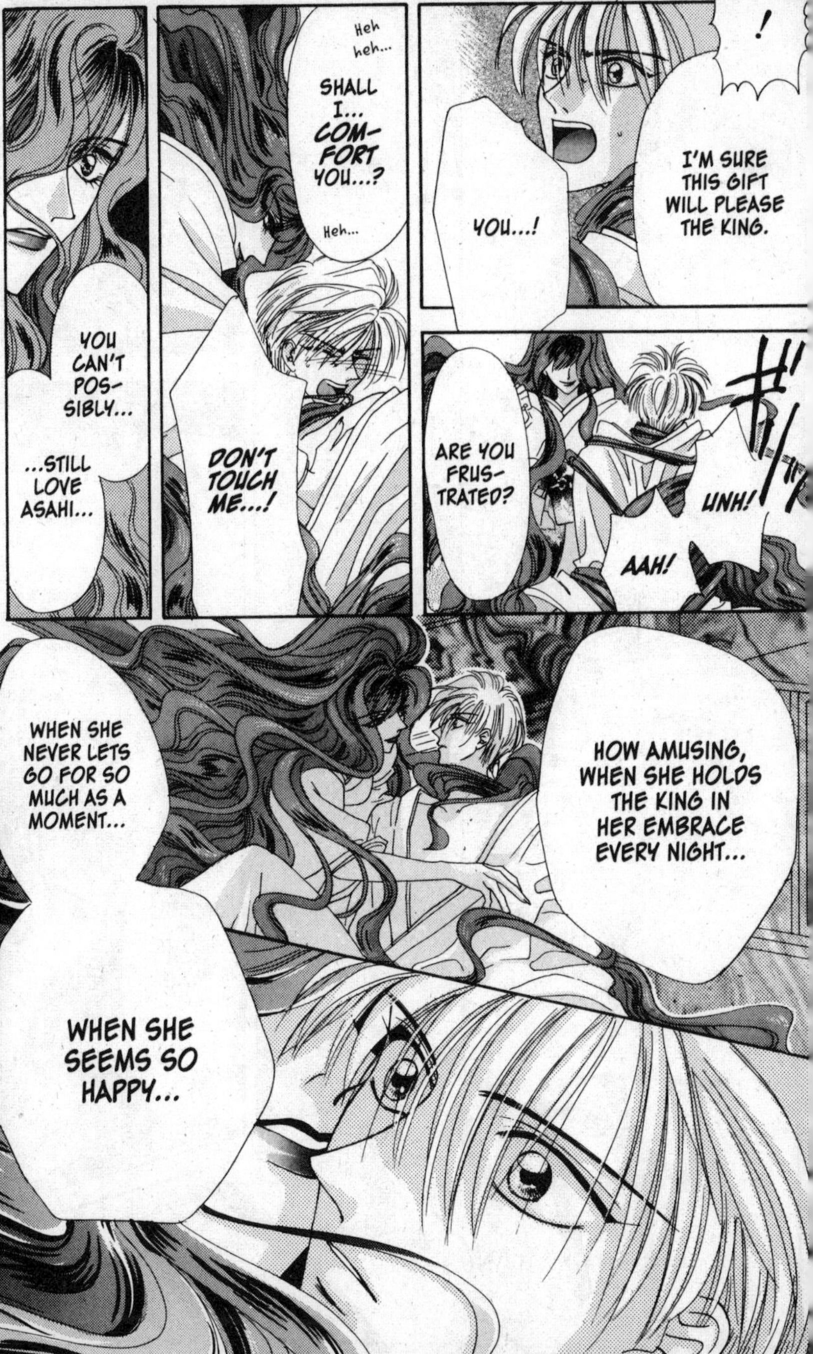
!
I'M SURE THIS GIFT WILL PLEASE THE KING.
YOU...!
ARE YOU FRUS-TRATED?
UNH!
AAH!
Heh heh...
SHALL I... COM-FORT YOU...?
Heh...
DON'T TOUCH ME...!
YOU CAN'T POS-SIBLY...
...STILL LOVE ASAHI...
HOW AMUSING, WHEN SHE HOLDS THE KING IN HER EMBRACE EVERY NIGHT...
WHEN SHE NEVER LETS GO FOR SO MUCH AS A MOMENT...
WHEN SHE SEEMS SO HAPPY...

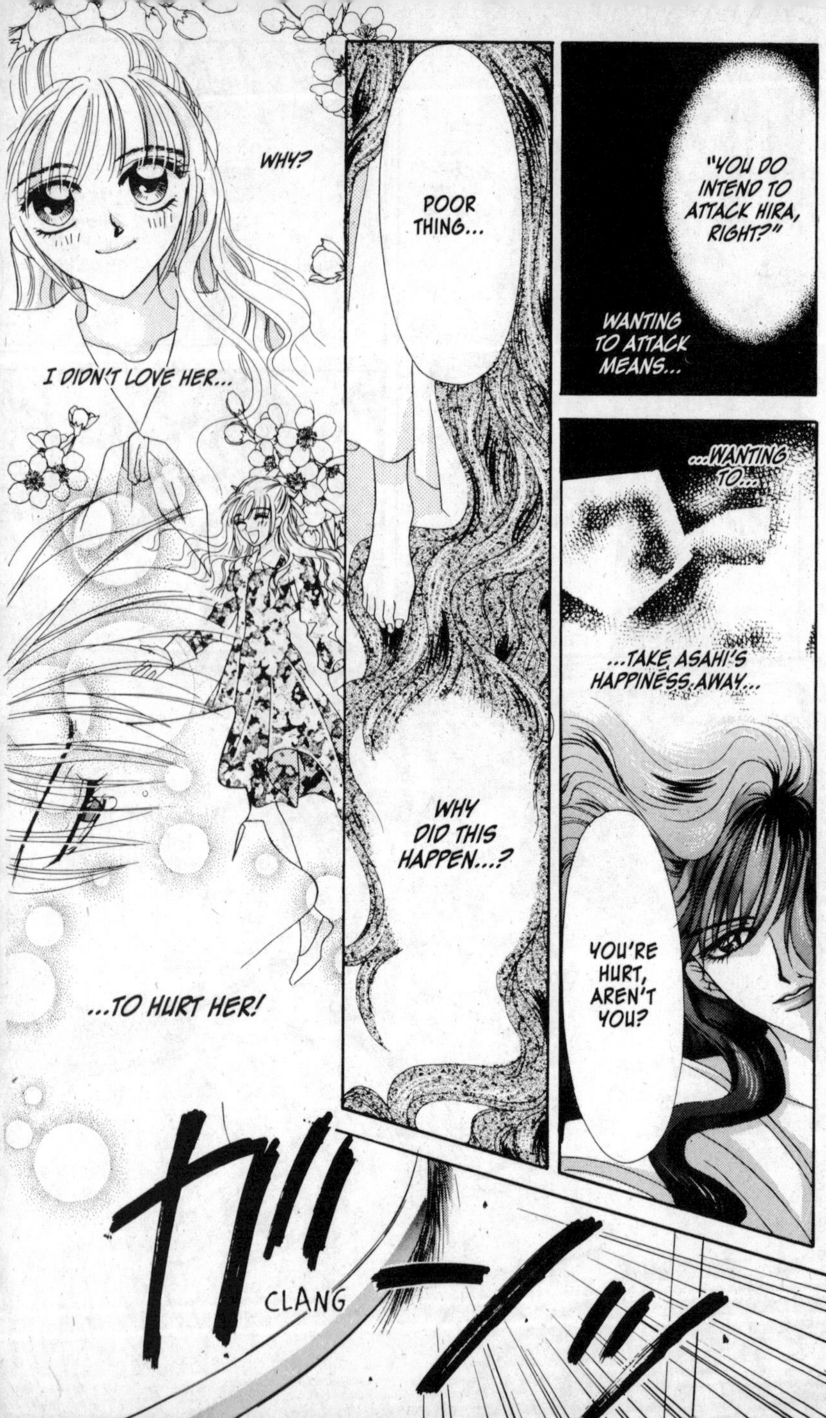
"YOU DO INTEND TO ATTACK HIRA, RIGHT?"
WANTING TO ATTACK MEANS...
...WANTING TO...
...TAKE ASAHI'S HAPPINESS AWAY...
YOU'RE HURT, AREN'T YOU?
POOR THING...
WHY DID THIS HAPPEN...?
WHY?
I DIDN'T LOVE HER...
...TO HURT HER!
CLANG

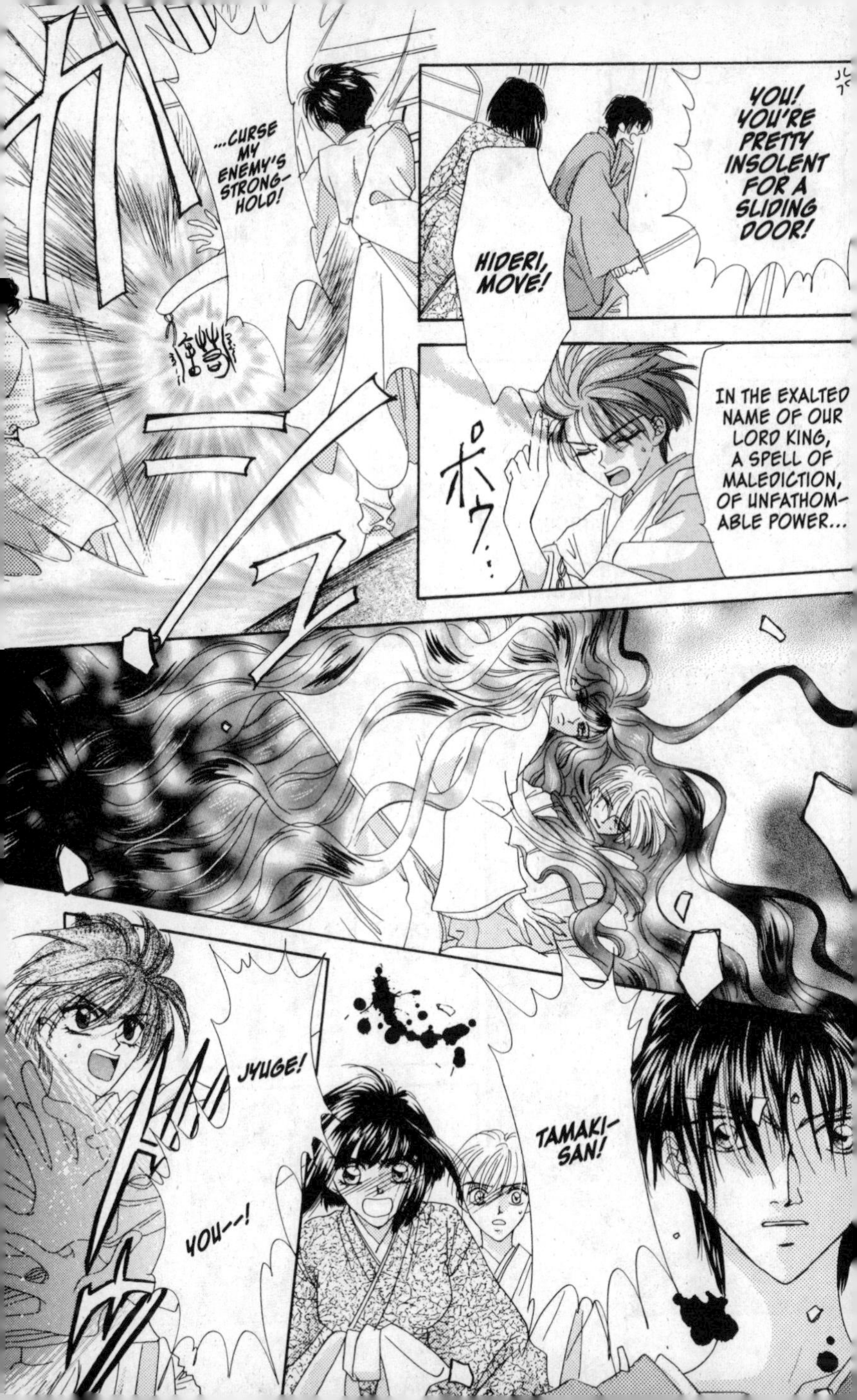
YOU! YOU'RE PRETTY INSOLENT FOR A SLIDING DOOR!
HIDERI, MOVE!
IN THE EXALTED NAME OF OUR LORD KING, A SPELL OF MALEDICTION, OF UNFATHOMABLE POWER...
ポウ...
...CURSE MY ENEMY'S STRONG-HOLD!
TAMAKI-SAN!
JYUGE!
YOU--!

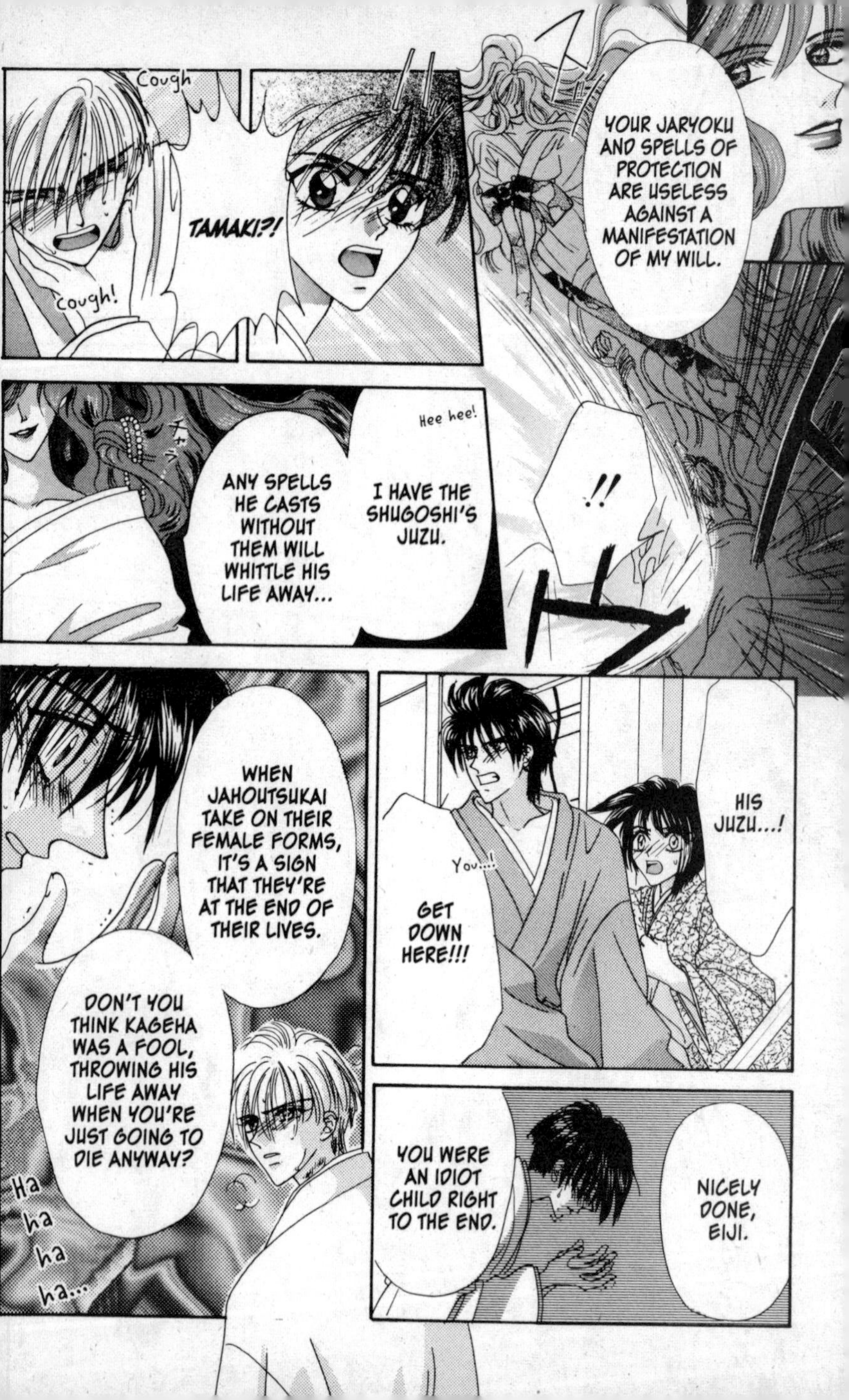
YOUR JARYOKU AND SPELLS OF PROTECTION ARE USELESS AGAINST A MANIFESTATION OF MY WILL.
TAMAKI?!
Cough
cough!
!!
Hee hee!
I HAVE THE SHUGOSHI'S JUZU.
ANY SPELLS HE CASTS WITHOUT THEM WILL WHITTLE HIS LIFE AWAY...
HIS JUZU...!
You...!
GET DOWN HERE!!!
NICELY DONE, EIJI.
YOU WERE AN IDIOT CHILD RIGHT TO THE END.
WHEN JAHOUTSUKAI TAKE ON THEIR FEMALE FORMS, IT'S A SIGN THAT THEY'RE AT THE END OF THEIR LIVES.
DON'T YOU THINK KAGEHA WAS A FOOL, THROWING HIS LIFE AWAY WHEN YOU'RE JUST GOING TO DIE ANYWAY?
Ha ha ha ha...

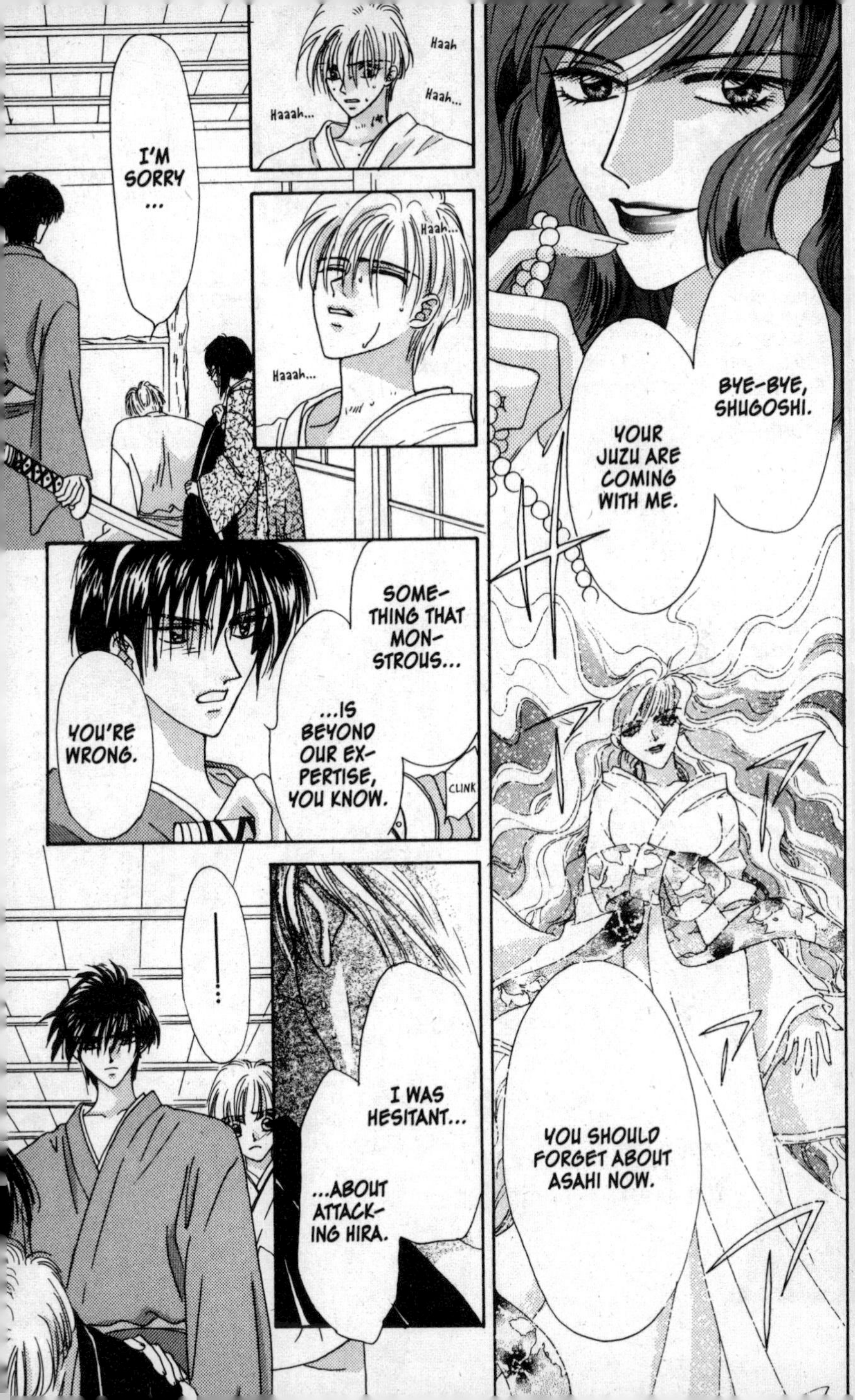

BYE-BYE, SHUGOSHI.
YOUR JUZU ARE COMING WITH ME.
YOU SHOULD FORGET ABOUT ASAHI NOW.
Haah
Haah...
Haaah...
Haah...
Haaah...
I'M SORRY...
SOME-THING THAT MON-STROUS...
...IS BEYOND OUR EX-PERTISE, YOU KNOW.
CLINK
YOU'RE WRONG.
I WAS HESITANT...
...ABOUT ATTACK-ING HIRA.
...!

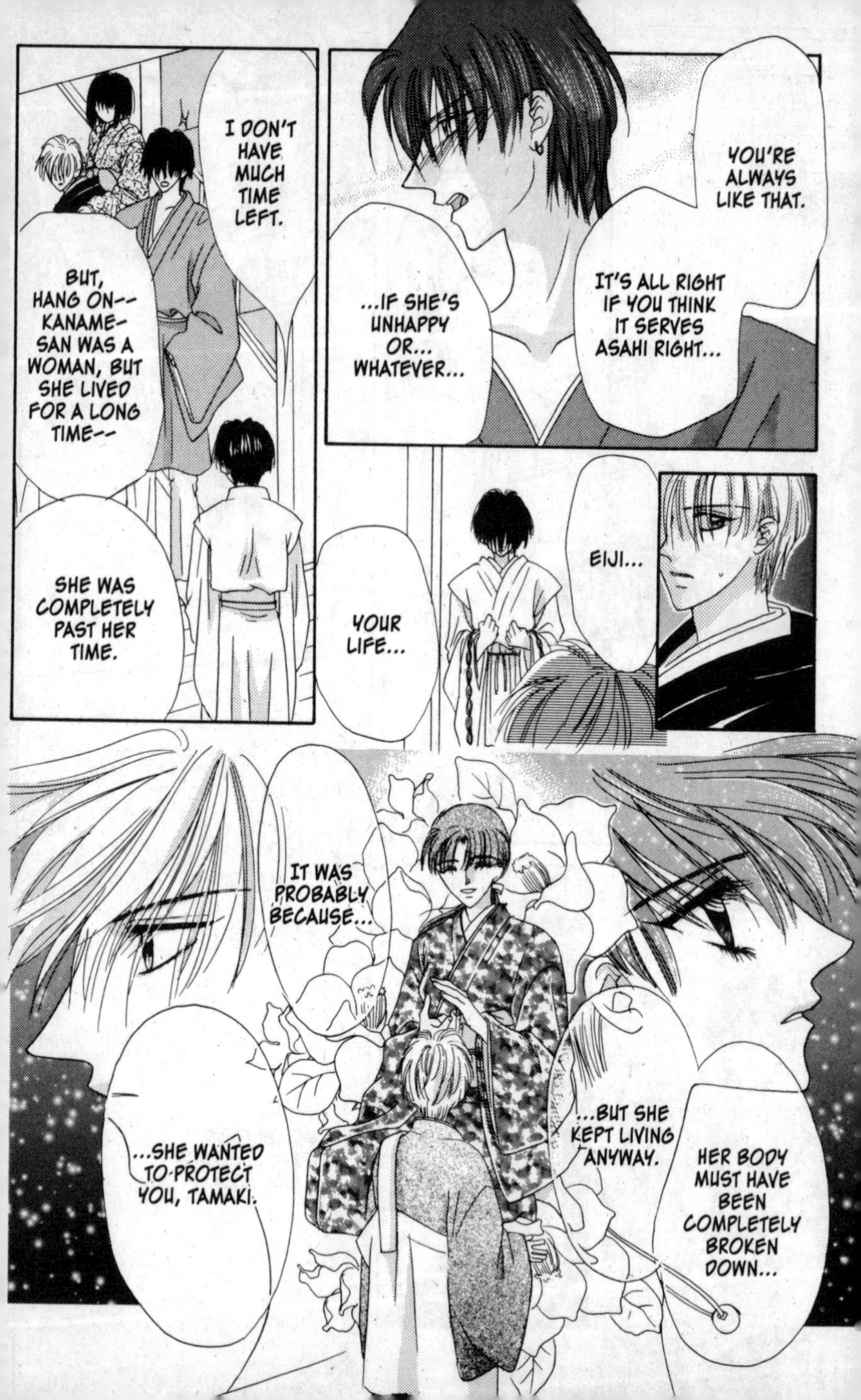
YOU'RE ALWAYS LIKE THAT.
IT'S ALL RIGHT IF YOU THINK IT SERVES ASAHI RIGHT...
...IF SHE'S UNHAPPY OR... WHATEVER...
EIJI...
YOUR LIFE...
I DON'T HAVE MUCH TIME LEFT.
BUT, HANG ON-- KANAME-SAN WAS A WOMAN, BUT SHE LIVED FOR A LONG TIME--
SHE WAS COMPLETELY PAST HER TIME.
HER BODY MUST HAVE BEEN COMPLETELY BROKEN DOWN...
...BUT SHE KEPT LIVING ANYWAY.
IT WAS PROBABLY BECAUSE...
...SHE WANTED TO PROTECT YOU, TAMAKI.

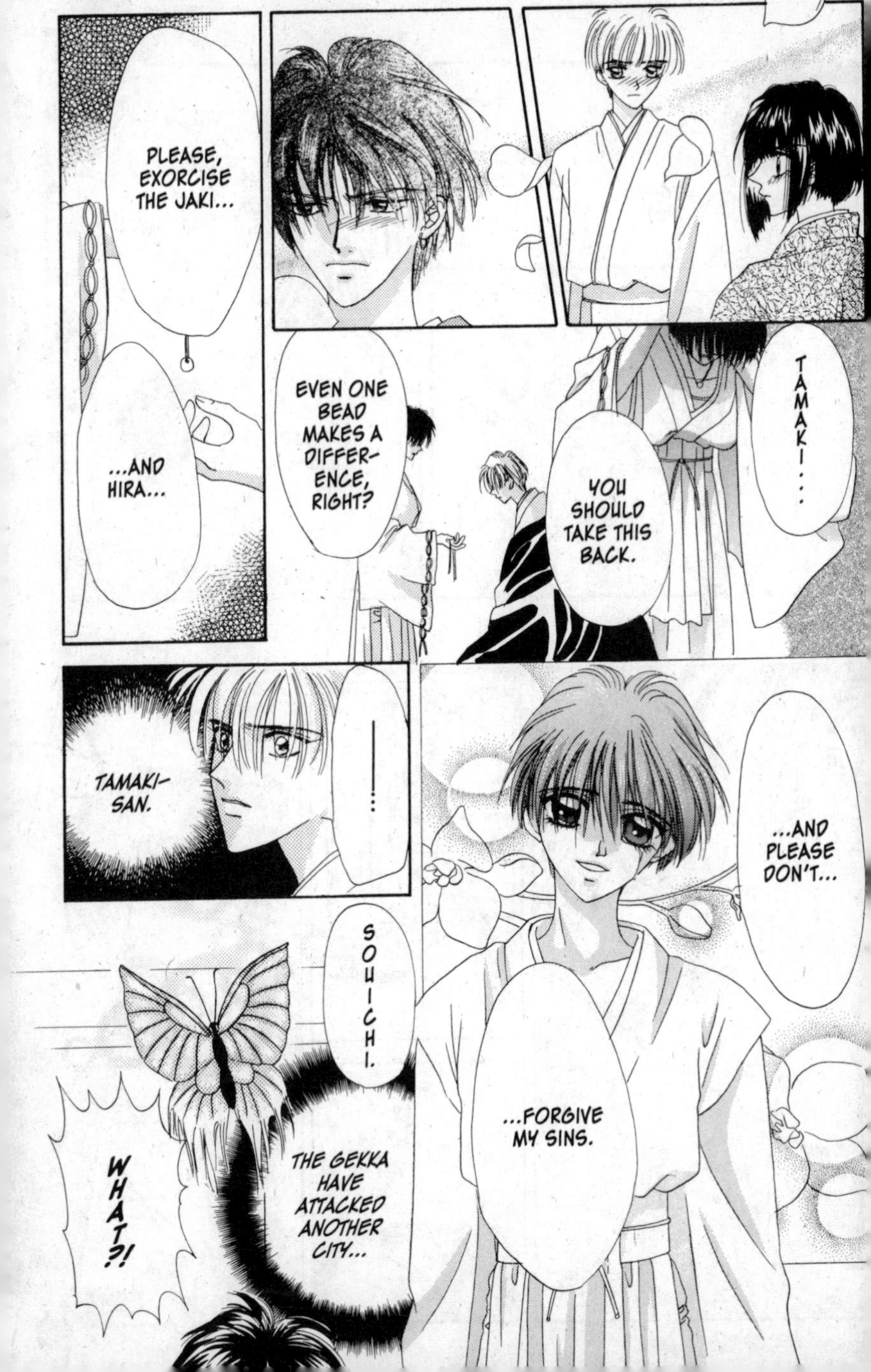
TAMAKI...
YOU SHOULD TAKE THIS BACK.
EVEN ONE BEAD MAKES A DIFFERENCE, RIGHT?
PLEASE, EXORCISE THE JAKI...
...AND HIRA...
...AND PLEASE DON'T...
...FORGIVE MY SINS.
—...
TAMAKI-SAN.
SOUICHI.
THE GEKKA HAVE ATTACKED ANOTHER CITY...
WHAT?!

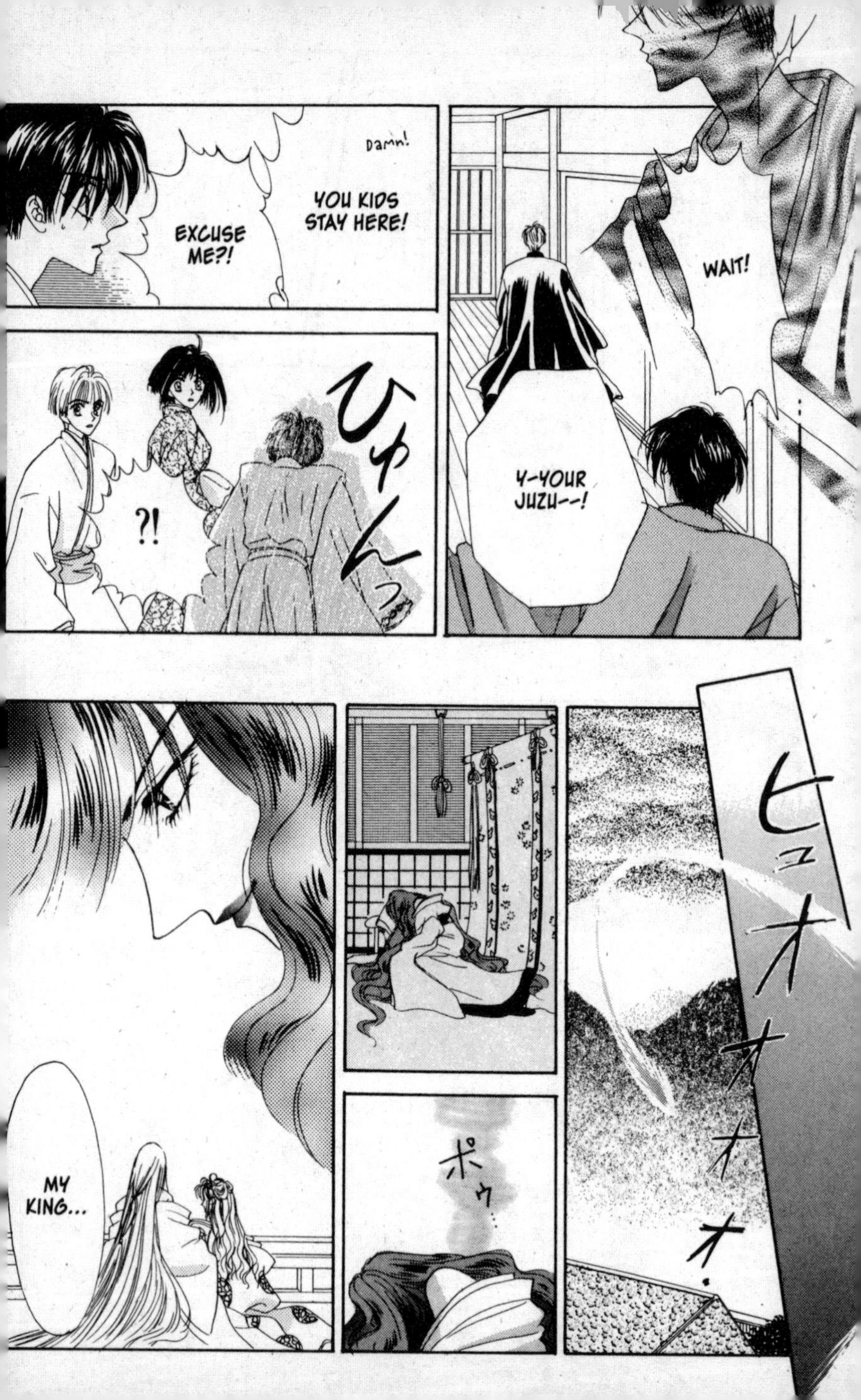
WAIT!
Y-YOUR JUZU--!
Damn!
YOU KIDS STAY HERE!
EXCUSE ME?!
ひゅんっ
?!
ヒュオオオオオ
ポゥ…
MY KING...

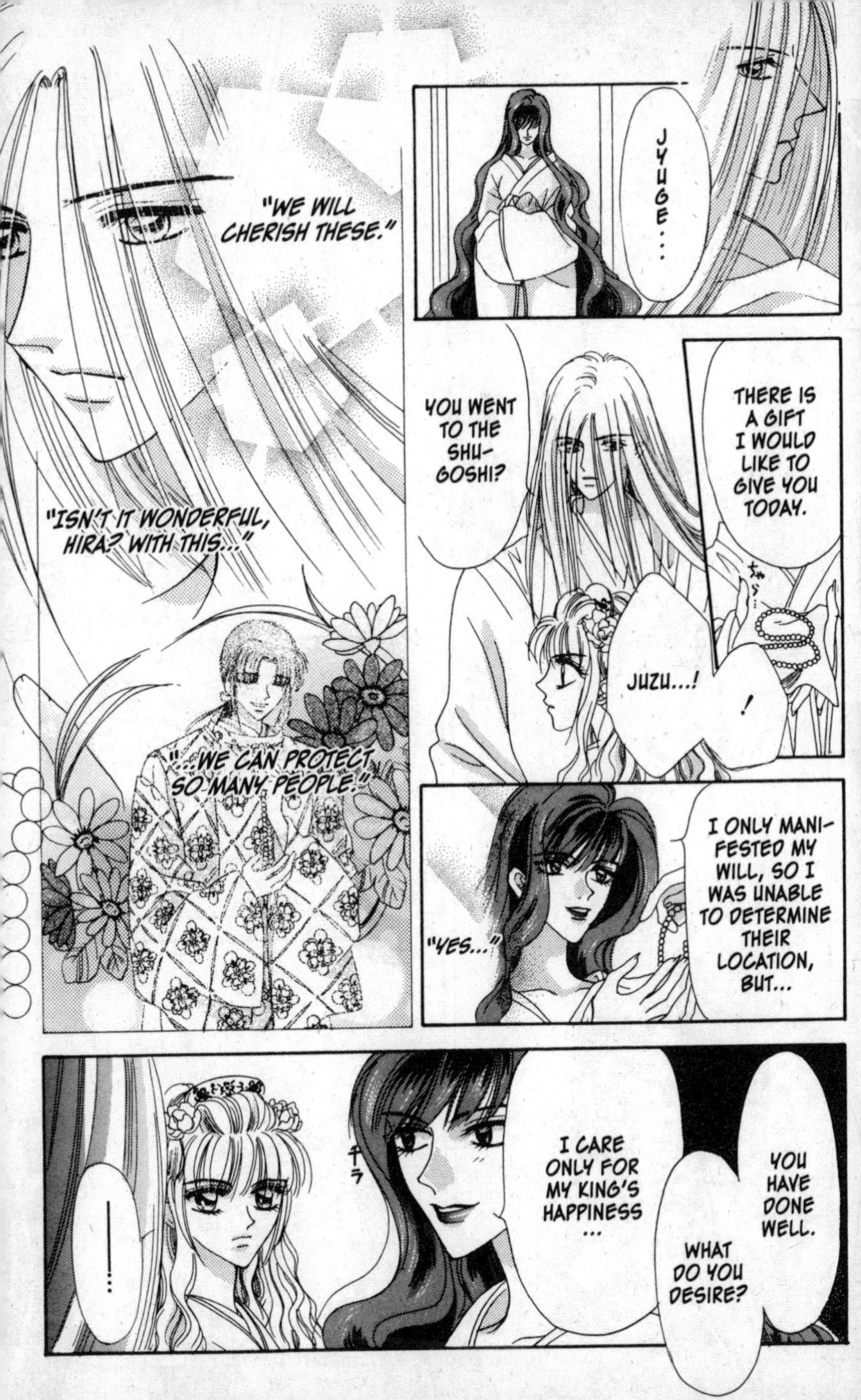
JYUGE...
THERE IS A GIFT I WOULD LIKE TO GIVE YOU TODAY.
!
YOU WENT TO THE SHU-GOSHI?
JUZU...!
I ONLY MANI-FESTED MY WILL, SO I WAS UNABLE TO DETERMINE THEIR LOCATION, BUT...
"YES..."
"WE WILL CHERISH THESE."
"ISN'T IT WONDERFUL, HIRA? WITH THIS..."
"...WE CAN PROTECT SO MANY PEOPLE."
YOU HAVE DONE WELL.
WHAT DO YOU DESIRE?
I CARE ONLY FOR MY KING'S HAPPINESS...
—......

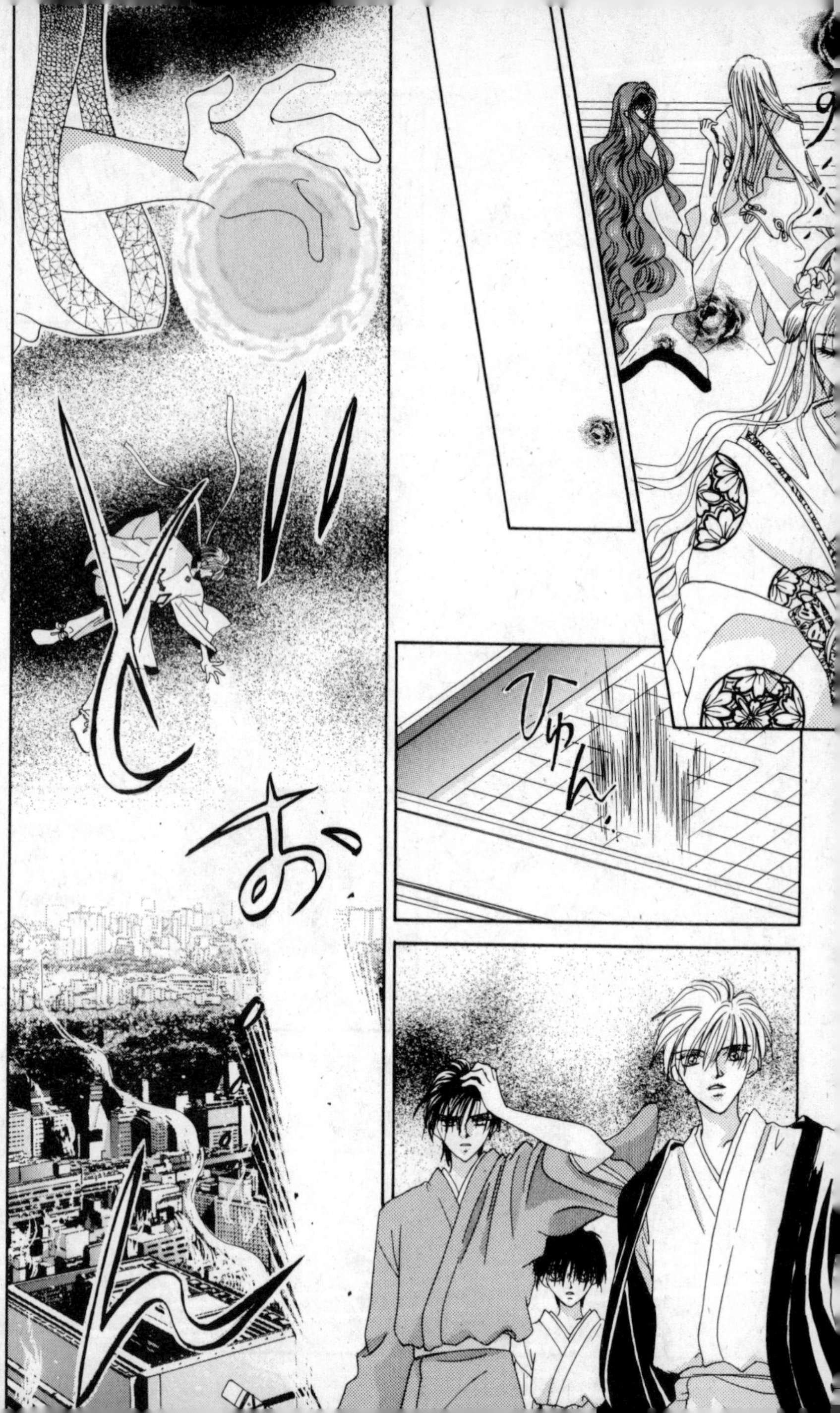
ひゅん
どおん

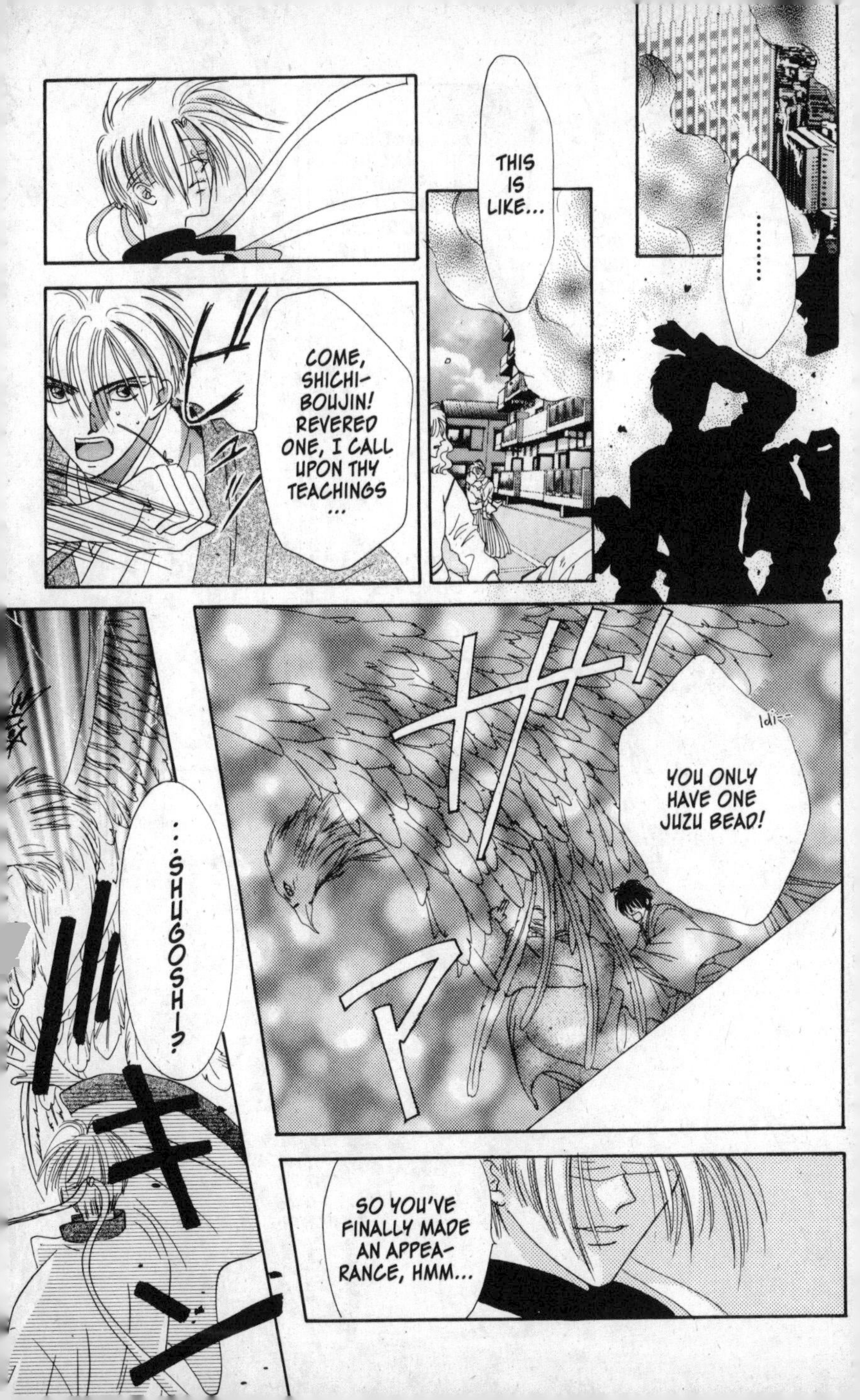
......
THIS IS LIKE...
COME, SHICHI-BOUJIN! REVERED ONE, I CALL UPON THY TEACHINGS ...
YOU ONLY HAVE ONE JUZU BEAD!
SO YOU'VE FINALLY MADE AN APPEARANCE, HMM...
...SHUGOSHI?

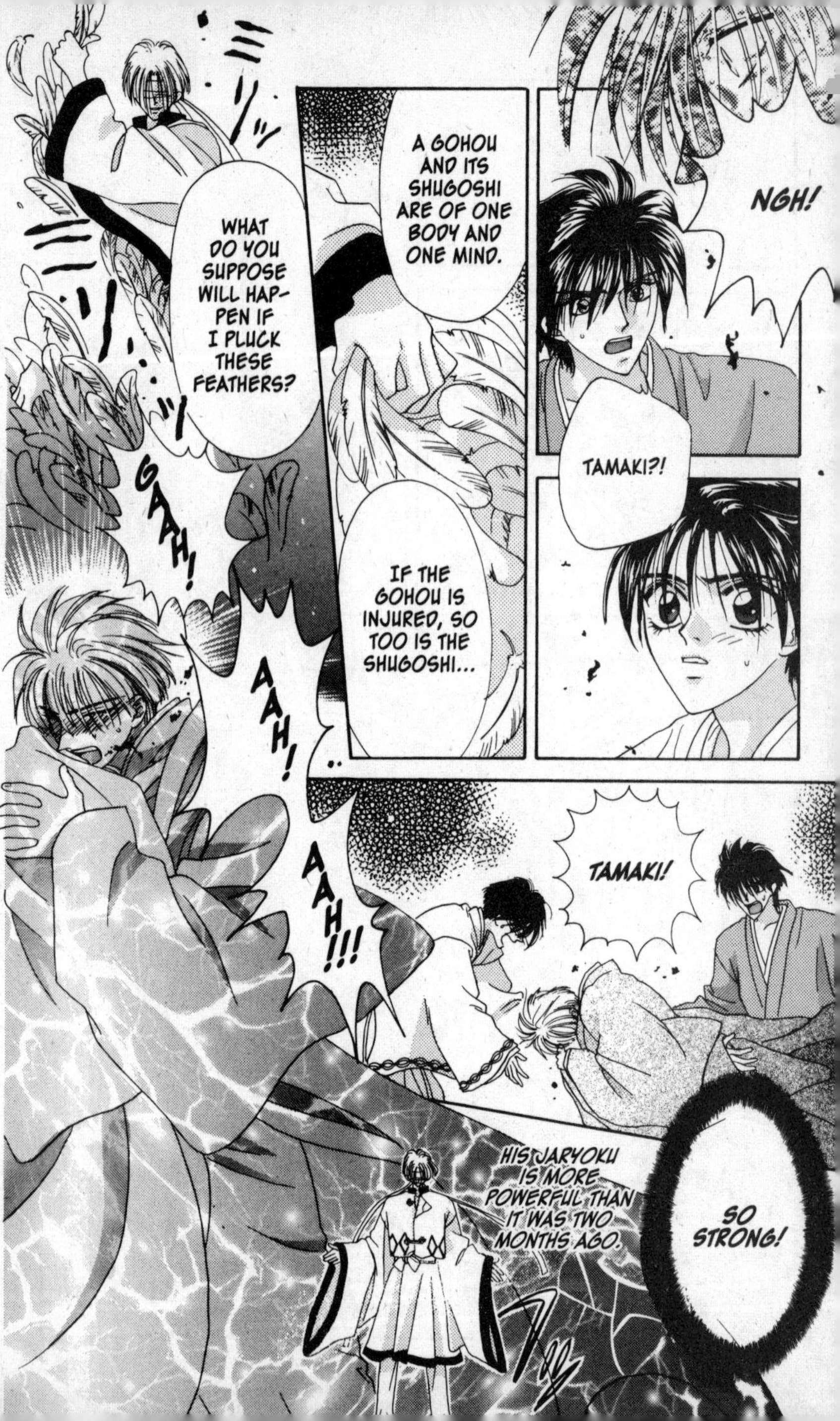
NGH!
TAMAKI?!
A GOHOU AND ITS SHUGOSHI ARE OF ONE BODY AND ONE MIND.
IF THE GOHOU IS INJURED, SO TOO IS THE SHUGOSHI...
WHAT DO YOU SUPPOSE WILL HAP-PEN IF I PLUCK THESE FEATHERS?
GAAH!
AAH!
AAH!!!
TAMAKI!
SO STRONG!
HIS JARYOKU IS MORE POWERFUL THAN IT WAS TWO MONTHS AGO.

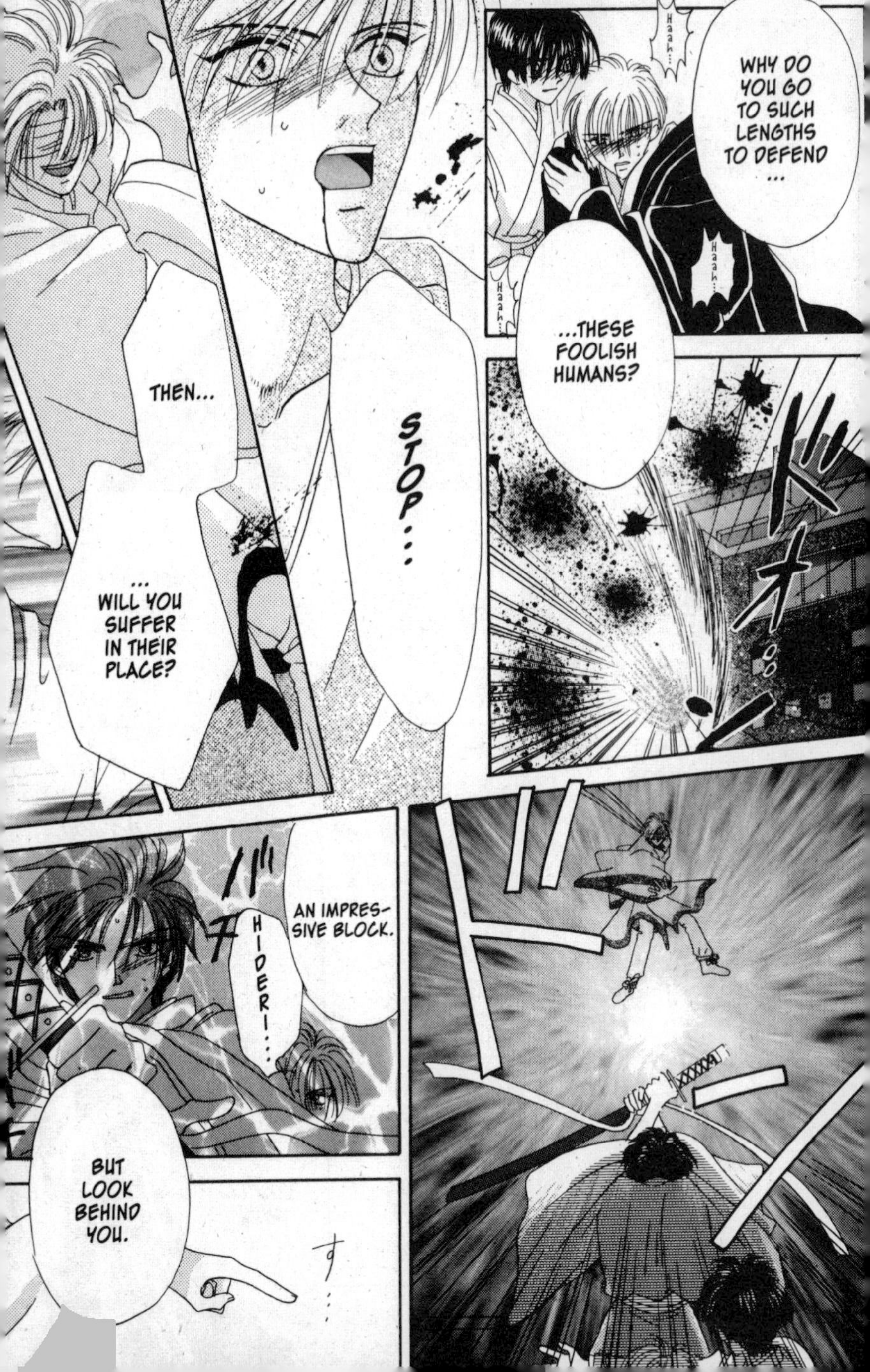
Haah...
Haah...
Haah...
WHY DO YOU GO TO SUCH LENGTHS TO DEFEND...
...THESE FOOLISH HUMANS?
STOP...
THEN...
...WILL YOU SUFFER IN THEIR PLACE?
AN IMPRES-SIVE BLOCK.
HIDERI...
BUT LOOK BEHIND YOU.
す...

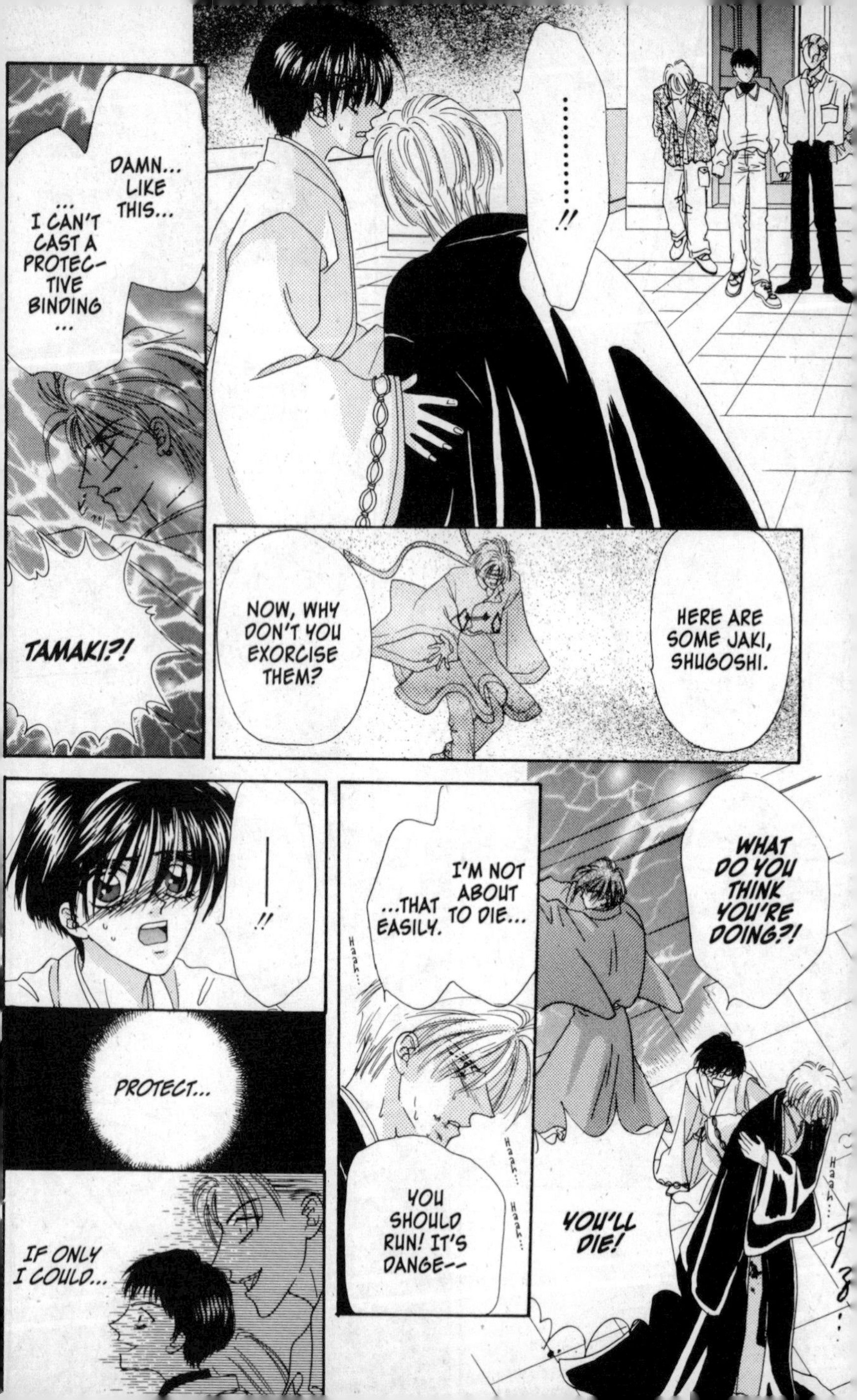
......!!
HERE ARE SOME JAKI, SHUGOSHI.
NOW, WHY DON'T YOU EXORCISE THEM?
DAMN... LIKE THIS...
... I CAN'T CAST A PROTECTIVE BINDING ...
TAMAKI?!
WHAT DO YOU THINK YOU'RE DOING?!
Haah...
YOU'LL DIE!
I'M NOT ABOUT TO DIE...
...THAT EASILY.
Haah...
Haah...
Haah...
YOU SHOULD RUN! IT'S DANGE--
—!!
PROTECT...
IF ONLY I COULD...

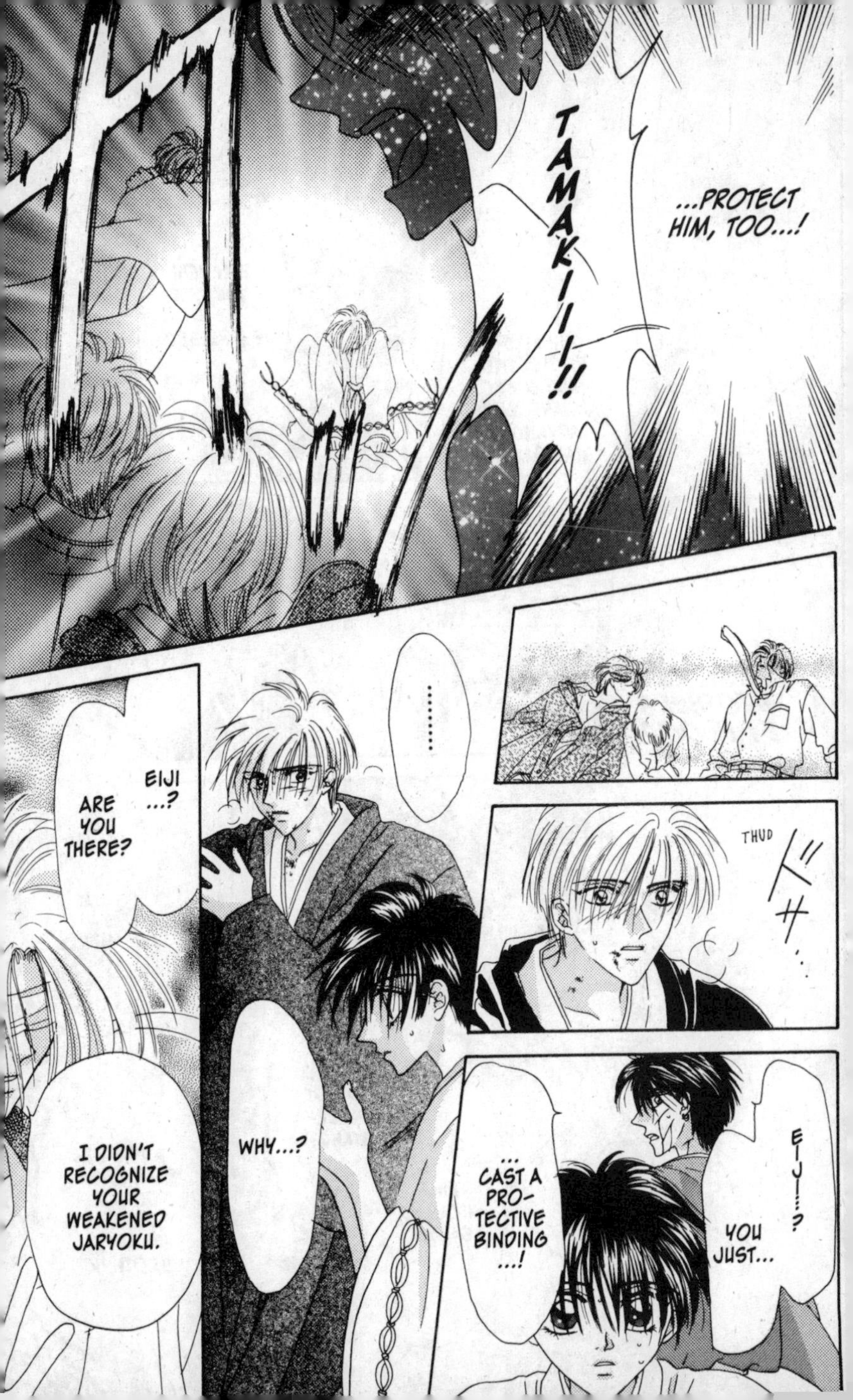
...PROTECT HIM, TOO...!
TAMAKI-I-I-I!!
THUD
ドサ..
EIJI...? YOU JUST...
...CAST A PRO-TECTIVE BINDING...!
......
WHY...?
EIJI...? ARE YOU THERE?
I DIDN'T RECOGNIZE YOUR WEAKENED JARYOKU.

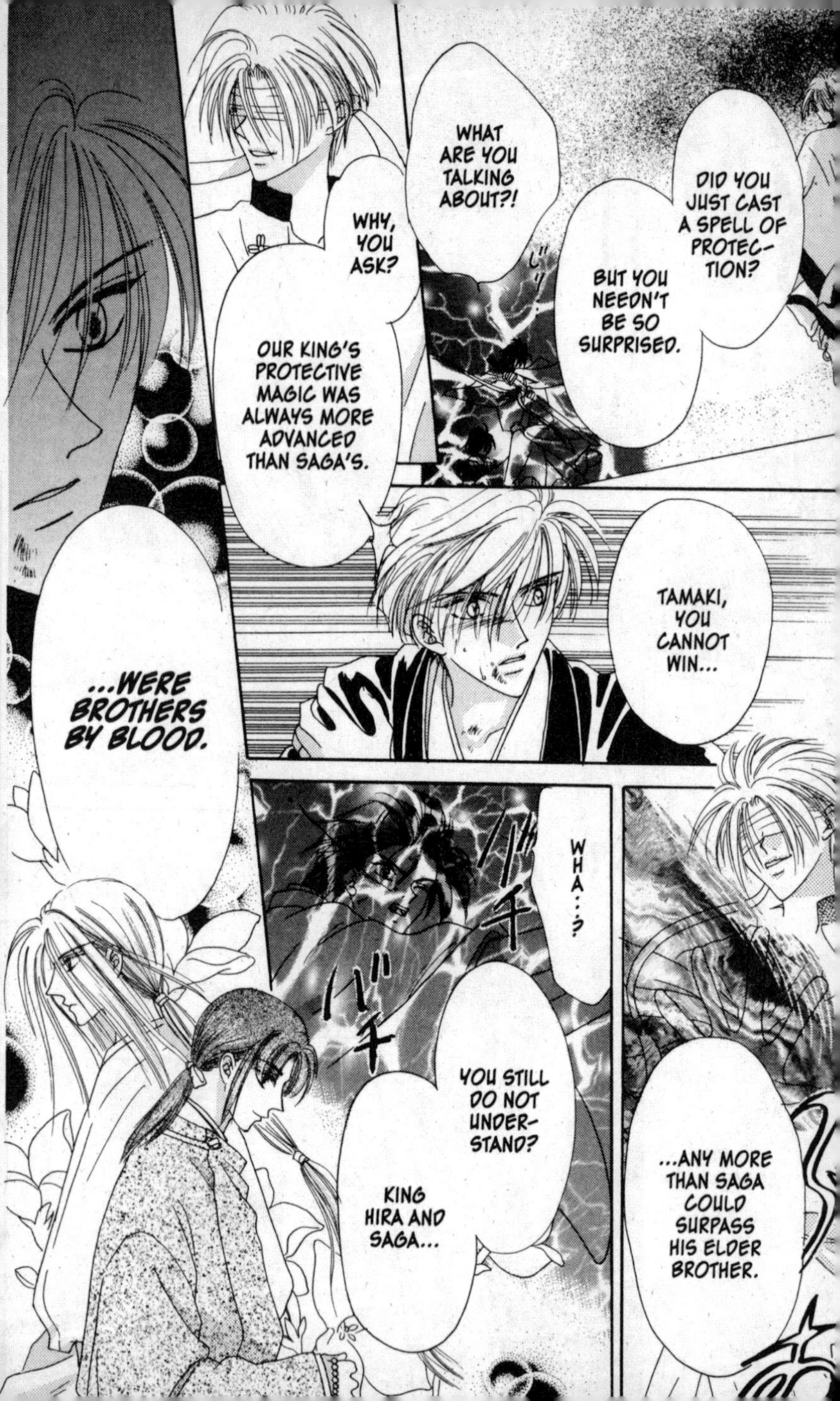
DID YOU JUST CAST A SPELL OF PROTECTION?
BUT YOU NEEDN'T BE SO SURPRISED.
WHAT ARE YOU TALKING ABOUT?!
WHY, YOU ASK?
OUR KING'S PROTECTIVE MAGIC WAS ALWAYS MORE ADVANCED THAN SAGA'S.
TAMAKI, YOU CANNOT WIN...
...ANY MORE THAN SAGA COULD SURPASS HIS ELDER BROTHER.
WHA...?
バチ
バチ
YOU STILL DO NOT UNDERSTAND?
KING HIRA AND SAGA...
...WERE BROTHERS BY BLOOD.

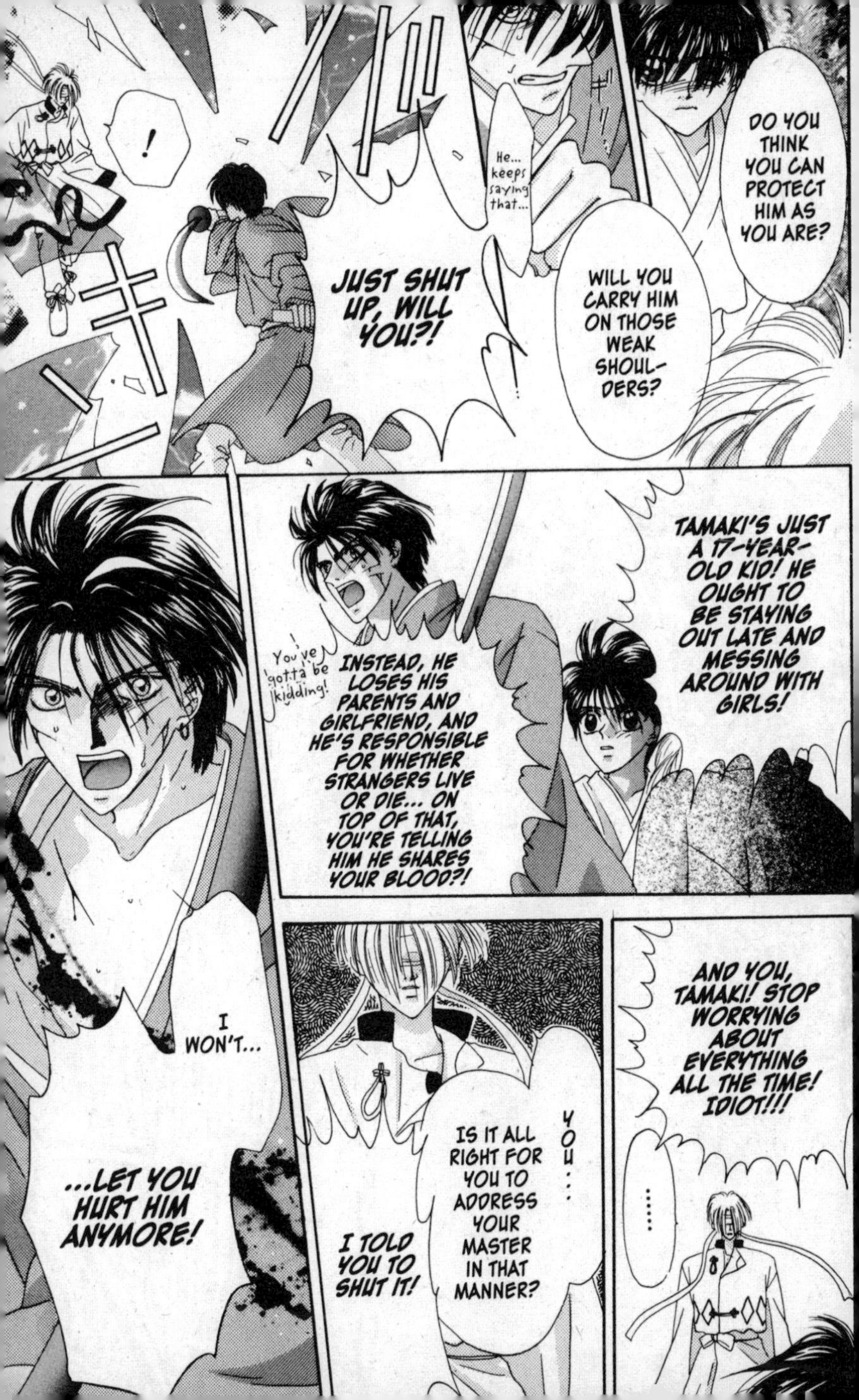
DO YOU THINK YOU CAN PROTECT HIM AS YOU ARE?
WILL YOU CARRY HIM ON THOSE WEAK SHOULDERS?
He... keeps saying that...
JUST SHUT UP, WILL YOU?!
!
TAMAKI'S JUST A 17-YEAR-OLD KID! HE OUGHT TO BE STAYING OUT LATE AND MESSING AROUND WITH GIRLS!
INSTEAD, HE LOSES HIS PARENTS AND GIRLFRIEND, AND HE'S RESPONSIBLE FOR WHETHER STRANGERS LIVE OR DIE... ON TOP OF THAT, YOU'RE TELLING HIM HE SHARES YOUR BLOOD?!
You've gotta be kidding!
AND YOU, TAMAKI! STOP WORRYING ABOUT EVERYTHING ALL THE TIME! IDIOT!!!
......
YOU...
IS IT ALL RIGHT FOR YOU TO ADDRESS YOUR MASTER IN THAT MANNER?
I TOLD YOU TO SHUT IT!
I WON'T...
...LET YOU HURT HIM ANYMORE!

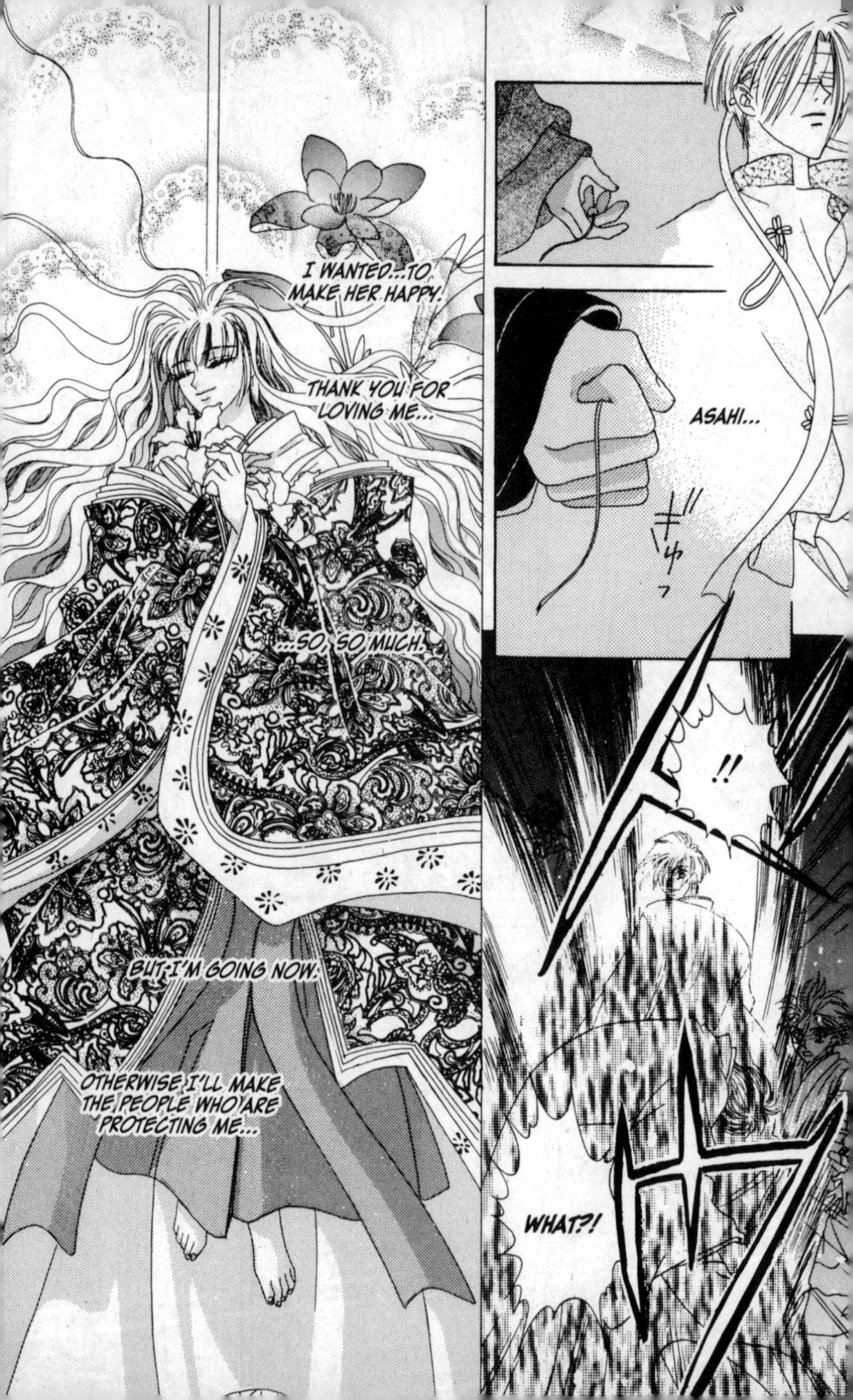
ASAHI...
!!
WHAT?!
I WANTED...TO MAKE HER HAPPY.
THANK YOU FOR LOVING ME...
...SO, SO MUCH.
BUT I'M GOING NOW.
OTHERWISE I'LL MAKE THE PEOPLE WHO ARE PROTECTING ME...

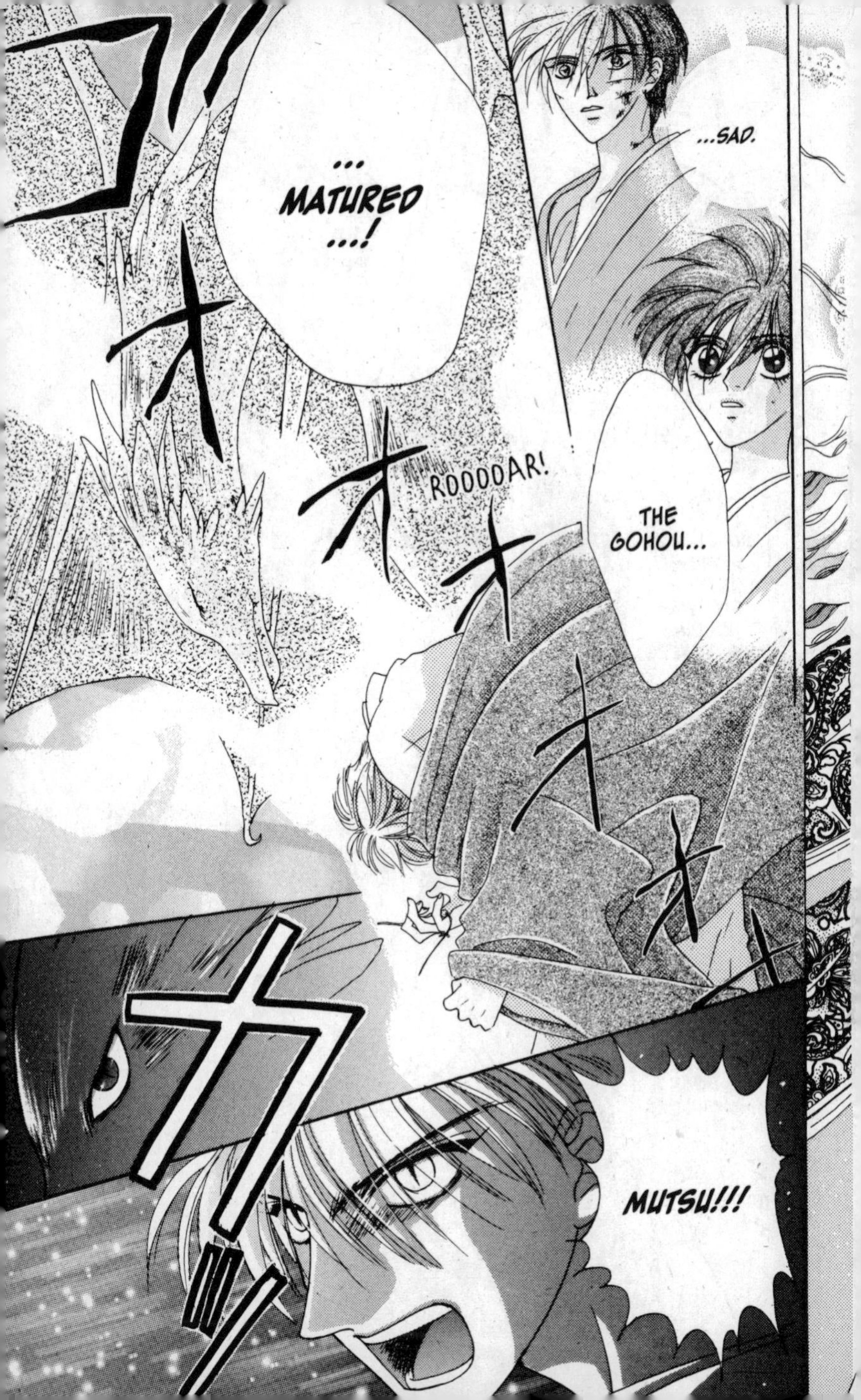
...SAD.
THE GOHOU...
...MATURED...!
ROOOOAR!
MUTSU!!!

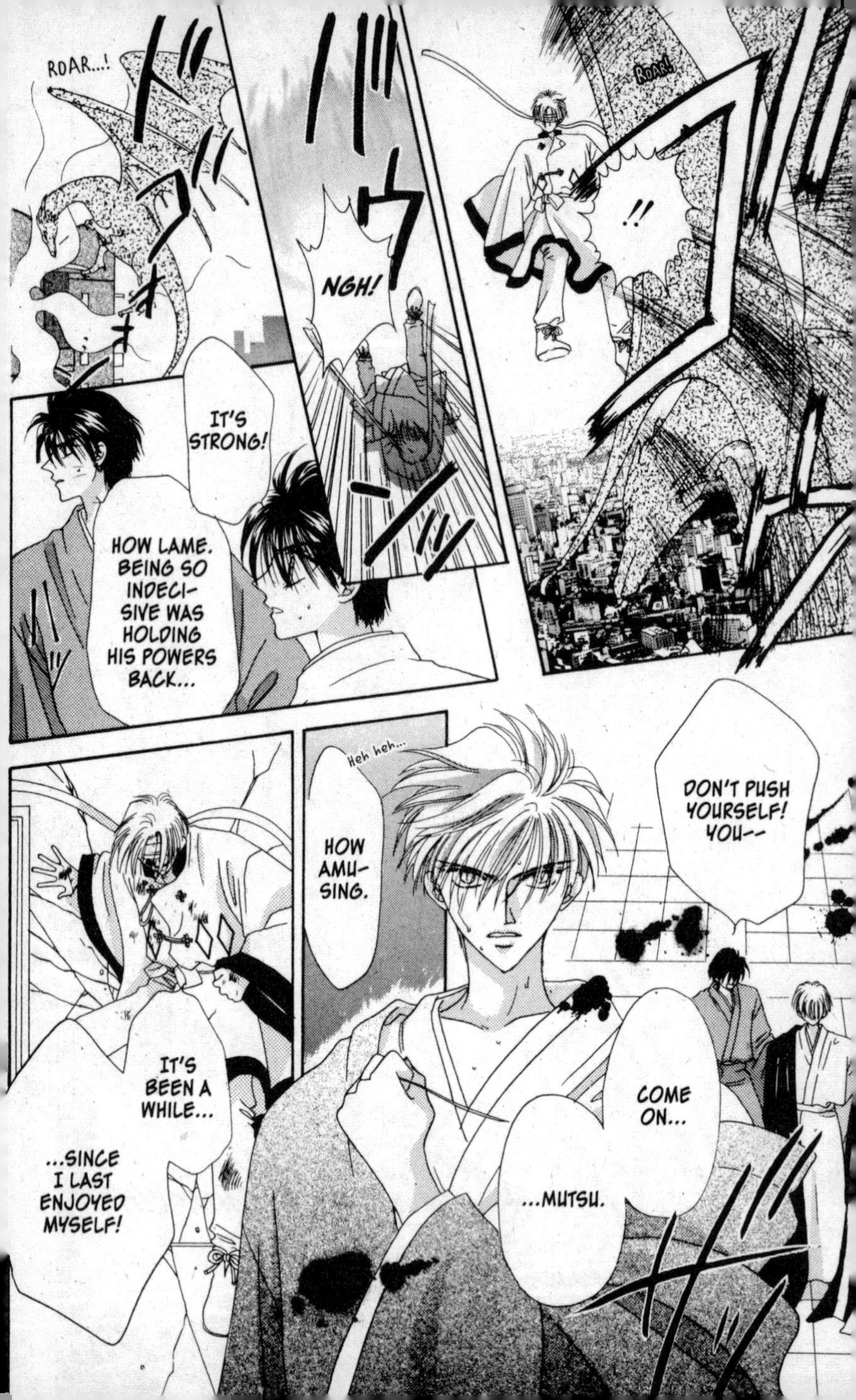
ROAR!
!!
NGH!
ROAR...!
IT'S STRONG!
HOW LAME. BEING SO INDECI-SIVE WAS HOLDING HIS POWERS BACK...
DON'T PUSH YOURSELF! YOU--
COME ON...
...MUTSU.
Heh heh...
HOW AMU-SING.
IT'S BEEN A WHILE...
...SINCE I LAST ENJOYED MYSELF!

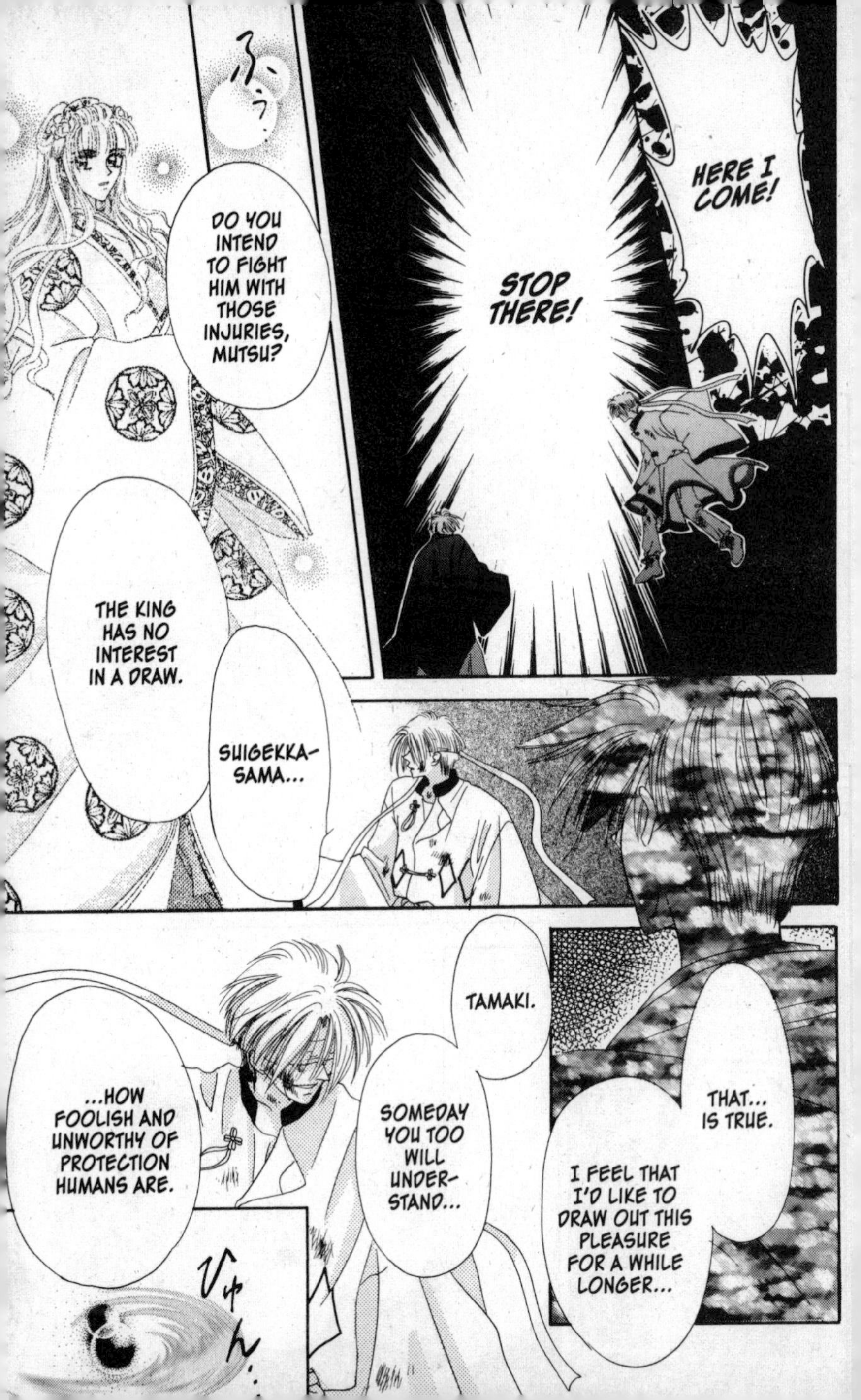
HERE I COME!
STOP THERE!
ふっ
DO YOU INTEND TO FIGHT HIM WITH THOSE INJURIES, MUTSU?
THE KING HAS NO INTEREST IN A DRAW.
SUIGEKKA-SAMA...
TAMAKI.
THAT... IS TRUE.
I FEEL THAT I'D LIKE TO DRAW OUT THIS PLEASURE FOR A WHILE LONGER...
SOMEDAY YOU TOO WILL UNDER-STAND...
...HOW FOOLISH AND UNWORTHY OF PROTECTION HUMANS ARE.
ひゅん

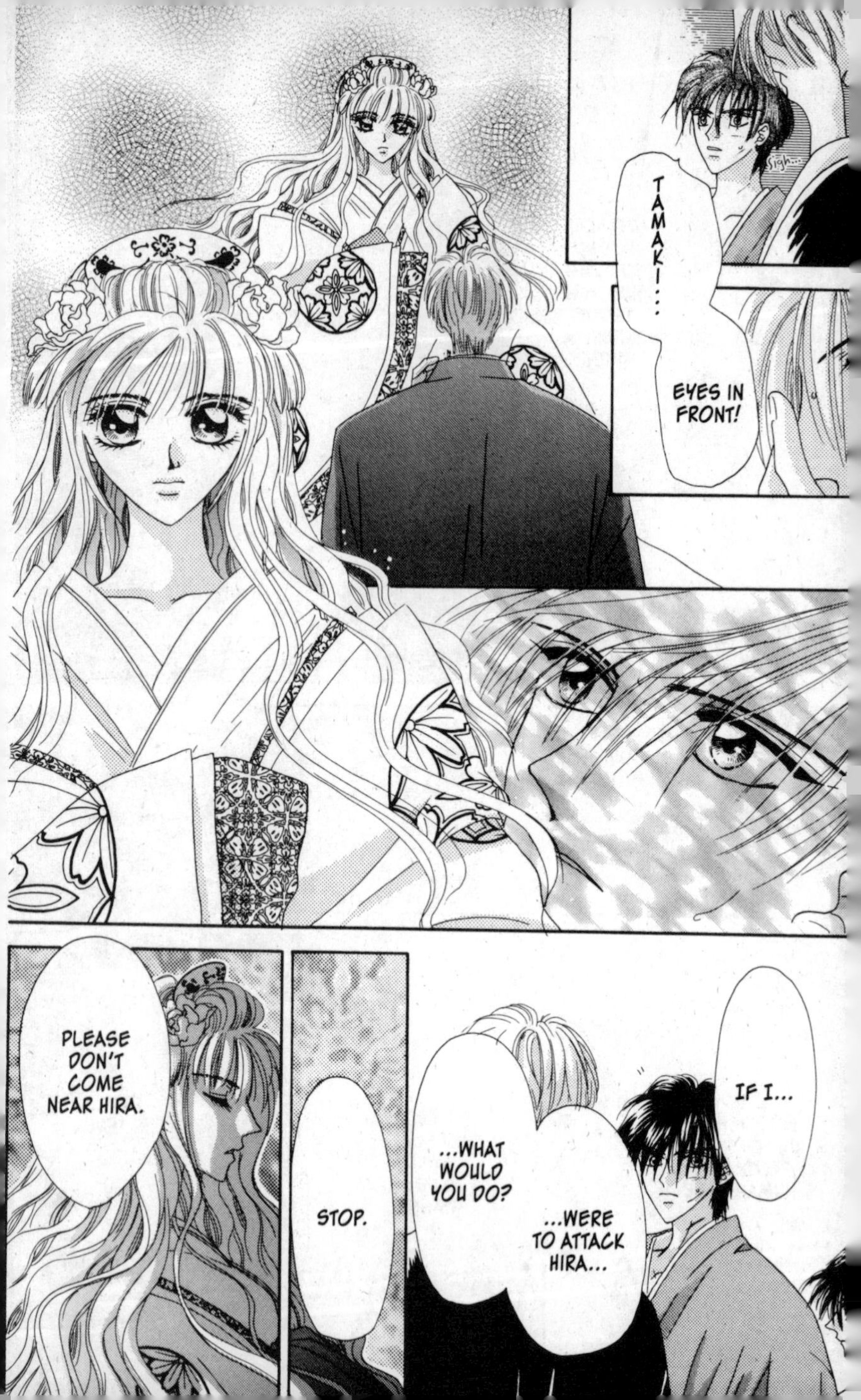
Sigh...
TAMAKI!...
EYES IN FRONT!
IF I...
...WERE TO ATTACK HIRA...
...WHAT WOULD YOU DO?
STOP.
PLEASE DON'T COME NEAR HIRA.

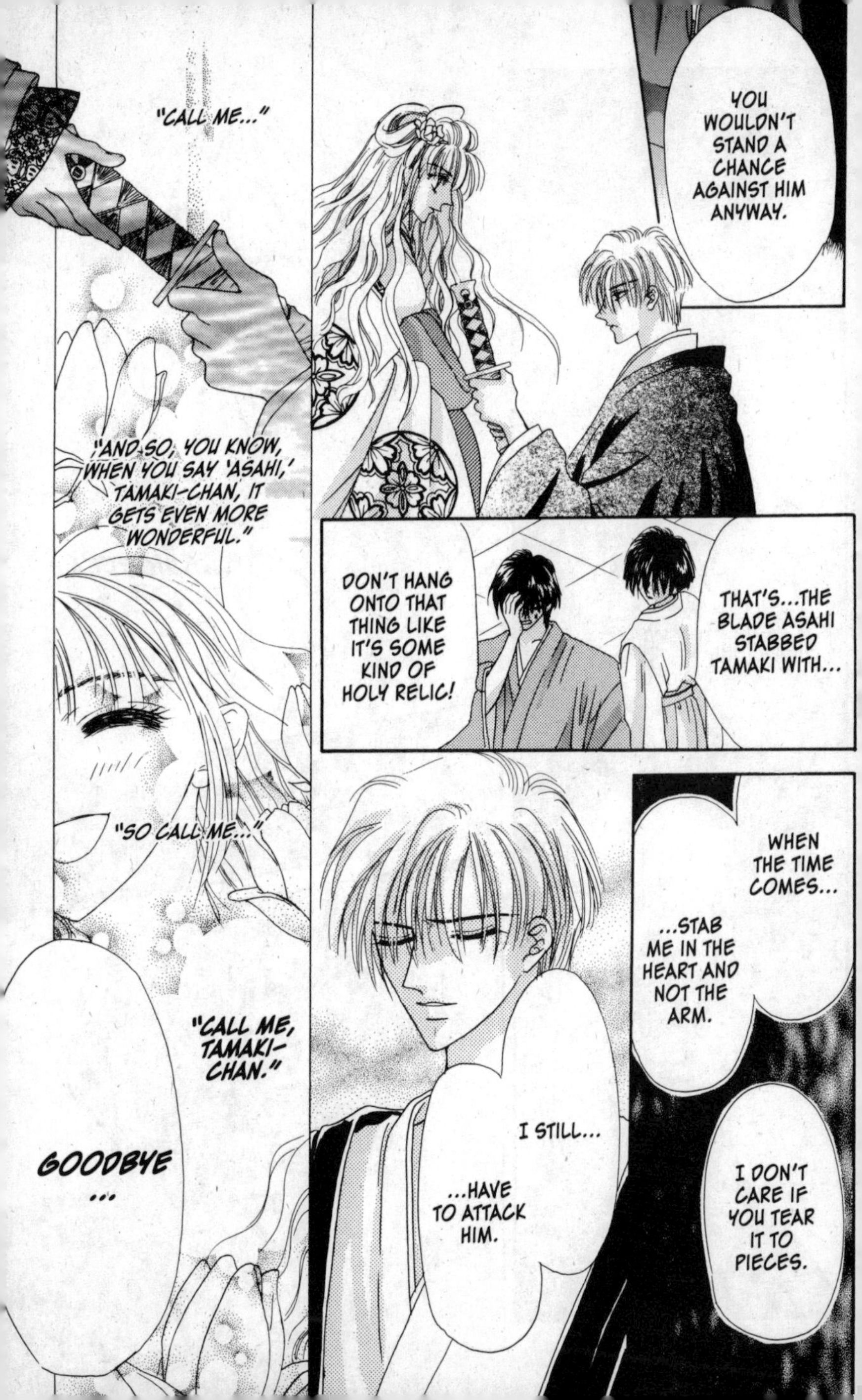
YOU WOULDN'T STAND A CHANCE AGAINST HIM ANYWAY.
THAT'S...THE BLADE ASAHI STABBED TAMAKI WITH...
DON'T HANG ONTO THAT THING LIKE IT'S SOME KIND OF HOLY RELIC!
WHEN THE TIME COMES...
...STAB ME IN THE HEART AND NOT THE ARM.
I DON'T CARE IF YOU TEAR IT TO PIECES.
I STILL...
...HAVE TO ATTACK HIM.
"CALL ME..."
"AND SO, YOU KNOW, WHEN YOU SAY 'ASAHI,' TAMAKI-CHAN, IT GETS EVEN MORE WONDERFUL."
"SO CALL ME..."
"CALL ME, TAMAKI-CHAN."
GOODBYE ...

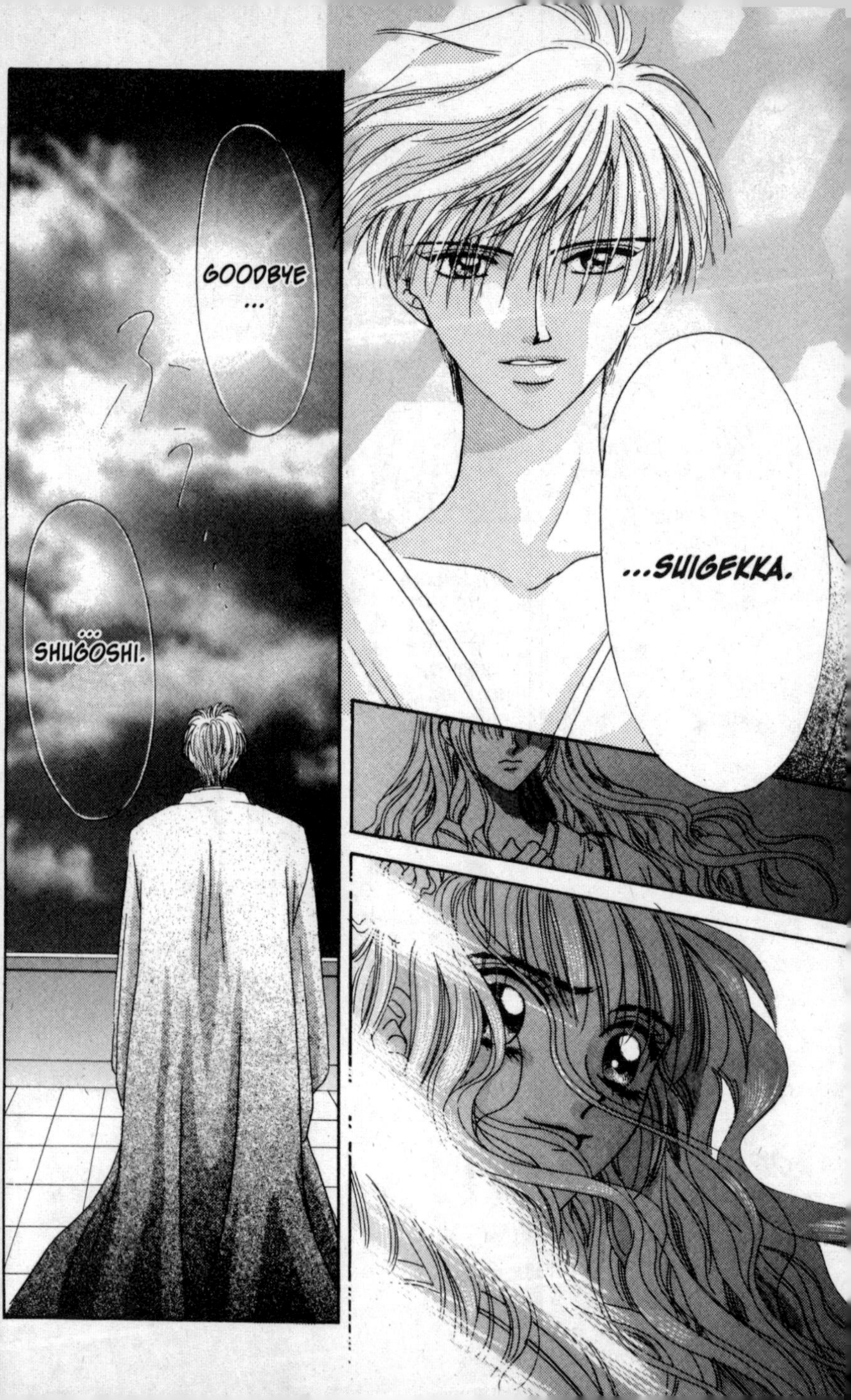
...SUIGEKKA.
GOODBYE ...
...SHUGOSHI.

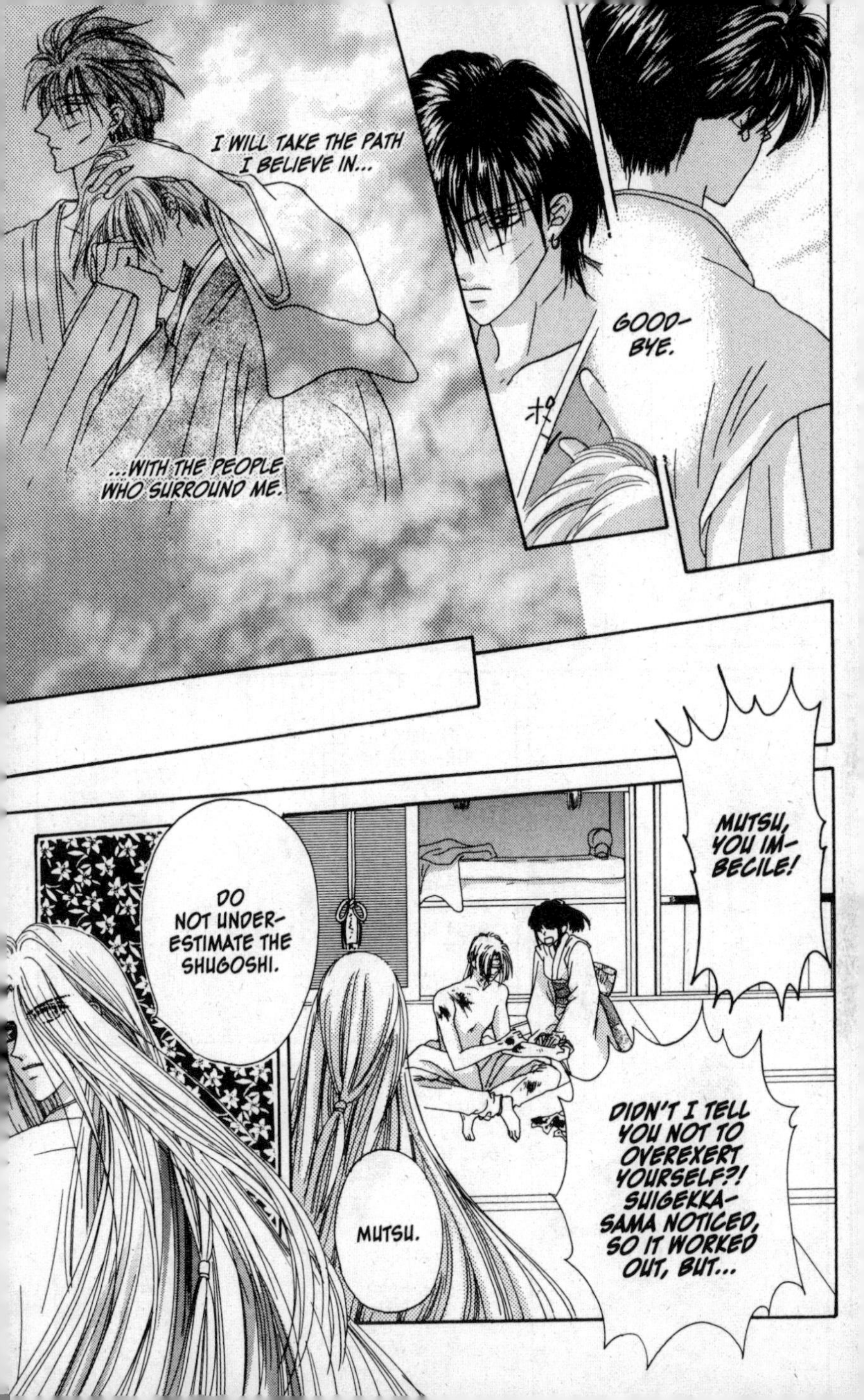
GOOD-BYE.
I WILL TAKE THE PATH I BELIEVE IN...
...WITH THE PEOPLE WHO SURROUND ME.
MUTSU, YOU IMBECILE!
DIDN'T I TELL YOU NOT TO OVEREXERT YOURSELF?! SUIGEKKA-SAMA NOTICED, SO IT WORKED OUT, BUT...
DO NOT UNDER-ESTIMATE THE SHUGOSHI.
MUTSU.

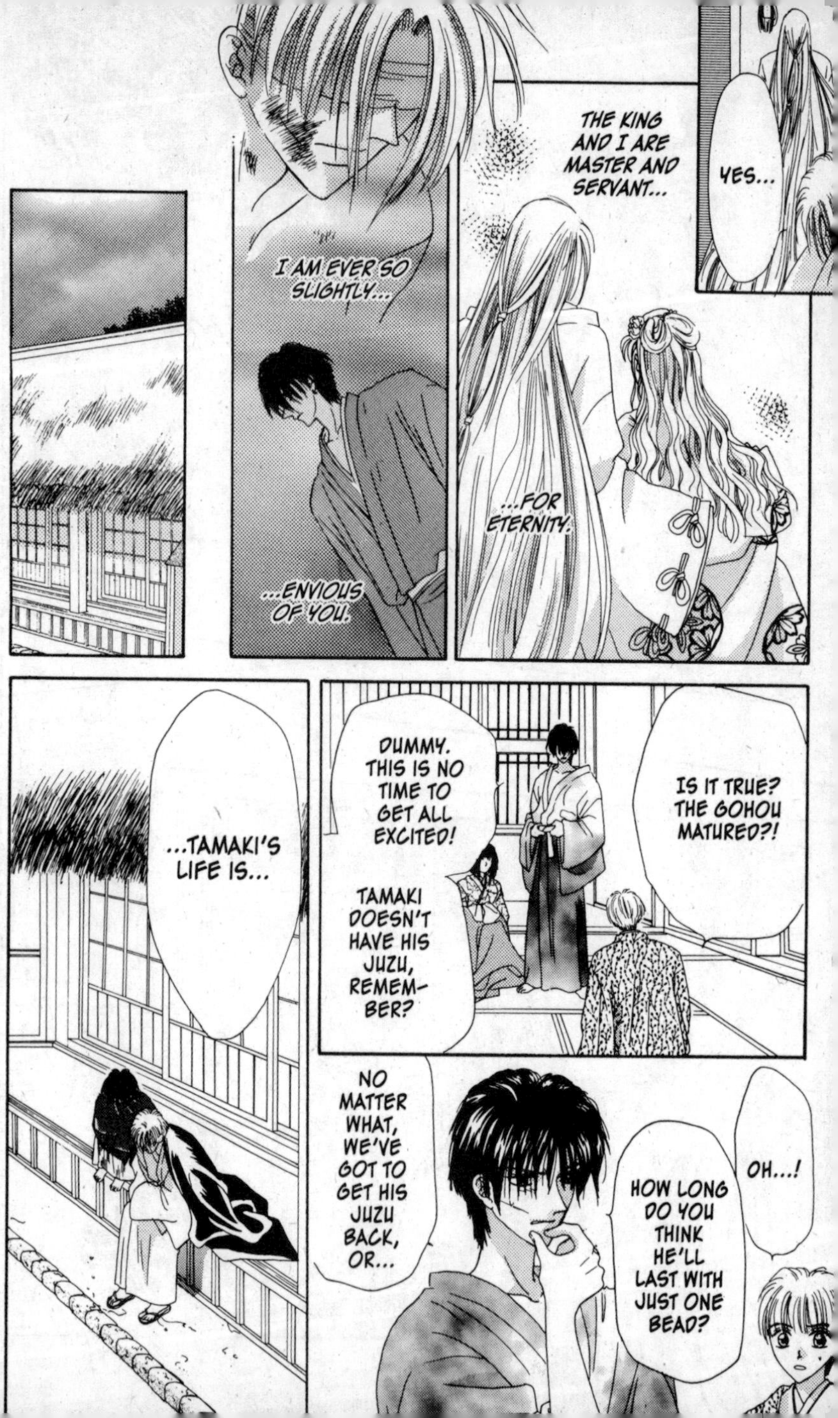
YES...
THE KING AND I ARE MASTER AND SERVANT...
...FOR ETERNITY.
I AM EVER SO SLIGHTLY...
...ENVIOUS OF YOU.
IS IT TRUE? THE GOHOU MATURED?!
DUMMY. THIS IS NO TIME TO GET ALL EXCITED!
TAMAKI DOESN'T HAVE HIS JUZU, REMEMBER?
OH...!
HOW LONG DO YOU THINK HE'LL LAST WITH JUST ONE BEAD?
NO MATTER WHAT, WE'VE GOT TO GET HIS JUZU BACK, OR...
...TAMAKI'S LIFE IS...

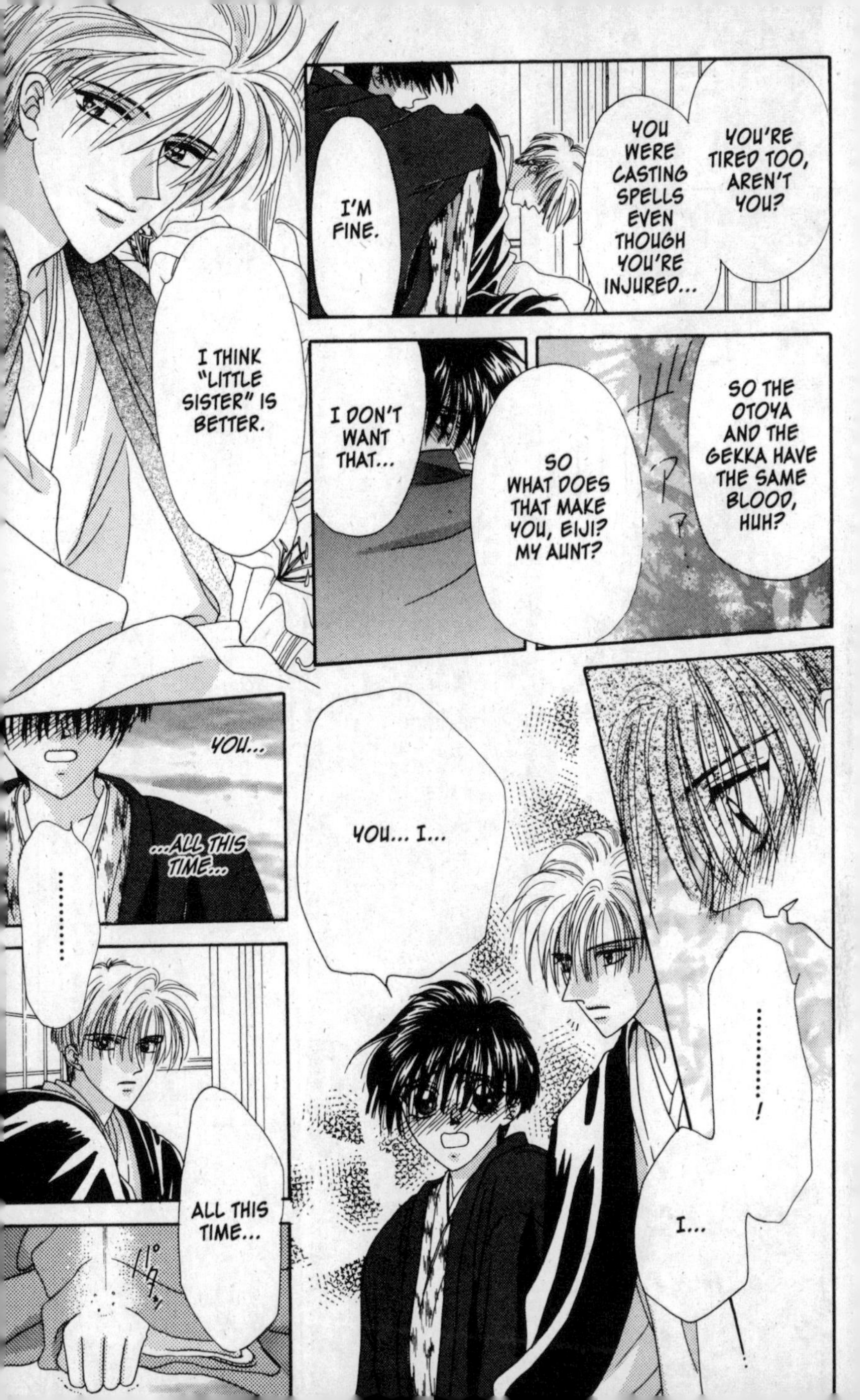
YOU'RE TIRED TOO, AREN'T YOU?
YOU WERE CASTING SPELLS EVEN THOUGH YOU'RE INJURED...
I'M FINE.
SO THE OTOYA AND THE GEKKA HAVE THE SAME BLOOD, HUH?
SO WHAT DOES THAT MAKE YOU, EIJI? MY AUNT?
I DON'T WANT THAT...
I THINK "LITTLE SISTER" IS BETTER.
......!
I...
YOU... I...
YOU...
...ALL THIS TIME...
......
ALL THIS TIME...

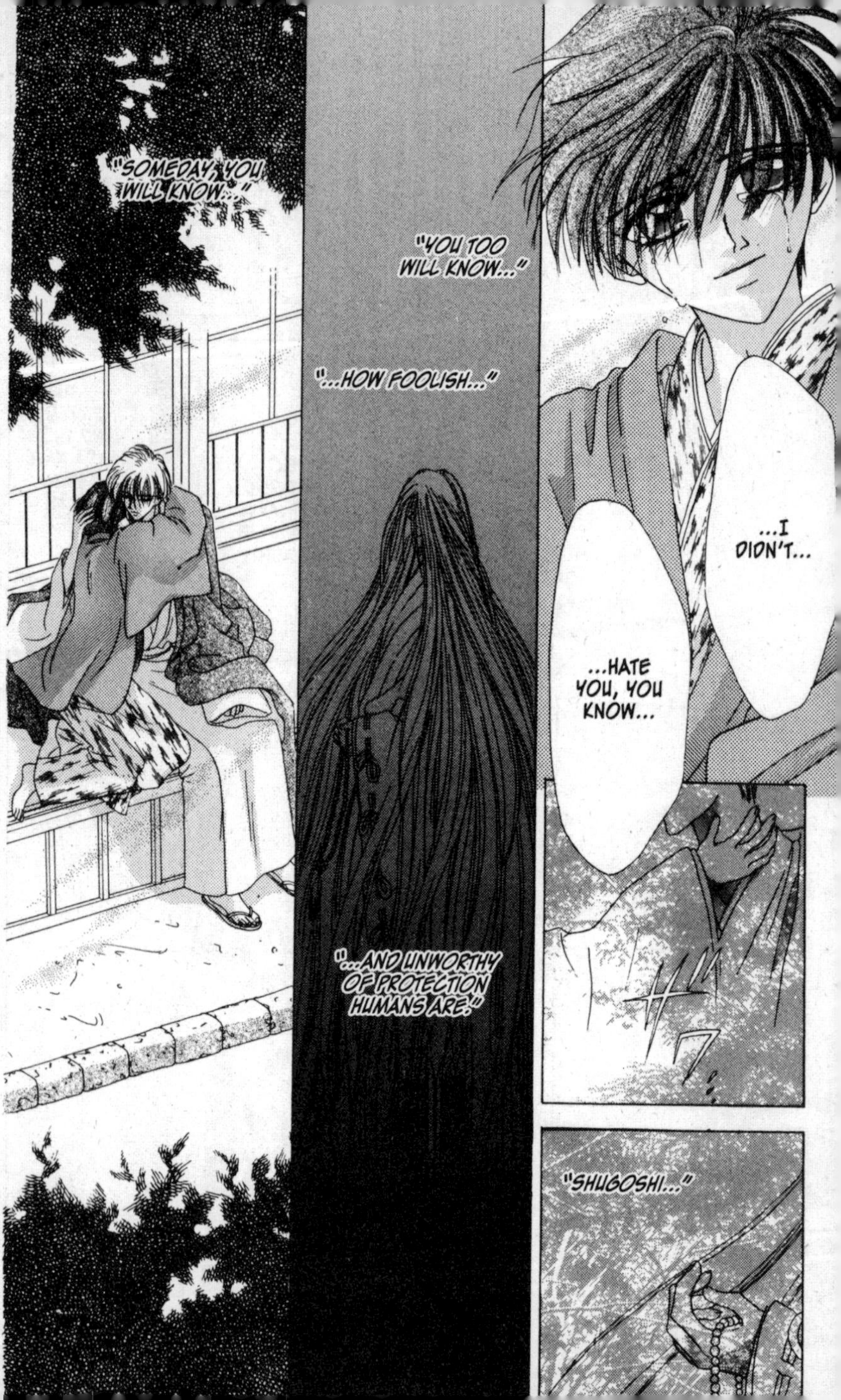
...I DIDN'T...
...HATE YOU, YOU KNOW...
"SHUGOSHI..."
"YOU TOO WILL KNOW..."
"...HOW FOOLISH..."
"...AND UNWORTHY OF PROTECTION HUMANS ARE."
"SOMEDAY, YOU WILL KNOW..."

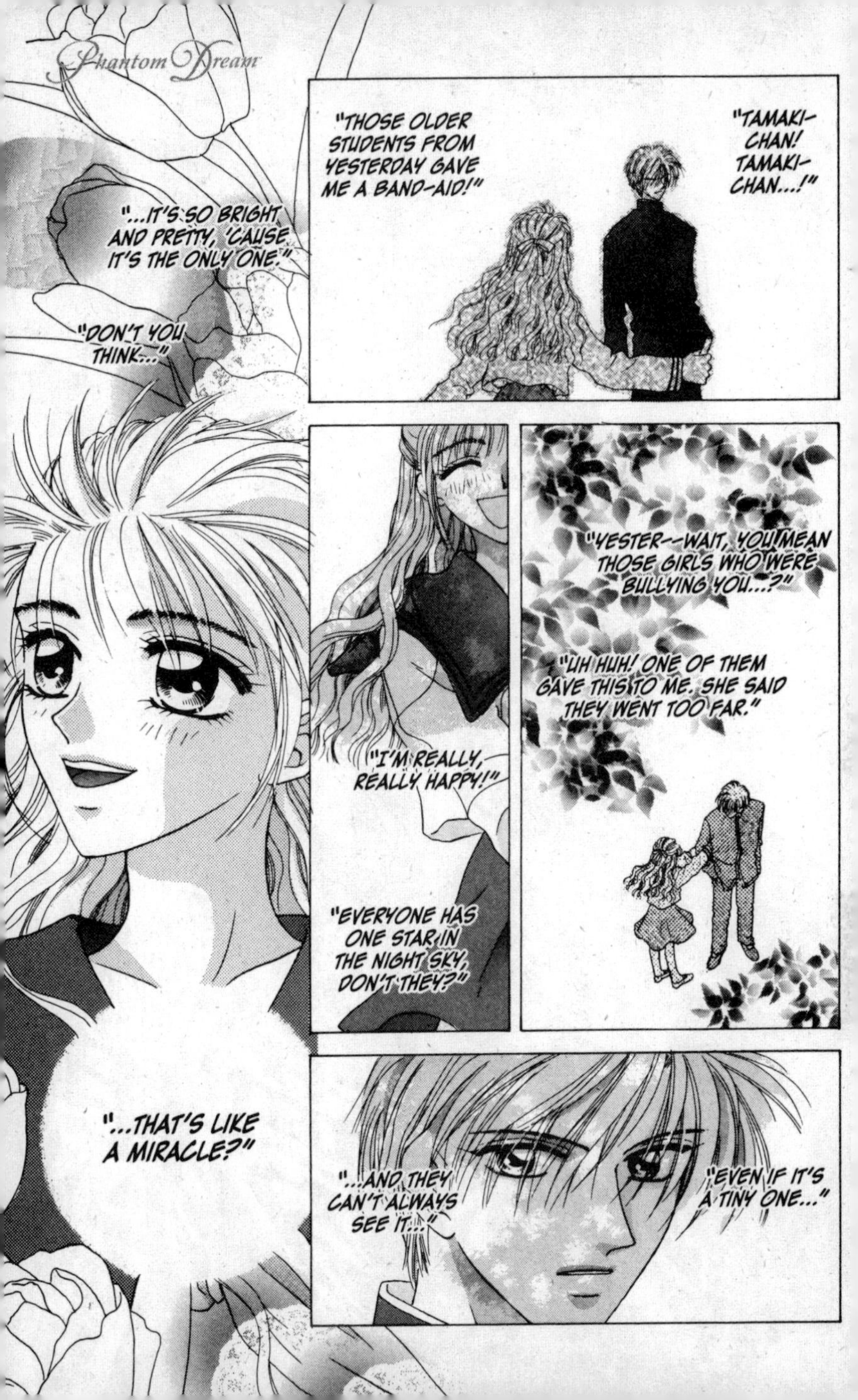
"TAMAKI-CHAN! TAMAKI-CHAN...!"
"THOSE OLDER STUDENTS FROM YESTERDAY GAVE ME A BAND-AID!"
"YESTER--WAIT, YOU MEAN THOSE GIRLS WHO WERE BULLYING YOU...?"
"UH HUH! ONE OF THEM GAVE THIS TO ME. SHE SAID THEY WENT TOO FAR."
"I'M REALLY, REALLY HAPPY!"
"EVERYONE HAS ONE STAR IN THE NIGHT SKY, DON'T THEY?"
"EVEN IF IT'S A TINY ONE..."
"...AND THEY CAN'T ALWAYS SEE IT..."
"...IT'S SO BRIGHT AND PRETTY, 'CAUSE IT'S THE ONLY ONE."
"DON'T YOU THINK..."
"...THAT'S LIKE A MIRACLE?"

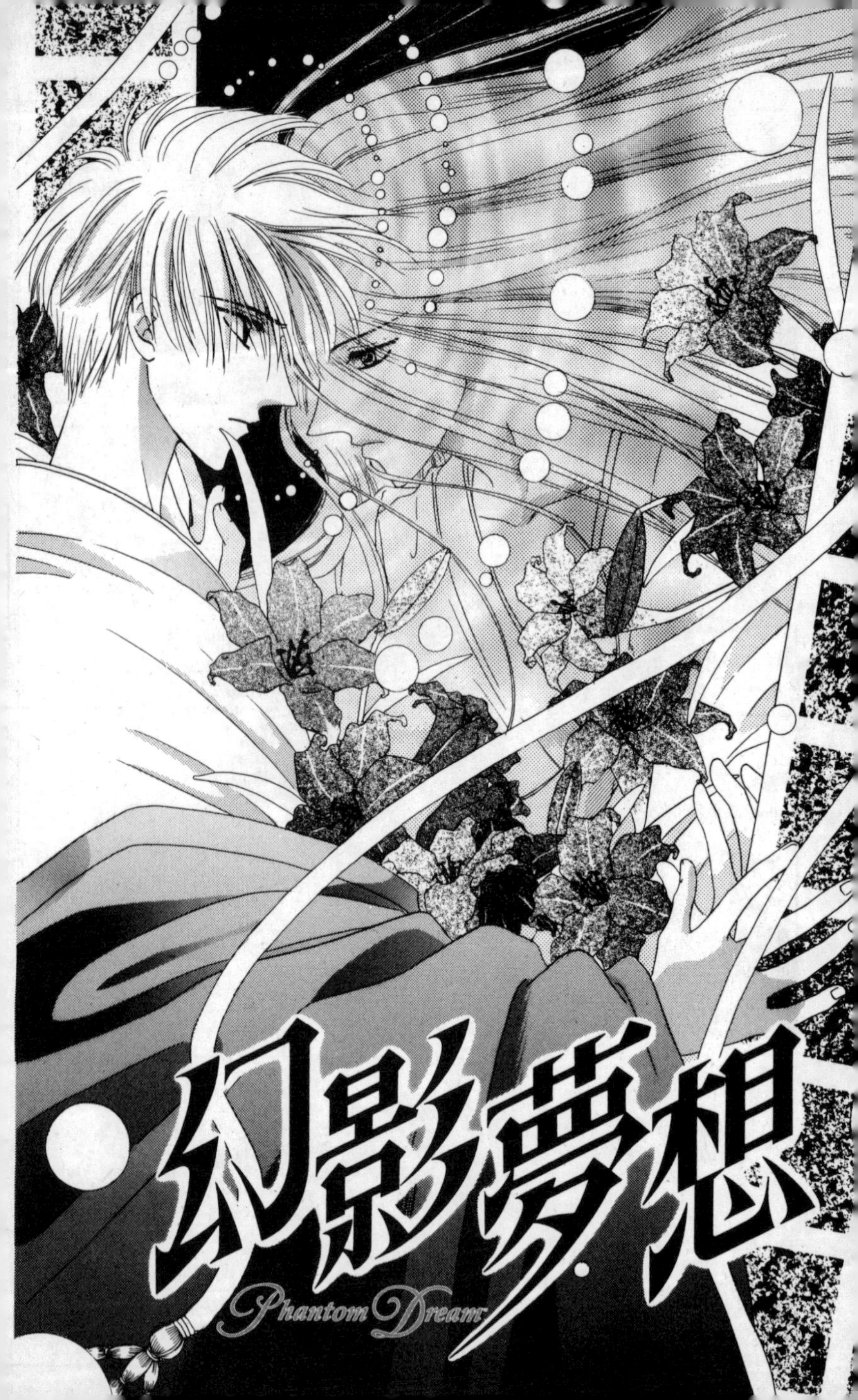
幻影夢想
Phantom Dream

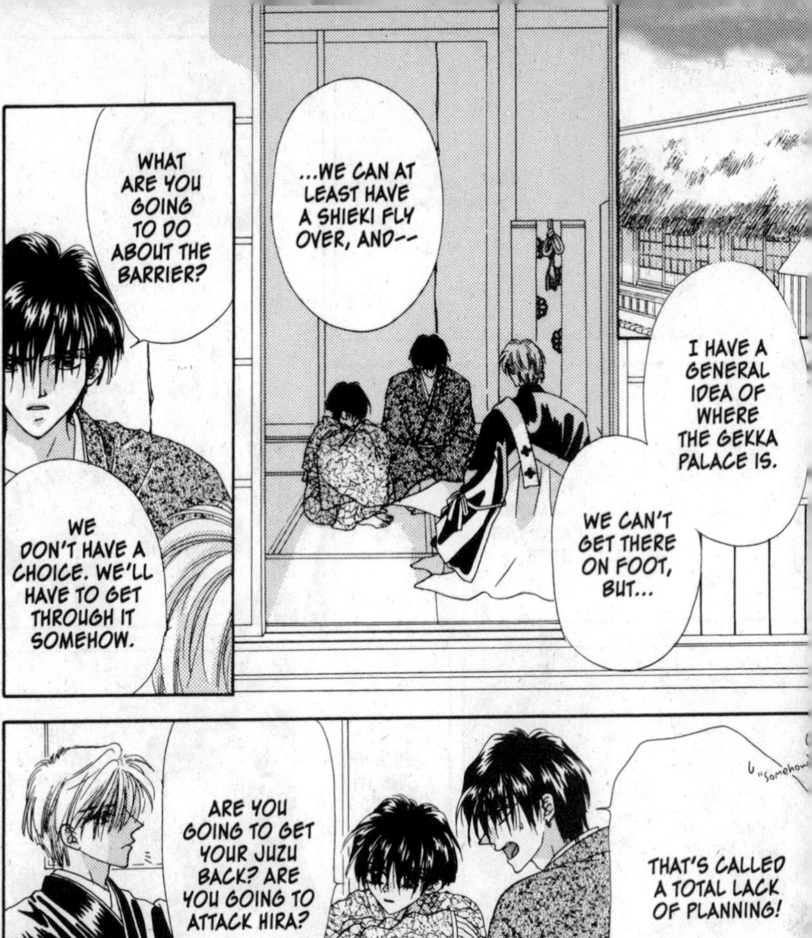
I HAVE A GENERAL IDEA OF WHERE THE GEKKA PALACE IS.
WE CAN'T GET THERE ON FOOT, BUT...
...WE CAN AT LEAST HAVE A SHIEKI FLY OVER, AND--
WHAT ARE YOU GOING TO DO ABOUT THE BARRIER?
WE DON'T HAVE A CHOICE. WE'LL HAVE TO GET THROUGH IT SOMEHOW.
"Somehow"
THAT'S CALLED A TOTAL LACK OF PLANNING!
ARE YOU GOING TO GET YOUR JUZU BACK? ARE YOU GOING TO ATTACK HIRA?

ULTRA SPECIAL *THINGS THAT DON'T MATTER III.*

Tamaki quit high school because of all the things that happened. That's the truth. (Asahi...who knows? [laughs]) Tokiwa and Migiri have taken temporary leaves of absence from school...probably. But Tamaki's the kind of person whose only hobby is sleeping, so he got to be smart (because he just keeps studying to pass the time). And he doesn't eat meat or fish! (Or ikura--see volume 1. Am I advertising?) He doesn't do it because Souetsu didn't...but look, now I'm explaining things about the main character even though we're already on the third volume. (Laughs) No, I can't seem to just write it into the story, so...sorry!

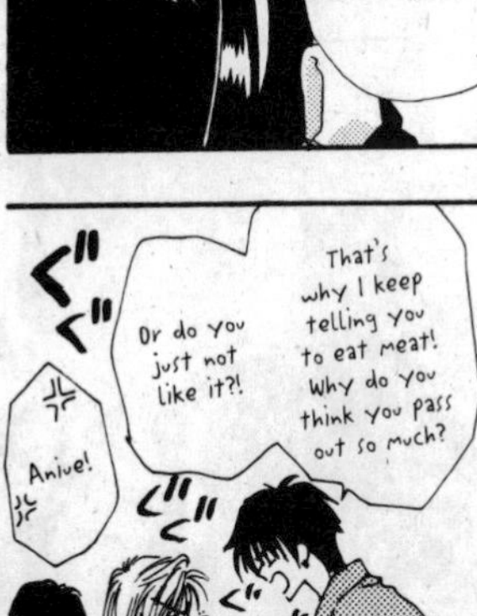
That's why I keep telling you to eat meat! Why do you think you pass out so much?
Or do you just not like it?!
Aniue!
Nose Pinch Attack

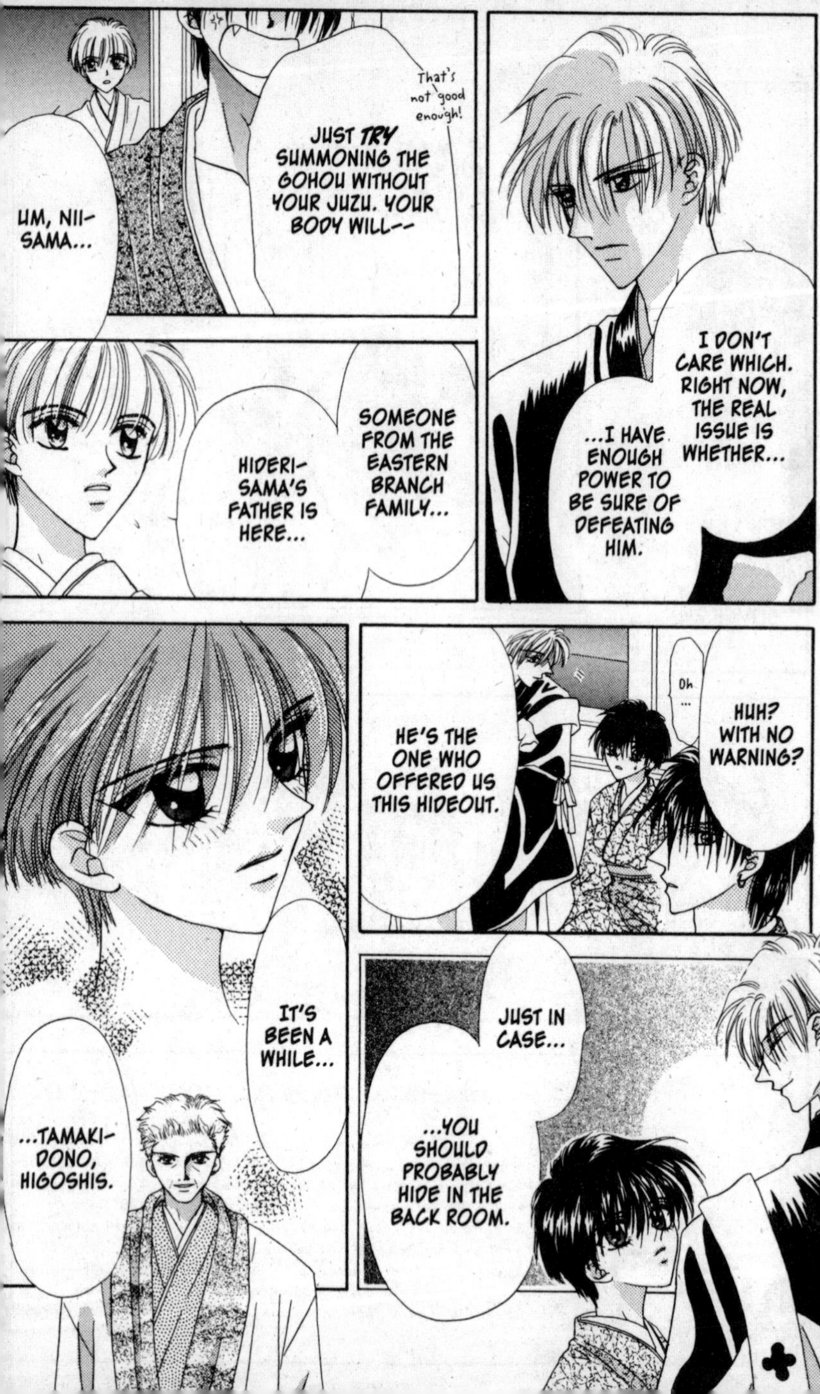
I DON'T CARE WHICH. RIGHT NOW, THE REAL ISSUE IS WHETHER...
...I HAVE ENOUGH POWER TO BE SURE OF DEFEATING HIM.
JUST TRY SUMMONING THE GOHOU WITHOUT YOUR JUZU. YOUR BODY WILL--
That's not good enough!
UM, NII-SAMA...
SOMEONE FROM THE EASTERN BRANCH FAMILY...
HIDERI-SAMA'S FATHER IS HERE...
HUH? WITH NO WARNING?
Oh...
HE'S THE ONE WHO OFFERED US THIS HIDEOUT.
JUST IN CASE...
...YOU SHOULD PROBABLY HIDE IN THE BACK ROOM.
IT'S BEEN A WHILE...
...TAMAKI-DONO, HIGOSHIS.

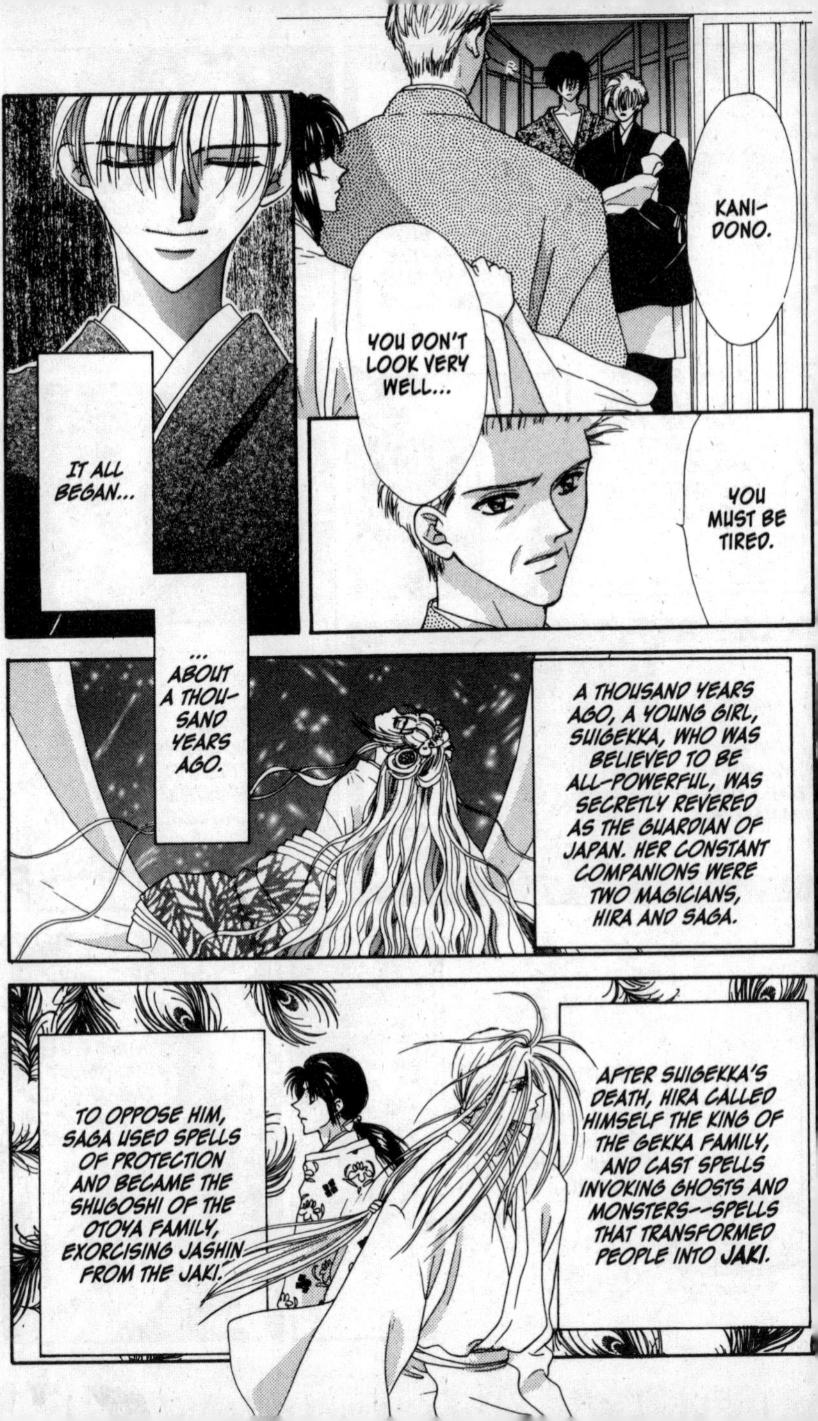
KANI-DONO.
YOU DON'T LOOK VERY WELL...
YOU MUST BE TIRED.
IT ALL BEGAN...
...ABOUT A THOUSAND YEARS AGO.
A THOUSAND YEARS AGO, A YOUNG GIRL, SUIGEKKA, WHO WAS BELIEVED TO BE ALL-POWERFUL, WAS SECRETLY REVERED AS THE GUARDIAN OF JAPAN. HER CONSTANT COMPANIONS WERE TWO MAGICIANS, HIRA AND SAGA.
AFTER SUIGEKKA'S DEATH, HIRA CALLED HIMSELF THE KING OF THE GEKKA FAMILY, AND CAST SPELLS INVOKING GHOSTS AND MONSTERS--SPELLS THAT TRANSFORMED PEOPLE INTO JAKI.
TO OPPOSE HIM, SAGA USED SPELLS OF PROTECTION AND BECAME THE SHUGOSHI OF THE OTOYA FAMILY, EXORCISING JASHIN FROM THE JAKI.

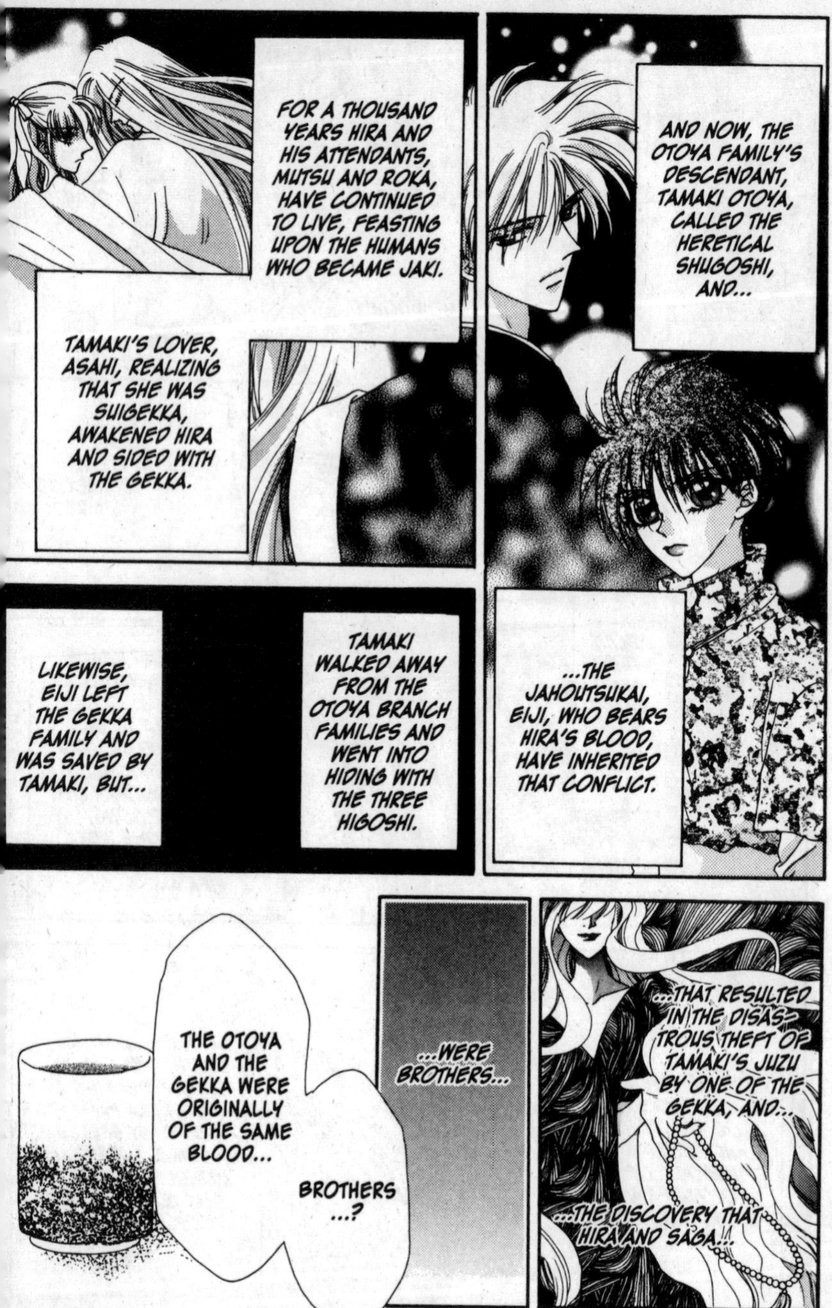
AND NOW, THE OTOYA FAMILY'S DESCENDANT, TAMAKI OTOYA, CALLED THE HERETICAL SHUGOSHI, AND...
...THE JAHOUTSUKAI, EIJI, WHO BEARS HIRA'S BLOOD, HAVE INHERITED THAT CONFLICT.
FOR A THOUSAND YEARS HIRA AND HIS ATTENDANTS, MUTSU AND ROKA, HAVE CONTINUED TO LIVE, FEASTING UPON THE HUMANS WHO BECAME JAKI.
TAMAKI'S LOVER, ASAHI, REALIZING THAT SHE WAS SUIGEKKA, AWAKENED HIRA AND SIDED WITH THE GEKKA.
TAMAKI WALKED AWAY FROM THE OTOYA BRANCH FAMILIES AND WENT INTO HIDING WITH THE THREE HIGOSHI.
LIKEWISE, EIJI LEFT THE GEKKA FAMILY AND WAS SAVED BY TAMAKI, BUT...
...THAT RESULTED IN THE DISASTROUS THEFT OF TAMAKI'S JUZU BY ONE OF THE GEKKA, AND...
...THE DISCOVERY THAT HIRA AND SAGA...!!
...WERE BROTHERS...
THE OTOYA AND THE GEKKA WERE ORIGINALLY OF THE SAME BLOOD...
BROTHERS ...?

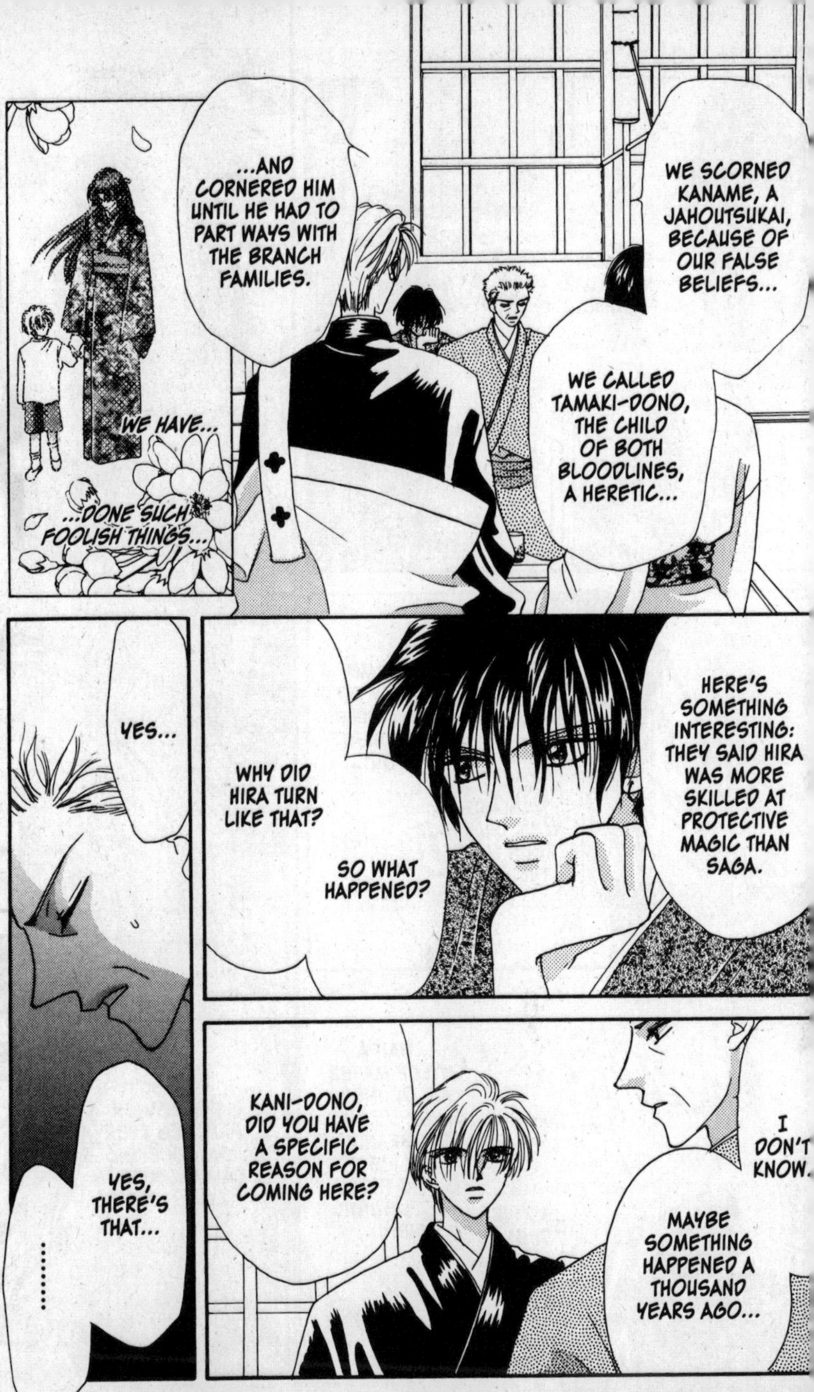
WE SCORNED KANAME, A JAHOUTSUKAI, BECAUSE OF OUR FALSE BELIEFS...
WE CALLED TAMAKI-DONO, THE CHILD OF BOTH BLOODLINES, A HERETIC...
...AND CORNERED HIM UNTIL HE HAD TO PART WAYS WITH THE BRANCH FAMILIES.
WE HAVE...
...DONE SUCH FOOLISH THINGS...
HERE'S SOMETHING INTERESTING: THEY SAID HIRA WAS MORE SKILLED AT PROTECTIVE MAGIC THAN SAGA.
WHY DID HIRA TURN LIKE THAT?
SO WHAT HAPPENED?
I DON'T KNOW.
MAYBE SOMETHING HAPPENED A THOUSAND YEARS AGO...
KANI-DONO, DID YOU HAVE A SPECIFIC REASON FOR COMING HERE?
YES...
YES, THERE'S THAT...
......

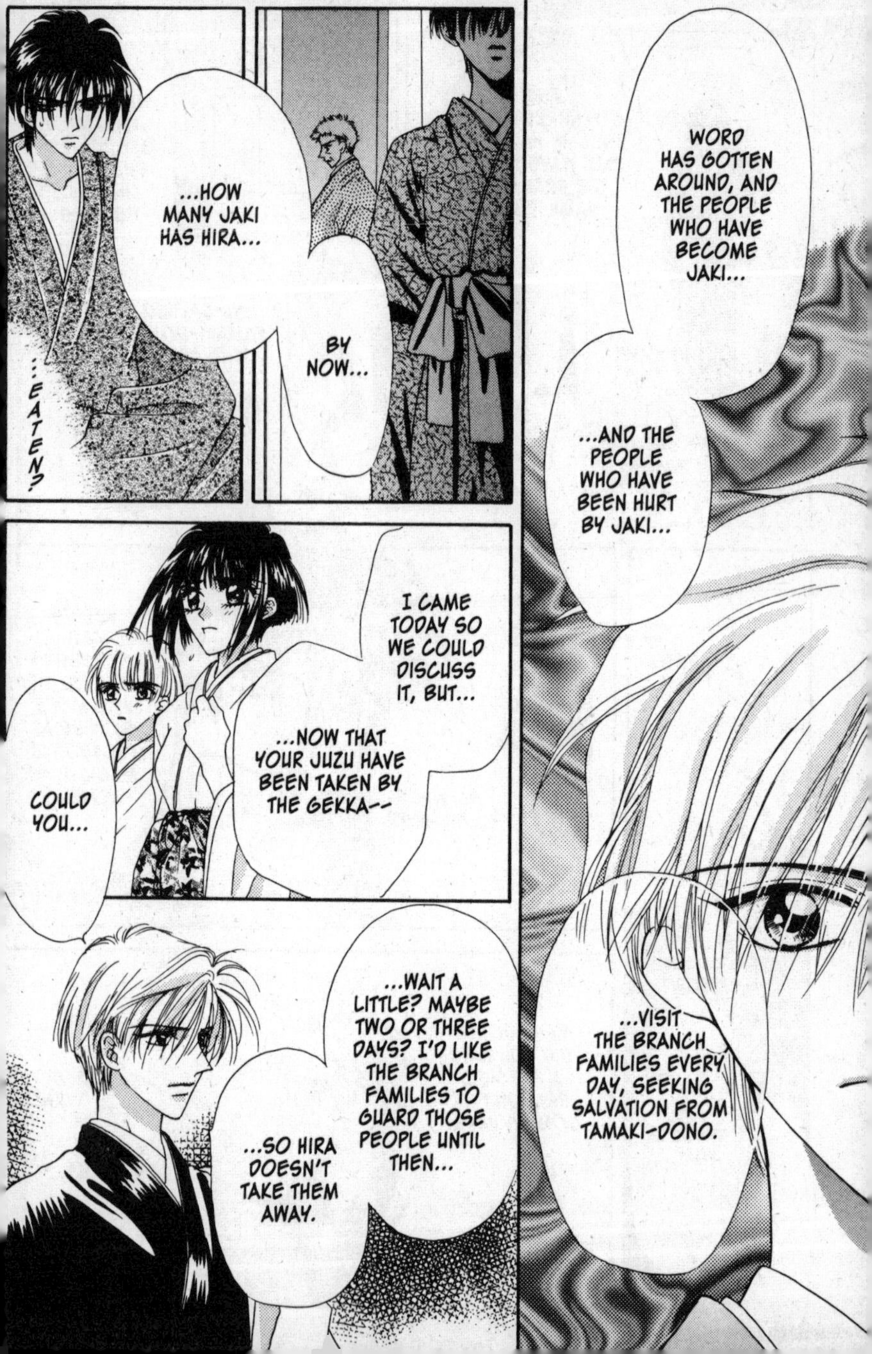
WORD HAS GOTTEN AROUND, AND THE PEOPLE WHO HAVE BECOME JAKI...
...AND THE PEOPLE WHO HAVE BEEN HURT BY JAKI...
...VISIT THE BRANCH FAMILIES EVERY DAY, SEEKING SALVATION FROM TAMAKI-DONO.
...HOW MANY JAKI HAS HIRA...
BY NOW...
...EATEN?
I CAME TODAY SO WE COULD DISCUSS IT, BUT...
...NOW THAT YOUR JUZU HAVE BEEN TAKEN BY THE GEKKA--
COULD YOU...
...WAIT A LITTLE? MAYBE TWO OR THREE DAYS? I'D LIKE THE BRANCH FAMILIES TO GUARD THOSE PEOPLE UNTIL THEN...
...SO HIRA DOESN'T TAKE THEM AWAY.

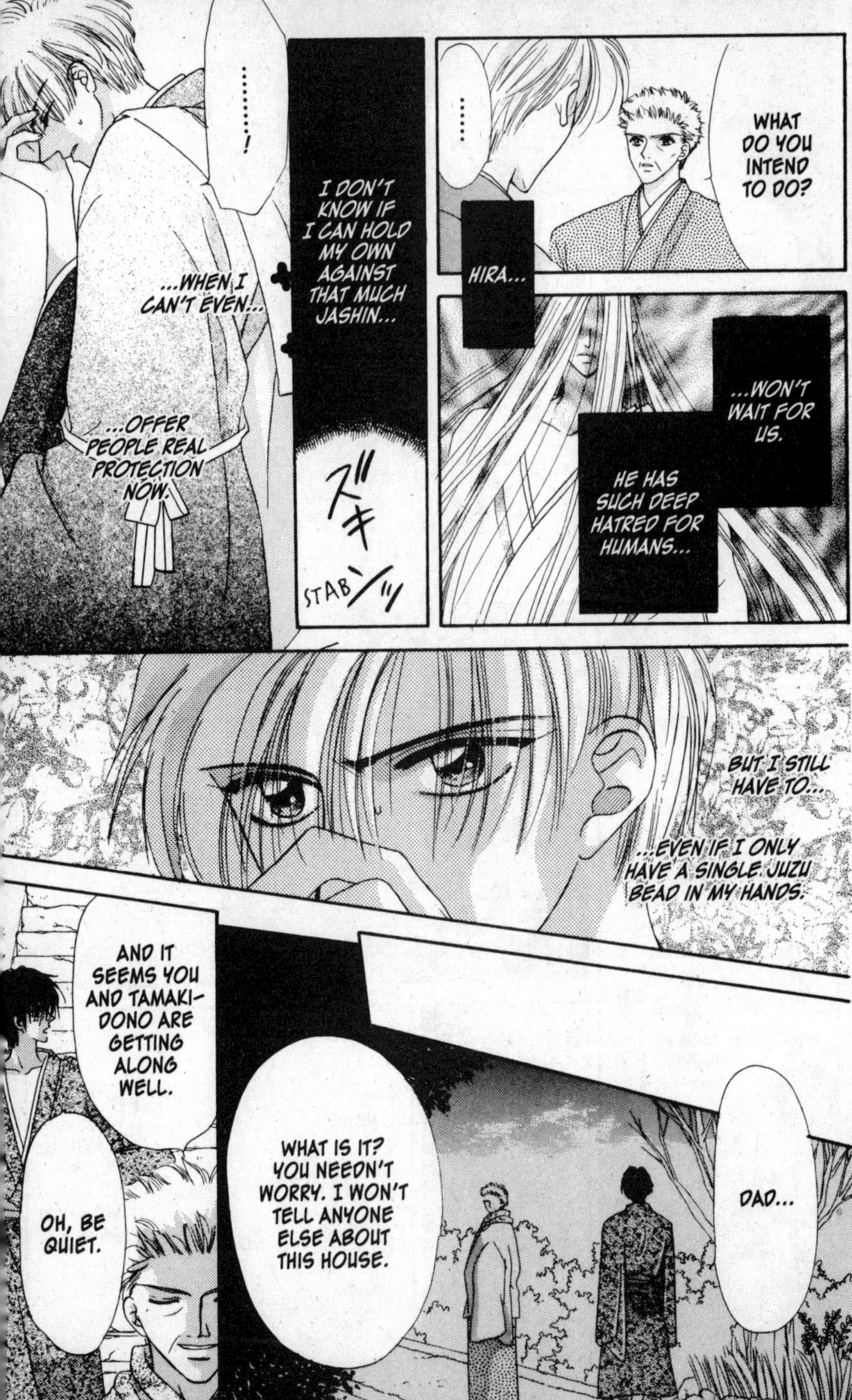

WHAT DO YOU INTEND TO DO?
......
HIRA...
...WON'T WAIT FOR US.
HE HAS SUCH DEEP HATRED FOR HUMANS...
I DON'T KNOW IF I CAN HOLD MY OWN AGAINST THAT MUCH JASHIN...
ズキ
STAB ンッ
......!
...WHEN I CAN'T EVEN...
...OFFER PEOPLE REAL PROTECTION NOW.
BUT I STILL HAVE TO...
...EVEN IF I ONLY HAVE A SINGLE JUZU BEAD IN MY HANDS.
DAD...
WHAT IS IT? YOU NEEDN'T WORRY. I WON'T TELL ANYONE ELSE ABOUT THIS HOUSE.
AND IT SEEMS YOU AND TAMAKI-DONO ARE GETTING ALONG WELL.
OH, BE QUIET.

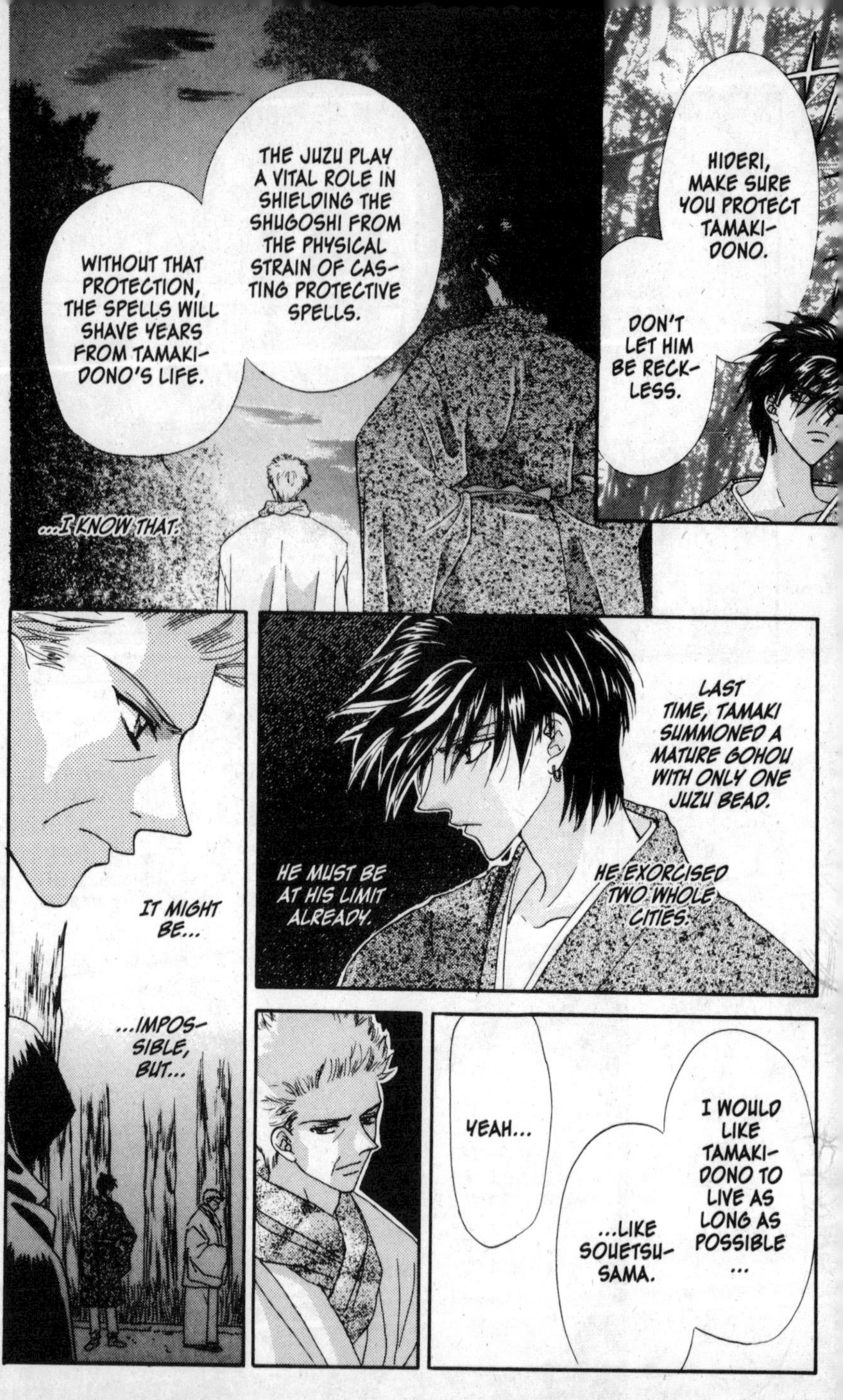
HIDERI, MAKE SURE YOU PROTECT TAMAKI-DONO.
DON'T LET HIM BE RECKLESS.
THE JUZU PLAY A VITAL ROLE IN SHIELDING THE SHUGOSHI FROM THE PHYSICAL STRAIN OF CASTING PROTECTIVE SPELLS.
WITHOUT THAT PROTECTION, THE SPELLS WILL SHAVE YEARS FROM TAMAKI-DONO'S LIFE.
...I KNOW THAT.
LAST TIME, TAMAKI SUMMONED A MATURE GOHOU WITH ONLY ONE JUZU BEAD.
HE EXORCISED TWO WHOLE CITIES.
HE MUST BE AT HIS LIMIT ALREADY.
IT MIGHT BE...
...IMPOSSIBLE, BUT...
I WOULD LIKE TAMAKI-DONO TO LIVE AS LONG AS POSSIBLE...
...LIKE SOUETSU-SAMA.
YEAH...

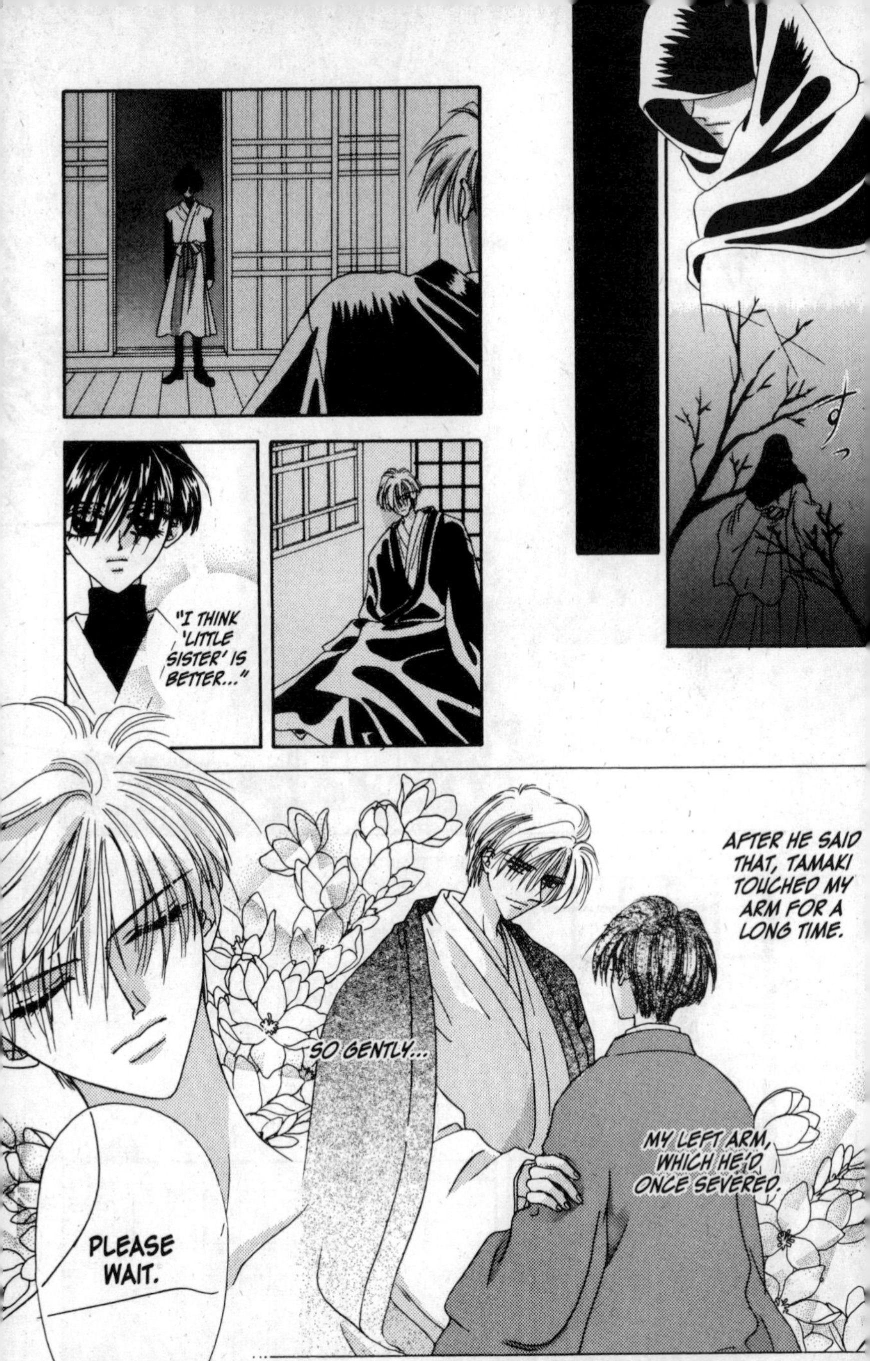
"I THINK 'LITTLE SISTER' IS BETTER..."
AFTER HE SAID THAT, TAMAKI TOUCHED MY ARM FOR A LONG TIME.
SO GENTLY...
MY LEFT ARM, WHICH HE'D ONCE SEVERED.
PLEASE WAIT.

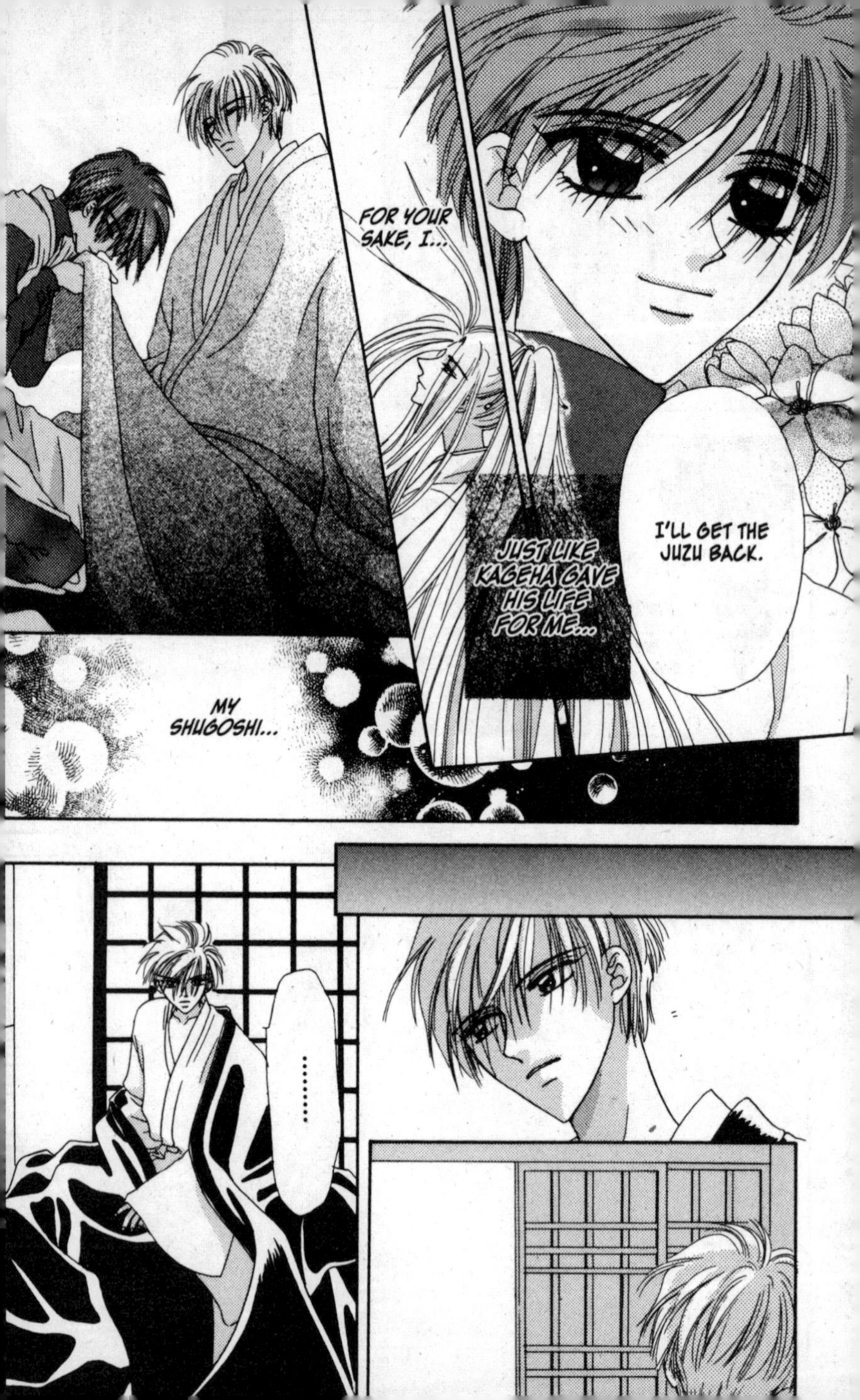
I'LL GET THE JUZU BACK.
JUST LIKE KAGEHA GAVE HIS LIFE FOR ME...
FOR YOUR SAKE, I...
MY SHUGOSHI...
......

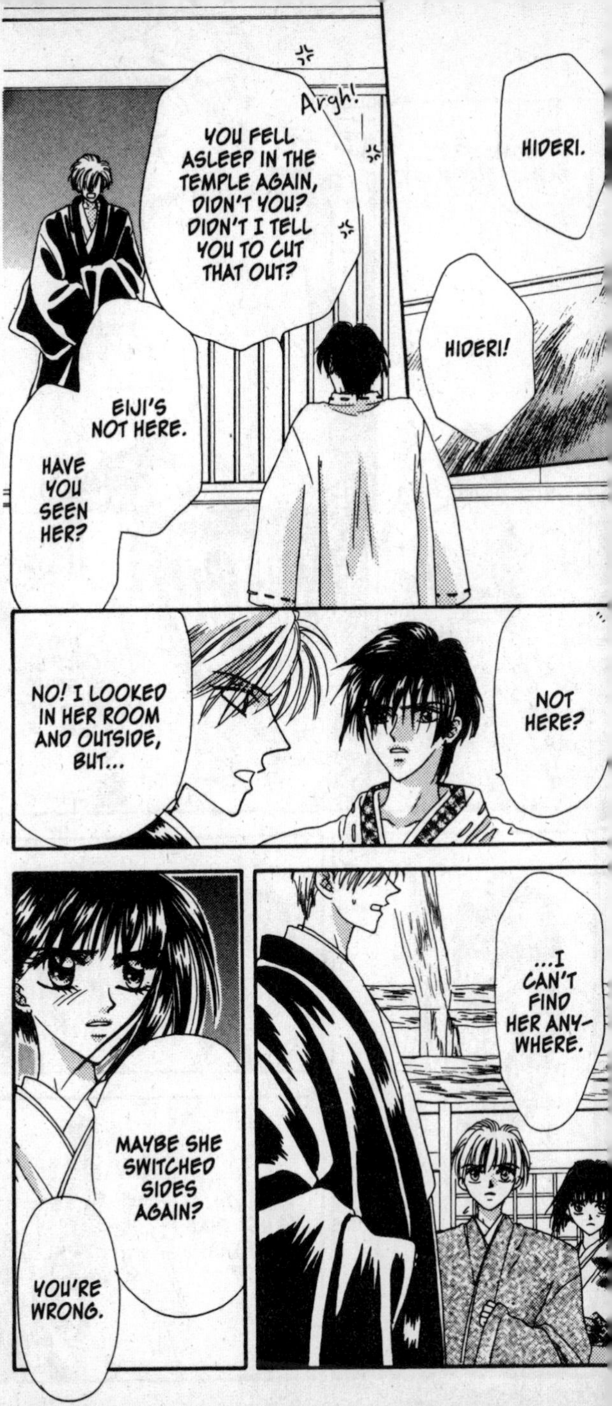
HIDERI.
HIDERI!
Argh!
YOU FELL ASLEEP IN THE TEMPLE AGAIN, DIDN'T YOU? DIDN'T I TELL YOU TO CUT THAT OUT?
EIJI'S NOT HERE.
HAVE YOU SEEN HER?
NOT HERE?
NO! I LOOKED IN HER ROOM AND OUTSIDE, BUT...
...I CAN'T FIND HER ANY-WHERE.
MAYBE SHE SWITCHED SIDES AGAIN?
YOU'RE WRONG.

Scroll Five

Everyone, do you remember your dreams? I mean, the dreams you have when you're asleep. I have a lot of similar dreams, usually about riding a train or bus and never getting where I want to go. Or I'm traveling and staying at a creepy hotel. Or I can't go home. Or I even go to school, of all things. Stuff like that. In short, I have a lot of nightmares. (laughs) But the thing is, I never make it to where I want to go, or I wind up somewhere scary. Why do you think that is? It makes me want to get my dreams analyzed or something. I vaguely know why I'm having these dreams, though. And every once in a while I do have a good one. Once I had a very happy dream where I was with Oyamada-san (from Cornelius), and we sat and watched the aurora borealis together...

My dreams have color and smells, and I can even feel things!

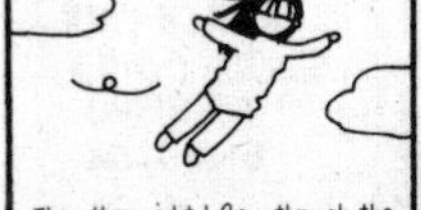

The other night I flew through the sky. I hadn't done that in a while.

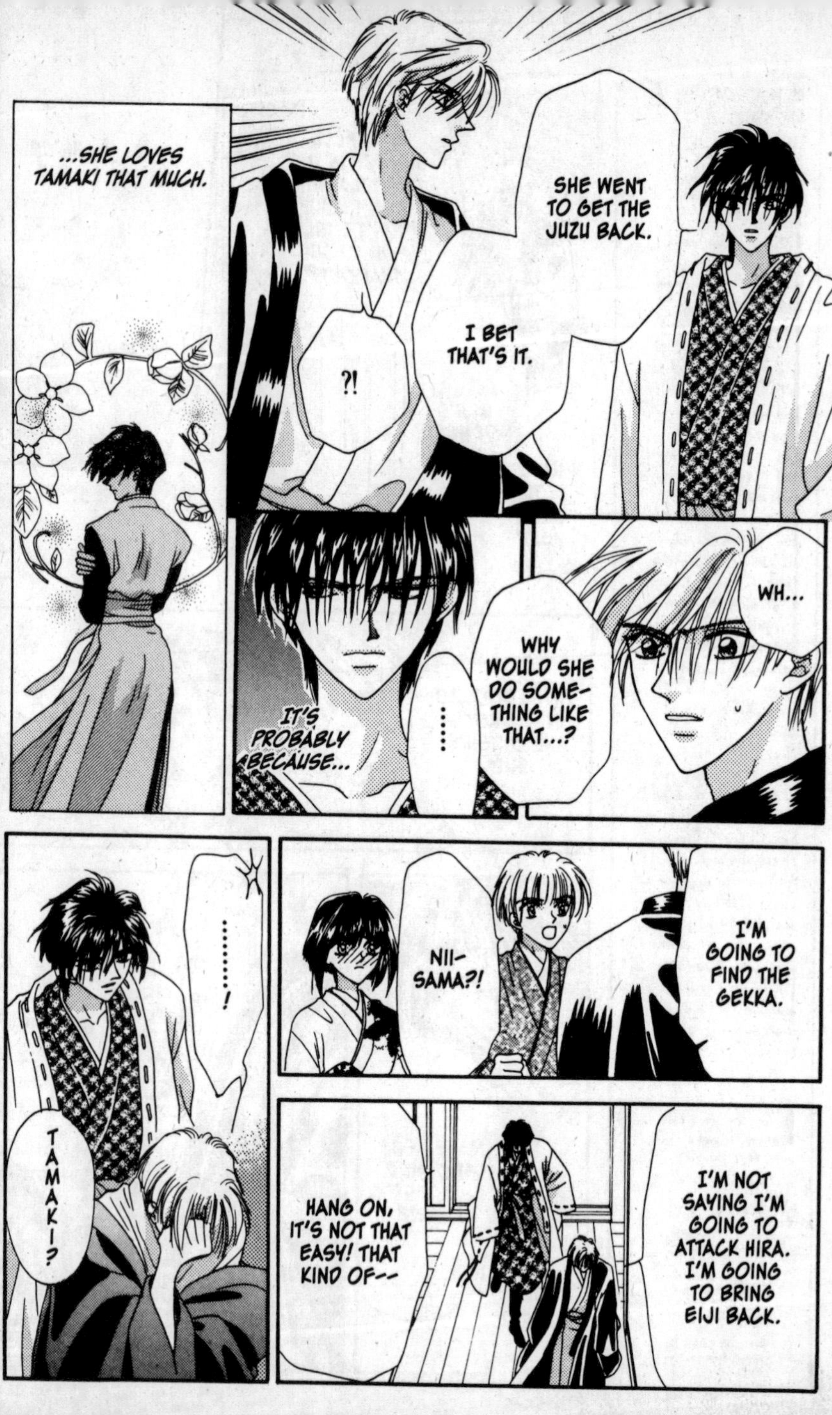
SHE WENT TO GET THE JUZU BACK.
I BET THAT'S IT.
?!
WH...
WHY WOULD SHE DO SOME-THING LIKE THAT...?
......
IT'S PROBABLY BECAUSE...
...SHE LOVES TAMAKI THAT MUCH.
I'M GOING TO FIND THE GEKKA.
NII-SAMA?!
I'M NOT SAYING I'M GOING TO ATTACK HIRA. I'M GOING TO BRING EIJI BACK.
HANG ON, IT'S NOT THAT EASY! THAT KIND OF--
......!
TAMAKI?

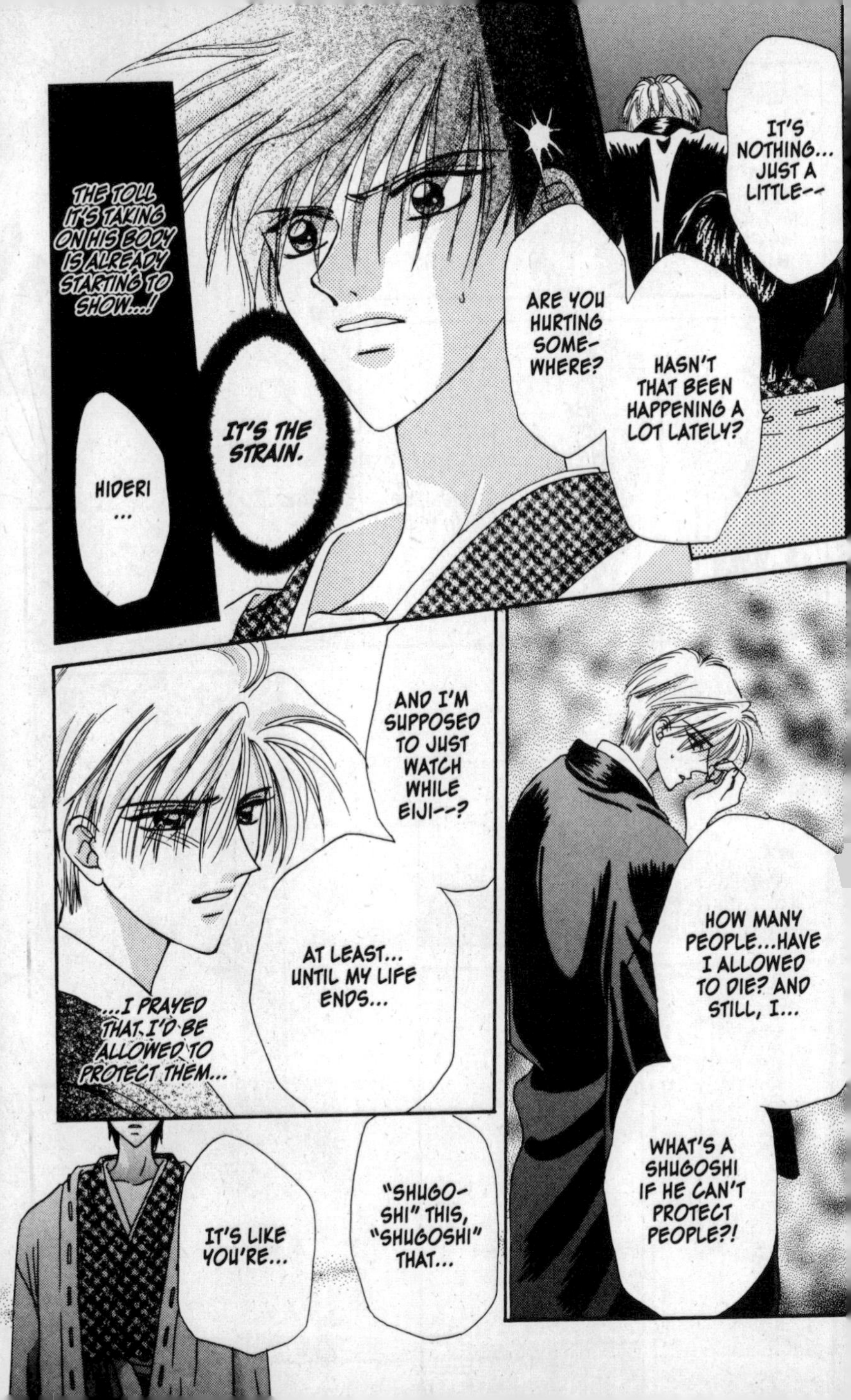
IT'S NOTHING... JUST A LITTLE--
ARE YOU HURTING SOME-WHERE?
HASN'T THAT BEEN HAPPENING A LOT LATELY?
IT'S THE STRAIN.
THE TOLL IT'S TAKING ON HIS BODY IS ALREADY STARTING TO SHOW...!
HIDERI...
HOW MANY PEOPLE...HAVE I ALLOWED TO DIE? AND STILL, I...
WHAT'S A SHUGOSHI IF HE CAN'T PROTECT PEOPLE?!
AND I'M SUPPOSED TO JUST WATCH WHILE EIJI--?
AT LEAST... UNTIL MY LIFE ENDS...
...I PRAYED THAT I'D BE ALLOWED TO PROTECT THEM...
"SHUGO-SHI" THIS, "SHUGOSHI" THAT...
IT'S LIKE YOU'RE...

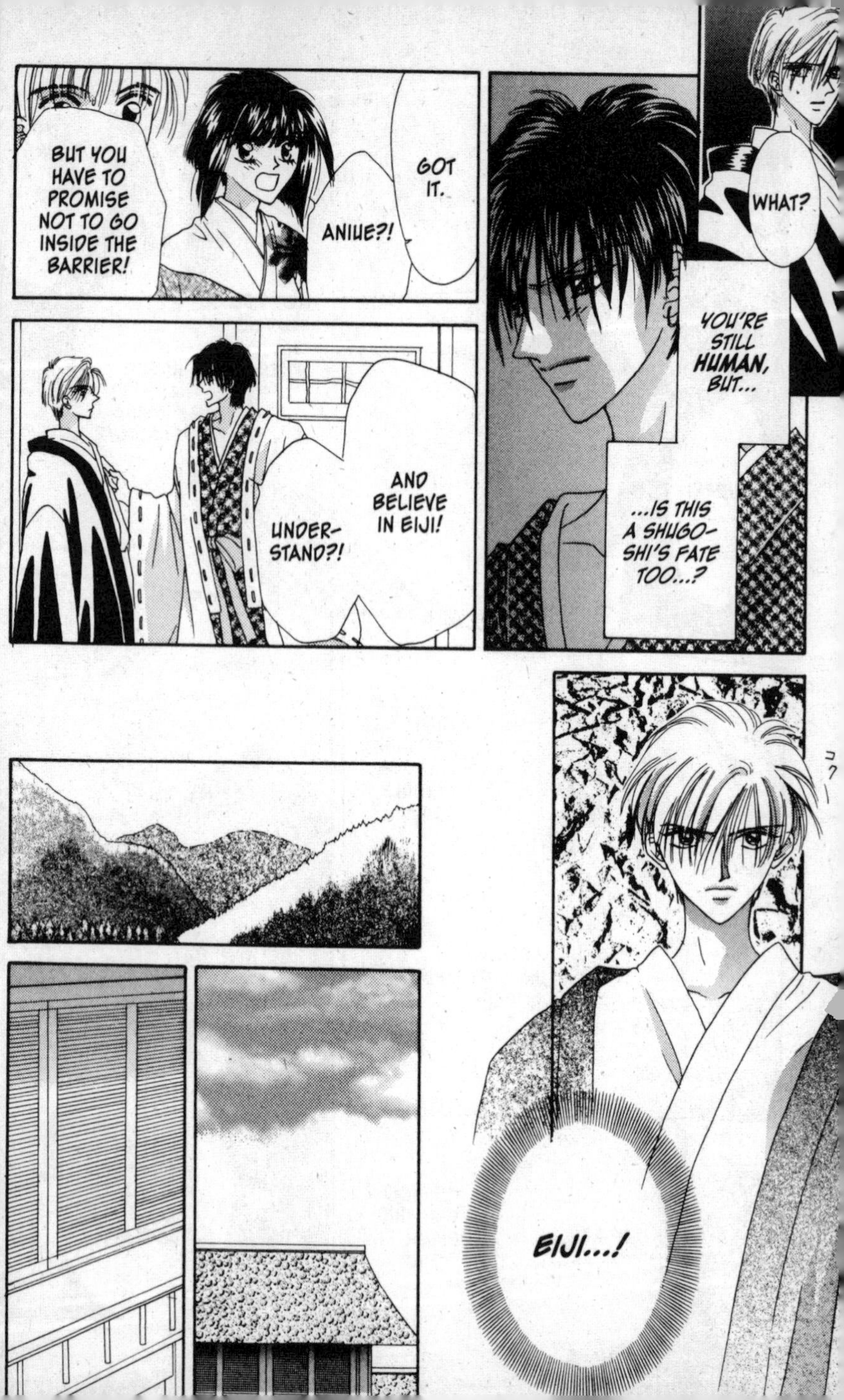
WHAT?
YOU'RE STILL HUMAN, BUT...
...IS THIS A SHUGO-SHI'S FATE TOO...?
GOT IT.
ANIUE?!
BUT YOU HAVE TO PROMISE NOT TO GO INSIDE THE BARRIER!
AND BELIEVE IN EIJI!
UNDER-STAND?!
EIJI...!

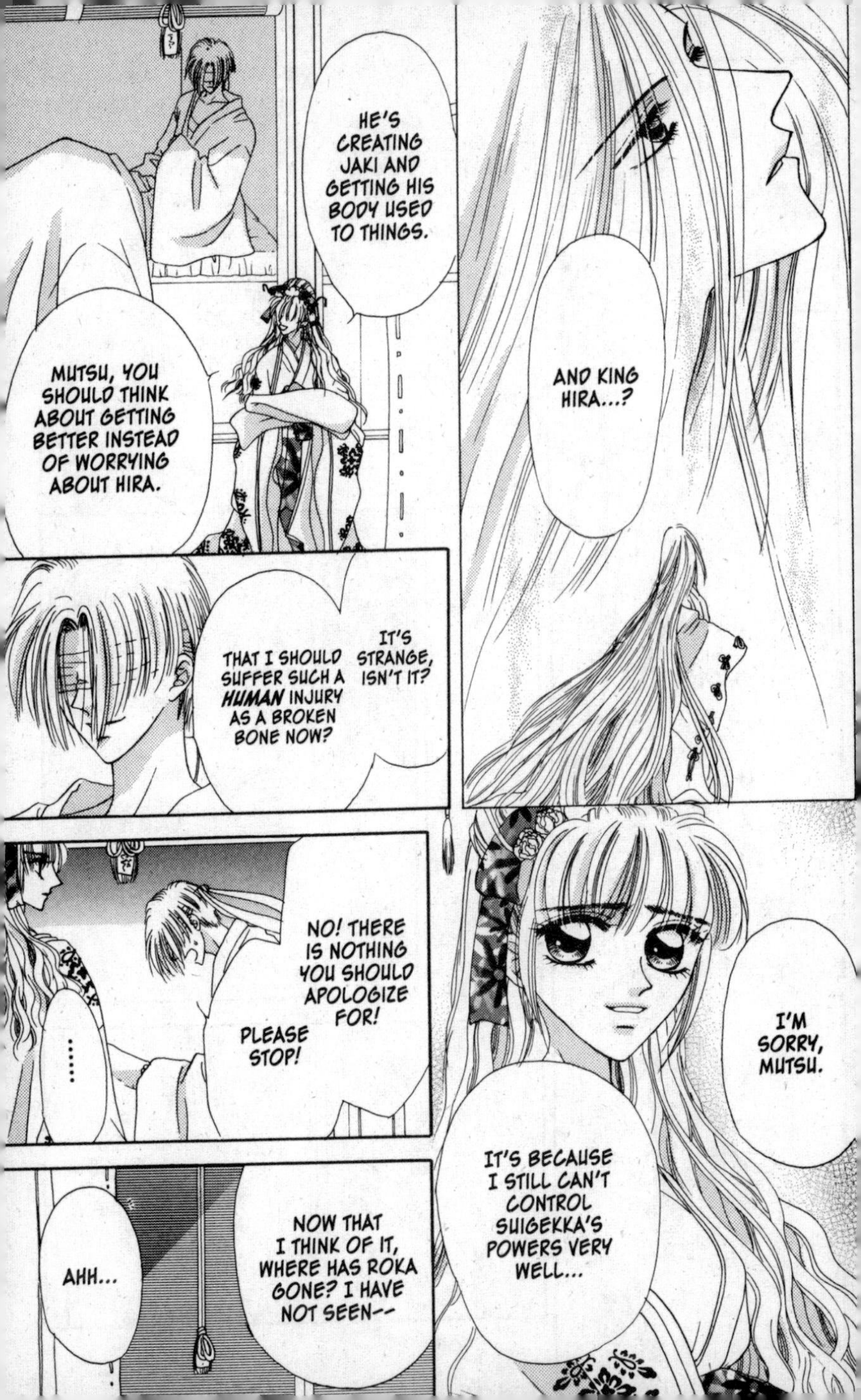
AND KING HIRA...?
HE'S CREATING JAKI AND GETTING HIS BODY USED TO THINGS.
MUTSU, YOU SHOULD THINK ABOUT GETTING BETTER INSTEAD OF WORRYING ABOUT HIRA.
IT'S STRANGE, ISN'T IT?
THAT I SHOULD SUFFER SUCH A *HUMAN* INJURY AS A BROKEN BONE NOW?
I'M SORRY, MUTSU.
IT'S BECAUSE I STILL CAN'T CONTROL SUIGEKKA'S POWERS VERY WELL...
NO! THERE IS NOTHING YOU SHOULD APOLOGIZE FOR!
PLEASE STOP!
......
NOW THAT I THINK OF IT, WHERE HAS ROKA GONE? I HAVE NOT SEEN--
AHH...

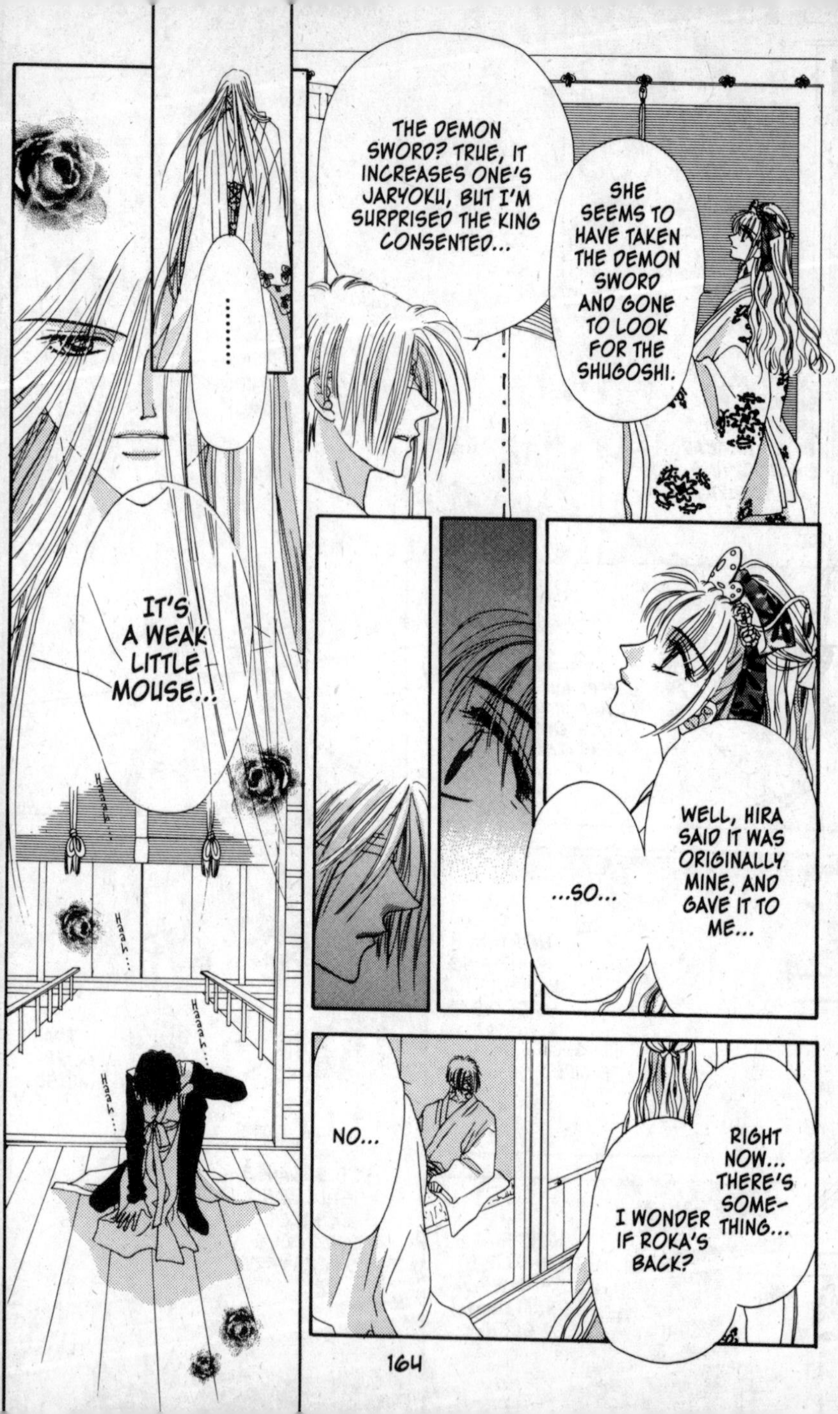
SHE SEEMS TO HAVE TAKEN THE DEMON SWORD AND GONE TO LOOK FOR THE SHUGOSHI.
THE DEMON SWORD? TRUE, IT INCREASES ONE'S JARYOKU, BUT I'M SURPRISED THE KING CONSENTED...
WELL, HIRA SAID IT WAS ORIGINALLY MINE, AND GAVE IT TO ME...
...SO...
RIGHT NOW... THERE'S SOME-THING...
I WONDER IF ROKA'S BACK?
NO...
......
IT'S A WEAK LITTLE MOUSE...
Haaah...
Haah...
Haaah...
Haah...

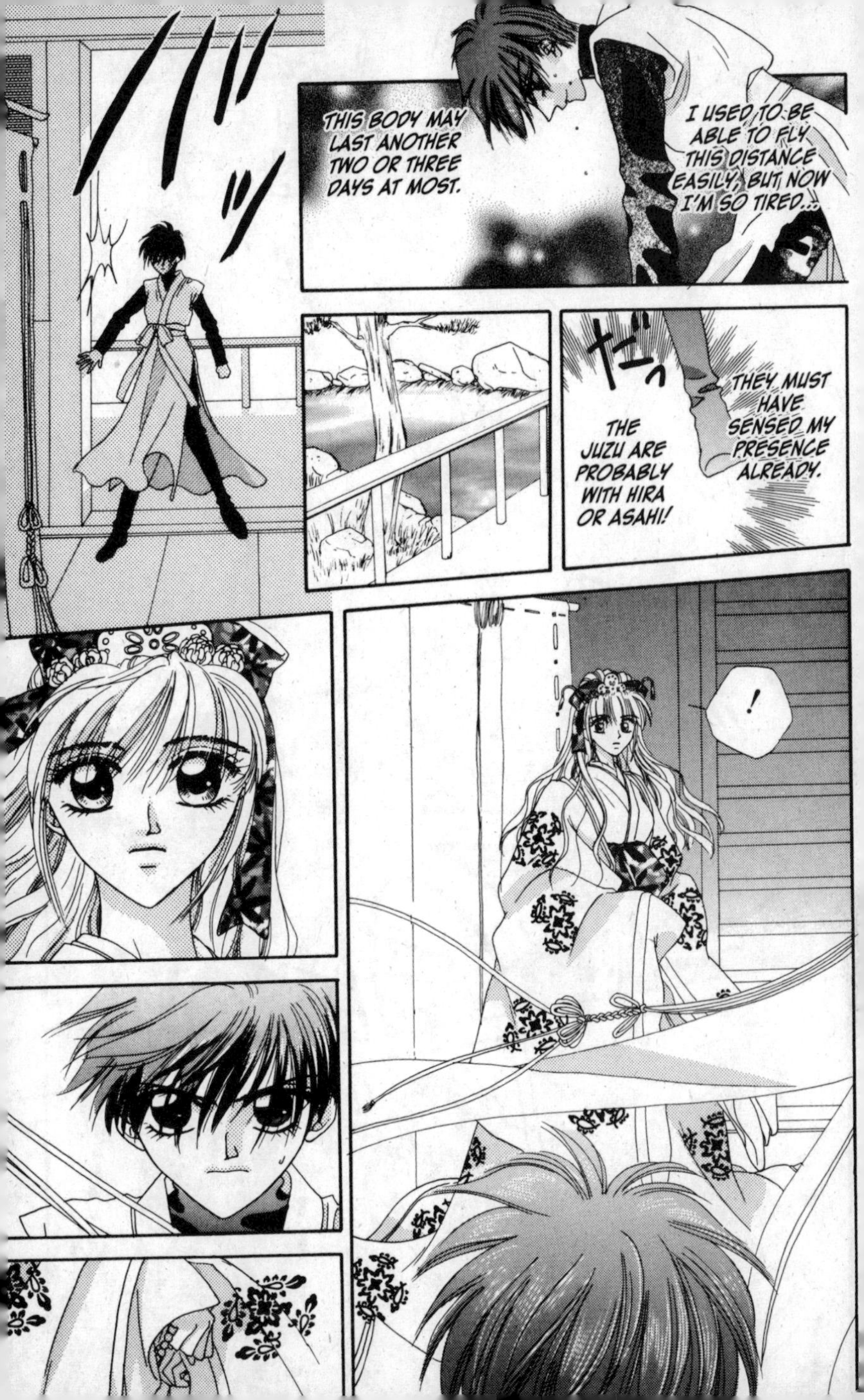

I USED TO BE ABLE TO FLY THIS DISTANCE EASILY, BUT NOW I'M SO TIRED...
THIS BODY MAY LAST ANOTHER TWO OR THREE DAYS AT MOST.
THEY MUST HAVE SENSED MY PRESENCE ALREADY.
THE JUZU ARE PROBABLY WITH HIRA OR ASAHI!
!

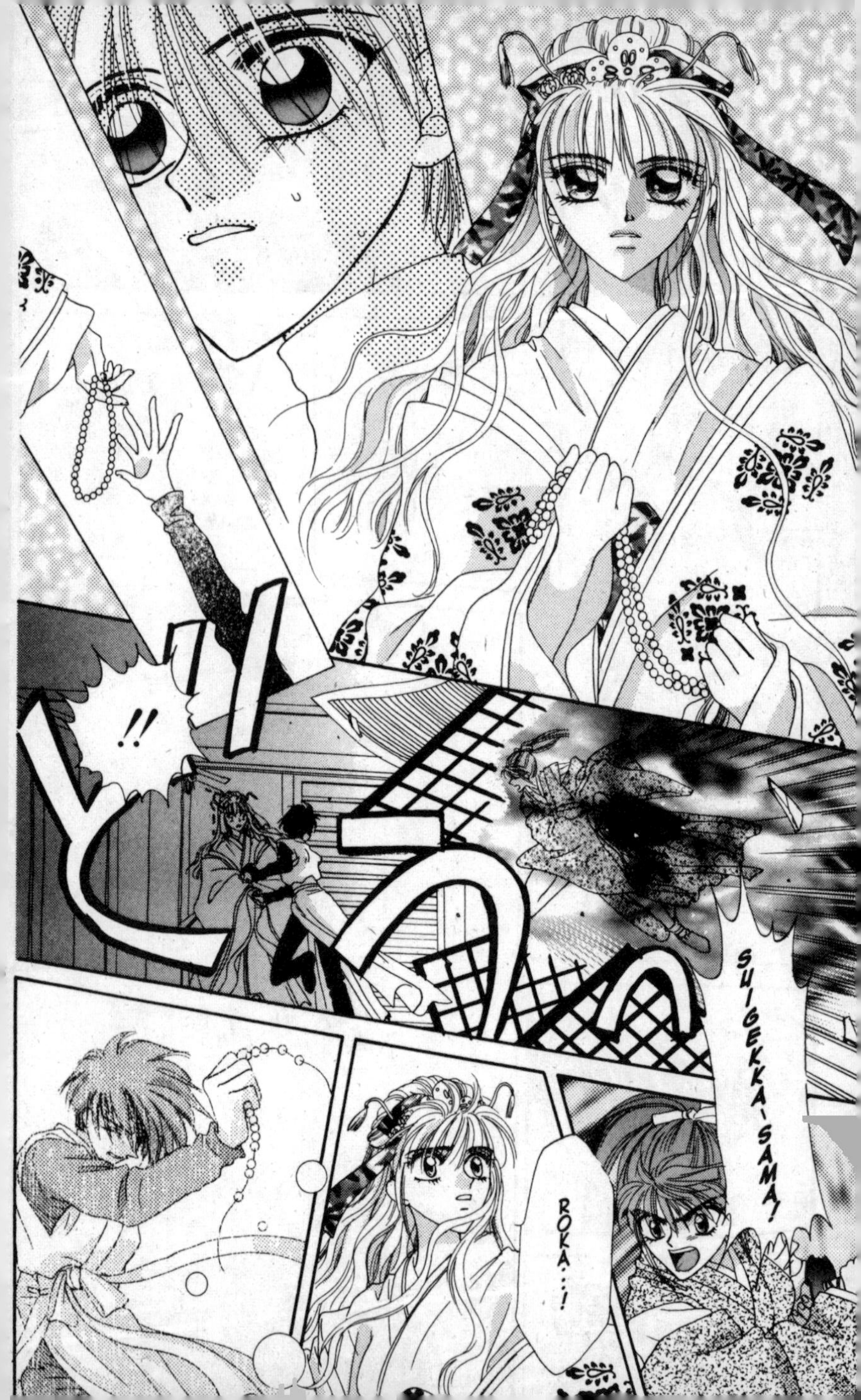
!!
SUIGEKKA-SAMA!
ROKA...!

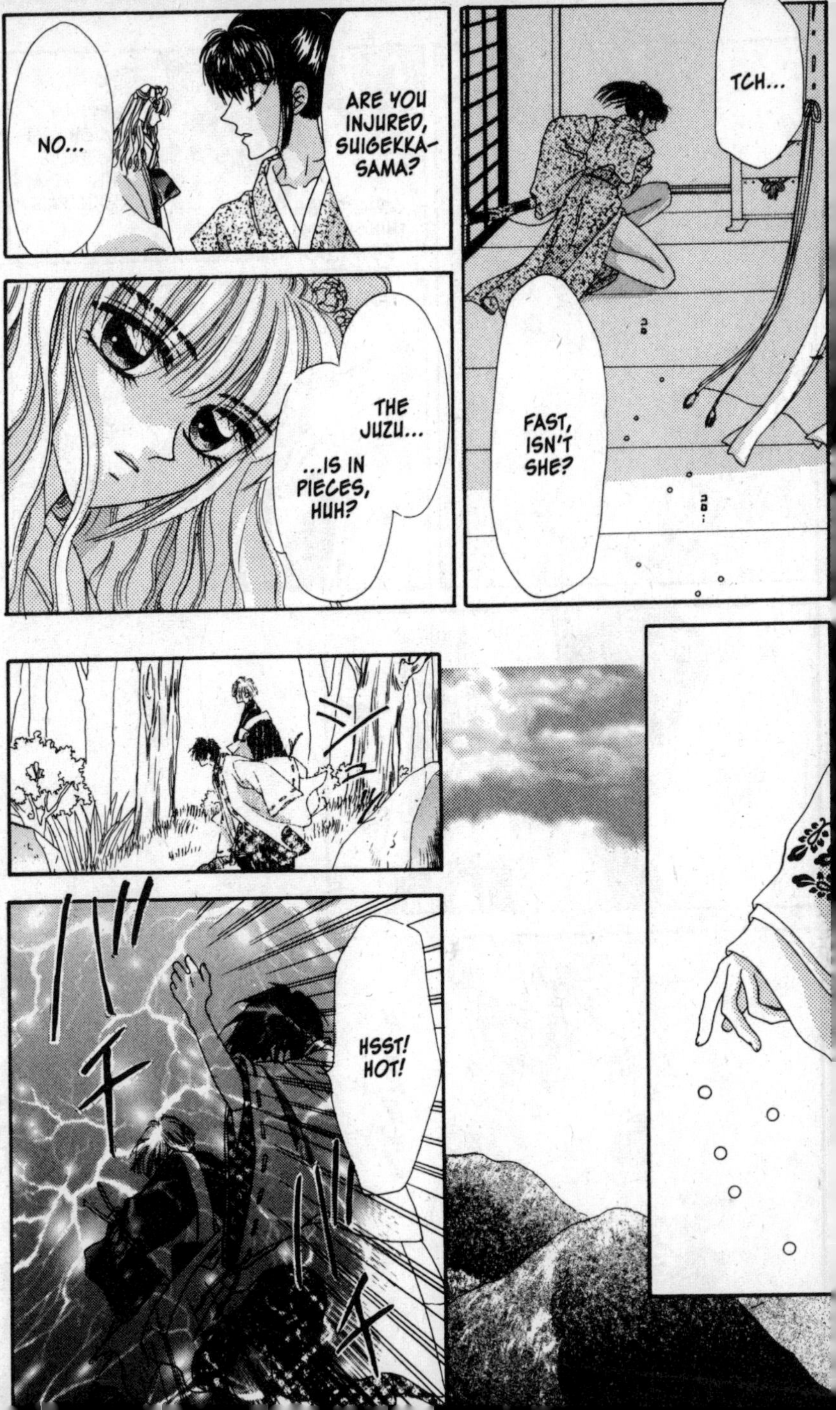
TCH...
FAST, ISN'T SHE?
ARE YOU INJURED, SUIGEKKA-SAMA?
NO...
THE JUZU...
...IS IN PIECES, HUH?
HSST! HOT!

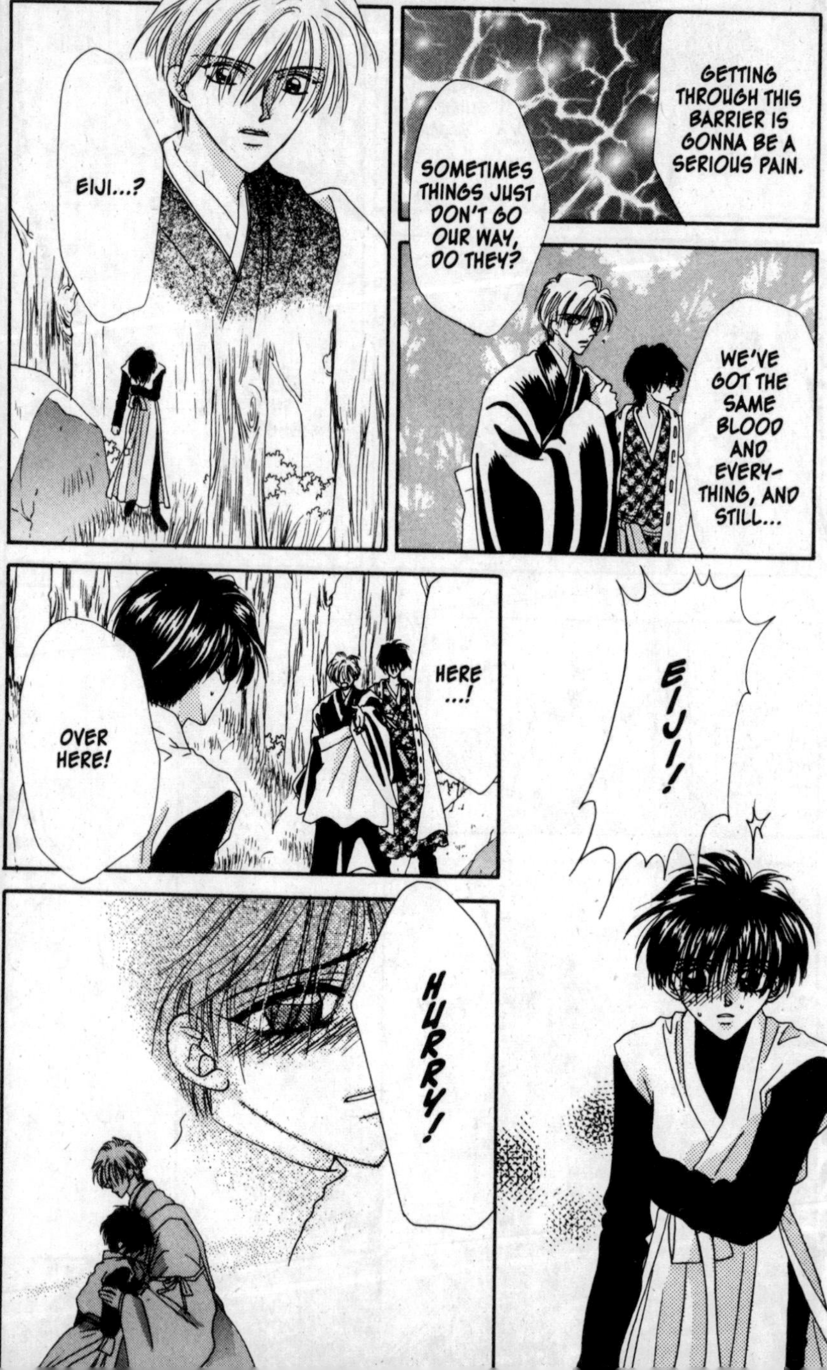
GETTING THROUGH THIS BARRIER IS GONNA BE A SERIOUS PAIN.
SOMETIMES THINGS JUST DON'T GO OUR WAY, DO THEY?
WE'VE GOT THE SAME BLOOD AND EVERY-THING, AND STILL...
EIJI...?
EIJI!!
HERE ...!
OVER HERE!
HURRY!

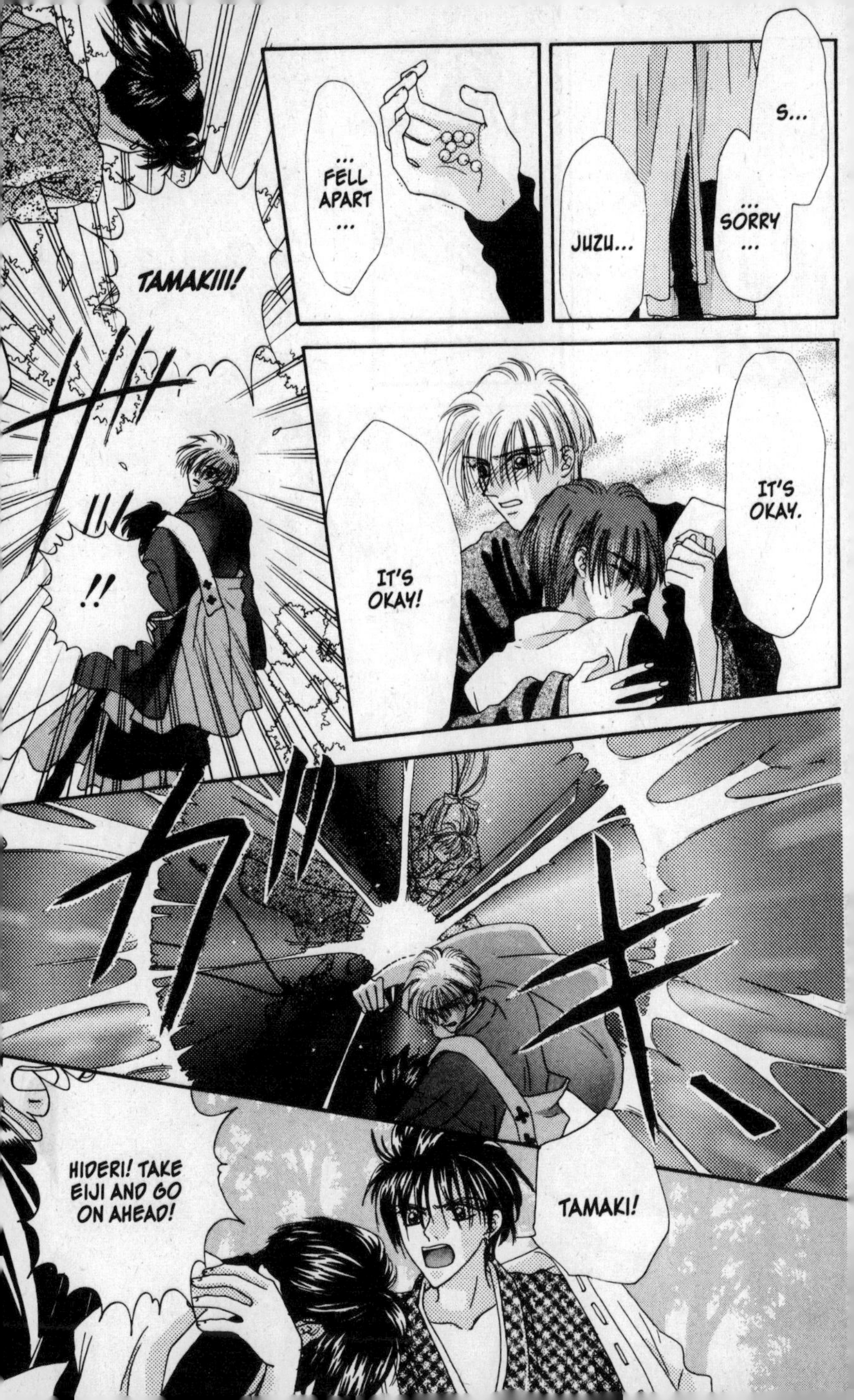
S...
...SORRY...
JUZU...
...FELL APART...
IT'S OKAY.
IT'S OKAY!
TAMAKIII!
!!
TAMAKI!
HIDERI! TAKE EIJI AND GO ON AHEAD!

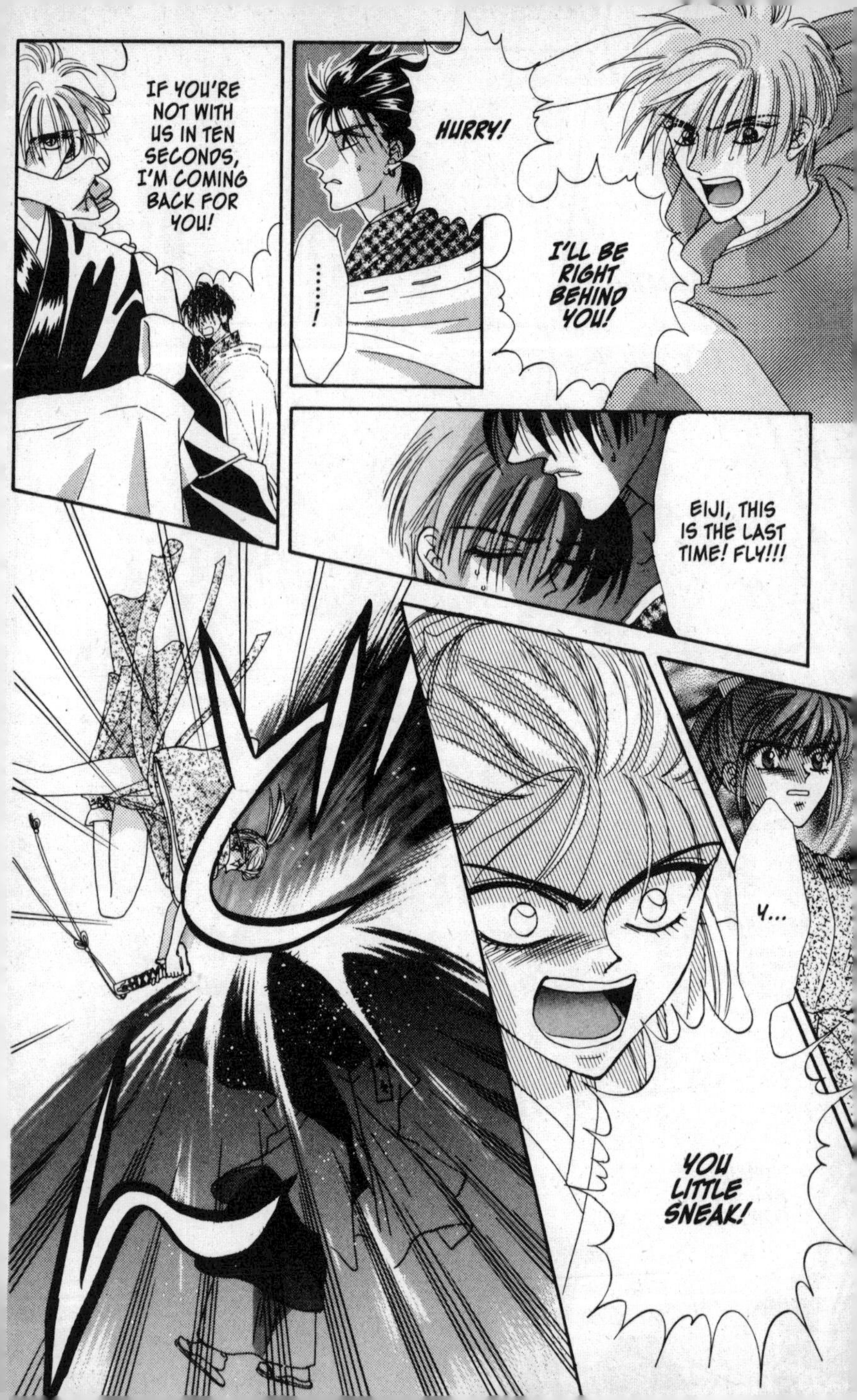
I'LL BE RIGHT BEHIND YOU!
HURRY!
......!
IF YOU'RE NOT WITH US IN TEN SECONDS, I'M COMING BACK FOR YOU!
EIJI, THIS IS THE LAST TIME! FLY!!!
Y...
YOU LITTLE SNEAK!

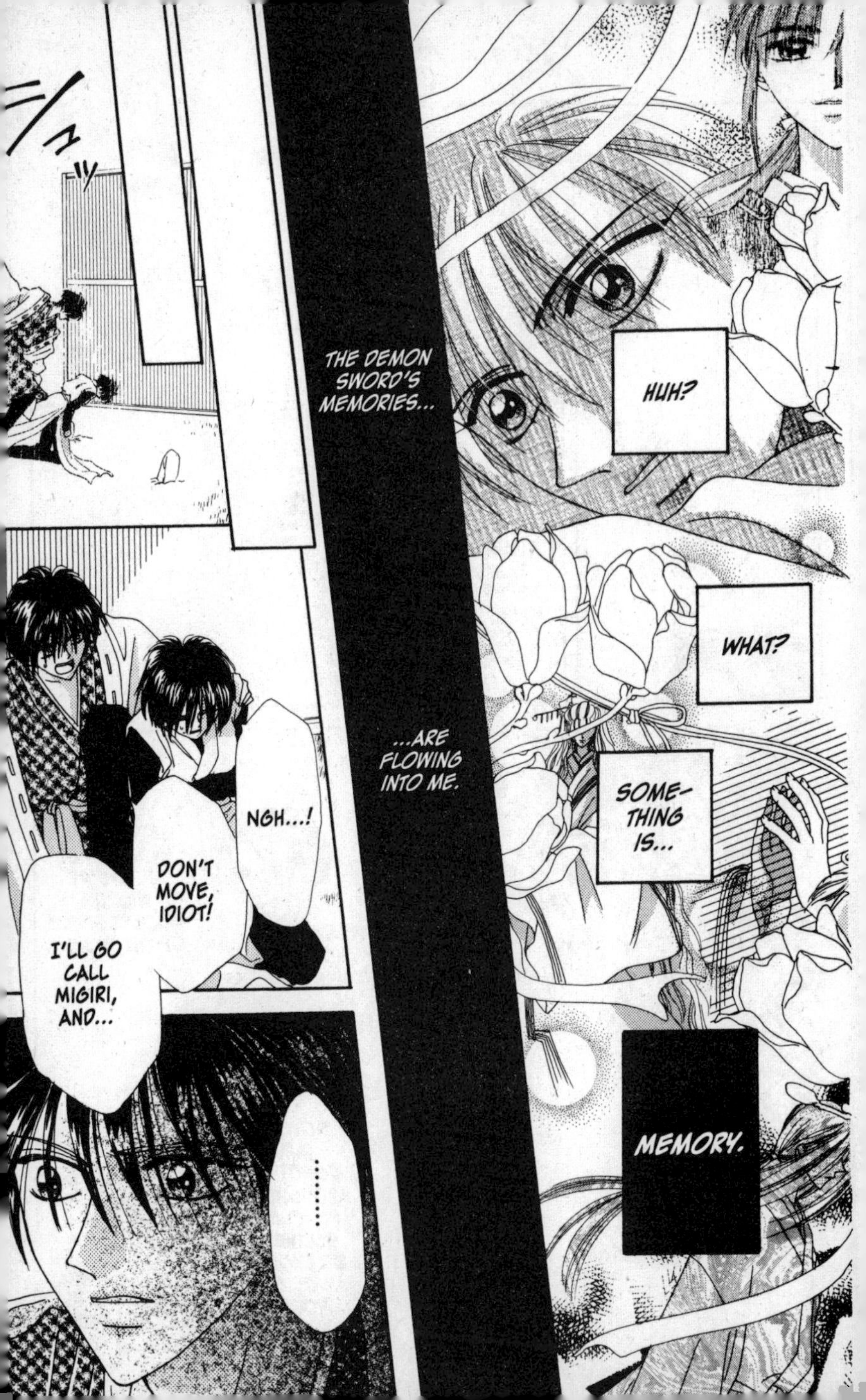
HUH?
WHAT?
SOME-THING IS...
MEMORY.
THE DEMON SWORD'S MEMORIES...
...ARE FLOWING INTO ME.
NGH...!
DON'T MOVE, IDIOT!
I'LL GO CALL MIGIRI, AND...
......

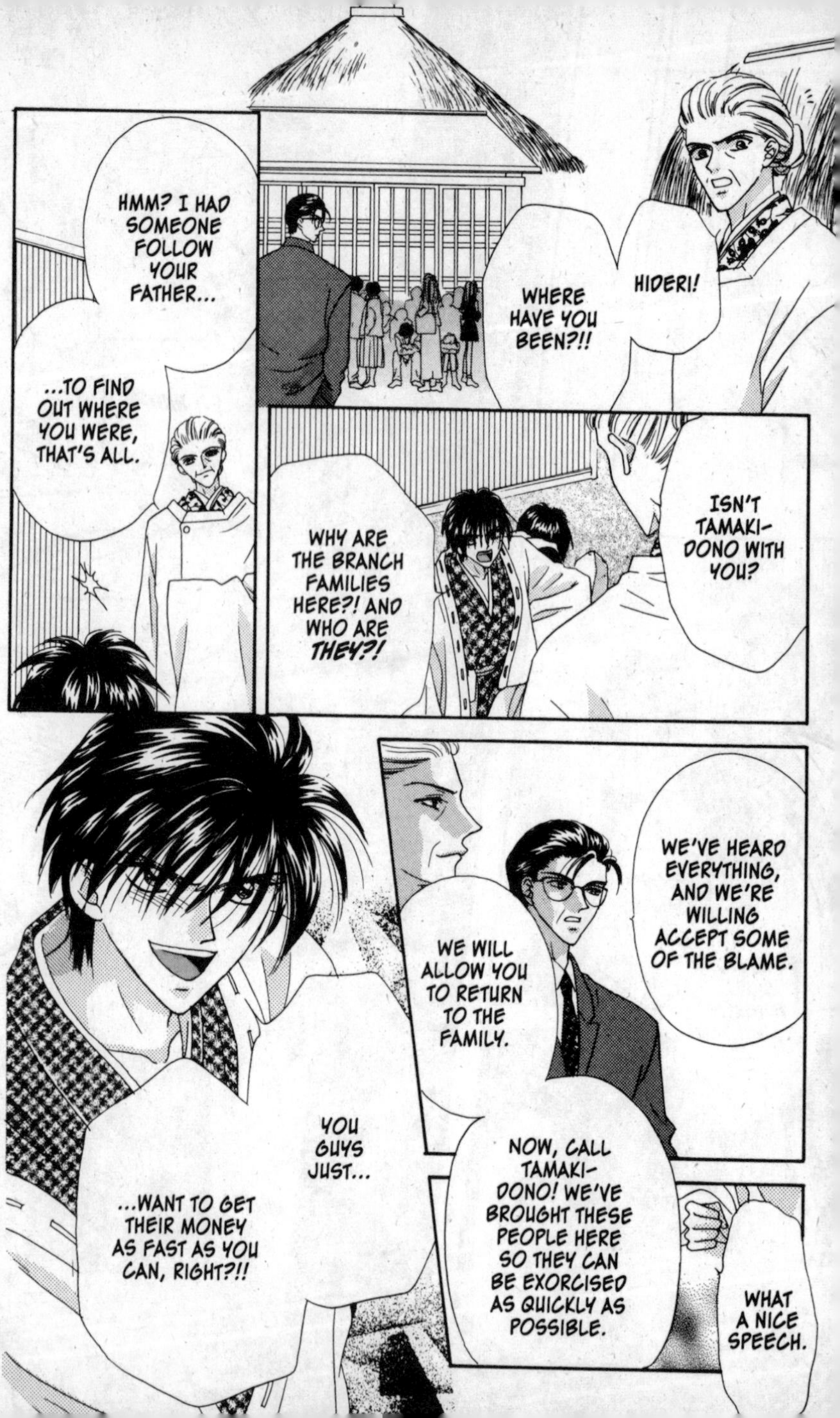
HIDERI!
WHERE HAVE YOU BEEN?!!
ISN'T TAMAKI-DONO WITH YOU?
WHY ARE THE BRANCH FAMILIES HERE?! AND WHO ARE *THEY?!*
HMM? I HAD SOMEONE FOLLOW YOUR FATHER...
...TO FIND OUT WHERE YOU WERE, THAT'S ALL.
WE'VE HEARD EVERYTHING, AND WE'RE WILLING ACCEPT SOME OF THE BLAME.
WE WILL ALLOW YOU TO RETURN TO THE FAMILY.
NOW, CALL TAMAKI-DONO! WE'VE BROUGHT THESE PEOPLE HERE SO THEY CAN BE EXORCISED AS QUICKLY AS POSSIBLE.
WHAT A NICE SPEECH.
YOU GUYS JUST...
...WANT TO GET THEIR MONEY AS FAST AS YOU CAN, RIGHT?!!

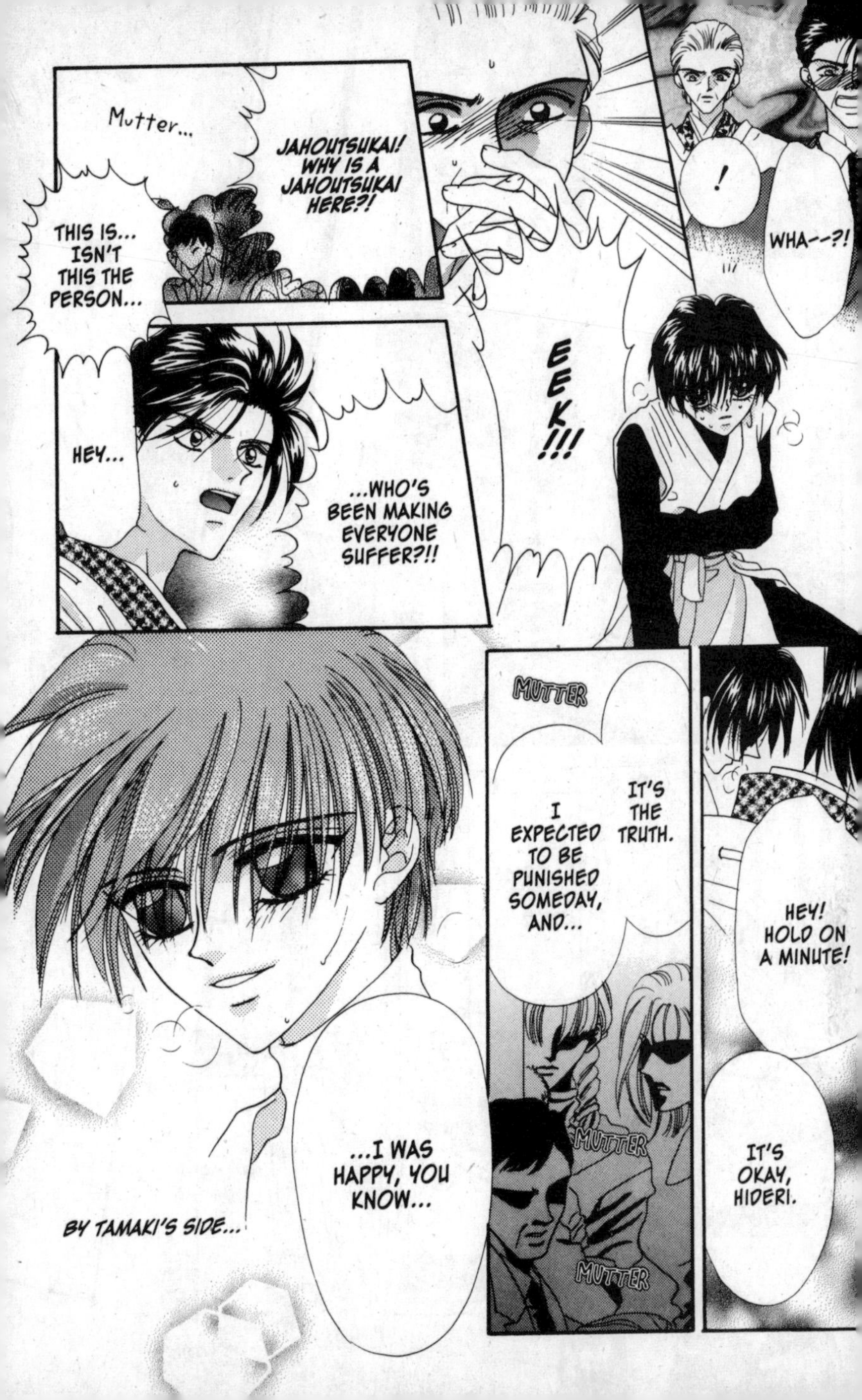
!
WHA--?!
JAHOUTSUKAI! WHY IS A JAHOUTSUKAI HERE?!
Mutter...
THIS IS... ISN'T THIS THE PERSON...
EEK!!!
HEY...
...WHO'S BEEN MAKING EVERYONE SUFFER?!!
HEY! HOLD ON A MINUTE!
IT'S OKAY, HIDERI.
MUTTER
IT'S THE TRUTH.
I EXPECTED TO BE PUNISHED SOMEDAY, AND...
MUTTER
MUTTER
...I WAS HAPPY, YOU KNOW...
BY TAMAKI'S SIDE...

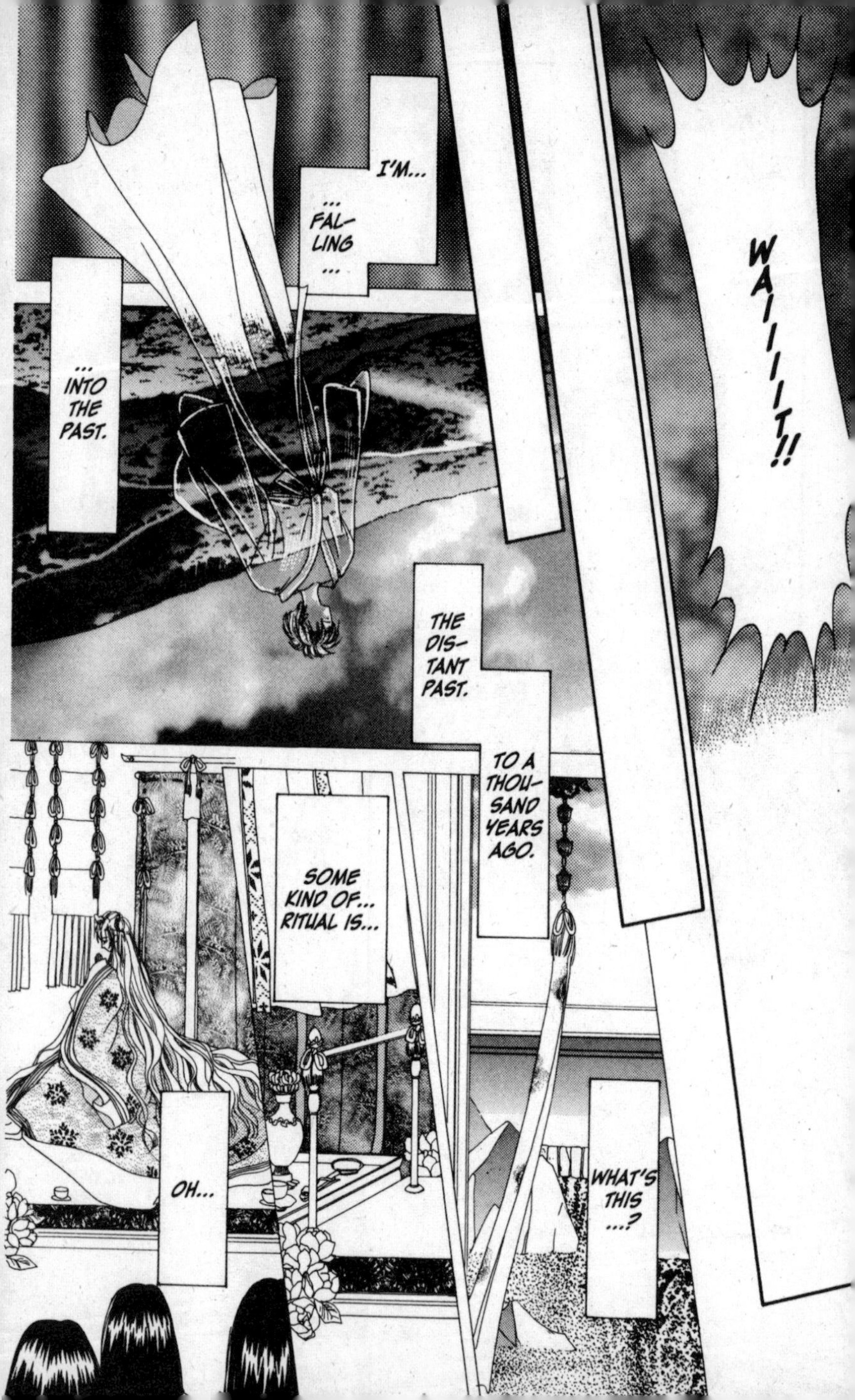

WAIIIIT!!
I'M...
...FALLING...
...INTO THE PAST.
THE DISTANT PAST.
TO A THOUSAND YEARS AGO.
SOME KIND OF... RITUAL IS...
WHAT'S THIS ...?
OH...

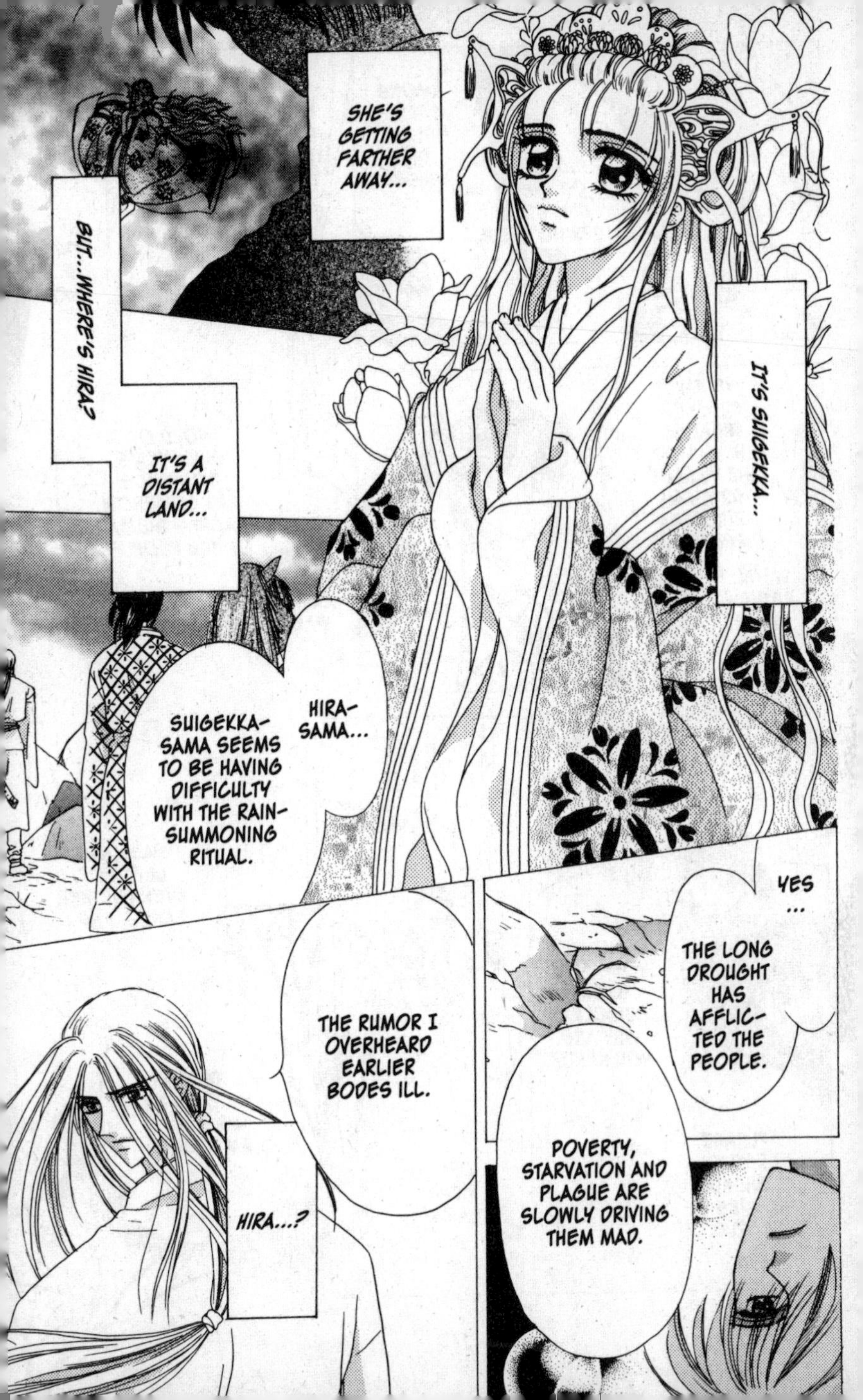
IT'S SUIGEKKA...
SHE'S GETTING FARTHER AWAY...
IT'S A DISTANT LAND...
BUT...WHERE'S HIRA?
HIRA-SAMA...
SUIGEKKA-SAMA SEEMS TO BE HAVING DIFFICULTY WITH THE RAIN-SUMMONING RITUAL.
YES...
THE LONG DROUGHT HAS AFFLICTED THE PEOPLE.
POVERTY, STARVATION AND PLAGUE ARE SLOWLY DRIVING THEM MAD.
THE RUMOR I OVERHEARD EARLIER BODES ILL.
HIRA...?

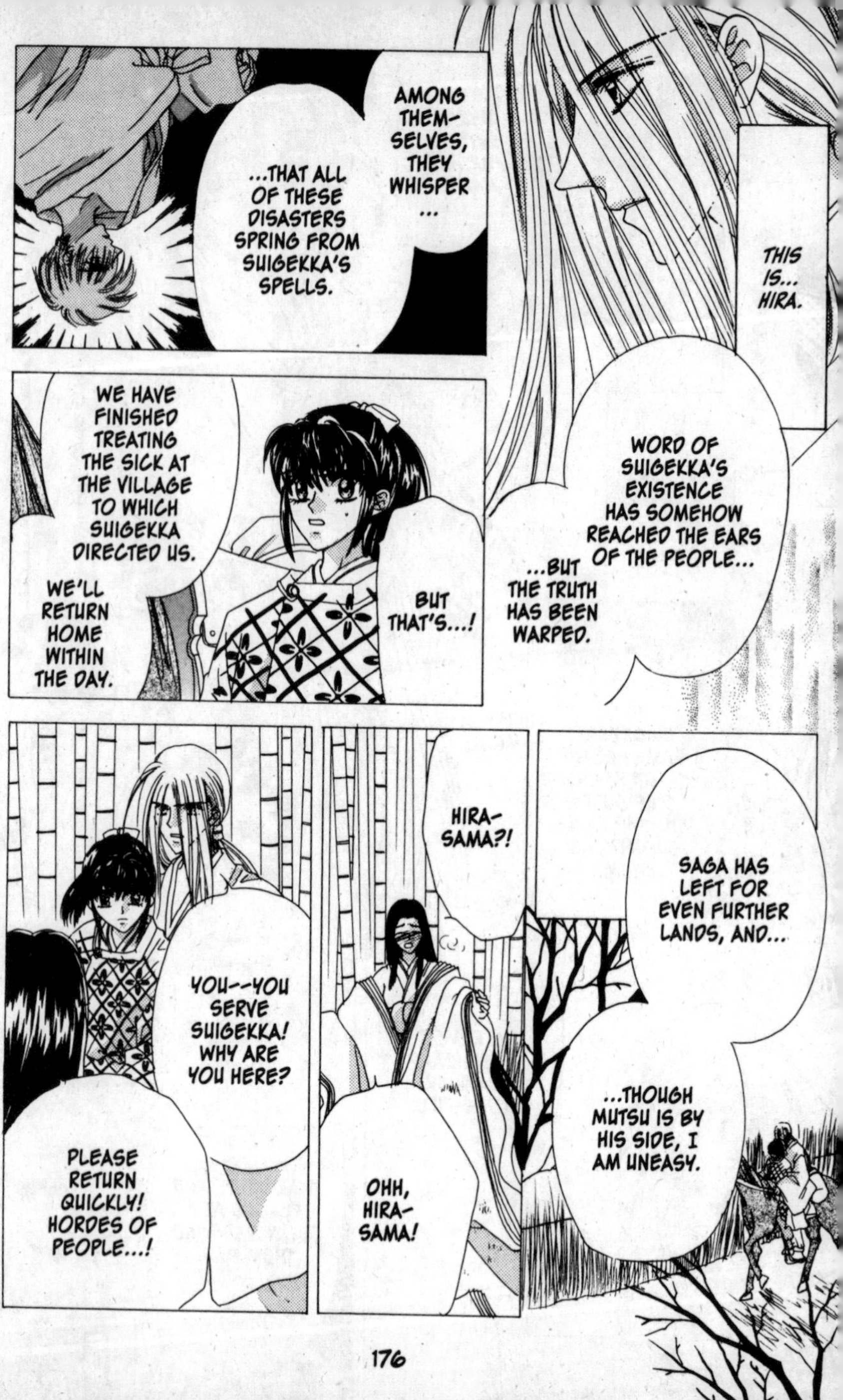
THIS IS... HIRA.
WORD OF SUIGEKKA'S EXISTENCE HAS SOMEHOW REACHED THE EARS OF THE PEOPLE...
...BUT THE TRUTH HAS BEEN WARPED.
AMONG THEM-SELVES, THEY WHISPER...
...THAT ALL OF THESE DISASTERS SPRING FROM SUIGEKKA'S SPELLS.
BUT THAT'S...!
WE HAVE FINISHED TREATING THE SICK AT THE VILLAGE TO WHICH SUIGEKKA DIRECTED US.
WE'LL RETURN HOME WITHIN THE DAY.
SAGA HAS LEFT FOR EVEN FURTHER LANDS, AND...
...THOUGH MUTSU IS BY HIS SIDE, I AM UNEASY.
HIRA-SAMA?!
OHH, HIRA-SAMA!
YOU--YOU SERVE SUIGEKKA! WHY ARE YOU HERE?
PLEASE RETURN QUICKLY! HORDES OF PEOPLE...!

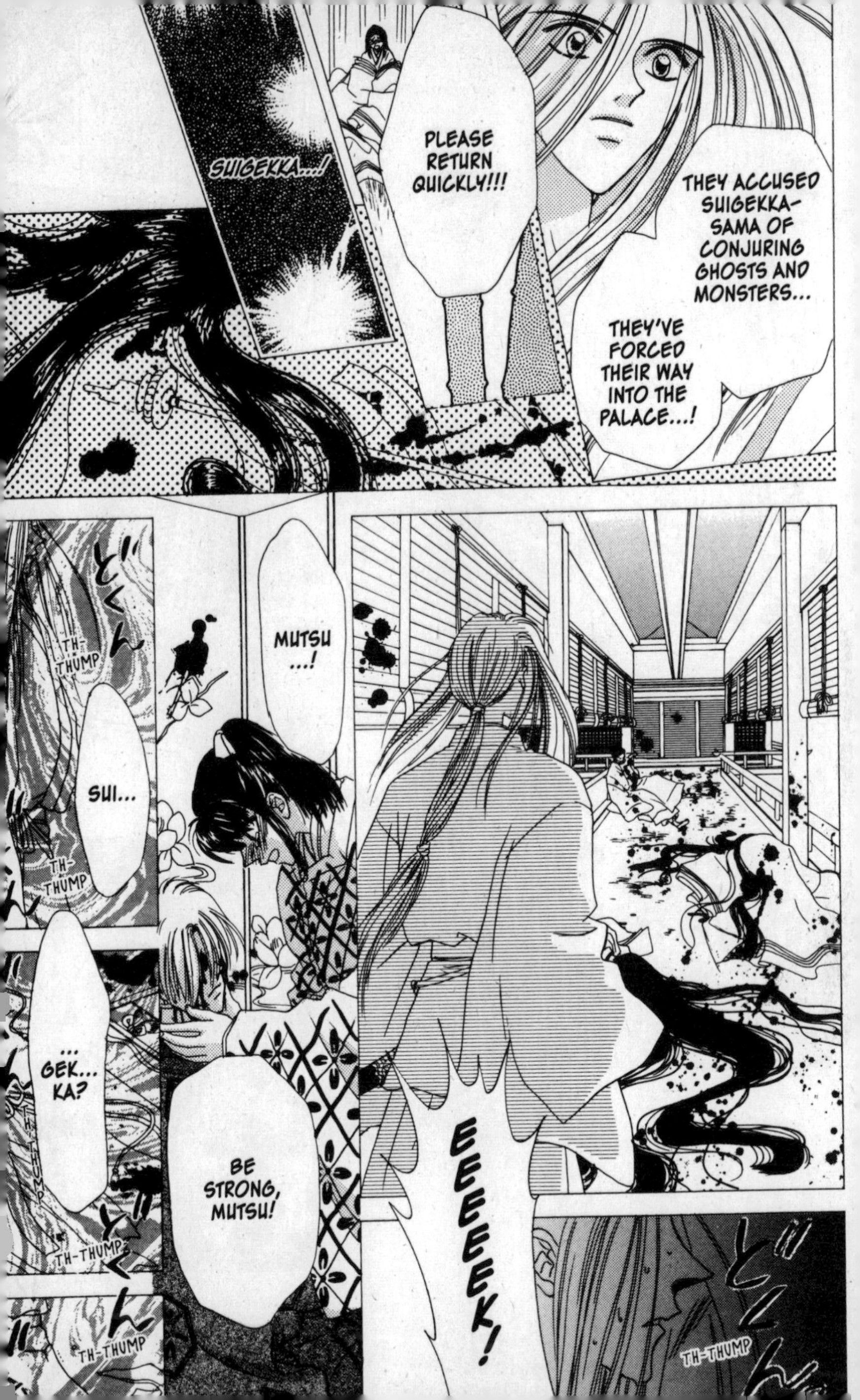
THEY ACCUSED SUIGEKKA-SAMA OF CONJURING GHOSTS AND MONSTERS...
THEY'VE FORCED THEIR WAY INTO THE PALACE...!
PLEASE RETURN QUICKLY!!!
SUIGEKKA...!
EEEEEEK!
TH-THUMP
MUTSU...!
BE STRONG, MUTSU!
TH-THUMP
SUI...
TH-THUMP
...GEK...KA?
TH-THUMP
TH-THUMP
TH-THUMP

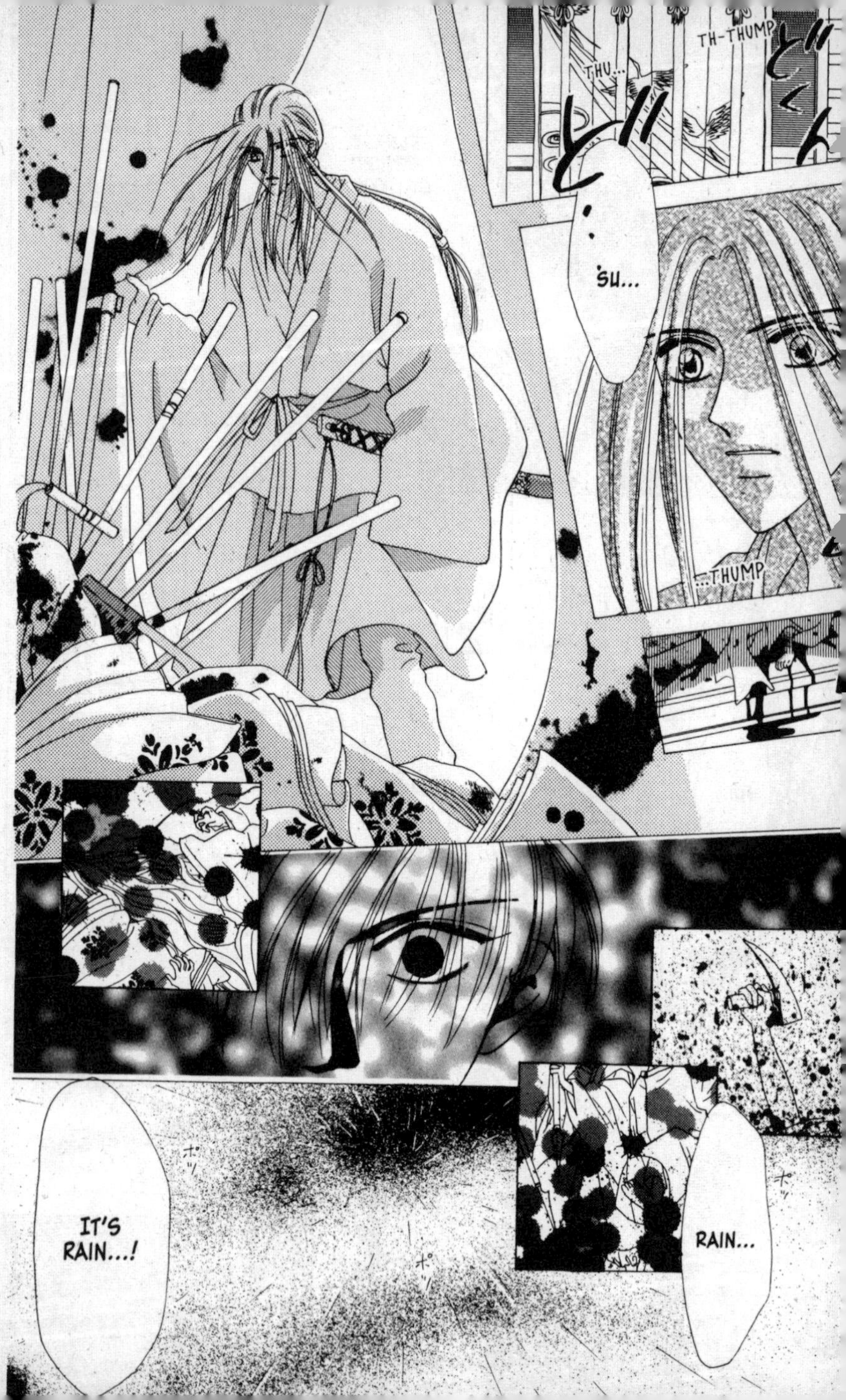
TH-THUMP
どくん
THU...
SU...
...THUMP
RAIN...
ポツ
IT'S RAIN...!
ポツ

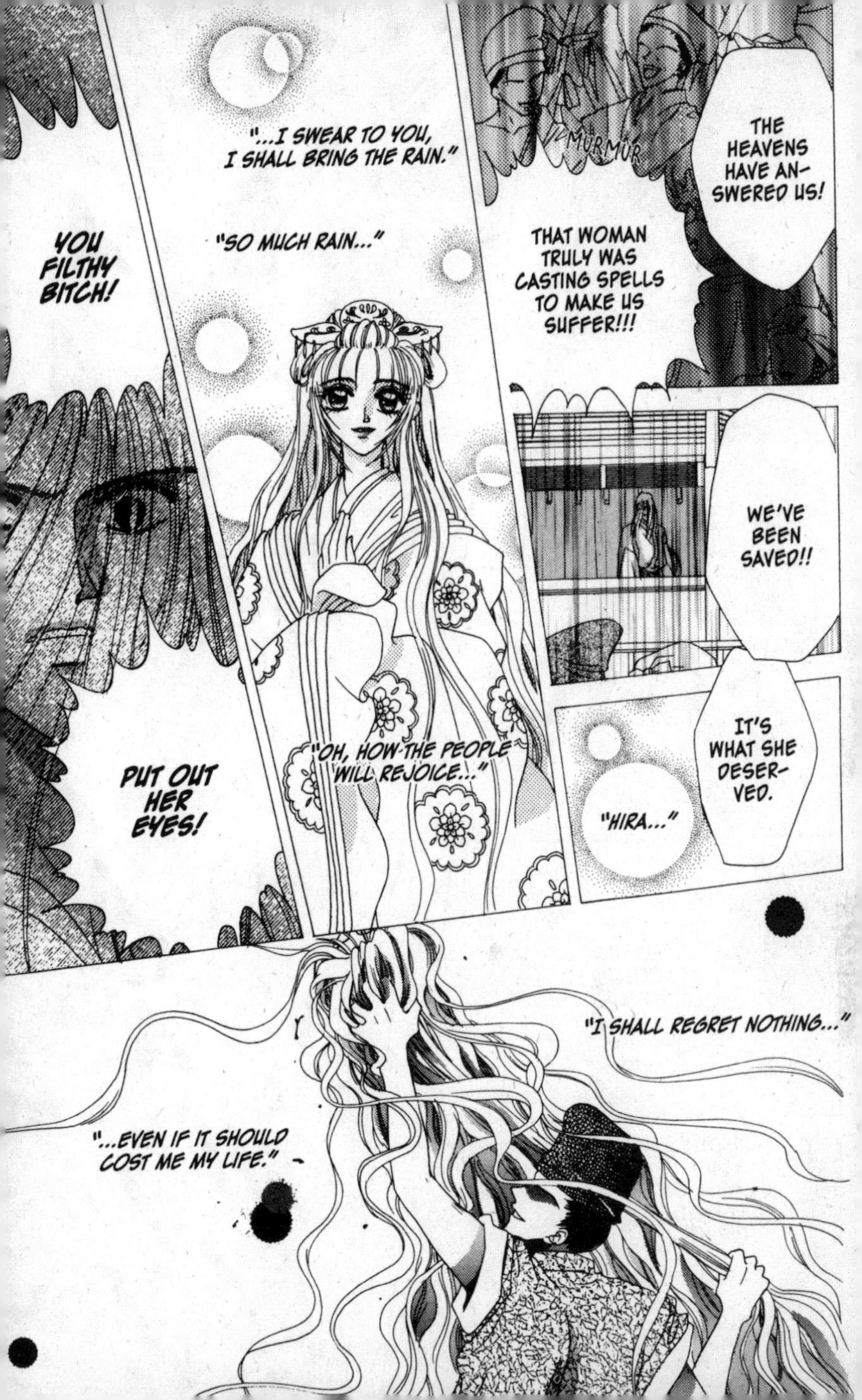
THE HEAVENS HAVE AN-SWERED US!
MURMUR
THAT WOMAN TRULY WAS CASTING SPELLS TO MAKE US SUFFER!!!
WE'VE BEEN SAVED!!
IT'S WHAT SHE DESER-VED.
"HIRA..."
"...I SWEAR TO YOU, I SHALL BRING THE RAIN."
"SO MUCH RAIN..."
"OH, HOW THE PEOPLE WILL REJOICE..."
YOU FILTHY BITCH!
PUT OUT HER EYES!
"I SHALL REGRET NOTHING..."
"...EVEN IF IT SHOULD COST ME MY LIFE."

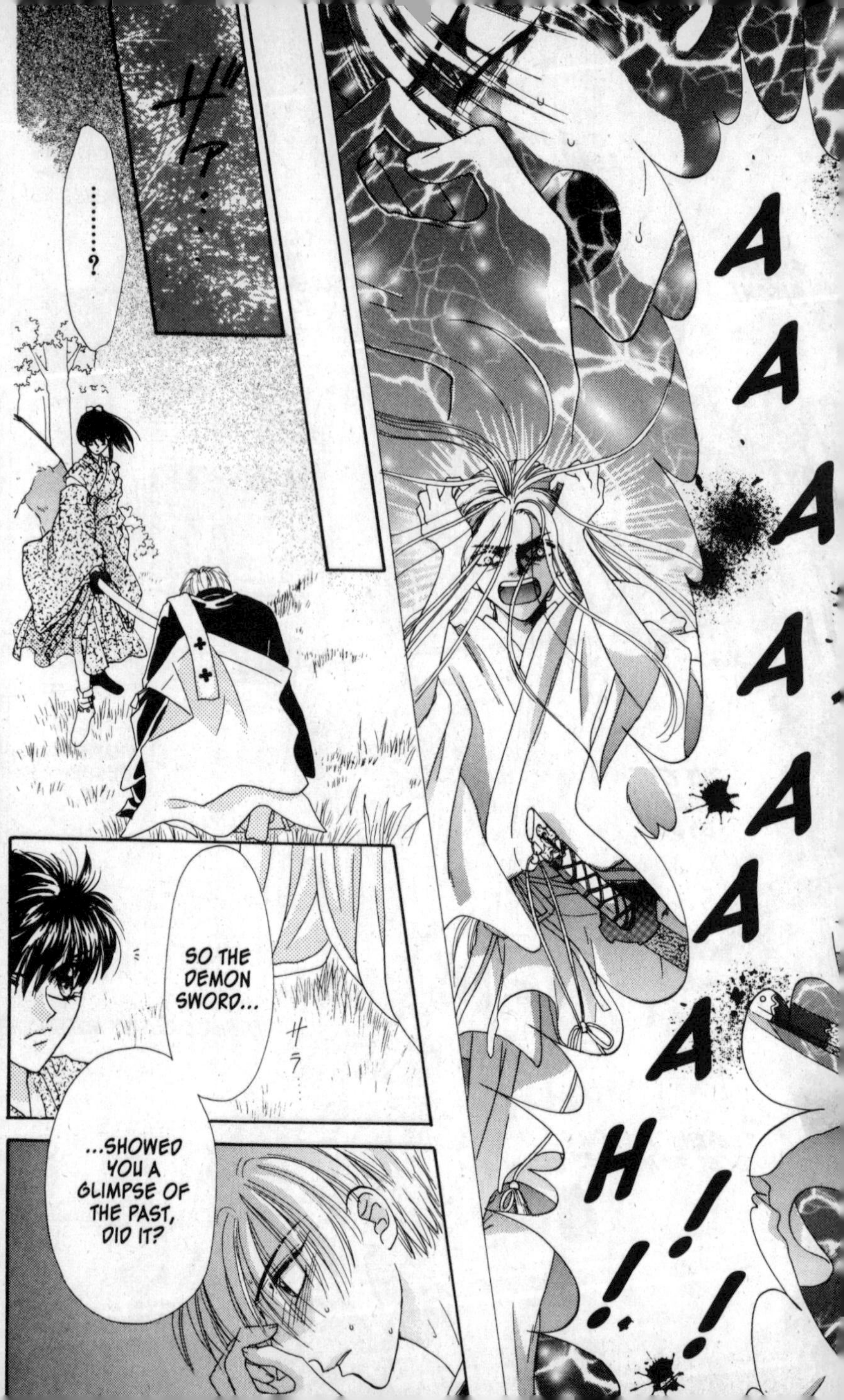
AAAAAAAH!!!
ザァ…
……?
SO THE DEMON SWORD...
...SHOWED YOU A GLIMPSE OF THE PAST, DID IT?

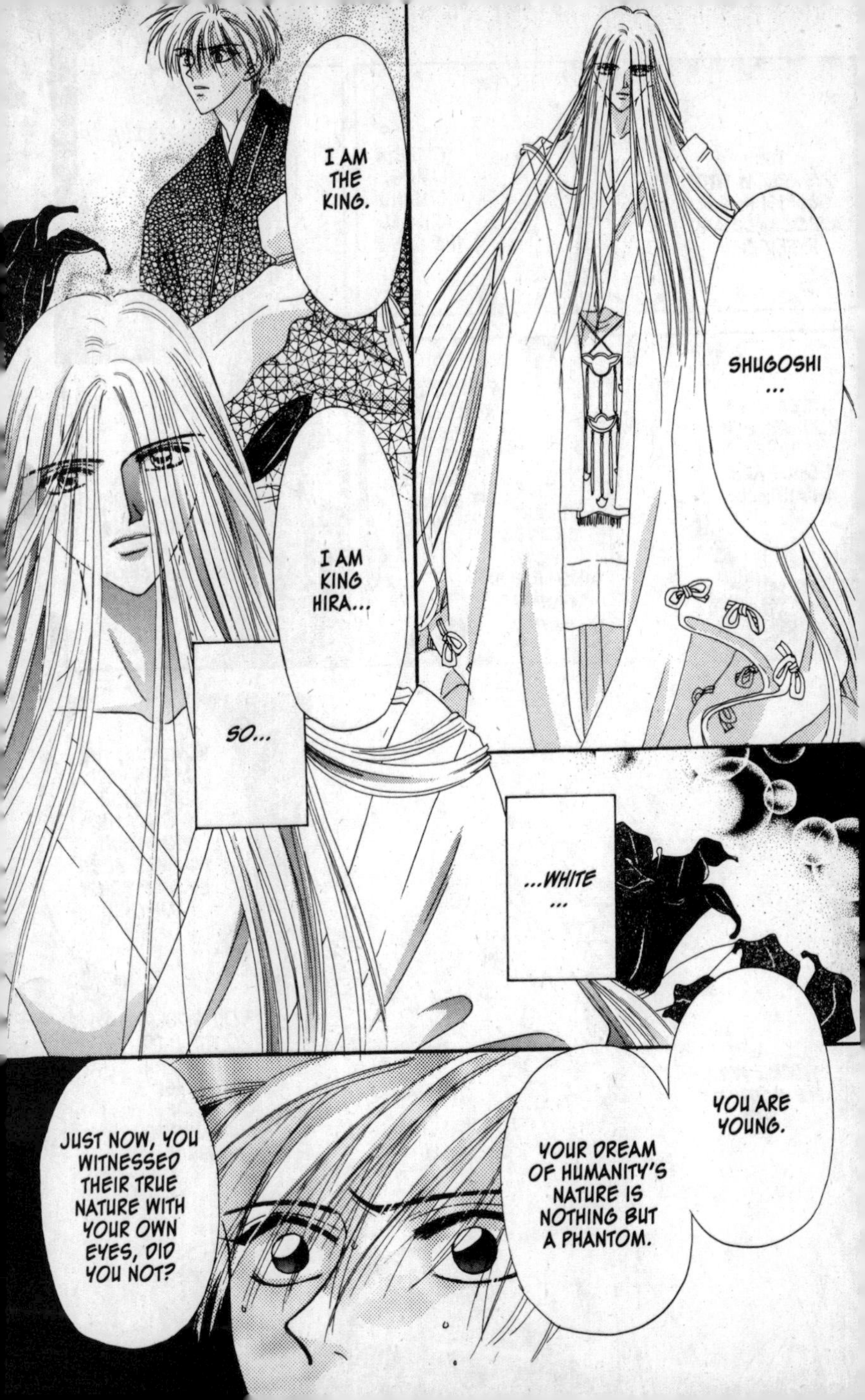
SHUGOSHI ...
...WHITE ...
I AM THE KING.
I AM KING HIRA...
SO...
YOU ARE YOUNG.
YOUR DREAM OF HUMANITY'S NATURE IS NOTHING BUT A PHANTOM.
JUST NOW, YOU WITNESSED THEIR TRUE NATURE WITH YOUR OWN EYES, DID YOU NOT?

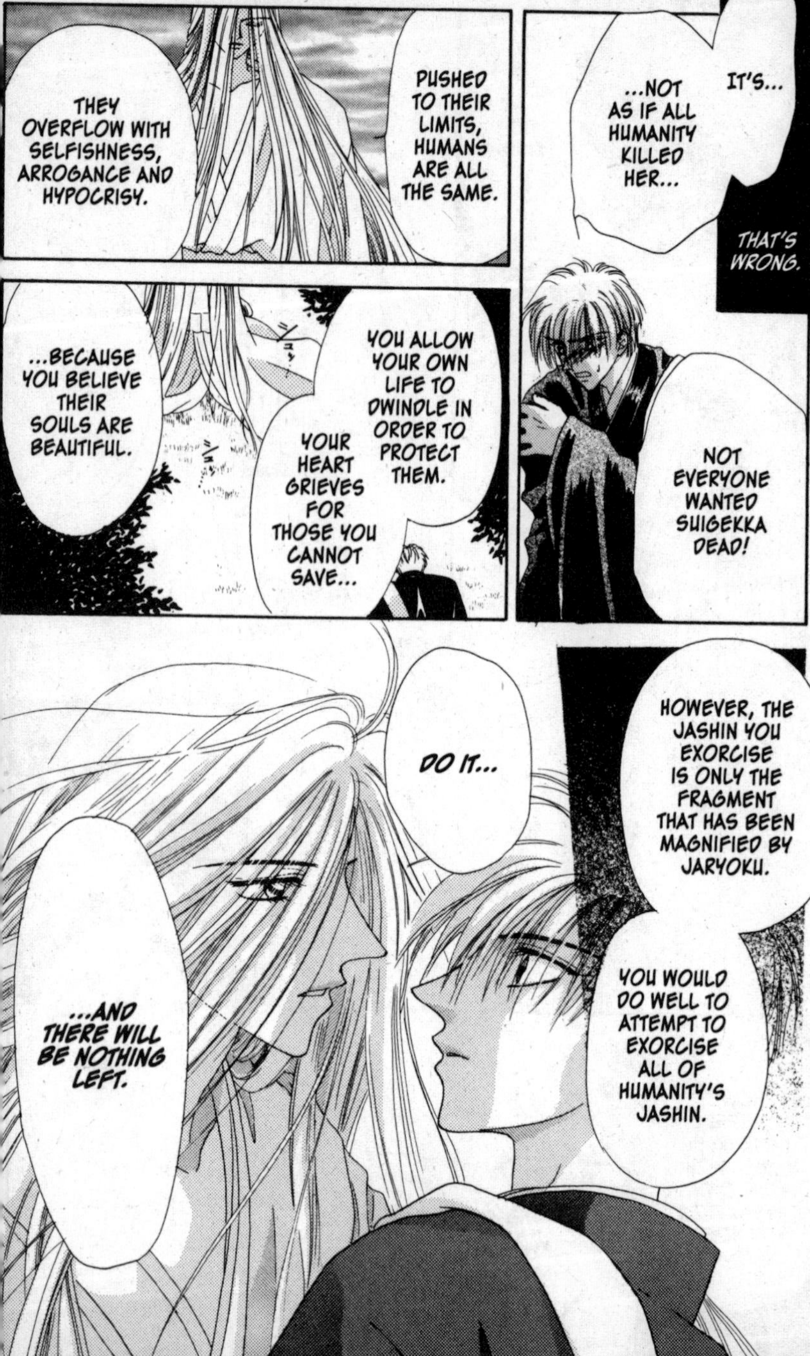
IT'S...
...NOT AS IF ALL HUMANITY KILLED HER...
THAT'S WRONG.
NOT EVERYONE WANTED SUIGEKKA DEAD!
PUSHED TO THEIR LIMITS, HUMANS ARE ALL THE SAME.
THEY OVERFLOW WITH SELFISHNESS, ARROGANCE AND HYPOCRISY.
YOU ALLOW YOUR OWN LIFE TO DWINDLE IN ORDER TO PROTECT THEM.
YOUR HEART GRIEVES FOR THOSE YOU CANNOT SAVE...
...BECAUSE YOU BELIEVE THEIR SOULS ARE BEAUTIFUL.
HOWEVER, THE JASHIN YOU EXORCISE IS ONLY THE FRAGMENT THAT HAS BEEN MAGNIFIED BY JARYOKU.
YOU WOULD DO WELL TO ATTEMPT TO EXORCISE ALL OF HUMANITY'S JASHIN.
DO IT...
...AND THERE WILL BE NOTHING LEFT.

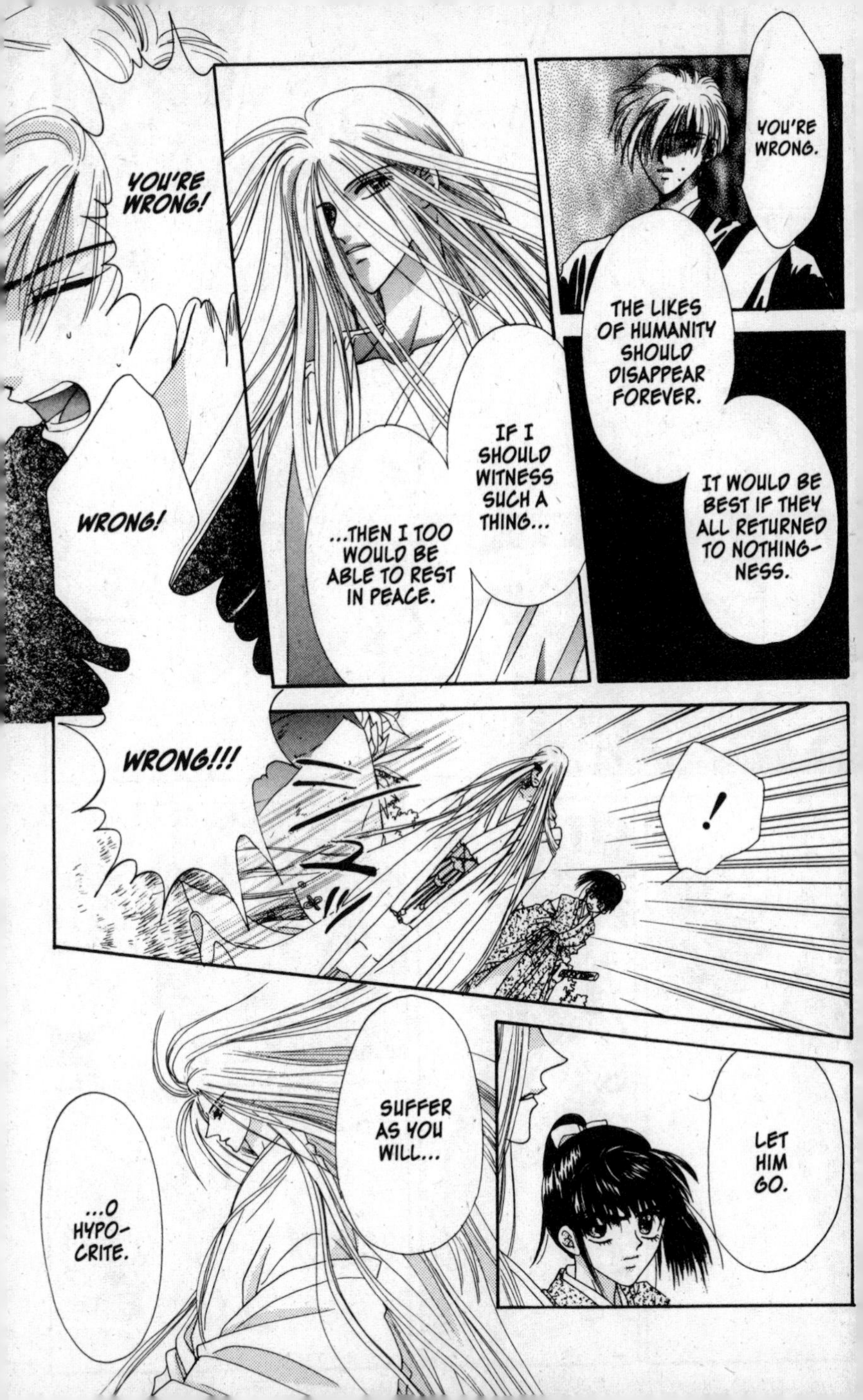
YOU'RE WRONG.
THE LIKES OF HUMANITY SHOULD DISAPPEAR FOREVER.
IT WOULD BE BEST IF THEY ALL RETURNED TO NOTHING-NESS.
IF I SHOULD WITNESS SUCH A THING...
...THEN I TOO WOULD BE ABLE TO REST IN PEACE.
YOU'RE WRONG!
WRONG!
!
WRONG!!!
LET HIM GO.
SUFFER AS YOU WILL...
...O HYPO-CRITE.

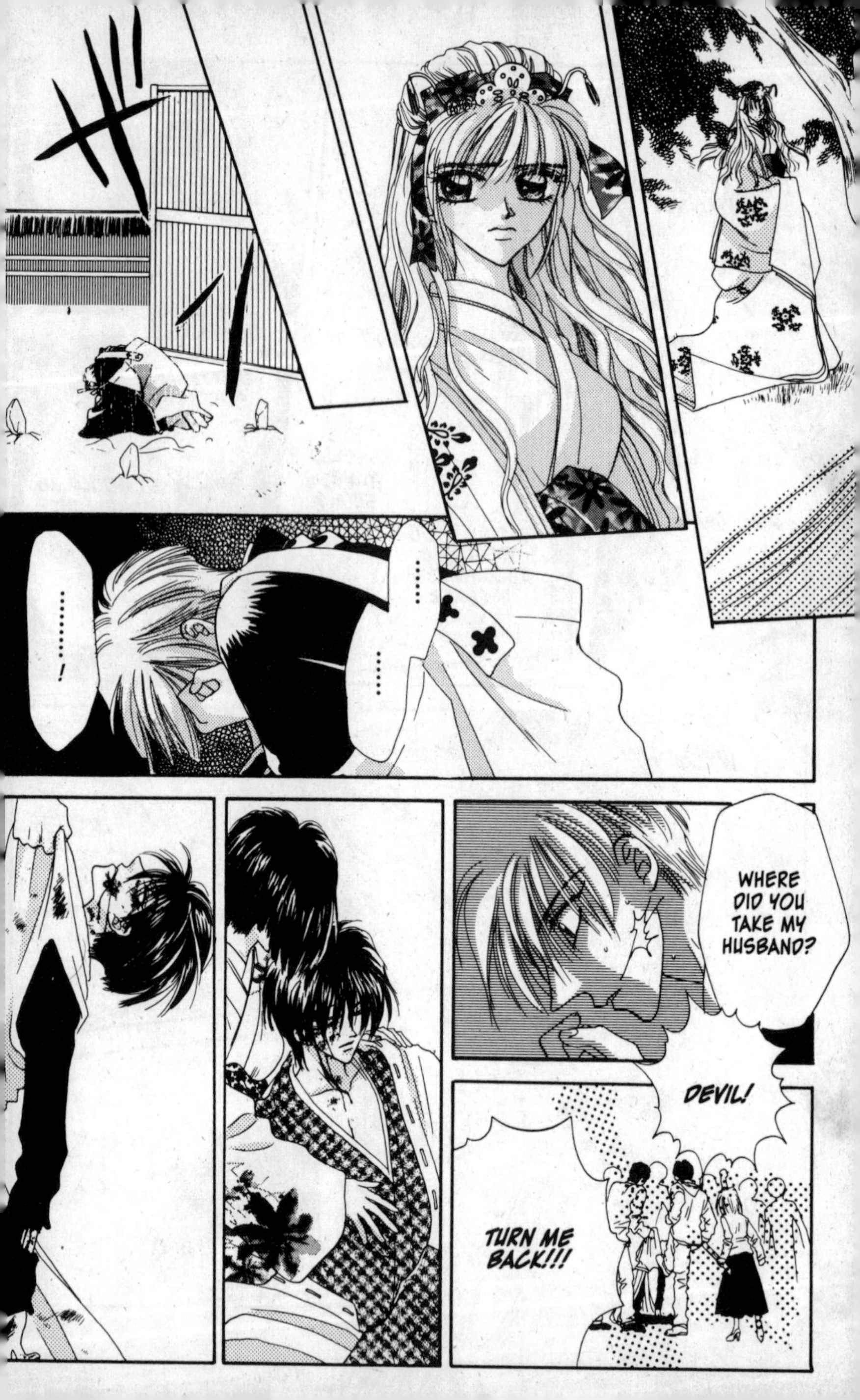
......
......!
WHERE DID YOU TAKE MY HUSBAND?
DEVIL!
TURN ME BACK!!!

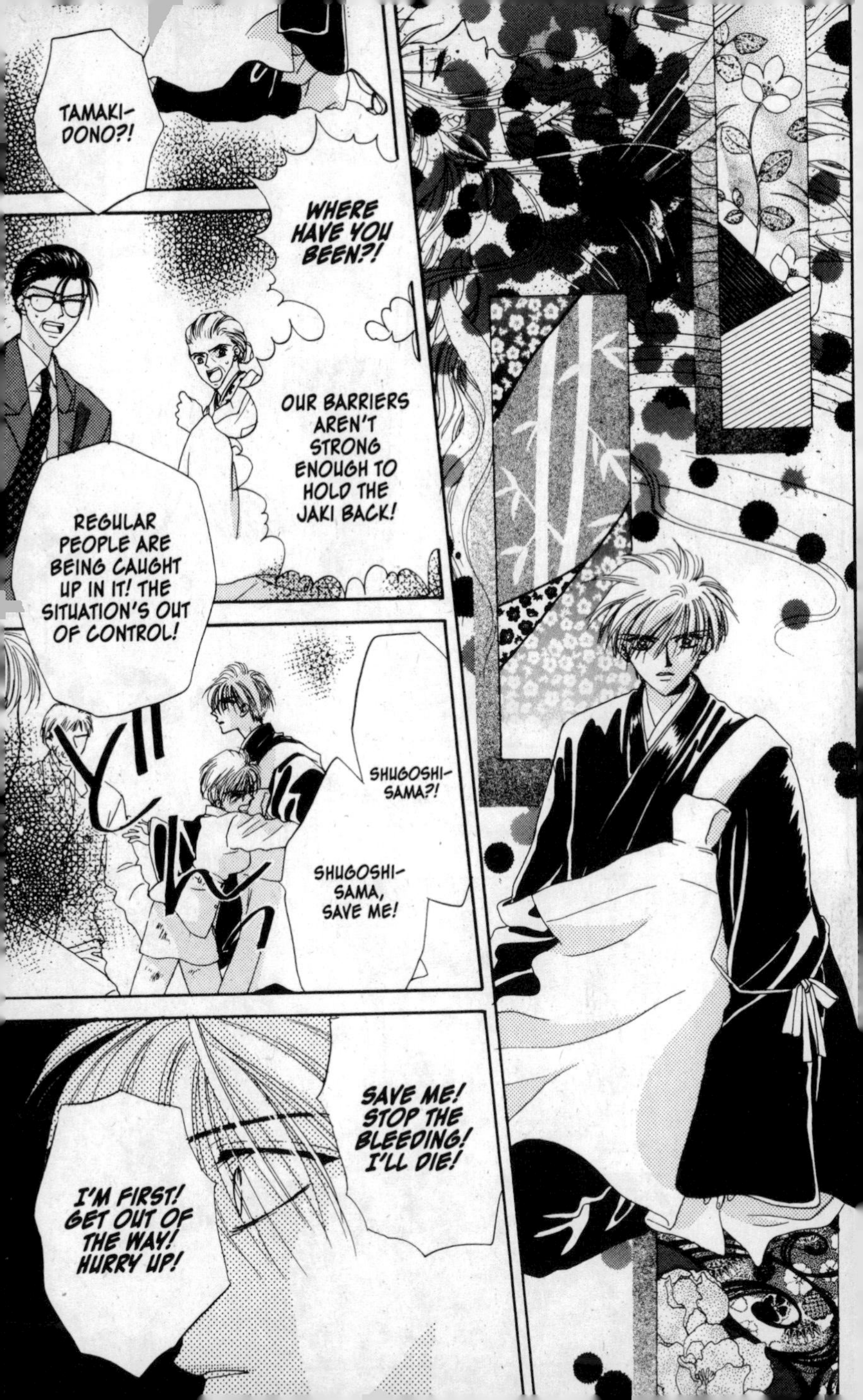
TAMAKI-DONO?!
WHERE HAVE YOU BEEN?!
OUR BARRIERS AREN'T STRONG ENOUGH TO HOLD THE JAKI BACK!
REGULAR PEOPLE ARE BEING CAUGHT UP IN IT! THE SITUATION'S OUT OF CONTROL!
SHUGOSHI-SAMA?!
SHUGOSHI-SAMA, SAVE ME!
SAVE ME! STOP THE BLEEDING! I'LL DIE!
I'M FIRST! GET OUT OF THE WAY! HURRY UP!

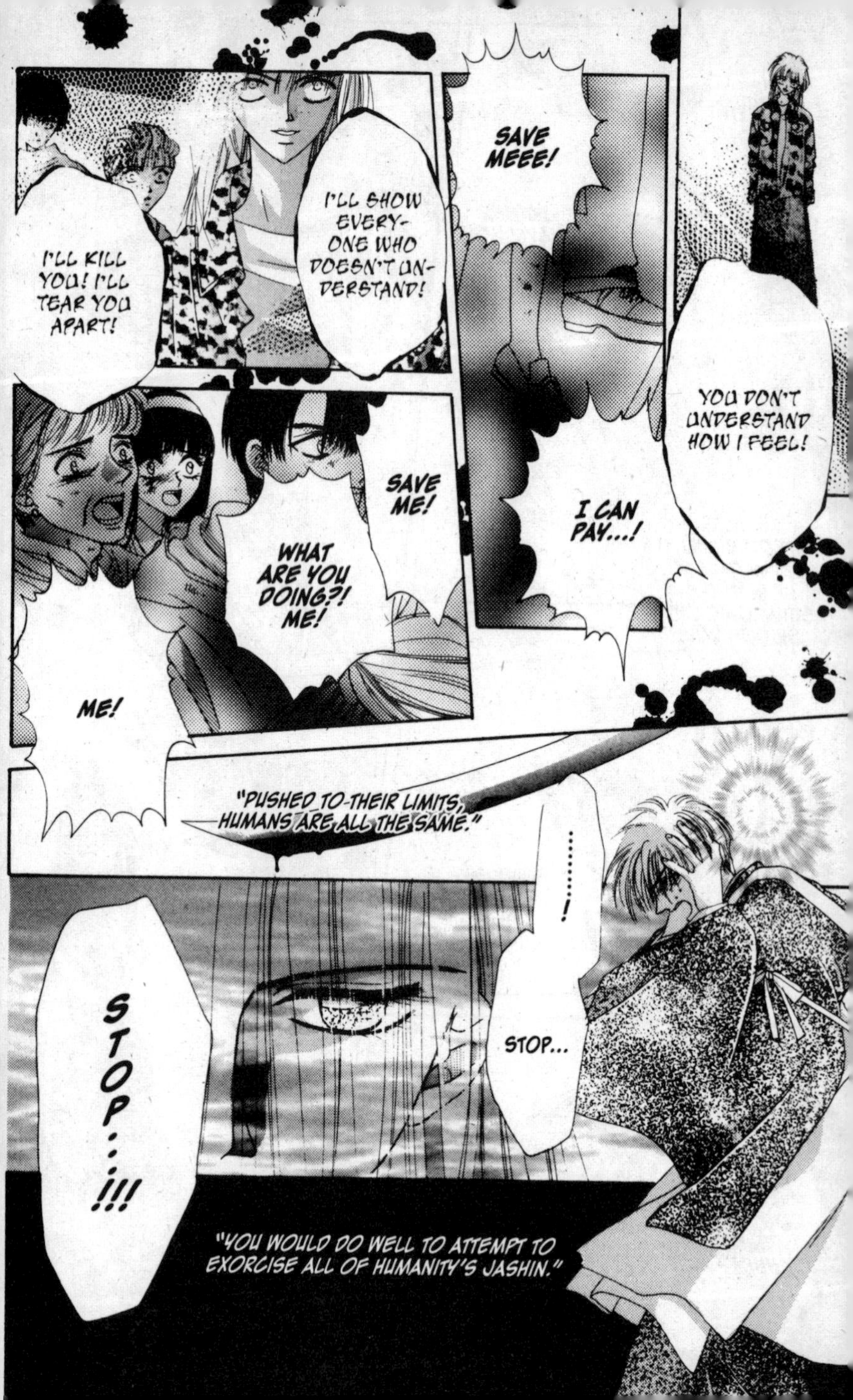
YOU DON'T UNDERSTAND HOW I FEEL!
SAVE MEEE!
I CAN PAY...!
I'LL SHOW EVERY-ONE WHO DOESN'T UN-DERSTAND!
I'LL KILL YOU! I'LL TEAR YOU APART!
SAVE ME!
WHAT ARE YOU DOING?! ME!
ME!
"PUSHED TO THEIR LIMITS, HUMANS ARE ALL THE SAME."
......!
STOP...
STOP...!!!
"YOU WOULD DO WELL TO ATTEMPT TO EXORCISE ALL OF HUMANITY'S JASHIN."

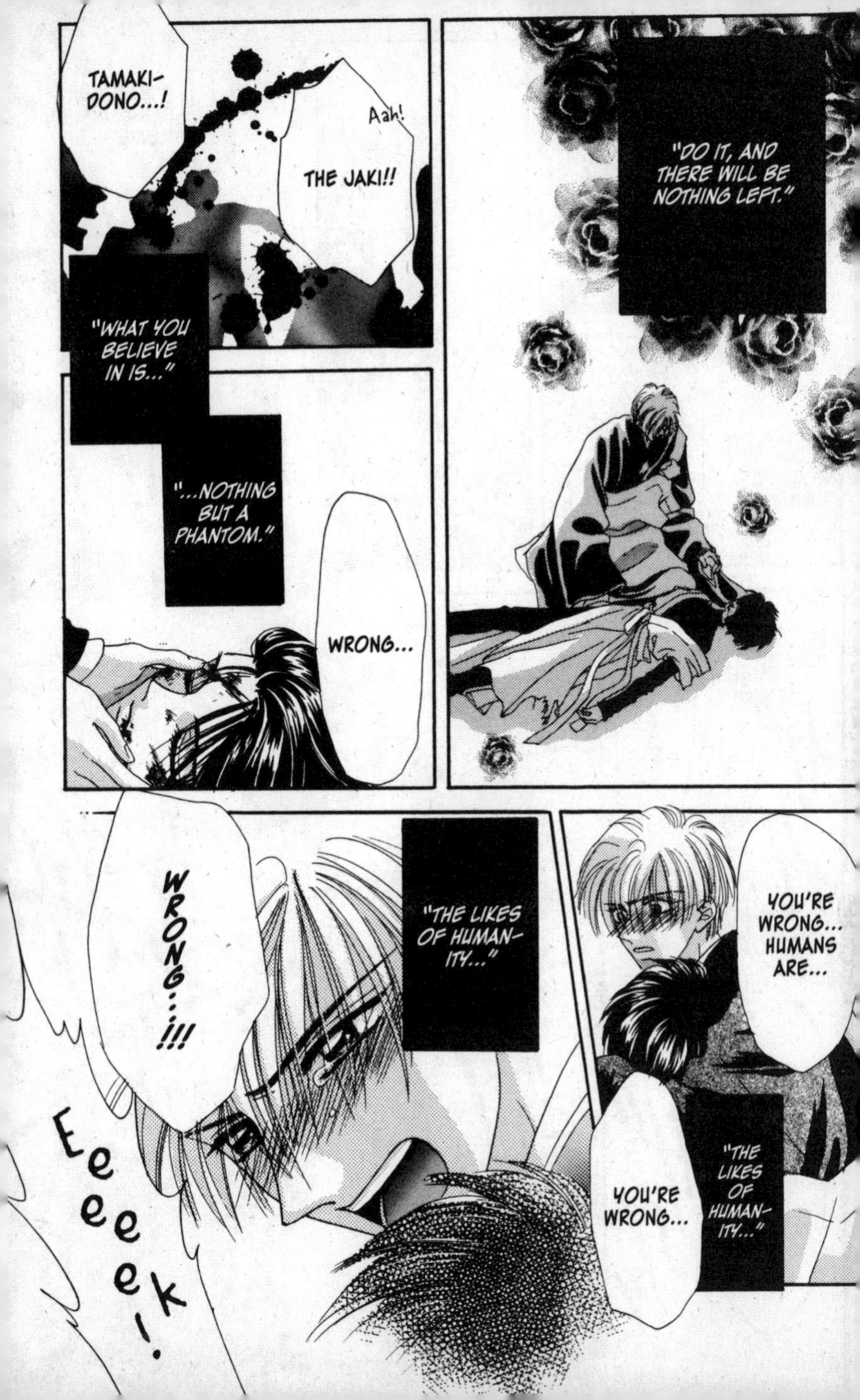
"DO IT, AND THERE WILL BE NOTHING LEFT."
Aah!
THE JAKI!!
TAMAKI-DONO...!
"WHAT YOU BELIEVE IN IS..."
"...NOTHING BUT A PHANTOM."
WRONG...
YOU'RE WRONG... HUMANS ARE...
"THE LIKES OF HUMAN-ITY..."
YOU'RE WRONG...
"THE LIKES OF HUMAN-ITY..."
WRONG...!!!
Eeeeek!

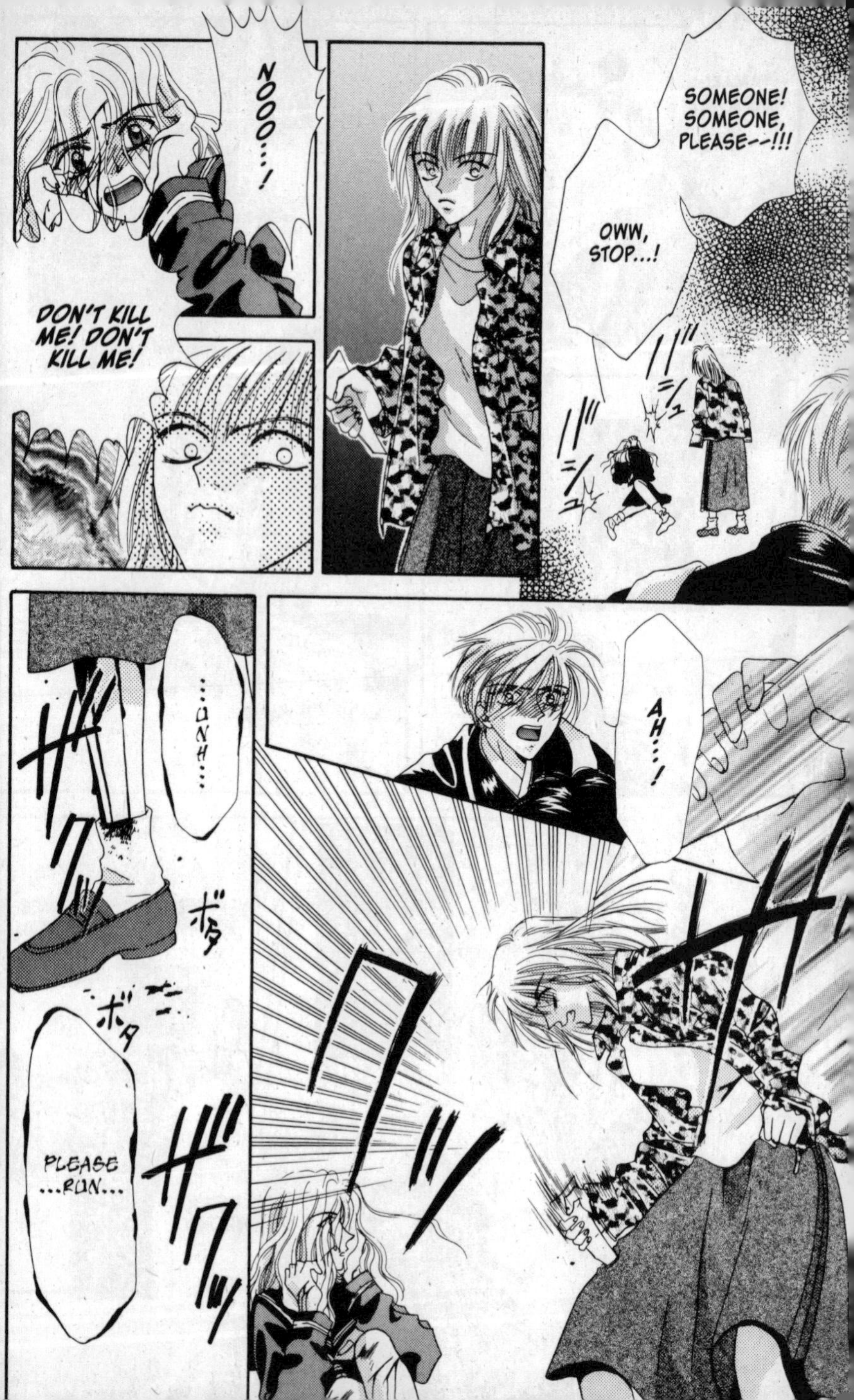
SOMEONE! SOMEONE, PLEASE--!!!
OWW, STOP...!
NOOO...!
DON'T KILL ME! DON'T KILL ME!
AH...!
...UNH...
ボタ
ボタ
PLEASE ...RUN...

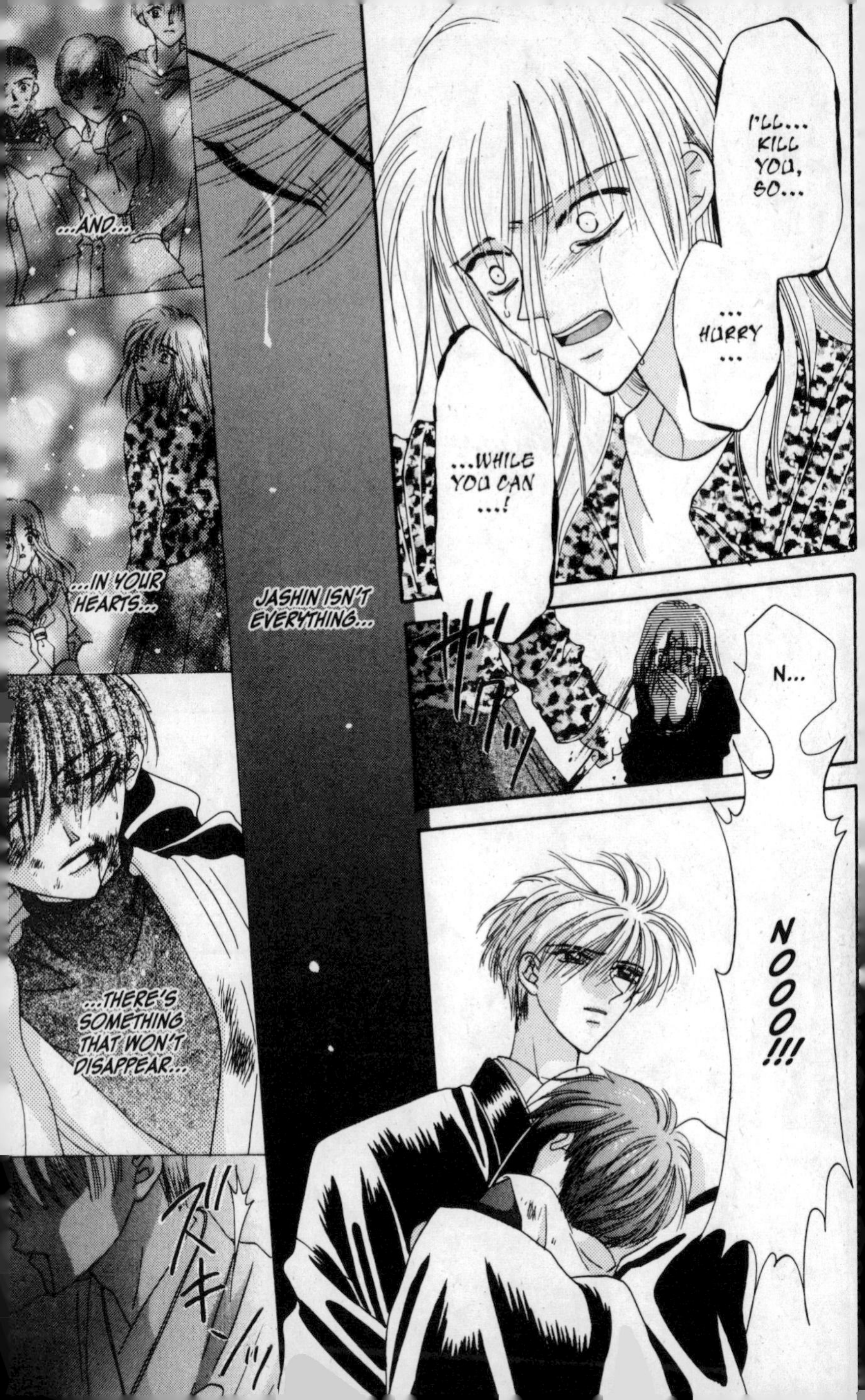
I'LL... KILL YOU, SO...
... HURRY ...
...WHILE YOU CAN ...!
N...
NOOOO!!!
JASHIN ISN'T EVERYTHING...
...AND...
...IN YOUR HEARTS...
...THERE'S SOMETHING THAT WON'T DISAPPEAR...

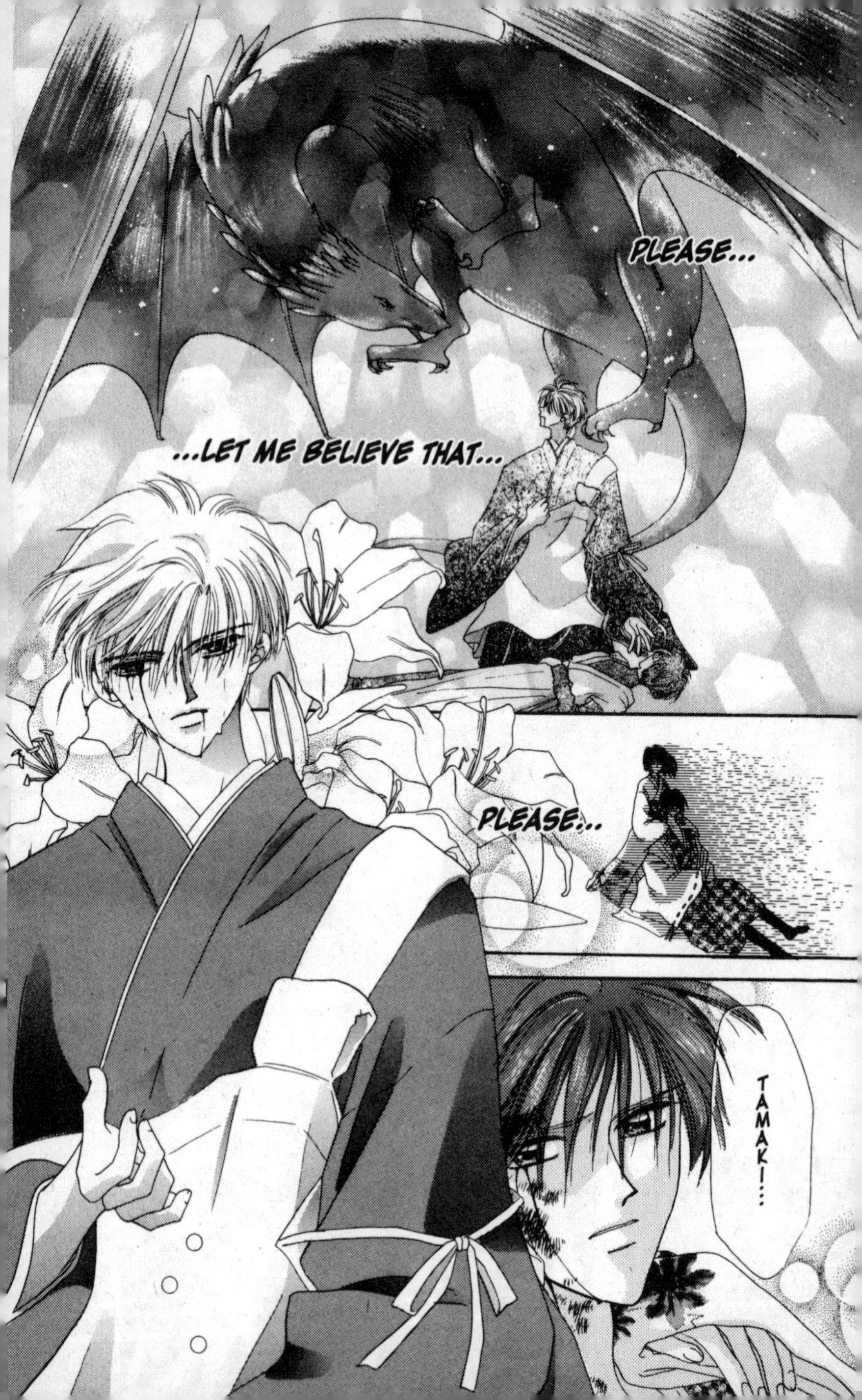
PLEASE...
...LET ME BELIEVE THAT...
PLEASE...
TAMAKI!..

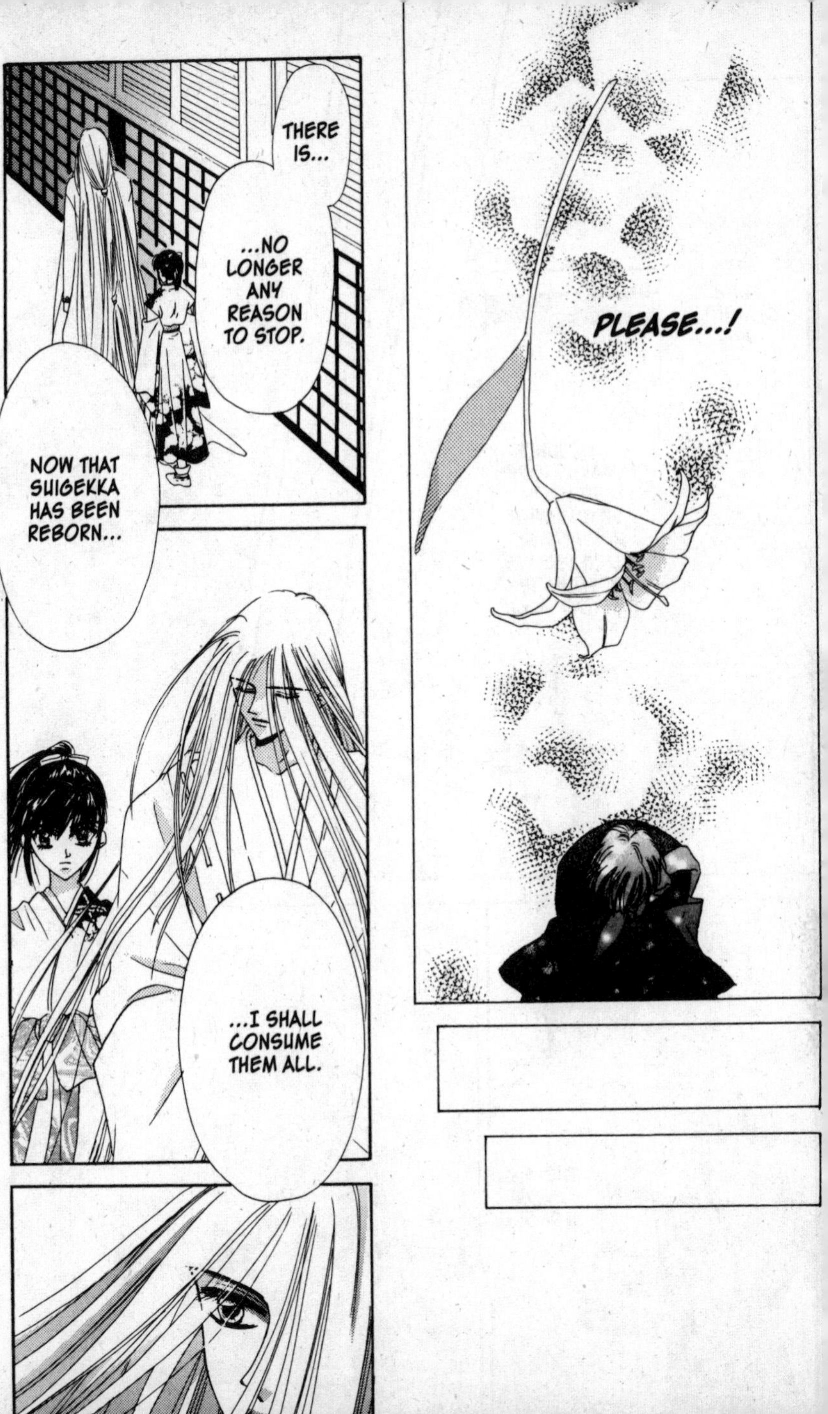
PLEASE...!
THERE IS...
...NO LONGER ANY REASON TO STOP.
NOW THAT SUIGEKKA HAS BEEN REBORN...
...I SHALL CONSUME THEM ALL.

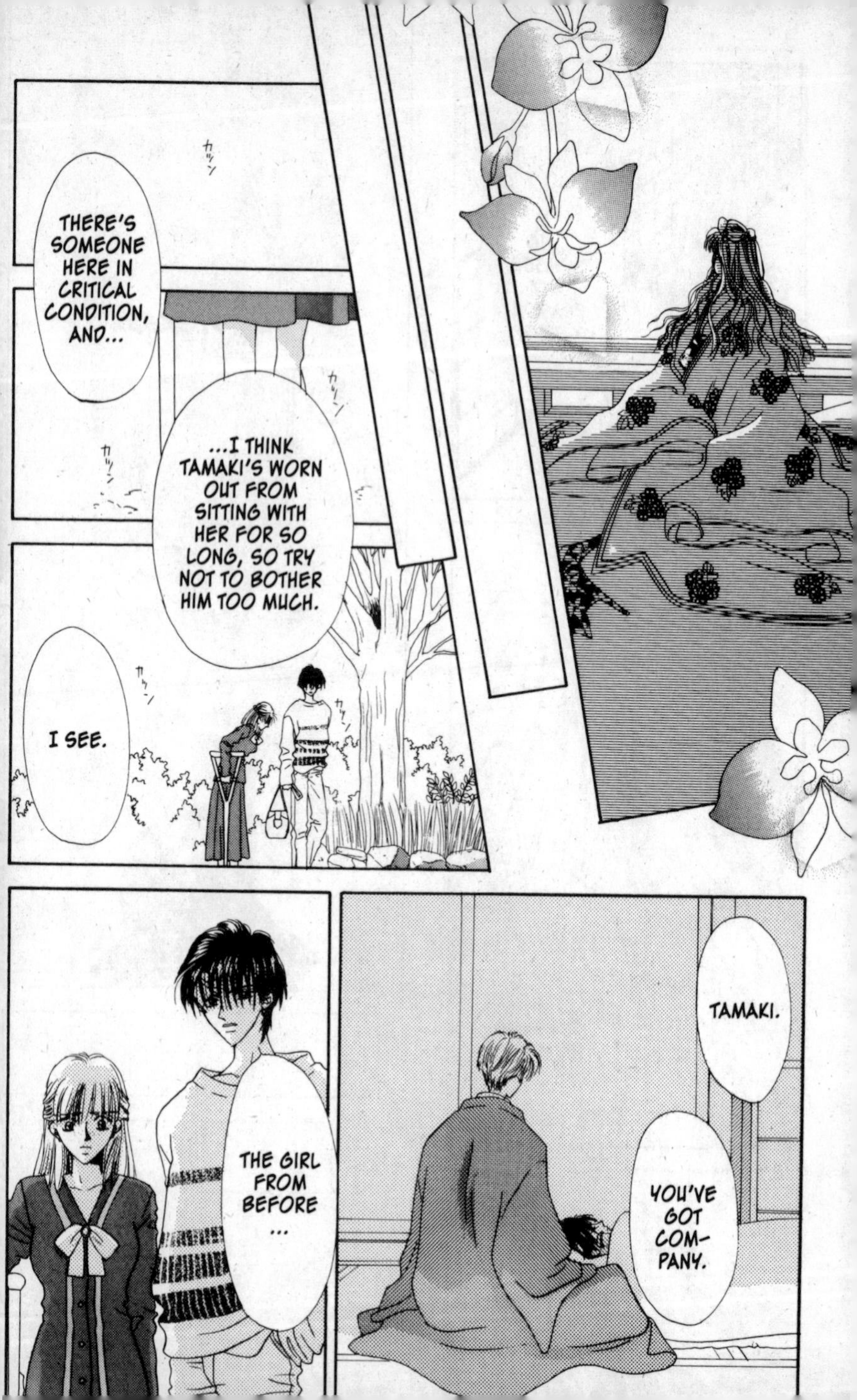
THERE'S SOMEONE HERE IN CRITICAL CONDITION, AND...
...I THINK TAMAKI'S WORN OUT FROM SITTING WITH HER FOR SO LONG, SO TRY NOT TO BOTHER HIM TOO MUCH.
I SEE.
TAMAKI.
YOU'VE GOT COM-PANY.
THE GIRL FROM BEFORE ...

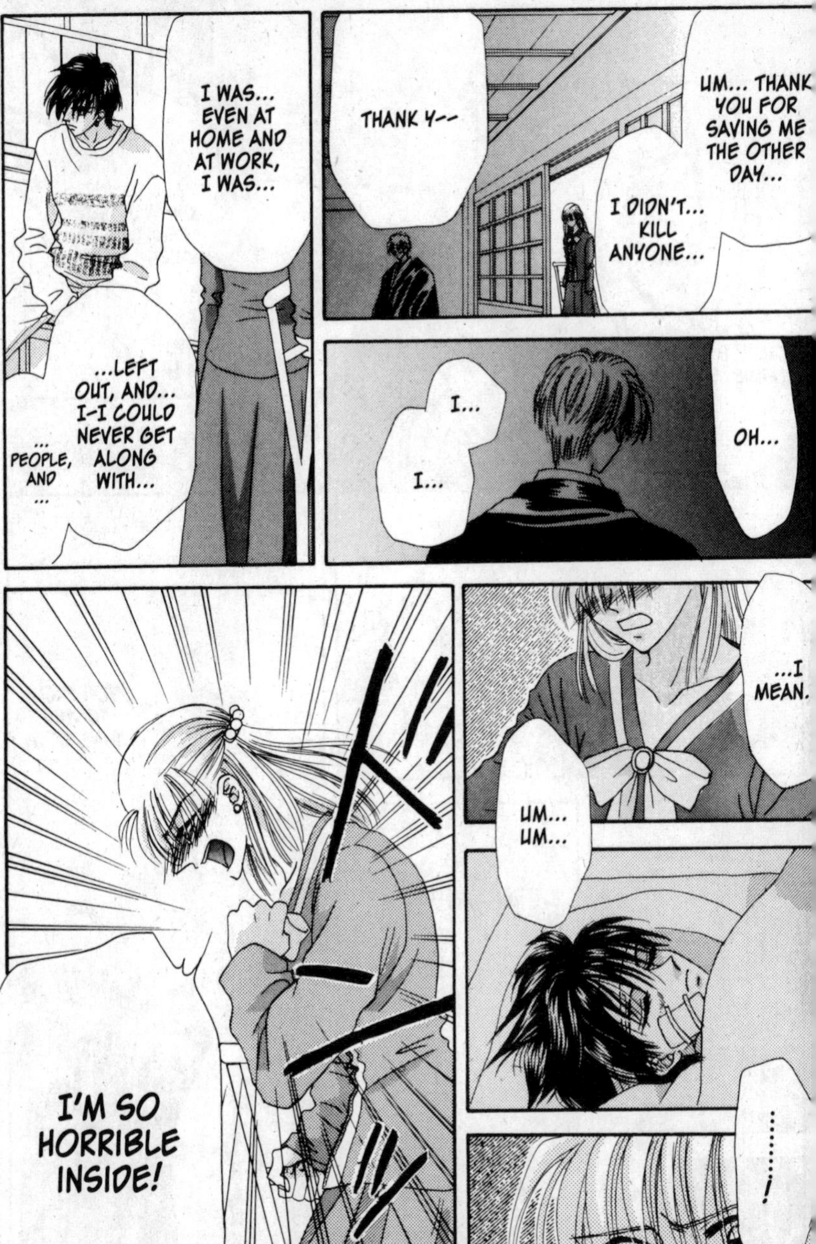
UM... THANK YOU FOR SAVING ME THE OTHER DAY...
THANK Y--
I DIDN'T... KILL ANYONE...
OH...
I...
I...
I WAS... EVEN AT HOME AND AT WORK, I WAS...
...LEFT OUT, AND... I-I COULD NEVER GET ALONG WITH...
... PEOPLE, AND ...
...I MEAN.
UM... UM...
......!
I'M SO HORRIBLE INSIDE!

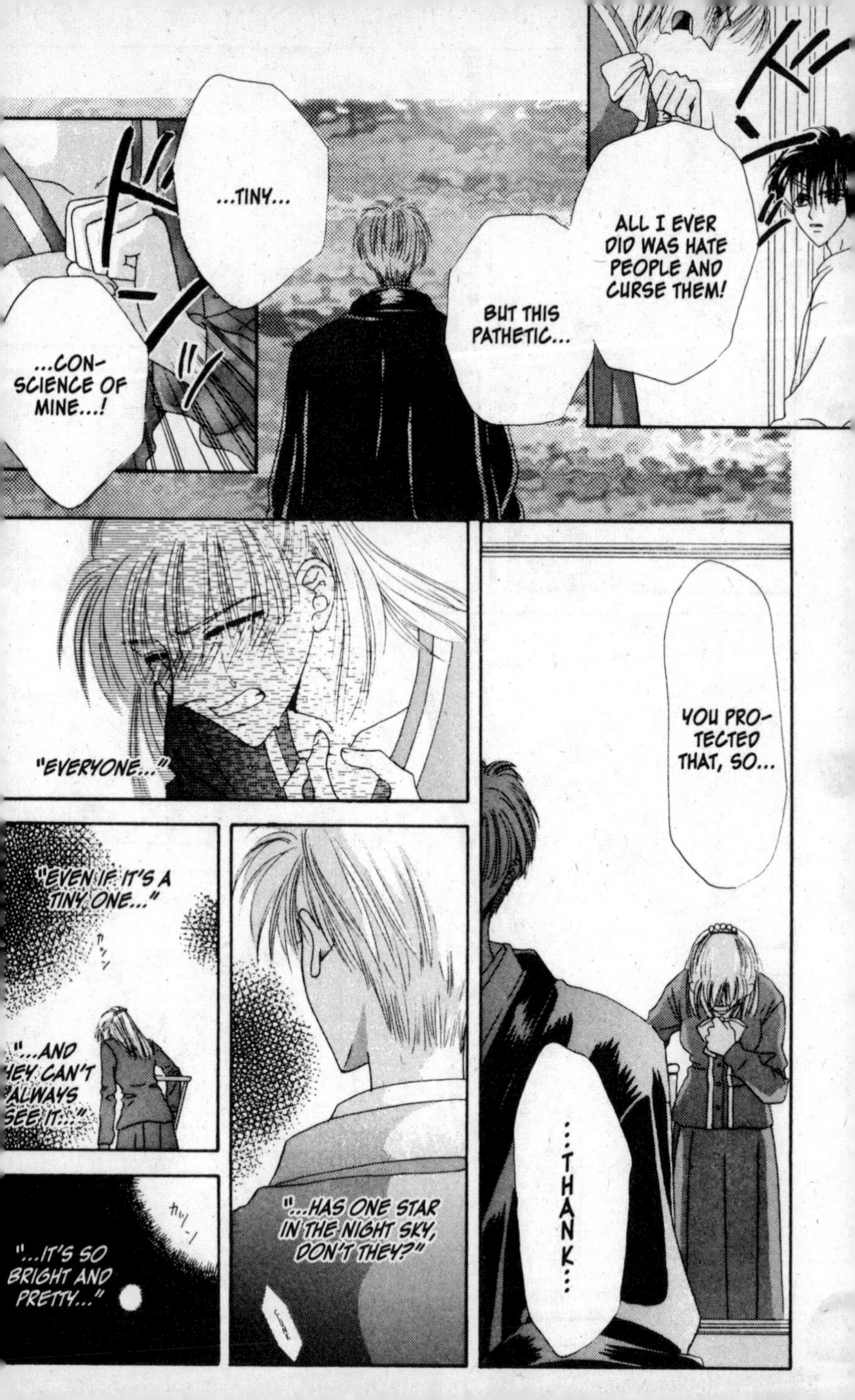
ALL I EVER DID WAS HATE PEOPLE AND CURSE THEM!
BUT THIS PATHETIC...
...TINY...
...CON- SCIENCE OF MINE...!
YOU PRO- TECTED THAT, SO...
...THANK...
"EVERYONE..."
"...HAS ONE STAR IN THE NIGHT SKY, DON'T THEY?"
"EVEN IF IT'S A TINY ONE..."
"...AND HEY CAN'T ALWAYS SEE IT..."
"...IT'S SO BRIGHT AND PRETTY..."

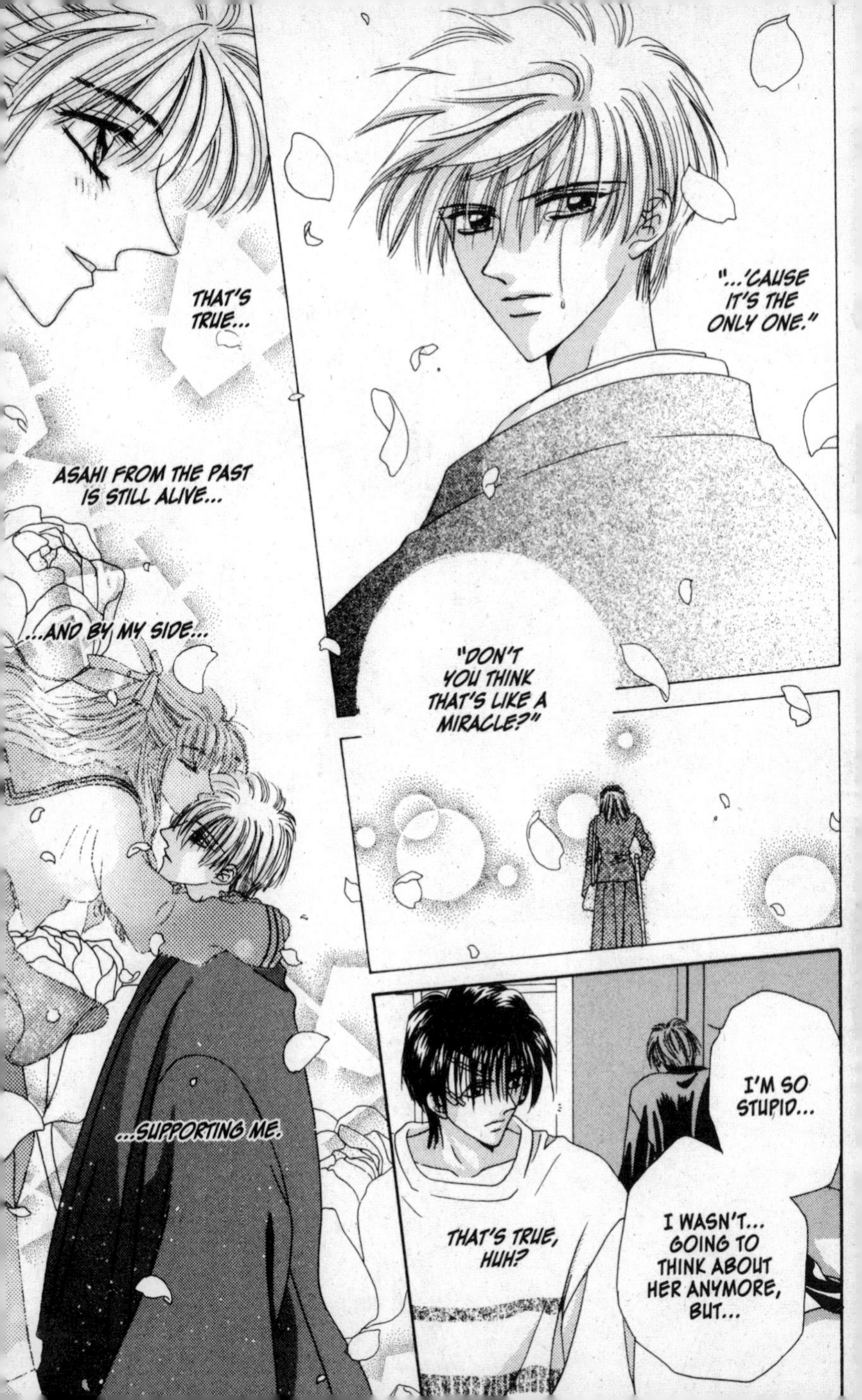
"...'CAUSE IT'S THE ONLY ONE."
"DON'T YOU THINK THAT'S LIKE A MIRACLE?"
I'M SO STUPID...
I WASN'T... GOING TO THINK ABOUT HER ANYMORE, BUT...
THAT'S TRUE, HUH?
THAT'S TRUE...
ASAHI FROM THE PAST IS STILL ALIVE...
...AND BY MY SIDE...
...SUPPORTING ME.

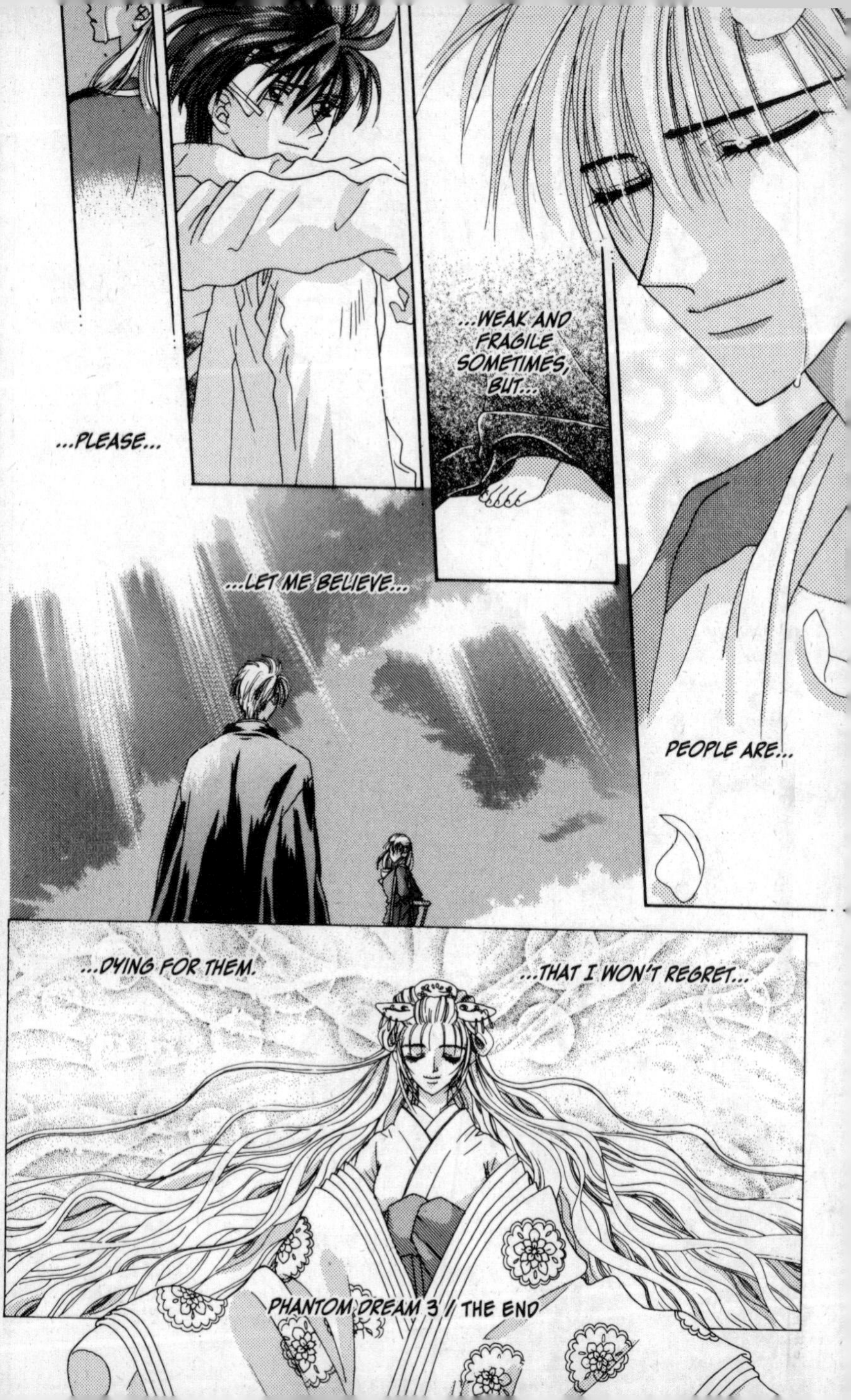
PEOPLE ARE...
...WEAK AND FRAGILE SOMETIMES, BUT...
...PLEASE...
...LET ME BELIEVE...
...THAT I WON'T REGRET...
...DYING FOR THEM.
PHANTOM DREAM 3 / THE END

Natsuki Takaya's Just Between Us

People kept saying, "I hate him, I hate him! And just when I thought I might like him after all...he died." There were so many people who said that about Kageha. Spring came too late for him. (laughs)

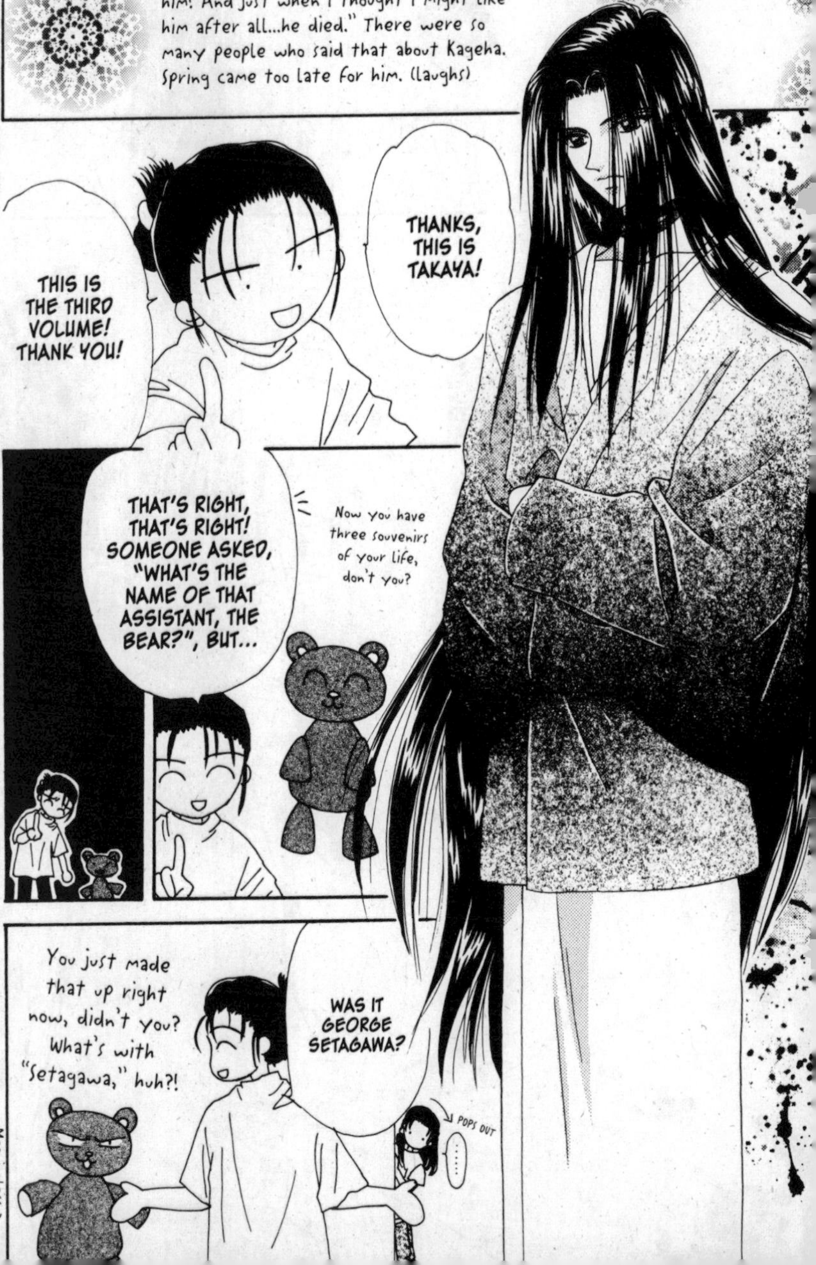
THANKS, THIS IS TAKAYA!
THIS IS THE THIRD VOLUME! THANK YOU!
Now you have three souvenirs of your life, don't you?
THAT'S RIGHT, THAT'S RIGHT! SOMEONE ASKED, "WHAT'S THE NAME OF THAT ASSISTANT, THE BEAR?", BUT...
WAS IT GEORGE SETAGAWA?
You just made that up right now, didn't you? What's with "Setagawa," huh?!
POPS OUT
......
Meaningless...

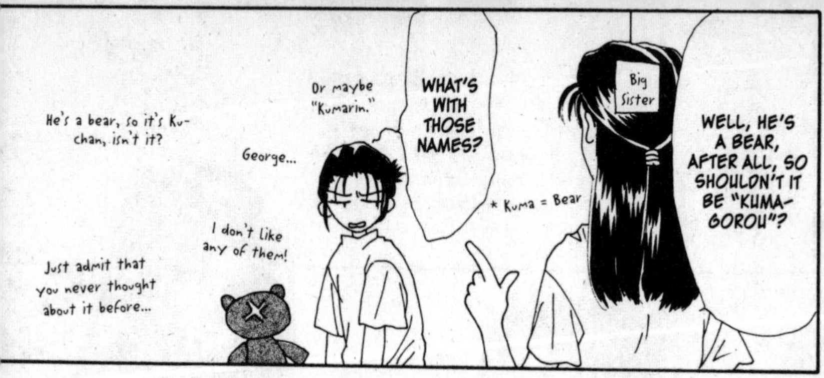
Big Sister
WELL, HE'S A BEAR, AFTER ALL, SO SHOULDN'T IT BE "KUMA-GOROU"?
* Kuma = Bear
WHAT'S WITH THOSE NAMES?
Or maybe "Kumarin."
George...
He's a bear, so it's Ku-chan, isn't it?
I don't like any of them!
Just admit that you never thought about it before...

She really said that.

About the Manga

The members of the Gekka family finally make an appearance! For the time being, people who get turned into jaki become part of the family too (although they're going to get eaten...). Every once in a while I get a letter asking what Mutsu's face looks like under that headband (?), but the truth is I don't know myself... I've never drawn it. Maybe it's because I think that's his real face or something? Well... But there is that saying, "Mask Handsome," so... (laughs) I don't know whether Mutsu is "Mask Handsome" or not, but... (laughs) But you can't really figure out people's expressions from just their mouths, huh? So it's really hard.

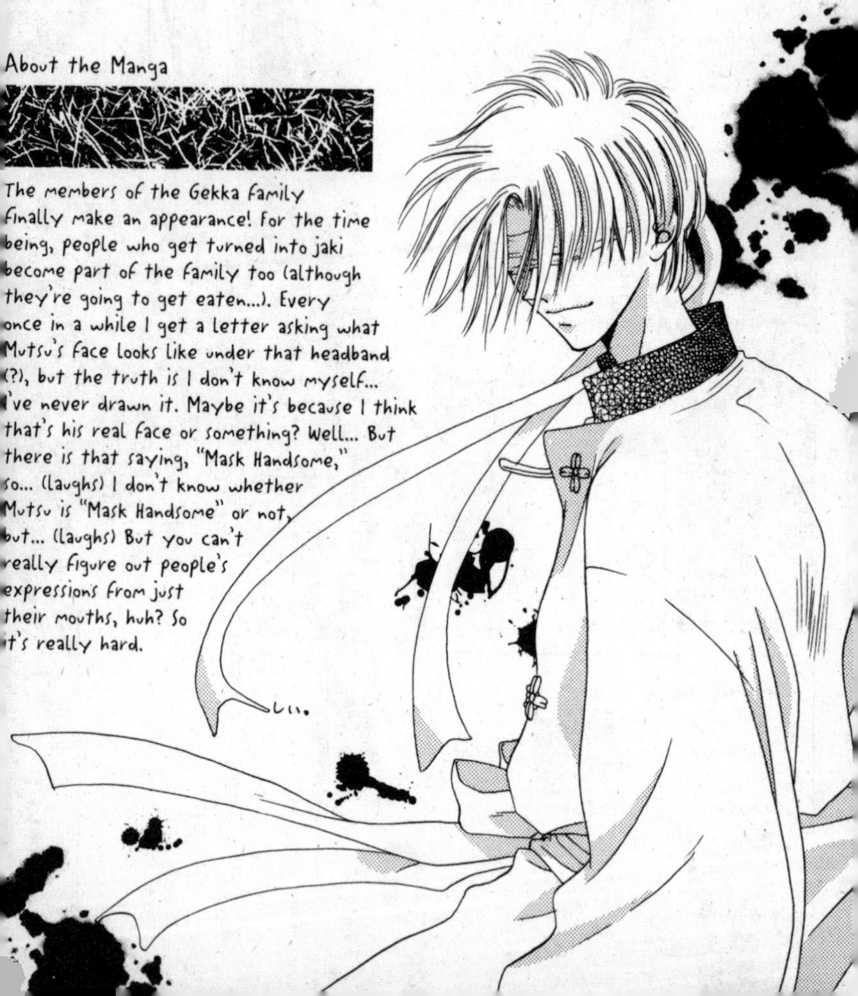

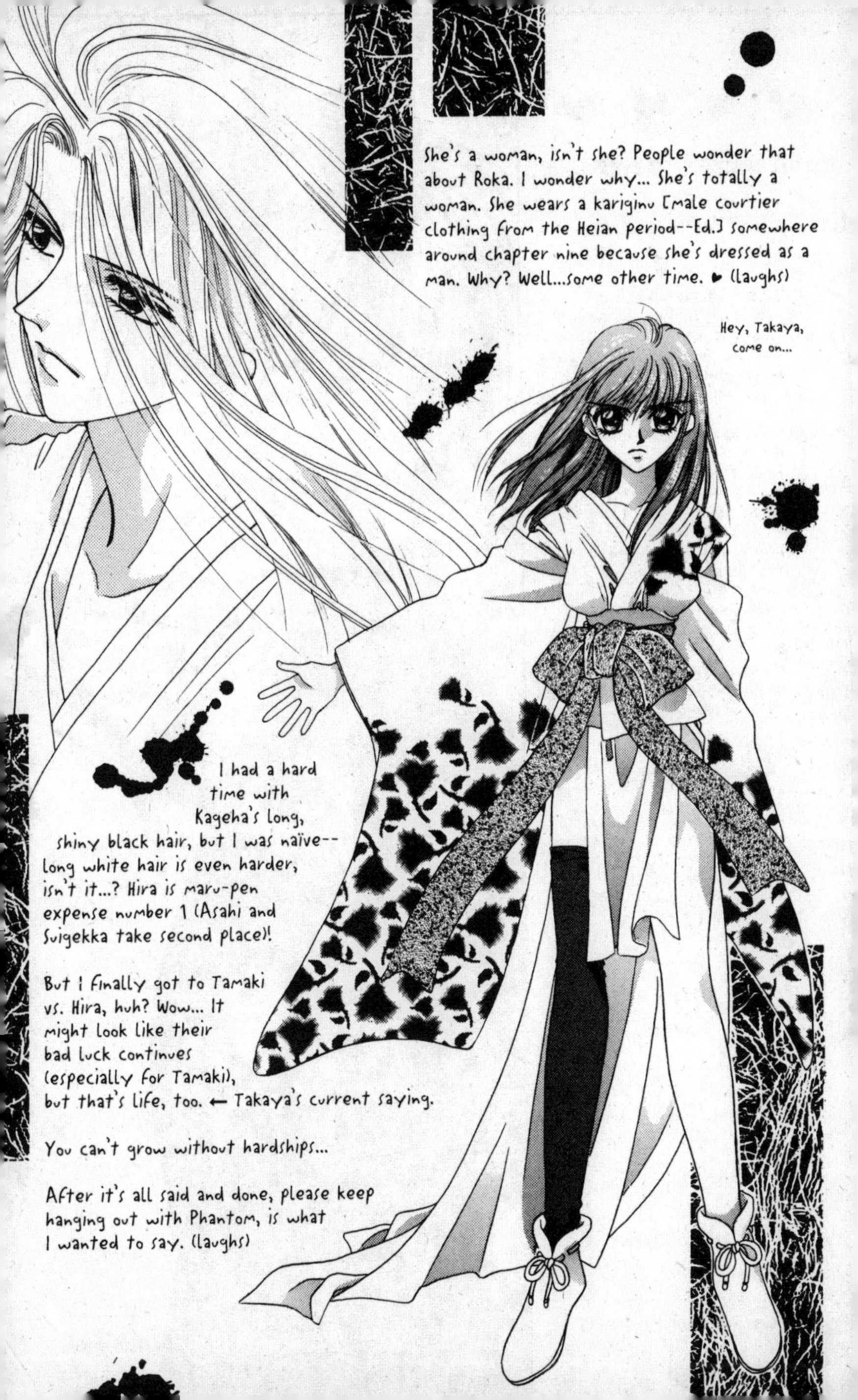
Hey, Takaya, come on...

She's a woman, isn't she? People wonder that about Roka. I wonder why... She's totally a woman. She wears a kariginu [male courtier clothing from the Heian period--Ed.] somewhere around chapter nine because she's dressed as a man. Why? Well...some other time. ♥ (laughs)

I had a hard time with Kageha's long, shiny black hair, but I was naïve--long white hair is even harder, isn't it...? Hira is maru-pen expense number 1 (Asahi and Suigekka take second place)!

But I finally got to Tamaki vs. Hira, huh? Wow... It might look like their bad luck continues (especially for Tamaki), but that's life, too. ← Takaya's current saying.

You can't grow without hardships...

After it's all said and done, please keep hanging out with Phantom, is what I wanted to say. (laughs)

I'M SO GRATEFUL TO EVERYONE!

To the people who read this, the people who sent me letters and the people who bought this, thank you! People who send me letters every time, thank you too! (Come to think of it, real letters spiked around chapter eight, when Tamaki and Asahi broke up. That's when I really realized that Asahi was a huge presence in this manga!) Who knows what I'm saying... How did you like Phantom Dream 3? I'm looking forward to your opinions.

So my words of gratitude are a bit late, sorry... Takemura-sama of Naht, I am in your debt every time. Thank you!

Well, then--see you later!

This was Natsuki Takaya.♡

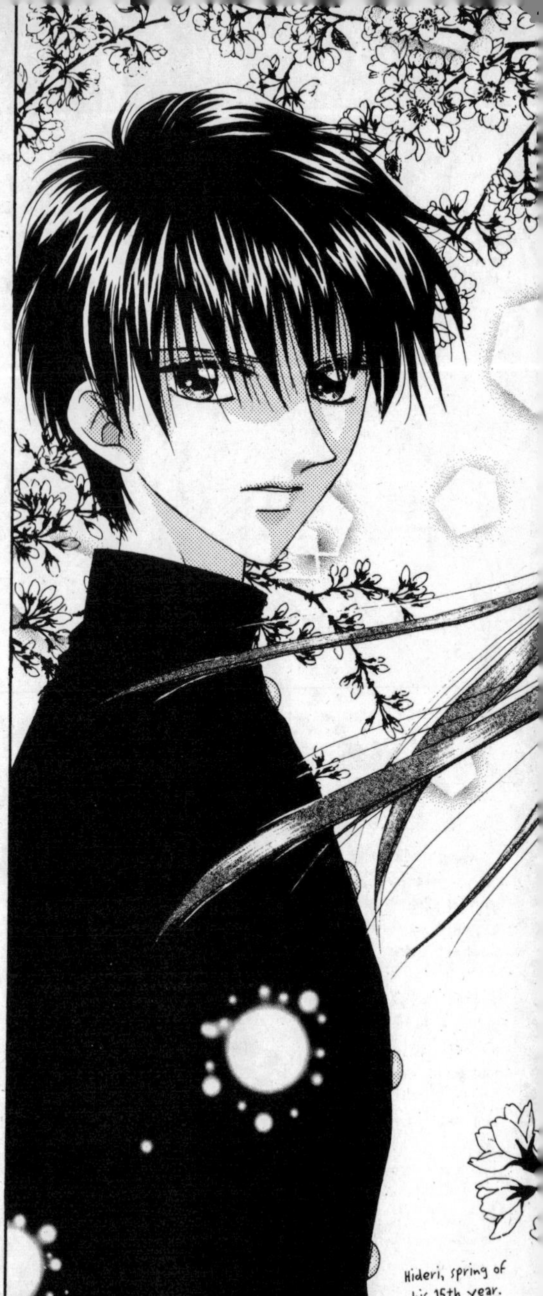
Hideri, spring of his 15th year.

NATSUKI TAKAYA'S "JUST BETWEEN US" / THE END

IN THE NEXT VOLUME OF

Phantom Dream

EIJI'S LIFE HANGS IN THE BALANCE AS
FACTIONS ONCE AGAIN SHIFT AND REALIGN.
ASAHI STRUGGLES WITH HER NEW POWERS, AND
GUILT OVER WHAT HAPPENED IN THE PAST, AND
TAMAKI STRIVES TO CONTROL THE CONTINUING
OUTBREAK OF CHAOS IN THE PRESENT. AND A
MYSTERIOUS NEW FIGURE EMERGES TO JOIN
THE BATTLE, BUT IS HE AN ALLY OR AN ENEMY?!

Is the World's #1 Shojo Manga

**Fruits Basket Ultimate Editions
Volumes 1-3**

**Fruits Basket
Fan Book -Cat-**

**Fruits Basket
Sticker Collection**

**Fruits Basket
Journal**

**Fruits Basket 18-month
Planner**

FOR MORE INFORMATION VISIT: WWW.TOKYOPOP.COM

STOP!

This is the back of the book.
You wouldn't want to spoil a great ending!

This book is printed "manga-style," in the authentic Japanese right-to-left format. Since none of the artwork has been flipped or altered, readers get to experience the story just as the creator intended. You've been asking for it, so TOKYOPOP® delivered: authentic, hot-off-the-press, and far more fun!

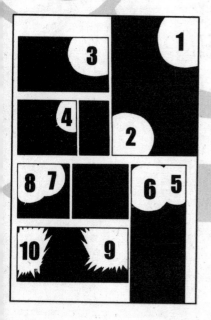

DIRECTIONS

If this is your first time reading manga-style, here's a quick guide to help you understand how it works.

It's easy... just start in the top right panel and follow the numbers. Have fun, and look for more 100% authentic manga from TOKYOPOP®!